Perception and the Physical World

Perception and the Physical World

Psychological and Philosophical Issues in Perception

DIETER HEYER

University of Halle, Germany

and

RAINER MAUSFELD

Kiel University, Germany

JOHN WILEY & SONS, LTD

Other Wiley Editorial Offices

John Wiley & Sons, Inc., 605 Third Avenue,
New York, NY 10158-0012, USA

WILEY-VCH Verlag GmbH, Pappelallee 3,
D-69469 Weinheim, Germany

John Wiley & Sons Australia, Ltd., 33 Park Road, Milton,
Queensland 4064, Australia

John Wiley & Sons (Asia) Pte, Ltd., 2 Clementi Loop #02-01,
Jin Xing Distripark, Singapore 129809

John Wiley & Sons (Canada), Ltd., 22 Worcester Road,
Rexdale, Ontario M9W 1L1, Canada

British Library Cataloging in Publication Data

A catalogue record for this book is available from the British Library

ISBN 0-471-49149-7

Typeset in 10/12pt Times from the author's disks by TechBooks, New Delhi, India
Printed and bound in Great Britain by TJ International, Ltd, Padstow, Cornwall
This book is printed on acid-free paper responsibly manufactured from sustainable forestry,
in which at least two trees are planted for each one used for paper production.

Contents

vi   *Contents*

About the Editors

Dieter Heyer graduated in Psychology and Mathematics at the University of Bonn and received his Ph.D. in Psychology from the University of Kiel. He is Professor of Psychology at the University of Halle, where he teaches statistics, mathematical psychology, and visual perception. His main research interests lie in the field of visual perception with a special focus on colour theory and the phenomenology of picture perception, and in the theory of probabilistic measurement.

Rainer Mausfeld is Professor of Cognitive Science at the Christian-Albrechts University at Kiel. His main research interests are centred upon issues of "meaning" in perception, in particular the structure of representational primitives underlying colour perception. Additional scientific interests include abstract measurement and meaningfulness theory and the history of perception.

About the Authors

Larry Arend has been a research psychologist at NASA Ames Research Center since 1997. He designs electronic maps and "map-like" information visualizations for the cockpit and air traffic control. He received his B.A. in Psychology from Stanford University (1965) and a Ph.D. in Psychology from Duke University (1970). Over the following 20 years he taught and conducted research in visual perception at the University of Pennsylvania, Brandeis University, and The Schepens Eye Research Institute of Harvard Medical School. Following several years of research on information visualization at the Sarnoff Corporation, he joined the ZiF study group.

Margaret Atherton is a Professor of Philosophy at the University of Wisconsin-Milwaukee. Her primary field of interest is the History of Early Modern Philosophy, with a particular interest in issues concerning perception. She is the author of *Berkeley's Revolution in Vision* as well as two edited anthologies and numerous articles.

Horace Barlow has worked in Vision and Perception for 50 years. He contributed to the experimental discovery of bug-detectors and lateral inhibition in the frog retina, motion detection in the rabbit retina, and selectivity for disparity in the cat cortex. As a theoretician, he has argued that exploiting the redundancy of natural stimuli is important for effective perception and cognition, and the absolute statistical efficiencies provide the most informative measure of the work involved.

Bruce M. Bennett received his Ph.D. in Pure Mathematics at Columbia University in New York under H. Hironaka in algebraic geometry and singularity theory. In the 1980s he became interested in perception, working on mathematical models of specific visual capacities, as well as on formalisms for general perceptual modelling and the logic of perceptual inference. He is a coauthor with Don Hoffman and Chetan Prakash of *Observer Mechanics* (Academic Press, 1989). In recent years he has worked on dynamical probabilistic inference, which is the subject of the article in this volume, and on algebraic–geometric codes. He was on the mathematics faculty at Harvard and Stanford before coming to the University of California at Irvine, where he is now a Professor of Mathematics.

Andrea J. van Doorn graduated in Physics and Mathematics in 1971 at Utrecht University. She has participated in research on vision at Groningen University and is now connected with the Department of Industrial Design of Delft Technical University and with the Helmholtz Instituut of the Universiteit Utrecht. She works on a variety of topics in visual psychophysics and modelling of visual functions in humans.

Gary Hatfield received the PhD from the University of Wisconsin-Madison, in 1979, then taught at Harvard and Johns Hopkins before coming to Penn in 1987, where he is Adam Seybert Professor in Moral and Intellectual Philosophy. He works in the history of modern philosophy and the philosophy of psychology. In 1990 he published *The Natural and the Normative: Theories of Spatial Perception from Kant to Helmholtz*; his translation of Kant's *Prolegomena to Any Future Metaphysics* appeared in 1997, and he has been working on books on Descartes and on the philosophy of psychology.

Heiko Hecht is research scientist at the Man–Vehicle Laboratory of the Massachusetts Institute of Technology, Cambridge, MA, where he oversees the research on artificial gravity. He investigates the effects of unusual environments on our senses, such as being weightless or experiencing a virtual reality simulation. Dr. Hecht has published on issues of picture perception, dynamic event perception, and skilled human performance in tasks typical for pilots and astronauts.

Donald D. Hoffman received his B.A. summa cum laude in Quantitative Psychology from the University of California at Los Angeles (1978), and his Ph.D. in Computational Psychology from the Massachusetts Institute of Technology (1983). He is author of the book *Visual Intelligence* and a Professor of Cognitive Science at the University of California, Irvine.

Mark Kaplan is Professor of Philosophy at the University of Wisconsin-Milwaukee. Author of *Decision Theory as Philosophy* (Cambridge, 1996) and numerous articles on Bayesianism and epistemology, he has been a National Science Foundation grant recipient, a Senior Fellow of the the the American Council of Learned Societies, and a Visiting Fellow of the School of Advanced Studies at the University of London.

Daniel Kersten studied undergraduate and graduate-level mathematics at the Massachusetts Institute of Technology and the University of Minnesota. He obtained his Ph.D. in Psychology from the University of Minnesota in 1983 and then moved to Cambridge University for post-doctoral studies. He joined the faculty of Brown University in 1984. He has been with the Psychology Department at the University of Minnesota since 1989.

Jan J. Koenderink graduated in Physics and Mathematics in 1967 at Utrecht University. He has been associate professor in Experimental Psychology at the Universiteit of Groningen, in the 1970's returned to the Universiteit Utrecht where he holds a chair in the Department of Physics and Astronomy. He founded the Helmholtz Instituut in which multidisciplinary work in biology, medicine, physics, and computer science is coordinated. He has received an honorific degree (D.Sc.) in Medicine from the University of Leuven and is a member of the Royal Netherlands Academy of Arts and Sciences. Research interests include cognitive science, ecological physics and machine intelligence.

Laurence T. Maloney is Associate Professor of Psychology and Neural Science at New York University. His work concerns human visual perception and decision making, specifically, how human observers combine information from different visual cues to arrive at estimates of shape, surface color and contour in scenes. He graduated from Stanford University with a doctorate in Psychology and a master's degree in mathematical statistics. In 1987, he received the Troland Award of the National Academy of Sciences (USA).

Chetan Prakash received his Ph.D. in Applied Mathematics from Cornell University in 1982. His thesis was supervised by Leonard Gross and Michael Fisher, and was on classical statistical mechanics. Specifically, it employed techniques originated by Dobrushin in the study of Markov random fields. Dr. Prakash began working on mathematical theories of perception with Bruce Bennett and Don Hoffman in 1985; in collaboration with them he has written the book *Observer Mechanics* and several papers related to perception and structure from motion. He is a Professor of Mathematics at the California State University in San Bernardino and has been a visiting professor at U.C. Irvine.

Paul Schrater received his Ph.D. degree in Neuroscience from the University of Pennsylvania in 1999 and is now Assistant Professor jointly in the departments of Psychology and Computer Science. He works on human and computer vision and the control of reach and grasp.

Robert Schwartz is Professor of Philosophy at the University of Wisconsin-Milwaukee. His primary field of interest is the Philosophy of Psychology. He has written papers on issues concerning language, non-linguistic representation, mathematical cognition and perception. He is the author of *Vision: Variations on Some Berkeleian Themes* and editor of *Perception: Blackwell Readings in Philosophy* (forthcoming).

Dejan Todorović works at the Department of Psychology, University of Belgrade, Yugoslavia. He is interested in mathematical analyses, computer simulations, and experimental investigations of lightness, space, and motion perception, as well as in history of perception.

Preface

Among the disciplines of cognitive science hardly any other field is as rewarding and instructive for students' apprenticeship to cognitive science as perception theory. Perception is at the interface of the mental and the physical. Inquiries into its nature have, since the beginnings of rational inquiry, played a prominent role in our attempts to gain a theoretical understanding of the world within the framework of the natural sciences. In fact, such inquiries mark the historical origin of fields as diverse as physics, psychology, and epistemology. In the context of today's cognitive sciences they provide a microcosmos of multidisciplinary research in which perceptual and developmental psychologists, philosophers, neurophysiologists, and researchers from the field of artificial intelligence investigate a single realm of phenomena. Perception theory, as the oldest and most mature field of scientific psychology, naturally became a field of paradigmatic interest for investigations into fundamental aspects of the cognitive sciences; its importance for all the cognitive sciences is also derived from the reasonable conjecture that in evolutionary history perceptual representations provided the structural germ for the development of "higher" cognitive processes.

The present volume emerged from a research project at the Zentrum für interdisziplinäre Forschung (ZiF) of the University of Bielefeld (Germany) in which scholars from various disciplines attempted to identify, among the huge masses of current experimental and theoretical research, a few threads running through the intellectual history of the field that they considered to be of particular importance for our attempts to theoretically understand "how the mind works". As we are still far from a deeper theoretical understanding of the principles of the mind and often have not even agreed on what conceptual framework and what level of analysis to use for phrasing our questions, it is a well-known observation that individual assessments of what constitutes the important issues differ greatly. The present volume is no exception in this regard. Still there are a few common threads discernable that point to foundational and unresolved issues of continuing interest. These issues concern the general nature of the relation between the external world (i.e. the world as described by physics) on the one hand, and the world as it appears to us on the other, and how to describe "what's within" and "what's outside". Their urgency and significance derive from the observation of a huge discrepancy between the information that the senses have at their disposal and the perceptual achievement. Because of this gap the structure of perceptual representations cannot simply be accounted for by the information available in the sensory input. This discrepancy is not only of great concern in perception theory but also in epistemology. In perceptual psychology corresponding observations, dating back almost a thousand years, have given rise to a great variety of intuitions about how this gap could be bridged in explanatory accounts of perception and have resulted in the invocation of concepts like "unconscious inference", "higher order" processes, learning schemes, or Gestalt principles. Recently, under the heading of Bayesian approaches to perception, fascinating developments that provide a framework for formulating intuitions about inference-like mediating processes in a precise manner, and for exploring their potential fruitfulness in a much deeper way, have emerged in perceptual psychology. The Bayesian approach can be considered as currently the most sophisticated and most promising overarching framework in perception theory. This thread, which refers to the observation of an explanatory gap between the information available to the perceptual system and its achievement and the venerable intuitions it brought forth in the history of the field, is also mirrored in the book. It is intimately interwoven with issues concerning the sensation–perception distinction, the relation between proximal and distal stimuli, and inference-like mediating processes, as captured by the Bayesian approach—issues that constitute a major part of the present volume.

Of the 17 contributors to this book, 13 would count primarily as vision researchers (one of them with an emphasis on neurophysiology, 5 of them with a foot in the field of ecological physics and machine vision), 4 primarily as philosophers (2 of them with an emphasis on the intellectual history of perception science). The style of the chapters varies, in accord with the subject matter they cover, and in the degree to which they are written in the style of essays and personal assessments, systematic expositions, elaborations of theoretical ideas, or experimental case studies. The chapters are not intended to constitute a representative survey of contemporary thinking in perception science, which would be an almost impossible goal for a single volume. Nevertheless, they indubitably centre on fundamental issues of the field that are of continuing interest and importance to anyone interested in the cognitive sciences.

The arrangement of the chapters follows, very loosely, a line from the more general as well as the more introductory to the more specific and more technical, though individual chapters are often open-worked with respect to these aspects. The first chapter, by *Atherton*, picks up the thread concerning the relation between the external world and the world as it appears to us from the perspective of the conceptual history of the field. By describing and comparing the different conceptions of the perceptual process of Descartes, Malebranche, Reid, and Berkeley she brings out the different motives and underlying assumptions that gave rise to the emergence of sensation–perception distinctions. Todorovic, in his chapter, presents a review of some conceptual issues and empirical findings in the perception of size, shape, orientation, direction, and achromatic and chromatic colours. For all attributes, the organization of the discussion has the same formal structure in order to stress the basic commonalities of issues. For both the distal and the proximal variable a corresponding phenomenal variable is considered. Such distinctions apply, in principle, to all attributes considered. The chapter discusses the ways in which the two phenomenal types of variables can be defined and studied. Brief reviews of relevant empirical findings are presented, and the fruitfulness of this approach for the analysis of important notions such as perceptual constancies and illusions is demonstrated.

In the following chapter, *Barlow*, utilizing the analogy of code-breaking, outlines a model for cognitive systems that are both innately determined and capable of being modified by experience. His leading idea is to consider the incoming stream of sensations as a code to be broken to give sense. This analogy illuminates the relation between innate knowledge of the world and the statistical properties of the input in cognition, and it makes one look again at the form this prior knowledge might take in the cortex. The chapter by Mausfeld outlines, by using what he dubs the physicalistic trap as a contrasting background, a sign theoretic approach to perception that is inspired by ethology. He argues that attempts to derive the structure of perceptual representations in an empiricist way from structural properties of the sensory input are inappropriate. According to his account the structure of internal representations is not only determined by properties of the external world but also by internal functional constraints, by internal architectural constraints and by contingent properties of internal coding, and is based on a rich set of representational primitives. In a historical appendix he sketches the tradition of sign theories from Alhazen, Descartes, Reid, and Cudworth to Helmholtz. *Hatfield's* chapter examines unconscious inference or unnoticed judgment accounts of perception from Alhazen to Rock, using size perception and colour constancy as examples. He identifies and analyses three problems facing such theories: the cognitive machinery problem, the sophisticated content problem, and the phenomenal experience problem. If a theory posits unnoticed or unconscious judgments, it should specify the cognitive resources underlying such judgments. If the judgments or inferences contain premises exhibiting sophisticated content, such as "spectral reflectance distribution", then the resources needed for expressing such content should be attributed to the perceptual or inference drawing system, or an explanation should be provided why such resources need not be attributed. Finally, theories should explain how unconscious inferences or judgments could produce perceptual experience (in vision, "the way things look").

Chapters 6 to 9 are all concerned with the Bayesian approach to visual perception. *Maloney's* chapter provides a clear introduction to statistical decision theory, including Bayesian decision theory as a special case, and a careful discussion of the relevance for modelling visual perception using the formal language of Bayesian statistics. Discussing the concept of an "Ideal Bayesian Observer" Maloney comes to the conclusion that "Non-ideal Bayesian Observers" are more plausible choices for modelling biological visual processing than are "Ideal Bayesian Observers". Finally, Maloney compares the current status of Bayesian models in cognition and perception and contrasts the failure of these models in explaining human conscious judgments with the belief in vision science that the Bayesian framework will be adequate and natural for understanding "unconscious inferences". The view that "the language of Bayesian inference is fundamental to quantitatively describe how reliable answers about the world can be obtained from image patterns", that Bayesian formalism will prove to be as crucial for theories of vision as calculus has been for the development of physics is strongly promoted by *Kersten* and *Schrater* in their contribution. Starting from a discussion of signal detection theory, ideal observer analysis and a review of recent applications of Bayes' nets and pattern theory to vision they end up with an abstract theory of inference, called "pattern inference theory", a set of general principles and concepts to formulate predictive and testable models of vision. Several recent examples of pattern inference theory are reviewed. In their chapter about perceptual evolution *Bennett*, *Hoffman*, and *Prakash* take advantage of recent advances in the study of Bayesian approaches to vision and offer a natural way to formulate the evolutionary question as a problem of convergence of measures. They develop this formulation and find that it is possible to ask and answer precise and interesting questions about conditions in which perceptual evolution can, and cannot, profitably occur. In the following chapter *Kaplan* gives a critical analysis of both the usage of the term "unconscious probabilistic inference" in philosophy and theories of perception from a philosopher's point of view. He offers thoughtful arguments showing that the idea of perception conceptualized as a process of unconscious probabilistic inference leads to severe conceptual problems, for which reason he unequivocally concludes that the probabilistic-inference model should be abandoned. He points out, however, that to model perceptual processes in the context of a probabilistic machinery does in no way depend on being construed as an attempt to reconstruct a process of unconscious probabilistic inference.

The next two chapters deal with picture perception though from quite different perspectives. *Schwartz* examines the general relation between vision and cognition in the area of picture perception. He offers a somewhat different analysis of the "visuality" that is thought to be distinctive of pictorial representation. On the basis of this analysis, he explores such matters as: (i) the special status accorded perspective renderings, (ii) the significance of infant and cross cultural findings, (iii) where diagrams, maps, haptic pictures, Cubist renderings, etc., fit into the scheme, and (iv) an alternative framework for considering station point problems associated with the "robustness" of perspective and differential rotation effects. In their chapter *Koenderink*, *van Doorn*, *Arend* and *Hecht* study both theoretically and empirically the pictorial relief in photographs of real objects. In their experiment they explore a variety of illuminations that yield a variety of shadings and have the effect of losing part of the contour of the pictorial object used. The authors investigate the question of whether observers know where the invisible contour runs and examine follow-up questions that relate to the perceptions of shape within the contour: Is the perception of shape influenced by the omission of (part of) the contour, is it influenced by "amodally completed" contours? They approach these questions from a psychophysical angle, taking essentials of ecological physics into account.

The final chapter by *Barlow* draws the arc back to general issues concerning the social function of perception and consciousness. The idea is that natural selection has moulded perception under the requirement that perceptions be communicable to conspecifics. It is argued that conscious experience occurs when the communicable representation is activated and that the communications that may result provide the main survival value of our conscious perception.

Of what use can these chapters be? It is the hope of the editors and the authors that the chapters not only provide a rewarding reading by themselves that stimulates and guides more detailed reading of current research literature, but also that the collection as a whole broadens the horizon of advanced students in all subfields of cognitive science and can serve as an invitation to join the fascinating field of cognitive science.

The volume originated from a research year that a group of scholars from various academic disciplines spent at the ZiF during the academic year 1995/96: the contributors to the volume were among the participants. The major focus of this research year was to discuss, within a broad historical and interdisciplinary perspective, foundational aspects of perception. As other academic disciplines, notably in the cognitive sciences, perception science suffers from a high degree of compartmentalization. For the participants of this research group it was an exciting experience that, on the individual level, at least some of these barriers can be broken down by laying bare and explicating the purposes and goals one pursues and the underlying tacit assumptions and intuitions that motivate the specific theoretical language and the conceptual vocabulary that one uses in formulating problems of perception. Still, different purposes, goals and ways of conceptualizing problems are an obstacle in perception theory that cannot be fully surmounted, despite tentative agreements about a common core of fundamental problems. The chapters in this volume exemplify this endeavour to dig into the same mountain from different directions, as it were.

The generous financial and organizational support of the ZiF during the research years 1995–1996 and for subsequent conferences was invaluable in enabling us to carry out this endeavour. All the authors join us in expressing our gratitude to the members of staff of the ZiF. Their commitment, hospitality and support created an atmosphere that made our project year and the concomitant conferences a most pleasant and intellectually rewarding experience.

Finally we would like to extend our appreciation and thanks to the staff of Wiley for their continuing encouragement and help in all the steps leading to the publication of this volume.

Dieter Heyer
Rainer Mausfeld

1

The Origins of the Sensation/Perception Distinction

Department of Philosophy, University of Wisconsin-Milwaukee, USA

> *It can be predicted at the outset that few people will not be taken aback by the following general proposition, viz., that we have no sensation of external objects that does not involve one or more false judgments. It is well known that most people do not even think there is any judgment, true or false in our sensations. Consequently, these people, surprised by the novelty of this proposition, will undoubtedly say to themselves: but how can that be? I do not judge that this wall is white, I see that it is; I do not judge that there is pain in my hand, I assuredly feel it there: and who can doubt what is so certain unless he senses things in a way different from mine? Their inclination toward childish prejudices will eventually lead them much further, and if they do not go on to insult and despise those whom they believe to be of another opinion, they will undoubtedly deserve to be counted among reasonable people.*
>
> (Nicolas Malebranche, *The Search after Truth*)[1]

Present-day readers of Malebranche, unlike the readers of his own day, may not find quite so novel the suggestion that perceiving a visual world is a complex and not a simple event, with judgmental or quasi-judgmental aspects, but many such readers may find themselves nevertheless saying with Malebranche's imagined reader, How can this be? I see the white wall and I feel the painful hand. These contemporary readers may suppose, moreover, that they have history on their side. For throughout the twentieth century, theorists have been inclined to agree with these "childish prejudices" and to suppose that visual perception is not the accomplishment of a two-stage process, in which perceivers come to see a visual world through their awareness of their sensations. Psychologists have, on the whole, accepted the verdict of the Gestalt

Perception and the Physical World: Psychological and Philosophical Issues in Perception.
Edited by Dieter Heyer and Rainer Mausfeld. © 2002 John Wiley & Sons, Ltd.

psychologists that introspective attempts to discover the true sensory world of sensa-tions are irrelevant to an understanding of the world we perceive. And philosophers today most often reject out of hand any suggestion that sense data have a role to play in our perception of objects.

The reason for rejecting this view has often been because the notion of a sensation has seemed problematic. For, when I see a white wall, what is it I am supposed to sense? Sensations seem to be annoying, extra little entities, elliptically shaped quasi-objects, for example, that somehow intervene between the round dish and our perception of it as round. So it has seemed good to many to dispense with sensations entirely. And yet, the distinction between sensation and perception refuses to go away. Perhaps in addition to the uniform whiteness we see the wall to be, it seems useful to talk about the different ways the wall looks in sunshine and shadow. So the distinction between sensation and perception resurfaces, for example, in J. J. Gibson's talk of a distinction between visual field and visual world or Irvin Rock's of proximal mode and world mode.[2] I propose therefore to re-open the question, Does an account of visual perception require a distinction between sensation and perception? by returning to a time when the question was new, and when it could be answered unashamedly in the affirmative. I hope through an understanding of what was at stake when the distinction between sensation and perception was first introduced, it will be possible to become clearer about what is involved in accepting or rejecting the distinction, or, if not clearer, at least to become more aware of the complexities involved. I propose to begin, not with Malebranche, but with Malebranche's immediate predecessor, René Descartes, from whom Malebranche learned about the nature of sensation.

DESCARTES

The most straightforward place where Descartes indicates he considers perception to be a multi-stage process occurs in the Sixth Set of Replies to the Objections to the *Meditations*. In this passage, Descartes develops a set of categories that are replicated in one way or another throughout the period. The passage runs as follows:

> If we are to get a clear view of what sort of certainty attaches to the senses, we must distinguish three grades of sensory response. The first is limited to the immediate stimu-lation of the bodily organs by external objects; this can consist in nothing but the motion of the particles of the organs, and any change of shape and position resulting from this motion. The second grade comprises all the immediate effects produced in the mind as a result of its being united with a bodily organ which is affected in this way. Such effects include the perceptions of pain, pleasure, thirst, hunger, colours, sound, taste, smell, heat, cold, and the like, which arise from the union and as it were the intermingling of mind and body, as explained in the Sixth Meditation. The third grade includes all the judgements about things outside us which we have been accustomed to make from our earliest years—judgements which are occasioned by the movements of these bodily organs.[3]

This passage puts forward a clear statement that, in addition to a physiological grade, sense perception includes two psychological grades. The problem then is to

understand why Descartes thought sense perception requires two different psychological processes and to discover the criteria by which he identified each grade.[4]

The nature of the physiological stage is relatively unproblematic[5] although it might
be questioned why he included it at all in a description of sensory information.
Descartes' subsequent example makes clear, however, that he thinks a knowledge of
physiology will reveal that it cannot be that the wall looks white simply because it
is white. He wants his readers to be clear that things do *not* look as they do because
"certain 'intentional forms' fly off the stick toward the eye" (*CSM*, 295, *AT*, IX–1,
236–237). We don't see by means of images copying for the eye the ways things
are, rather "rays of light are reflected off the stick and set up certain movements in
the optic nerve and, via the optic nerve, in the brain" (*CSM*, 295. *AT*, IX–1, 237).
When, with the second grade of sensing, Descartes looks at the question, Why do
things look as they do? his answer then seems to be that things look as they do
because the proximal stimuli are as they are, that what we sense is determined by
the excitations in our sense organs caused by the light rays reflected from the object.
This, in turn, suggests a way of thinking about Descartes' reasons for singling out
the second grade of sensory response: he is identifying this level with the locus of
proximal stimulation.

Gary Hatfield and William Epstein offer an interpretation of Descartes' theory
that adopts this approach.[6] "The second grade of sensation", they say, "is a mental
representation of the retinal image; the third grade is the ostensibly direct experience of
solid objects at a distance, which actually results from unnoticed judgmental processes
performed upon the unnoticed sensory core" (p. 377). Hatfield and Epstein point out,
however, that, given their interpretation, the presence of the stage which they call the
sensory core, corresponding to the retinal image, causes problems for Descartes. As
a psychological element, it should be conscious, but we are aware of what they call
the visual world, and not of anything corresponding to the retinal image. Since there
is no phenomenological evidence for the second grade of sensation, they suggest that
it is actually a "hypothetical construct" introduced into Descartes' theory in order to
preserve the topographical features of the retinal image into his account of perception
and transmogrified into a psychological state as a result of Descartes' distinction
between mind and body. On their account, the sensation as a psychological element
has slipped into perceptual theory as a result of Descartes' metaphysical predelictions
and, by implication, if these are removed, so is the sensation.

There are several considerations that suggest to me, however, that things are not
quite that simple. The first is that when Descartes introduces the second grade of
sensing, he identifies it by means of a set of phenomenologically available sensible qualities: "pain, pleasure, thirst, hunger, colours, sound, taste, smell, heat, cold
and the like". While Descartes clearly supposes there to be an extremely tight connection between these sensible qualities and immediate physiological stimulation,
it does not seem correct to say that these qualities are identified by Descartes by
reading them off the various areas of physiological stimulation rather than through
conscious introspection. Secondly, it is not obvious that Descartes' third grade can be
straightforwardly identified with Hatfield and Epstein's visual world, "the ostensibly

direct experience of solid objects at a distance". Both in his initial description of this grade and in his subsequent example, Descartes stresses the judgmental nature of this grade. "But suppose that, as a result of being affected by this sensation of colour, I judge that a stick, located outside me, is coloured; and suppose that on the basis of the extension of the colour and its boundaries together with its position in relation to the parts of the brain, I make a rational calculation about the size, shape and distance of the stick: although such reasoning is commonly assigned to the senses (which is why I have here referred it to the third grade of sensory response), it is clear that it depends solely on the intellect" (*CSM*, 295, *AT*, IX–1, 237). From this passage it appears that Descartes thinks there are discrepancies between the spatial judgments we can make about what we see and the spatial array of the sensation. The third stage is necessary to account for these discrepancies. The exact nature of this third stage, however, remains problematic. Margaret Wilson points out, in as much as the purpose of the passage is to delineate the area of certainty in sensing, that it is quite plausible that Descartes intended to limit the area of uncertainty to the second grade, holding it is only this grade for which our sensory systems are responsible, while the third grade consists not of a direct experience of the visual world, but of intellectually generated beliefs about the visual world.[7] On this reading, it is not the sensory grade which goes unnoticed, instead we fail to notice our beliefs "go beyond" and fail to match what we apprehend in sensation.

It should be noted, however, that, as Wilson recognizes, the interpretation which accords most readily with the passage in the Sixth Set of Replies is not the most natural reading in all cases in Descartes' various discussions of sense perception.[8] For example, in the Sixth Discourse of the *Dioptrics*, Descartes says: "It is obvious too that we judge shape by the knowledge or opinion that we have of the position of the various parts of an object, and not by the resemblance of the pictures in our eyes. For these pictures usually contain only ovals and rhombuses, when they make us see circles and squares" (*CSM*, 172, *AT*, VI, 140–141). While it would not be completely out of the question to maintain that Descartes is here saying we sense ovals and believe them to be circles, a more natural reading would be closer to the lines proposed by Hatfield and Epstein, that, thanks to the operations of our visual system, we are caused to see circles and squares. Even if we accept this reading however, the exact nature of the processes of the visual system remains unclear. That Descartes several times described a particular visual process, such as perceiving the distance of an object, as taking place "as if by a natural geometry"[9] suggests the circles and squares we end up seeing are the product of some sort of calculation-like process in which the ovals and diamond shapes in the retinal image play an unnoticed role. Thomas Hall, however, in a gloss on the use of the phrase about natural geometry in *Treatise on Man*, suggests a physiological interpretation for the phrase. His idea is: Descartes supposes that the convergence of right and left eyes on the object sends different flows of animal spirits to the pineal gland. "These differences in flow", he writes, "occur automatically, according to Descartes, but the soul is affected by them and obtains information from them about the different patterns of activation of the muscles of the right and left eyes and hence of the eye's convergence. It does this without recognizing that this is the sort of information it is using."[10] On this sort of interpretation, then, the thrust of Descartes' account is to argue that processes like distance perception take place as a result of non-resembling corporeal changes.

As the originator of the sensation/perception distinction, it is not surprising that Descartes' conclusion is somewhat equivocal. It seems clear that Descartes holds there to be an aspect to sense perception, the one he describes as the second grade of sensation, which is importantly psychophysical in nature. In this sensory grade, there is something present to the mind which is as it is because of corporeal excitations.[11] I have argued that, at least in the first instance, Descartes did not intend to identify features of the sensation by means of any particular physical state, such as the retinal image. Indeed, part of his project is to argue that the retinal image qua image plays no role in sensation. Instead, his position seems to be that we know we sense light and colors because light and colors are present to the mind, we know this is due to the brain, which is necessary for sensation, so the process of sensation will require the transmittal of stimulation from external objects through nerves to the brain.[12] Ultimately, what is sensed depends upon and reflects the character of the brain states. It is also clear that, in some sense, Descartes thinks sensing, so understood, does not tell the whole story of visual perception but how he would want to complete the story is far less clear. In particular, it is not clear whether he thinks the story is to be completed by talking about intellectual states belonging to the perceiver or whether he wishes to attribute a certain amount of processing to the visual system. It is not clear whether Descartes thinks the problem of what we end up perceiving is a problem to be solved by studying the cognitive history of perceivers or by studying the visual system itself. And if, in fact, the visual system is the locus of visual processing for Descartes, it is still unclear whether he thinks visual processing poses a problem to be solved by attributing calculation-like processes to the visual system or whether he would limit himself to physiological processes, such as the flow of animal spirits in the nerves. Descartes' understanding of the nature of sensation led him to suppose we perceive more than we sense, but what exactly is accomplished in perception remains uncertain.

MALEBRANCHE

Malebranche's account of sense perception owes sufficiently to Descartes to maintain many of the ambiguities already found in Descartes himself. In developing his theory, however, Malebranche makes some useful distinctions and clarifications. In its general outlines, however, Malebranche's debt to Descartes is obvious. Early on in his discussion of sensory processes in *The Search after Truth*, Malebranche makes a list of "four things we confuse in each sensation" which is clearly reminiscent of Descartes' three grades of sensing. Malebranche's list runs as follows:

> The first is the *action* of the object, i.e. in heat, for example, the motion and *impact* of the particles of wood against the fibers of the hand.

The second is the *passion* of the sense organ, i.e. the agitation of the fibers of the hand caused by the agitation of the tiny particles of fire, which agitation is communicated to the brain, because otherwise the soul would sense nothing.

The third is the *passion*, sensation, or perception of the soul, i.e. what each of us feels when near the fire.

The fourth is the *judgment* the soul makes that what it perceives is in the hand and in the fire. Now this natural judgment is only a sensation but the sensation or natural judgment is almost always followed by another, free judgment that the soul makes so habitually that it is almost unable to avoid it.[13]

Malebranche differs from Descartes in breaking the first or physiological level into two, that which acts externally, and that in the sense organ which suffers the action, but the details of the process, culminating in a brain state, do not differ significantly from Descartes' own description. Malebranche's attention is focused quite directly on the ways sensation can mislead, and among the ways that interest him particularly are those in which the composition of the various sense organs and especially individual differences among the sense organs possessed by different perceivers can influence and alter the resulting sensations. In making the point, for example, that color sensations do not immediately reflect qualities in objects, Malebranche points out that individual variation in color sensation is so great that "[t]here are some people who see certain objects yellow with one eye and as green or blue with the other" (*OC*, I, XIII, vi, 153, *LO*, 66). Malebranche provides considerably greater detail than Descartes, but is following the outlines of Descartes' approach.

Malebranche's third category, "what each of us feels", corresponds neatly to Descartes' second grade. Indeed, Malebranche is explicit in his "Three Letters concerning M. Arnauld's Defense", that it was from Descartes he had learned sensations such as color, heat and pain are modifications of the soul,[14] modifications which he says in *The Search after Truth* are "in relation to what takes place in the body to which it is joined" (*OC*, I, XIII, I, 143, *LO*, 61). Because of the laws of our nature, certain changes in the body are followed by changes in the soul, which Malebranche says, we can't help but apprehend. Color sensations, for example, are immediately apparent to us. They are that mode of awareness which happens to the sighted as soon as they open their eyes and which never happens to the blind.

It is in the final category that Malebranche's account diverges from Descartes'. Like Descartes, he refers to this final stage as judgmental, but unlike Descartes, he distinguishes between "natural judgments" and "free judgments". The exact nature of the mechanisms by means of which natural judgments occur is not entirely clear, but the nature of the circumstances in which natural judgments take place can be readily understood. Malebranche gives the following example:

When we look at a cube, for example, it is certain that the sides of it that we see almost never project an image of equal size in the fundus of our eyes. This is so because the image of each of its sides that appears on the retina, or optic nerve, is very like a cube painted in perspective; and consequently the sensation we have of it ought to present the faces of the cube to us as being unequal, since they are unequal in a cube in perspective. Nonetheless, we see them as equal, and we are not deceived. (*OC*, I, VII. iv, 96, *LO*, 34)

Malebranche is claiming there are cases where we see something which is not what we would have expected to see, given what we know about the way in which light from the object impacts on our body—that is, given what we know about the patterns of excitation on the retina. In these cases, he thinks, we must account for the discrepancy and the means he is proposing is the natural judgment. In addition to the example given above of shape constancy, Malebranche early on instances size constancy and distance as phenomena needing explanation in terms of natural judgments.

Malebranche also distinguishes natural judgments from free judgments. Free judgments are judgments that I, the perceiver, am responsible for making. I can believe the external world has the sizes, shapes and distances I visually perceive them to have or I can withhold assent from this sort of proposition. The natural judgments are not made by the perceiver, but by the visual system belonging to the perceiver, or rather, as Malebranche prefers to put it, by God as the creator of the visual system. In calling what God does by means of the visual system "judgmental", Malebranche is stressing there are predictable connections between what occurs corporeally on the retina and the visual world we end up seeing, predictable because they are like what we could judge had we knowledge enough. "God fashions [these natural judgments] in such a way that we could form them ourselves if we knew optics and geometry as God does, if we knew everything that occurs in our eyes and our brain, and if our soul could act on its own and cause its own sensations" (*OC*, I, IX, iii, 120, *LO*, 46–47) What we end up seeing is a geometrical transformation performed by the visual system on the retinal display back in the direction of the origin of the light rays producing the retinal image.[15]

Thus Malebranche's distinction between natural judgments and free judgments makes clear, as far as he is concerned, that the optical system itself is responsible for a further element in visual perception, in addition to sensations. By the time he develops his account in the Elucidation on Optics, the processes he attributes to the visual system are quite complex.

> Among other things I see at about a hundred steps from me a large white horse running toward the right at full gallop. How can I see it thus according to the assumption I have made; this is how.
>
> I know . . . that all rays of light travel in a straight line and that those reflected from above the unknown object, i.e. from the horse, upon entering my eyes converge on the retina, and that the principal ray, the one that is the common axis of the two small cones . . . disturbs it the most. I must therefore judge that this ray falls on it perpendicularly and that therefore this horse is somewhere on this perpendicular line; but I do not yet know its distance.
>
> Second. I know that it is standing with its head turned to the right, although its image is reversed on my retina. For since I know that my retina is not flat but concave, geometry teaches me that perpendicular lines on a concave surface necessarily cross and that they can be parallel to each other only when they fall on a plane surface, and that therefore I must judge that its situation is opposite to that of its image.
>
> Third. I know also that it is about one hundred steps away, because I simultaneously have on my retina its image and that of the ground which it is on, by which I know roughly its distance; I judge its distance this way and by other means as well that need not be explained here.

Fourth. I know it is a large horse, for since I know its distance, the size of its image, and the diameter of my eyes, I construct this proportion: as the diameter of my eyes stands to its image, so the distance of the horse stands to its size; and comparing its size with that of other horses I have seen, I judge that it is one of the large horses.

Fifth. I know that it is running because its image changes place in my eyes, and that it is running at full gallop because I know the space its image quickly traverses on my retina; from this I conclude, by constructing the same proportion I just did, that it traverses a large space in a short time.

Sixth. I know it is white, because I know what kind of disturbance the rays it reflects produce on my retina, and since I can act on myself, I give myself, without ever erring, a given sensation when there is a given disturbance on my retina, and through it, in my brain.

Seventh. Finally, if I incline my head or lie down on the grass while looking at the horse, its image will change place on my retina and no longer disturb precisely the same fibers in it; yet I shall always see it the same. Or assuming that it stops and I begin to run while steadily looking at it, its image will change place in the fundus of my eyes, and yet I shall see it as immobile. This is because I at the same time know (a) that I have my head inclined and (b) what the situation of my eyes is, or the precise amount of motion I am giving myself by running, and because reasoning properly, I discover that the motion belongs only to me.

Eighth. If I approach the horse while looking at it, I shall see it as having the same size although its image continuously increases on my retina, and the height of this image is ten times greater when I am not more than ten steps from it than when I was a hundred. This is because optics teaches me that the various heights of the images of an object stand to each other as the inverse of the distances from the object, and because knowing that at each step I take this proportion remains the same, I continue to give myself the same sensation. (*OC*, III, Eclaircissement XVII, 43, 343–345, *LO*, Elucidation in Optics, pp. 745–746)

Perceivers end up with a spatially organized visual world containing a large white horse a hundred steps away running to the right only thanks to vast machinations, calculations and computations of the visual system. In the case of Malebranche it is quite clear that this complexly organized visual picture is instantaneously available to the perceiver, and is not the product of any calculations or any beliefs on the part of the perceiver. Rather, the calculations are the ones needed to be assigned to the visual system in order to account for the visual picture we end up with when our retinas are stimulated. The task Malebranche sets himself as a visual theorist is to ask: Given the complexly organized visual picture we succeed in seeing, what steps, if taken by the visual system, would be sufficient to account for this success?

Because this visual world is not the result of any action taken by a perceiver, it is not clear what sort of a relationship obtains between this visual picture and the other sensory grade available to perceivers, the sensation. In the case of Descartes, it seems most likely that he thought the judgments of the third stage were about the sensations of the second stage: this seems plain from the example Descartes gives about seeing the stick. I have suggested, however, there does not seem to be a compelling reason to identify Descartes' sensations with retinal images. In the case of Malebranche, similar considerations apply, although in somewhat different circumstances, leading to a somewhat different conclusion. Malebranche indubitably thinks the visual world is the result of a calculation in which the retinal image serves as a step in the calculation. But, since, for Malebranche, the calculation is performed by the visual system, not the perceiver, there is no reason to suppose Malebranche thinks there is anything sensed corresponding to the retinal image. There is no reason, that is, to suppose, for Malebranche, that sensations constitute a stage or a sensory core on the way to constructing a visual field. For Malebranche, the reason why the construction of the visual world is a multi-stage process is because the initial stage at which the external world acts on the visual system is insufficient to account for the spatially organized visual world Malebranche thinks we end up seeing. While the having of sensations is not similarly multi-stage, there is no reason to suppose Malebranche is thinking we at any time sense colors laid out in the spatial array they would be in if we sensed our retinal image and then subsequently perceive a differently organized visual display. So sensations for Malebranche are undoubtedly a part of what we perceive but they are not a step on the way to our perceiving, and, inasmuch as Malebranche refers to natural judgments as compound sensations, it seems likely he considers the entire visual picture containing the running white horse as a way of sensing a mind falls into upon appropriate stimulation.

BERKELEY

George Berkeley introduces a somewhat different vocabulary into his account of visual perception as a multi-stage process, so a part of the problem in assessing Berkeley's contribution to the history of the sensation/perception distinction will be to decide the extent to which his terms coincide with the concepts already introduced. Berkeley's claim is, in visual perception, that the proper and immediate ideas of sense are connected with mediate ideas via suggestion. In *Theory of Vision Vindicated*[16] he gives an account of this process, explaining what he means by his special terminology.

> By a sensible object I understand that which is properly perceived by sense. Things properly perceived by sense are immediately perceived. Besides things properly and immediately perceived by any sense, there may be also other things suggested to the mind by means of those proper and immediate objects. Which things so suggested are not objects of that sense, being in truth only objects of the imagination, and originally belonging to some other sense or faculty. Thus sounds are the proper objects of hearing, being properly and immediately perceived by that, and by no other sense. But, by the mediation of sounds or words, all other things may be suggested to the mind, and yet things so suggested are not thought the object of hearing. (*TVV*, 9)

In *Essay towards a Theory of Vision*, Berkeley most frequently identifies colors or sometimes light and colors as constituting the immediate objects of sight (*NTV*, 43, 103), while among the things we see only mediately he mentions coaches, also distance, the fixed sizes of objects and their situation. And, as Berkeley argues at length in *Three Dialogues between Hylas and Philonous*, the proper and immediate objects of sight are affections of the mind, ways of sensing the mind falls into, which cannot exist except as immediately perceived.

Berkeley's immediate objects of sight, like Descartes' and Malebranche's sensory level, are modifications of the mind that, in Malebranche's words, are what "each of us feels". Although Berkeley seems to think it is plain that, visually speaking, what each of us feels is light and color, because he is also going to be arguing for a somewhat restricted understanding of what is immediately perceived, he also provides some thought-experiments to help his readers recover this notion. Berkeley thinks what is immediately perceived by sight are the proper objects of that sense, so we immediately perceive by sight all and only what we could not perceive unless we had sight. The proper objects are what we perceive simply because we are sighted—we have a visual sensory system. Berkeley repeatedly tries to get his readers to think themselves back into the condition a person would be in "at first receiving of his sight" (*NTV*, 103) by asking them to consider the experiences of a man born blind when first made to see. The purpose of this thought-experiment is to help his readers find themselves in a state in which we see variety of light and color, but not coaches, distances or fixed sizes. In stressing the importance of such thought-experiments, I am disagreeing with Hatfield's and Epstein's contention that Berkeley took over uncritically the view that the sensory core could be identified with the retinal image. Although Berkeley didn't think facts about the retina are irrelevant to identifying what we can see, and he explicitly agreed with Descartes and Malebranche that we don't immediately perceive distance, because objects at different distances along the same line of sight cannot affect the retina differently, like Descartes, Berkeley wanted to stress that the retinal image is non-visual in nature and quite clearly thought there were phenomenological means for identifying the proper objects of vision.

Where Berkeley diverges most dramatically from earlier accounts is in his characterization of the next stage, that which is perceived mediately. Berkeley's concern is to show when we perceive by sight that which cannot be immediately perceived, this is neither the result of the functioning of the visual system itself, nor is such perception to be attributed to beliefs intellectually arrived at. Rather, Berkeley tries to demonstrate that we can explain how the visual system gets supplemented by relying on other sensory means. Thus, if we perceive objects by sight at a distance, even though distance cannot be registered by the visual system, or if we perceive objects as being of fixed size, even though the blobs of color we apprehend visually are of almost any size, this is because distance and fixed size are apprehended tangibly and kinesthetically. Berkeley frequently glosses his term for this process, "suggestion", by means of an analogy with language. We learn, he says, over the course of time, and by habit, to read our visual experiences by assigning to them meanings derived from other senses, so that, for example, a small faint patch of color will be seen as a larger object at a considerable distance off (*NTV*, 51). On Berkeley's account, a good deal less of what we take ourselves to be seeing is actually due to the proper functioning of the visual system. Instead of asking, with Malebranche, What knowledge must be attributed to the visual system in order to account for my perception of the white horse? Berkeley is proposing that we investigate what information is available to us from other sensory systems in addition to the light and color properly perceived by sight. Thus, as may be the case in Descartes' account of vision in the Sixth Set of Replies, Berkeley is proposing what we learn by studying the visual system is limited to the level of sensation, but, unlike Descartes, Berkeley thinks the beliefs informing our visual sensations derive from, in his terms, the imagination, not the intellect. The beliefs that give meaning to visual sensations are themselves sensory in nature.

REID

Reid is the first of those in the history we have been exploring to introduce explicitly the terminology of sensation and perception into discussions of vision. As the following passage from *An Inquiry into the Human Mind*[17] shows, however, his general understanding of the nature of the sensory processes does not differ overmuch from that first found in Descartes:

> Although there is no reasoning in perception, yet there are certain means and instruments, which, by the appointment of nature, must intervene between the object and our perception of it; and, by these our perceptions are limited and regulated. First, if the object is not in contact with the organ of sense, there must be some medium which passes between them. Thus, in vision, the rays of light; in hearing, the vibrations of elastic air; in smelling, the effluvia of the body smelled, must pass from the object to the organ; otherwise we have no perception. Secondly, there must be some action or impression upon the organ of sense, either by the immediate application of the object, or by the medium that goes between them. Thirdly, the nerves which go from the brain to the organ, must receive some impression by means of that which was made upon the organ; and probably by means of the nerves, some impression must be made upon the brain. Fourthly, the impression made upon the organ, nerves, and brain, is followed by a sensation. And, last of all, this sensation is followed by the perception of the object.
>
> (*IHM*, Chap. 6, sect. XXI, p. 214)

While Reid, like Malebranche before him, has expanded upon the details of Descartes's first physiological grade, the general outline of the account has otherwise not altered one whit. Following upon physiological events in the sense organs, nerves and brain are two psychological stages, first the sensation, then the perception. What then, for Reid, is a sensation and what is a perception?

As Reid asserts in *Essays on the Intellectual Powers of Man*,[18] he intends by his notion of a sensation what he takes Berkeley to mean by a sensible idea. Reid writes:

> As there can be no notion or thought but in a thinking being; so there can be no sensation but in a sentient being. It is the act, or feeling of a sentient being; its very essence consists in its being felt. Nothing can resemble a sensation, but a similar sensation in the same, or in some other mind. To think that any quality in a thing that is inanimate can resemble a sensation, is a great absurdity. In all this, I cannot but agree perfectly with bishop Berkeley. (*EIPM*, II, X, 191).[19]

Reid, that is, takes himself to share with Berkeley the view that sentient beings have characteristic responses in consciousness to physiological events. Sensations are ways in which we feel, available phenomenologically. What Reid, like Berkeley before him, wants to stress is that there can be nothing more to a sensation than the way it is felt. It is a term needed to describe the way sentient beings feel.

When Reid describes what he means by perception, however, he diverges quite explicitly from Berkeley. Reid spells out what he takes to be involved in perception as follows:

> If, therefore, we attend to that act of our mind which we call the perception of an external object of sense, we shall find in it these three things. *First*, some conception or notion of the object perceived. *Secondly*, A strong and irresistible conviction and belief of its present existence. And, *thirdly*, that this conviction and belief are immediate, and not the effect of reasoning. (*EIPM*, II, V, 111–112)

For Reid, what is to be explained by referring to perceptions is the ineluctable belief perceivers have that what they are perceiving has a mind-independent existence. When I am pricked by a pin or when I see and smell a rose, the prick that I feel, the aroma and the color as it appears are accompanied by a belief in the external existence of the pin and the rose. But what is believed to have external existence is not, of course, the prick, which is a mind-dependent sensation, as are the aroma and the color appearance. What is believed to have external existence is the hard, sharp pin and the colored, scented rose, but these conceptions are quite other than the sensations which they accompany. Perceptions are belief states of perceivers, to which Reid appeals in order to account for some cognitive content of perceiving, content which is also quite different from the content of sensing. Thus, for Reid, there is no suggestion that perception is a transformation of sensation, perception is an entirely independent cognitive process from sensation, although, as it happens, when we sense we also perceive. We don't derive the content of our concept of the pin as hard and sharp from sensations of being pricked and we don't derive the content of our concept of the rose as colored and scented from the aromas and color-appearances we sense. While Reid takes it to be a law of our nature that perception accompanies sensation, just as it is a law of our nature that sensation accompanies physiological impressions, he supposes it is in principle possible to have perceptions without sensation just as it is in principle possible to have sensations without impressions.

The problem Reid introduced the concept of perception to solve was, in essence, an epistemological problem. If, as Berkeley thought, we are conscious only of our sensations, then Reid feared, we may find we are not in a position to assert the existence of a material world independent of our sensations and, indeed, may be tempted to deny that such a material world exists.

So Reid claimed that Berkeley has provided insufficient analysis of the content of our cognitive states: they contain not just mind-dependent sensations but perceptions of mind-independent objects. The nature of Reid's project often leaves his account phenomenologically obscure. Because our interest is in the objects of perception, Reid says, we often pay no attention to the sensations accompanying perception, and may fail to notice they are present at all, particularly when such sensations are not forceful or painful. This means that Reid is apparently willing to say when I perceive the red chair by my desk, that I am paying no attention to the sensuous sensation, but only to what Reid takes to be the proper referent of my term "red", namely the external piece of the world that is the origin of the psychological states in me. But since Reid also admits that the nature of the external cause is unknown, it is puzzling to imagine to what Reid thinks I am attending when I perceive my red chair. Whatever the conceptual content of my perceiving, however, one aspect that Reid is intending to capture is my conviction, deemed by him immediate and unlearned, that the chair exists.

SOME IMPLICATIONS

One very striking result of putting together these early accounts of the sensation/ perception distinction is the uniformity seeming to obtain in the way the concept of sensation is handled. From Descartes to Reid, there is agreement that, in accounts of perceiving, it is necessary to identify that stage that is the way perceivers feel when the appropriate sensory system is stimulated, altered and changed. Part of what might be imagined to produce this uniformity is a common acceptance of the view, originally articulated by Descartes, but often repeated, that it is the mind which senses and the mind which sees.[20] It should be stressed that for Descartes, as for the others, the mind that senses is an embodied mind and that the sensations it apprehends are the result of some appropriate corporeal changes. Nevertheless the conviction is that in order to talk about perception, we need to talk about something happening to perceivers because they are bodies that are emminded—bodies which respond to some sorts of corporeal changes with mental modifications or ways of feeling. Typically, these ways of feeling or sensations are identified by a list of phenomenal qualities which does not vary overmuch: light, colors, sounds, aromas, heat, cold, pleasure, pain, etc. In general, the thought seems to be that these qualities express ways in which we feel when a given sensory system is operating and which we lose when it is not.

Even more striking, because perhaps more counterintuitive, is the lack of uniformity found in the understanding of the second, or perceptual stage. This second stage is presumably what we all do as successful perceivers, yet there has been no agreement at all in the various accounts under review, about what successful perceiving is like. The uncertainties that initially surfaced in trying to decide the nature of Descartes' account of perception replicate themselves in the very different sets of assumptions about the nature of what is accomplished in perception found in subsequent theories. In the case of Malebranche, the perceptual achievement is taken to be a highly articulated visual picture. For Berkeley, what is perceived is visual sensation rendered meaningful by other sensible information. Reid claims that to perceive is to believe in the existence of a mind-independent world. Thus, rather startlingly, there is no clear agreement at all about the nature of the final stage in perception, the stage perceptual theory is presumably supposed to explain.

These conflicting accounts of the outcome of perception seem to rest in part on different assumptions about how much of the activity of perceiving by sight is visual in nature, how much, that is, is due to the operation of the visual sensory system alone. Part of the confusion in dealing with Descartes stemmed from difficulties in deciding whether he took the accomplishment of perception to be due to the actions of the visual system or to be the result of intellectually generated beliefs. Does Descartes, we must wonder, think that, thanks to the operation of the visual system, perceivers see, for example, a cube of fixed size and equal sides, or does he think we believe something sensed with varying sizes and shapes is a uniformly sized, shaped cube? Subsequent authors take a range of positions on this issue. Malebranche supposes the perceptual outcome to be a visual picture delivered entirely by the visual system, about which the perceiver can later make free judgments. Perceiving a cube of fixed size is therefore a problem to be solved by the visual system alone, while the perceiver "freely" develops beliefs about the veracity of the visual system. Reid, on the other hand, is located on the other end of this particular spectrum. He describes the perceptual stage as consisting in beliefs about the perceptual world, beliefs which are quite independent of the content of the senses. For Reid, to perceive a cube is to believe in the presence of a mind-independent cube. Such beliefs, however, are not ones we are free to accept or reject, but are the result of our cognitive nature. Berkeley is located somewhere in the middle here. Like Reid, Berkeley limits the output of the visual system to its proper objects—all that we can strictly be said to see are light and colors, but Berkeley holds that we learn to supplement this visual information with further beliefs derived from the other senses. As far as Berkeley is concerned, when we perceive a cube, what we see by means of our visual system has varying shapes and sizes. To say we see it as a cube, for Berkeley, is to say that we take what we see to stand for characteristic tangible and kinesthetic experiences. There is, then, no real agreement among our various authors about what a theory of the visual system is supposed to explain.

Given the wide variety of accounts of the nature of the perceptual stage, it is not surprising that there is also no one theory about how the perceptual stage relates to the sensational. In the case of Berkeley, it seems that perceptions result from sensations in the sense that we have or are aware of visual sensations which suggest their perceptual meanings. There are two identifiable psychological processes, both of which are open to introspection, although Berkeley insists there are not two separate temporal stages. Rather, we perceive when we sense meaningfully. In the case of Malebranche, the situation is somewhat less clear. Malebranche, however, sometimes refers to his second stage as that of "compound sensation", suggesting a picture in which perception is not triggered by sensation, but perhaps merely incorporates visual sensations as a part of the visual outcome. That this is Malebranche's approach is supported by his example of seeing the white horse, where "white" is part of what we give ourselves, thanks to our visual system, along with "large" and "running to the right". Reid's account is different still. Like Berkeley, he seems to think that sensations trigger perceptions, and like Berkeley, he thinks the content of perception is other than the content of sensation, but Reid thinks the objects of perceptions are their external world objects and not the sensations accompanying them. Because

Reid sets great store by the epistemological superiority of perceptions, he tends to emphasize their independence from sensations, so sensations, for Reid, are reduced to the role of frequently overlooked accompaniments to perception. Thus there is uniform agreement that we have sensations and agreement about what it means to say we have sensations, but there is no agreement among these authors about how or even whether sensations help us have perceptions.

If there is a lesson of wider import to be extracted from this history, it is that the significance or usefulness of a distinction between sensation and perception cannot be addressed until the concept of "perception" has been squarely addressed. Clearly, it makes no sense to try to decide whether or not we do or we do not need sensations in order to perceive unless we have a principled means of identifying when the stage of perception has been successfully accomplished. All of the authors we have been looking at agree that perceivers have a number of different beliefs about what they see. But there has been a lot of shifting about when it comes to identifying which beliefs are due to the proper functioning of the visual system and hence form part of the problem area for vision science and which fall outside the concerns of vision science. Before we can tackle the question, Why do things look as they do? we have to be able to say how things look. Among these early originators of the sensation/perception distinction, there is no agreement about how things look.

What I have said seems to imply that if there are problems with the sensation/perception distinction, they stem primarily from problems with the notion of "perception" and not with the more heavily criticized notion of sensation. That there was widespread agreement back in the seventeenth and eighteenth centuries about the use of this concept is certainly no argument that it retains its usefulness today. It is interesting to point out, however, that these early accounts of sensation do not present all of those features that were often singled out for criticism by those rejecting the notion of sensation. Koffka, for example, assumed that the distinction between a field of sensations and a field of perceptions was a distinction between a sense field that corresponded exactly to the proximal stimuli and a perceptual field which had through experience been corrected in the direction of reality.[21] This sort of theory does indeed give rise to some odd implications or suggestions: that perceivers, for example, are carrying around in consciousness two separate arrays, an unnoticed sensed array in one spatial orientation and a perceived array in another orientation. In such circumstances, to suppose that sensations are mere artifacts of the theory is quite natural. But among the early authors here under discussion, while the general thought behind the concept of sensation has certainly been that perceivers sense as they do because their proximal stimuli are as they are, there is no attempt at this period to define or locate sensations in terms of specific places of proximal stimulation. Sensations are identified broadly and phenomenologically as the proper objects of some sensory system, rather than specifically or physiologically with some particular area of reception, such as the retinal image. That perceivers sense as well as perceive is not a claim that there is a stage in consciousness in which perceivers are aware of a mosaic of sensory points displayed in a space that is isomorphic to the retinal image. In the way in which these early authors described sensation, it is more likely to be incorporated into, rather than in conflict with, perception. To the extent that conflicts are identified, they are more likely to be between what we believe and what we sense or to reflect the operations of more than one sensory system, than to be between differing deliverances of the same visual system. The theory that Koffka subjects to criticism, therefore, reflects a later development of the theory of sensation and perception.

Returning to a time when the sensation/perception distinction was new is not, alas, a move that can release all the answers. We do not discover a theory in such a pure form that we can decisively accept or reject it on the spot. But neither do we discover theories that are hopelessly out of date because of some ignorant naïvetée. The theorists discussed here are not, for example, so wedded to a distinction between mind and body that they imagined that physiological facts had no role to play in our understanding of visual perception, and they clearly did not think that an understanding of physiological facts could adequately substitute for the use of the concept of sensation. Perhaps a more significant difference between early modern and contemporary theorists, however, is that the understanding of the relationship that existed between mind and body among the earlier theorists allowed them unabashedly to foreground the phenomenology of perception. At any rate, I do suppose that a retreat to the past can have its uses. Looking at the sensation/perception distinction from this remote angle can bring to the fore long ignored assumptions and raise questions that would repay redressing.[22]

NOTES

1. English translations from *The Search after Truth* are from the translation by Thomas M. Lennon and Paul J. Olscamp, Columbus, Ohio: Ohio State University Press, 1980, henceforth to be referred as *LO*. References will be to *LO*, page number and to Malebranche, *Oeuvres Completes,* ed. Genevieve Rodis-Lewis, Paris: J. Vrin, 1964, by volume number, book, chapter and page number, henceforth to be referred to as *OC*. This quotation is to be found in *OC*, III, Bk I, ch. XIV, 155, and in *LO*, 67.
2. James J. Gibson, *The Perception of the Visual World*, Boston, Houghton Mifflin, 1950 and Irvin Rock, *The Logic of Perception*, Cambridge, Mass., MIT Press, 1983.
3. English translations are based on those found in *Philosophical Writings of Descartes*, translated by John Cottingham, Robert Stoothoff and Dugald Murdoch, Cambridge: Cambridge University Press, 1984. References will be to *CSM* and page number, and to *Oeuvres de Descartes*, Charles Adam and Paul Tannery, Paris: J. Vrin, 1973, to be referred to as *AT* by volume and page number. This quotation is to be found in *CSM*, 294–295. *AT*, IX–1, 236.
4. Another, and perhaps prior, problem is to identify precisely what Descartes means by a "grade" here, and to understand how each grade is related to the others. When it is assumed that, for Descartes, corporeal and mental events are entirely separate and distinct, then the three grades are generally taken to be temporally distinct stages. Some, most notably Paul Hoffmann, has argued that Descartes admits the possibility of "straddling modes" so that the first and second grades here might be thought of as corporeal and mental versions of the same event. See, for example, "The Unity of Descartes's Man", Philosophical Review, XCV, No 3 (July, 1986) pp. 339–370.
5. Although the details of Descartes' account naturally require upgrading.
6. In "The Sensory Core and the Medieval Foundations of Early Modern Perceptual Theory". *ISIS*, 1979 (253) pp. 363–384.
7. Margaret Wilson, "Descartes on the Perception of Primary Qualities" in *Essays on the Philosophy and Science of Rene Descartes*, edited by Stephen Voss, New York, Oxford University Press, 1993, pp. 162–176.

8. The difficulties in putting together a single coherent account of the various things Descartes has written about visual perception has been discussed by Wilson in "Descartes on the Perception of Primary Qualities", Celia Wolf-Devane, *Descartes on Seeing: Epistemology and Visual Perception*, Carbondale and Edwardsville, Southern Illinois University Press, 1993, and myself in *Berkeley's Revolution in Vision*, Ithaca: Cornell University Press, 1990.

9. *Dioptrics, CSM*, 170, *AT*, VI, 137, *Treatise on Man, AT*, XI, 160.

10. *Treatise on Man*, French text with translation and commentary by Thomas Steele Hall, Cambridge, Mass.: Harvard University Press, 1972, p. 62.

11. Although the exact relationship between what is present to the mind and the physical state to which it corresponds is controversial.

12. For a fuller account of Descartes' version of this process, see the Fourth Discourse of the *Dioptrics, CSM*, 164–166, *AT*, VI, 109–114.

13. *OC*, Bk I, ch. 10, section vi, p. 129, *LO*, p. 52.

14. *OC*, vol. VI p. 201.

15. To put this distinction into the earlier discussion of Descartes, Wilson is suggesting that in the sixth set of replies the most natural interpretation of Descartes' third grade is as Malebranchian free judgments, but some of what Descartes says in the *Dioptrics* suggests that he is thinking of Malebranchian natural judgments.

16. All references will be to *The Works of George Berkeley, Bishop of Cloyne*, Volume I, edited by A. A. Luce and T. E. Jessop, London: Thomas Nelson and Sons, Ltd., 1948. References to *Theory of Vision Vindicated* will be as *TVV* and section number, to *Essays towards a New Theory of Vision* will be as *NTV* and section number.

17. Thomas Reid, *An Inquiry into the Human Mind*, edited by Timothy J. Duggan, Chicago: University of Chicago Press, 1970. All references will be to *IHM* and chapter, section and page number.

18. *Essays on the Intellectual Powers of Man*, Introduction by Baruch Brody, Cambridge, Mass., MIT Press, 1969. References will be to *EIPM*, essay number, section number, and page number.

19. Phillip Cummins has spelled out helpfully the usefulness of Reid's concept of sensation for understanding Berkeley's ideas of sense in "Berkeley's Ideas of Sense", *Nous*, vol. IX, no. 1 (March, 1975), 55–72.

20. *AT*, vi, 109, 141, *CSM*, 164, 172.

21. K. Koffka, *Principles of Gestalt Psychology*, New York: Harcourt Brace and World, Inc., 1935.

22. I owe a great debt to the members of the sensation/perception discussion group and to Paul Whittle in particular for convening this group. This has been instrumental in helping me to think about material in early modern philosophy through a rather different lens. I owe special thanks to Paul Whittle, Dejan Todorovic and Robert Schwartz for their comments on earlier drafts of this piece.

2

Cognition as Code-Breaking

HORACE BARLOW
Physiological Laboratory, University of Cambridge, UK

INTRODUCTION

No one can seriously hold that cognitive behaviour is either entirely gene-driven and innate, or entirely the result of learning, training and experience; there can be arguments about their relative importance, but the behaviour of higher mammals certainly depends upon both. There is not, however, any coherent view of how genetically determined structure and acquired experience fit together to produce our perception of the world and the resulting behaviour. Does experience simply enter a few parameter values in a program that is written by the genes? Is the developing brain like the accident report form of an insurance company, with slots waiting for important details to be entered? Does experience laboriously debug an error-ridden developmental program, as Marvin Minsky once proposed? Or do the genes merely bias a mechanism that is predominantly moulded by experience?

In this DNA-dominated world where a new gene for this or that is discovered every week, one should perhaps welcome a strong presentation of the case for nurture, such as is given by Elman et al. (1996), but their exaggerated claims and one-sided arguments are not convincing. For instance few people who have observed the growth of physiological knowledge of the cortex over the past 40 years would agree with their claim that " . . . there is no compelling evidence for innate representations in the cortex". They also fail to appreciate that both the brain and behaviour have evolved dramatically during the comparatively recent evolution of *Homo Sapiens*, and that such changes depend upon heritable variation for natural selection to act upon. The fact that cortical size and the accompanying behaviour have changed so much so recently points to there being more than the usual amount of genetic variation in the cortex, and this genetic variation is surely of enormous interest to anyone interested in understanding our nature.

Perception and the Physical World: Psychological and Philosophical Issues in Perception.
Edited by Dieter Heyer and Rainer Mausfeld. © 2002 John Wiley & Sons, Ltd.

One must suspect that experience and innate structure are intertwined in very complex ways. Whereas most previous discussions have regarded nature and nurture as opposite explanations in competition with each other, the code-breaking analogy not only suggests that they cooperate, but also points to their respective roles. William James (1892) described the infant's subjective experience as "one big blooming buzzing Confusion", and the classical view is that this is converted into the more-or-less orderly succession of not-very-unexpected events that we normally experience by acquiring an immense amount of detailed knowledge of the world through experience. In this paper I shall examine the alternative idea that it is like code-breaking, where discovering the key enables a meaningless string of symbols to be converted into an intelligible message in a known language. This requires that the infant has an innate framework or "language of the brain" which has been honed by evolutionary selection to provide a suitable basis for our adult stream of consciousness about the world around us. We have very few other useful models or analogies that suggest how nature and nurture might cooperate rather than compete.

The analogy is not necessarily very close or complete, and it is the ancient, rather than the modern, aspects of cryptography and cryptanalysis that are relevant, but the theory of coding and code-breaking are now well understood, and I think they provide a guide to understanding some aspects of the process of cognitive development.

CODE-BREAKING AS AN ANALOGY FOR COGNITION

Coding converts a message in a known language, using a strictly-defined encryption procedure, into a stream of symbols that is initially meaningless to a recipient. The problem of code-breaking is to convert this stream back into the same language as the original, in other words to discover the inverse of the encryption process. The apparently meaningless stream of coded symbols is held to be analogous to the (initially unintelligible) stream of sensory messages received by the brain, while the meaningful message in a known language that is the result of code-breaking is the stream of meaningful information about the world that an experienced human or animal generates from its sensory messages.

Notice that according to the analogy the brain is not initially *tabula rasa*, for it is assumed that there is an innately determined "language of the brain" already there. It would be an impossible task to break a code encrypted from an unknown language, for reasons that will become clear when the process is described in greater detail. The result of the brain's code-breaking must be a grammatical, meaningful, message in the language of the brain, in the same way that the inverse of the encryption process has to produce a grammatical, meaningful, message in the original language.

If there is some similarity between code-breaking and cognition, what can one say about the encryption process? In our analogy, this is the process whereby sensory messages are generated from physical scenes and the events happening in them, but it is clearly unlike true encryption, which starts with messages in a particular language and is deliberately designed to conceal their meaning. It might be possible to elucidate some aspects of the "language of the brain" by developing this side of the analogy, but because of the clear differences this will not be pursued here.

One might be tempted by a simpler model, perhaps closer to the one Locke himself envisaged, in which there is nothing equivalent to this requirement of producing a legal message in a particular language and the brain is genuinely *tabula rasa*. One of the merits of the code-breaking analogy is that it shows that such a task is too difficult: for code-breaking, some prior knowledge is not just enormously helpful, but absolutely necessary, and the analogy suggests that this prior knowledge must be very extensive—something like the very thorough knowledge of a particular language that is an absolute necessity for anyone attempting to break codes originating in that language. This position is much closer to the one proposed by Kant in *The critique of pure reason*; although the roles proposed for nature and nurture are not necessarily the same as Kant's, I think it might be argued that they are more precisely defined in the analogy than they are in his or any other proposal about what occurs in the development of cognition.

There are circumstances in which we, as adults, experience a fragment of the transition from confusion to clarity that results from knowledge of the code-breaking key. If one emerges from an underground station in a not very familiar part of the city one may initially be hopelessly disoriented, but then one glimpses a familiar landmark on the skyline, or recognises a detail in the building opposite: suddenly one is wrenched around to become properly oriented in familiar surroundings, and one walks towards one's destination with complete confidence. Or one turns on the radio to hear a vaguely familiar noise, and this resolves itself over a period of several seconds into a particular moment in a particular movement of a well-known symphony. But it is not easy to analyse further the subjective experiences hinted at above, and what the model provides is a picture of the whole process of change from one state to the other that can help us to understand it. How we learn to make sense of the world is certainly an important problem in cognition: What can code-breaking, where a similar problem is solved, tell us about this process?

THE POSSIBILITY OF CODE-BREAKING

Code-breaking is not only possible, but very much easier than might be supposed. It is perhaps not surprising that it is easier than you or I suppose, but what is truly astonishing is that those who devise and use codes have often been deceived in the same way. Fletcher Pratt's book *Secret and Urgent* proves this with many fascinating stories, often concerned with Royalty, Assassination and Treason (Pratt 1939). When imprisoned, Mary Queen of Scots, for instance, communicated in code with the court of Spain and her unjailed Roman Catholic supporters in England, but her communications were regularly intercepted and decoded by the wily Walsingham, Elizabeth I's able secretary of state, and messages betraying a plot to assassinate Elizabeth led directly to Mary's trial and execution. Ironically, Walsingham had acquired his knowledge of cryptography in Rome, where the subject was being rapidly advanced as a result of the Vatican's great practical interest in it.

Three hundred years later codes and code-breaking played an important part in the Dreyfuss case, for an intercepted message from Pannizzardi, the Italian military attaché in Paris, to his home government was at first wrongly deciphered by the French Black Chamber, and appeared to incriminate Dreyfuss; an alternative decipherment was found, however, and this ended with the words "we do not know him here", exonerating Dreyfuss completely. To find which was the correct decipherment the Black Chamber fed a message, ostensibly from a French spy in Italy, to Pannizzardi and intercepted it as he sent it on to his home government; with the clear as well as the coded versions of this message before them they were able to prove conclusively that the exonerating decipherment was the correct one.

A final example of over-confidence in the security of codes is provided by the German armed forces in the Second World War, for they were convinced that their Enigma system could not be deciphered. This system depended upon a mechanical device, developed from a Polish prototype, that continuously changed the encryption code as the messages were fed through it, and the fascinating story of how the system was broken has been told many times, most recently in the book edited by Hinsley and Stripp (1993). It was a close run thing, and Allied success depended upon knowledge of the Polish prototype, the capture of an intact coding machine, and occasionally obtaining clear as well as coded versions of messages through accident or carelessness. For many periods of the war the code remained secure, but in the end it was broken through prodigious effort and ingenuity, aided by crude electro-mechanical proto-computers; but it *was* broken, with calamitous consequences for the Germans in many theatres of the war, and the methods used were essentially classical.

The history of cryptography shows that codes are becoming harder and harder to break, and the latest ones may be genuinely unbreakable, except by methods or accidents that we must agree to exclude. The principles of cryptography are now understood and it may no longer be true that even the experts underestimate the ease of breaking codes, but in the past this has certainly been the case. There are, however, two ways in which codes and code-breaking differ significantly from cognition.

First, the infant trying to make sense of the world has, by and large, a friendly and helpful environment. Parents will repeat messages, point at things, encourage self-discovery of the consequences of the infant's actions, and provide rewards and punishments of their own. In contrast the code-breaker is always confronted with a hostile world in which everything has deliberately been made as difficult as possible. We don't really want to include this malicious aspect in our analogy; the relationship between the infant's sensory messages and the real world is extremely complex and difficult, but, as Einstein said in another context, the Good Lord is "nicht boshaft".

The second difference is that our cognitive experience of the world does not allow us to reconstruct the causes of sensory messages without error, and almost certainly does not even allow us to reconstruct the sensory messages themselves at all completely. In other words sensory coding includes an irreversible loss of information as well as the reversible decoding that the analogy postulates. This is quite a serious objection, because information loss is certainly likely to be minimised for "useful" and "important" classes of sensory stimuli through natural selection, while it will be allowed or even encouraged for other types in order to reduce the overall load of information. Furthermore, it is far from clear that the reversible component can be conceptually separated from this lossy coding, for the two processes are likely to be closely interwoven. While acknowledging that this is the case I would argue that the reversible component is present, and it is this component that accounts for the improvements in perception with experience and the often remarkable extent to which we can accurately reconstruct the world surrounding us from our cognitive experience of it. The analogy suggests how nature and nurture conspire together to bring this about.

These differences mean that one must not push the analogy too far, and many of the fascinating modern developments in cryptography do not seem relevant. But since the principles are now understood the elementary applications can provide an enlightening model of the relation between innate and acquired knowledge of the world.

THE IMPORTANCE OF REDUNDANCY

Why is code-breaking relatively easy? It results from the enormous amount of redundancy in the messages that are encoded and then decoded. The importance of redundancy in perception is already quite well established (Attneave, 1954; Barlow, 1959, 2001; Atick, 1992), so we can see an immediate link with code-breaking, but we can be only dimly aware of the high redundancy of sensory inputs without quantitative measures. Shannon gave this in his paper on the entropy of printed English (Shannon, 1951). Initially one expects a stream of letters of the alphabet and spaces to convey $\log_2(27) = 4.755$ bits/symbol. He showed how the uneven frequencies of letters, digrams, and trigrams, which he obtained from Fletcher Pratt's book, reduce this to about 3 bits/symbol. Higher order multigram frequencies were not known, but human subjects know something about the higher order redundancy of English, for they improve in their capacity to guess the next letter in a string as the length of this string increases; by measuring this effect he was able to show that the 100th letter in a string conveys on average only 1 bit of extra information. Thus written English, after the first dozen words or so, is about 79% redundant.

The fact that written language is highly redundant, together with the detailed forms this redundancy takes, is the life-blood of code-breaking. In a simple substitution cipher you can find what stands for "e" simply by finding the commonest letter in the coded messages, and you can get a very good idea about "t" and "a" also. Word frequencies are also useful: "the" is the commonest word in English, with "of" as runner up, and "that" is the commonest four-letter word with "this" and "from" as runners up.

Such little linguistic scraps are constantly used, but their lesson is that language is redundant in extraordinarily intricate ways. There are some generally applicable statistics, such as the letter, digram, and trigram frequencies, but much of the redundancy consists of the fact that very large numbers of symbol combinations simply do not occur; there are almost 400 million possible sequences of 6 symbols each with 27 possible values, but only a very small fraction of these actually occur. Spell-checkers depend on this fact, for if it was not the case a large number of mis-spellings of one word would be correct spellings of another, and your spell-checker cannot reliably tell which meaning you intended.

Knowing that it is redundancy that makes codes easily breakable, it is obvious what the cryptographer must do to defeat the code-breakers, and the history of cryptography is largely the story of developing such techniques. This is fascinating in its own right, but it is not relevant here. The analogy would lose its value, however, if what is true of written language was not also true for the sensory messages likely to be generated by the natural environment. How redundant are they?

REDUNDANCY OF IMAGES

Some information is available about the redundancy of natural images. Kersten (1987) measured it using methods like Shannon's, and he was able to show from subjects' ability to fill in missing pixels that images are at least 50% redundant. Some image-compression methods allow reversible coding with less than 1 bit/pixel, implying much greater redundancy, and these codes only exploit its more obvious forms. The high redundancy of natural images is made obvious by considering images composed of random, independent, pixel values: how many such white-noise images would you have to look at before seeing *one* that is in the least like a natural scene? Here again real images seem to occupy only a tiny proportion of the available space, but we don't have the code-breakers, dictionarists, and cross-word-puzzle-solvers to tell us about the intricacies. Field (1994) says that images lie on cones in higher dimensional spaces and Ruderman (1994) likens the space to the froth on beer; however one describes it, most of the space is empty and natural images only occupy a tiny fraction of it.

Now these images are redundant because their cause, the natural world, is also redundant. It is, for instance, composed of objects at various distances that have relatively uniform surface properties and tend to move as wholes. One can see at once that representing a natural scene by the positions and poses of the objects in it would be enormously more compact than the directly coded images the scene actually produces, and cognition can perhaps be regarded as the process of deriving such an economical representation. The analogy with the code-breaker's task is immediately evident, for this is a matter of discovering transformation rules that convert an encrypted message into a sequence of words that is allowable in the language of the clear. Similarly understanding an image can be regarded as applying transformations that enable it to be interpreted as a set of known objects at determinate positions. Both cases require the matching of structure and regularity in the external world to structure and regularity that is held internally, and it is the matching that ultimately brings meaning to the coded symbols or the sensory messages.

GRAMMAR AND MEANING

Grammatical structure is a major source of redundancy in language. Linguists can be relied upon to object to the apparently derogatory description of grammar as a form of redundancy because of its importance in giving meaning to a sentence, but in fact there is no contradiction here: grammar restricts the allowable word sequences, so it undoubtedly contributes to redundancy, but this is not incompatible with its having an important role in generating meaning. In Shannon's experiment, different characteristics are used to guess the next letter as the symbol sequence available to the subject increases in length. For single letters, only the frequency of individual letters can be used; then come the digram and trigram frequencies; next one recognises the letter sequence of a plausible word; and somewhere between about 10 and 30 symbols one realises that a grammatical sentence is taking shape, and non-grammatical guesses can be excluded. Finally meaning emerges, and one may have enough prior knowledge of the topic to exclude certain meanings that are grammatical, but unlikely to be true. Grammar is a step to meaning, but that does not imply that it is not also a form of redundancy.

It is clear then that language has much structure or redundancy, and so does the world around us. It is an interesting speculation that the similarity between language and the world goes deeper than the mere presence of redundancy: their forms may also be similar. In written language, letters are made of elements that can be juxtaposed in many, but by no means all, different ways; the letters can be grouped to make many different words, but again by no means all groupings occur. Properly spelt words can be strung into a large, but again restricted, range of grammatical sentences, and the grammatical sentences may or may not be true and meaningful accounts of the world. At each stage the restrictions are forms of redundancy, and this hierarchical structure is reminiscent of scaling invariance in natural images: detailed statistical structure occurring on a small scale in images is repeated when larger parts are examined, and so on with yet larger parts. The hierarchical pattern of redundancy in language may be an important feature behind its richness and power in describing the world, or more likely, as we shall see in a moment, the brain may first have evolved a powerful scheme of description for the world which language naturally adopted for communication between individuals, that is for true language. But first we must clarify the roles of language in the analogy.

LANGUAGE IN THE ANALOGY AND IN REAL LIFE

Our scientific knowledge of language plays three roles in the analogy that is being developed, and it may avoid confusion to point them out. Its first role is as the language of the messages that are being coded, and we are beginning to see how important detailed knowledge of this language is in code-breaking. Second there is its role, through Shannon's experiment, in illustrating the nature of redundancy. And third it also has a role, not so far touched upon, as a model of cognitive development in its own right.

Pinker (1994) has given a persuasive exposition and development of Chomsky's views (1959, 1975) on the innate component of language. He claims that the facility with which normal humans acquire language would not be possible if they did not have a "language instinct". Bending this towards what I am suggesting here, this says that our brains are constructed to try to represent perceived speech in a particular way, in what amounts to an innate and universal language with its own special forms of redundancy, including grammar. During language learning the redundancy of the received messages is matched to the innately determined features of the language representation system. My argument suggests that this is more general and that the same is true of the whole of cognition. If so, the language instinct is one part of a very large mass of instinctive knowledge of the world, and it might indeed be illuminating to consider language acquisition in this light. Infants of all species face the problem of learning about the world, and the instincts enabling them to do this must precede our own language instincts in evolution; perhaps the language instinct is based on these more primitive instincts, and language itself is adapted to make use of instinctive "world knowledge".

When we look at how codes are broken we shall see that it is redundancy that makes code-breaking possible, and through the analogy we must suspect it is also the redundancy that makes cognition possible.

CODE-BREAKING

How are codes actually broken? The first step is to search for any kind of clue to the type of code that is in use, but this stage depends too much on historical and external knowledge to be of much interest here. If the code is a simple one it may retain the unequal frequency of symbols, digrams and trigrams of the original language, and by measuring these frequencies one can immediately start substituting candidate decoded symbols for the encrypted ones. This stage already requires knowledge of the symbol statistics of the original language, but then one goes on to the "little laws of language"; for example in English "l" is the most frequently doubled letter, "you" is one of the very few words with a terminal "u", and the restrictions a spell-checker exploits through the sparsely occupied space of possible words. These constraints limit the transformations that will produce meaningful language, and it is not necessarily the total amount of redundancy that decides how easy it is to find the right transformation, but the intricacy and variety of its forms. Finally grammar and meaning emerge. When this happens the code-breaker may think the job is done, but this can be a dangerous delusion: the French Black Chamber was smart enough to appreciate this trap after the first decipherment of Pannizzardi's telegram in the Dreyfuss case, and because they realised it they sought an alternative decipherment which was tested and proved to be correct.

The code-breaking analogy already suggests two lessons for cognition: the first is the crucial role of redundancy in sensory messages, and the second is the importance of prior knowledge of the statistics and structure of the language from which the messages have been encoded. For cognition, this means prior knowledge of the world we live in, for that is what cognition is about. We can get a little more from the analogy by considering more advanced codes.

These conceal the symbol statistics in various ways, and one is reduced to trying the inverses of transformations of types known to be used in codes, hoping that they will produce recognisable fragments of the original language. If this has to be done blind, without any guidance, the search space is so large that any progress at all is a matter of chance, but if you are lucky a break occurs. Very often this results from an additional item of information or a mistake on the part of the transmitter of the coded messages; for instance a copy of a message that has already been broken may be received in the unbroken code, or from other circumstances the clear of a portion of the received message may become known. The result is to decrease dramatically the search space for attempted solutions of part of the puzzle, and sometimes the whole problem then unravels as additional discoveries are made, each discovery decreasing the search space for the remainder of the problem.

The third lesson therefore has two parts. The first is the supreme importance of any prior information whatever, because this can sometimes be used to reduce the search space for the solution to a piece of the problem. The second part is that any knowledge obtained *must* be used to guide the search. To take a trivial example, if you can recognise "e", then you may be able to spot the occurrence of the word "the", which is much the commonest three letter word ending in "e", and so get strong hints about two more letters. In this way success can rapidly lead to further success, but this will only happen if the search for solutions is made in such a way that all knowledge gained is exploited. This would not necessarily happen if you simply accepted the solution to "e" as 1/27th of the solution to the whole problem; used properly it can point you to further solutions in restricted parts of the problem space.

GENETIC KNOWLEDGE

Because of the need for prior knowledge of the regularities of language, the analogy strongly suggests that prior knowledge of the real world is required in order for our brains to break the code in which sensory messages arrive. If you do not know the original language of your encoded message, you cannot break the code, because the redundancy is different in every language so you do not know what to match the redundancy of the received messages to. In the same way you cannot break the language of sensory messages originating in the outside world into the language of the brain unless the brain already "knows" about the redundancy of the world it inhabits. This redundancy, which really constitutes prior knowledge of the world, must of course come from our genes: it would be expressed in the innately determined pattern of connections and the innately determined activities and functional properties of our cortical and sub-cortical sensory neurons.

These ideas have been derived from the analogy, and with them in mind let us look again at what is known about how neurons in the visual cortex develop their adult properties.

PLASTICITY, DEPRIVATION, AND THE CORTICAL CODE

The analogy suggests that the first stage of matching internal redundancy to the redundancy of the messages will be based on the elementary statistical properties of the input. Ophthalmologists have long known that the visual system is very sensitive to abnormalities of the visual input during infancy, and Wiesel and Hubel (1963; also Hubel & Wiesel, 1970) discovered that the properties of neurons of the primary visual cortex (V1) were strongly influenced by procedures that, for instance, deprived the animal of vision through one eye, or induced an artificial strabismus. Unexpectedly, some neurons were found in young animals prior to any visual experience at all that had properties remarkably similar to those of fully experienced adults, and another unexpected result was that the neurons were much less affected by complete deprivation of all vision than they were by monocular deprivation.

For a period there was considerable disagreement about the extent to which the neurons of the primary visual cortex were innately specified or "hard-wired", and about their susceptibility to modification by experience or deprivation (see, for example, Barlow, 1975; Movshon & Van Sluyters, 1981). The main argument was between those who thought experience had a constructive effect, and those who thought that all the results could be explained by lack of experience having a destructive effect. Although there are fewer pattern selective neurons in the inexperienced cortex, and it is doubtful if they ever have such high contrast sensitivity and selectivity as is acquired after experience (Derrington, 1984; Blakemore & Vital-Durand, 1984), the consensus has gone the other way: there is sufficient innate structure to produce cortical neurons with the characteristic forms of selectivity that are found in the experienced adult (Freeman & Ohzawa, 1992; DeAngelis et al., 1993). However without appropriate experience during an early period of weeks (in kittens) or months (in rhesus monkeys) these forms of selectivity are not maintained and the majority of units become unresponsive. Thus the facts, initially difficult to assimilate, indicate that genes can form neurons with sensitivity and selectivity not far short of adult neurons, but that experience appropriate to what has been formed is also necessary for them to persist to adulthood.

What would the code-breaking analogy predict? Gaps are the most striking feature of the redundancy of language, typified by the fact that only a tiny fraction of the possible combinations of six or more symbols actually occurs. Hence a plausible way to form a system selectively sensitive to a language would be to start with an array of elements selective to very many different letter combinations, but to make them deprivation-sensitive, so that if that letter combination was not experienced selectivity for that letter combination would cease to exist. You would then end up with elements tuned just to the combinations that actually occurred. The matching of the pattern sensitivity of the neurons to the predominant patterns that actually occur would be achieved by selective survival of particular forms of pattern selectivity, and the non-survival of other forms. This scheme is unrealistic if one identifies the loss of pattern selective elements with the death of cortical neurons, for this does not occur on the scale required, but a more economical alternative will be proposed below.

Switching to vision, again a good way to form neurons with the appropriate selectivities would be to start with a wide range of units having different pattern selectivities, but to make them deprivation sensitive. You would then end up with units tuned to the spatio-temporal patterns actually present in the visual images received by the eyes. Remember that images composed of noise can readily be discriminated from real, natural, images because only a tiny fraction of possible images actually occurs. So if you compare what *does* happen with what *might* happen, one sees that normal experience is in fact a form of deprivation. If the innate mechanisms had produced neurons that better fitted what *does* happen, then there would be less need for deprivation sensitivity, but if the gene-selection scheme suggested below is correct, deprivation selectivity also allows the innate mechanism to be very versatile.

Notice that nature and nurture are working together in this scheme: the role of nature is to form an initial array of units with plausible patterns of selectivity—i.e. units that have a reasonable chance of being excited by naturally occurring images. The creation of this subset would be nature's contribution to the knowledge of the world held by the visual cortex. Experience would then promote the survival of a subset of these initial units, and this further selective process would constitute nurture's contribution.

Experimental support for such a scheme might be obtained by searching for patterns that excite immature units but fail to excite normal adult ones. These would be patterns that nature expected, but ones that nurture does not normally provide; if found, it should then be possible to preserve these into the adult cortex by providing the appropriate abnormal environment.

GENE-SELECTION AND CORTICAL PLASTICITY

The facts would thus make sense if experience prevented neurons dying, but we know that the fraction of neurons that die in the developing cortex is not high enough for this to be very effective: the selection process cannot depend solely on cell death. Edelman (1987) proposed a theory in which "neuronal groups" were the subject of such selection, but the nature of these groups was hard to fathom (Barlow, 1988). Now each cell contains a full complement of genes, and they could be reprogrammed by switching genes on and off; selection could therefore be occurring at this level. The presence of a high degree of selectivity in the inexperienced brain suggests that the cortex already "suspects" that the images to be delivered are likely to have oriented edges, that these edges are likely to move, will probably come in a variety of sizes, and be approximately lined up in the images provided by the two eyes. But such genetic suspicions are contained within every cell; therefore if a cell is "disappointed" by seldom experiencing the patterns to which it was initially tuned, it has the potential to develop a different form of selectivity.

On this view the genes impose the various forms of selectivity, but this could be done iteratively in several stages. Perhaps the genetic system does indeed know that oriented edges are frequent features of natural images, but it does not insist on making edge-detectors willy-nilly; instead it says in effect "Here, try this, see if it this elongated template is fitted by commonly appearing patterns". Often it would be, and that form of receptive field would persist, but occasionally it might not, and the genes would play their next card—they would generate an alternative to try out. Thus units like simple cells would survive and flourish only if the statistics of the images experienced at that stage of development included enough exemplars of their trigger features; if they had insufficient such experience, they would express different genes and this new form of selectivity would survive if the matching redundancy occurred in the sensory input; if not, new genes would be expressed and the try-out cycle would be re-entered. The same would be true for other forms of pattern selectivity such as motion selectivity and disparity selectivity.

Such a scheme would require additional rules. As set out above, there is nothing to stop the system generating only orientation selective units at the commonest appearing orientation, neglecting units with different orientations, or possessing directional or disparity selectivity. To avoid this the instruction should be more like "Try this and see if it is fitted by any commonly occurring pattern *that is not already causing another unit to respond*". In this way the system would generate an adequate number of units of each type, modifying the mix in accordance with the statistics of the images received. The model proposed by Földiák (1990) could take care of this requirement.

Notice that, if the scheme is to be versatile and useful, it should be able to generate a repertoire of types of response selectivity to be tried out, including some that would never be used if the course of development was completely normal. As already pointed out, this generate/test/try-again-if-necessary sequence could not involve new cells for each new try-out, because cell death does not occur at a sufficient rate in the developing brain, but it could be achieved by the successive expression of different genes, or sets of genes, in the same cell. Thus the genome could store knowledge of the expected statistical characteristics of images from the environment, and could bring this knowledge into play as required when generating the visual system, but the interaction of the genetic program and experience would be more intricate than cruder models have suggested.

One indication that this sort of thing happens is the remarkably good visual system that develops in the considerable section of the population that has little or no stereo-scopic vision. The generally accepted reason for the failure of stereopsis to develop in these people is that, from any of a variety of causes, concurrent stimulation of nearly corresponding points in the two eyes did not occur often enough during the critical stage of development. On the generate/test/try-again-if-necessary hypothesis, the ontogenetic system's disparity selective "try-outs" were presumably rejected be-cause they were not adequately stimulated. One would expect this disruption of the normal developmental process to have disastrous consequences in such a complex system, so the fact that the vision of stereo-blind individuals is normal in every other way is astonishing: it is as surprising as it would be to find that a vehicle designed as a four-wheeled car could be divided into two well-functioning motorbikes if it fell into the hands of two independent users of the vehicle. There is even evidence that stereo-blind individuals can have superior monocular acuity compared to those who have developed normal stereopsis (Freeman & Bradley, 1980), so neurons that had been tried out and failed for stereopsis may contribute to other tasks.

The requirements of the early visual system are probably rather stereotyped across individuals, and even species, so this is not a situation where the proposed try-out system would be most beneficial. At higher levels, where the space of possible combinations of inputs is much greater, the potentialities are also greater, and striking examples of plasticity occur. For instance the Siamese cat, with its grossly mis-wired visual cortex (Guillery, 1969), has a surprisingly effective visual system; one lived wild near our house in California, and it had no difficulty making a good living at the expense of the local birds and small mammals, indicating that the mis-wiring at the cortico-geniculate level must have been very effectively compensated by alterations to the normal patterns of connections at higher levels. Recovery after injury provides other examples, and a striking instance is the development of language capacities in the right cerebral hemispheres of young children with extensive damage to the left hemisphere, which normally has a near-monopoly of language functions.

The genetic system must impose structure on the brain in other ways than by determining the sensory patterns that cortical neurons respond to. Presumably it determines which sensory messages act as positive reinforcers, which as negative, in ordinary learning. Innate knowledge could also be expressed by neurons having other ontogenetically fixed properties, such as a certain fixed mean firing rate, or the requirement of firing as nearly as possible independently of other neurons, or at a certain time of day, or only after certain other neurons had fired, or in certain sequences and patterns. These would generate higher order structure in the patterns of neural activity in sensory representations, corresponding perhaps to the grammar of language in the analogy. The developing brain, like the adult brain, has a strong tendency to break into spontaneous rhythmic activities, and cognitive development may be the process of matching these spontaneous dreams to the reality of sensory messages actually received. At all events, the message of the analogy is clear: to understand how the brain learns to make sense of sensory messages, look for constraints, regularities, and redundancy in the activity of its sensory neurons, and in the innately determined rhythms and interactions of these neurons. It will make sense of the world to the extent that these types of redundancy can be matched to the redundancy of the sensory messages received from the outside world.

CONCLUSIONS

Code-breaking as an analogy for cognition makes one look at the problem of cognitive development through new eyes, for it suggests that experience does not write on a blank slate, but is a matter of matching patterns and sequences arriving in the sensory messages to marks already present on that slate. One previously puzzling feature that it helps to explain is the fact that plasticity in the critical period takes the form of sensitivity to deprivation, which is to be expected once one appreciates that redundancy in sensory messages, as in language, is mainly marked by the infrequent occurrence of particular subsets of patterns: deprivation of these patterns is a natural occurrence during normal development, and sensitivity to deprivation ensures that neurons become tuned to the patterns and sequences that actually occur. The idea also suggests novel experiments: for instance, are there patterns and sequences to which the immature brain is *more* sensitive than the adult brain? There should be, if the notion is correct that the tuning of the brain to the statistics of the natural world results from the normal absence of experience of a large subset of possible patterns and sequences.

Finally, the fact that breaking a code is easier than even the experts expect points to the plausibility of the Lockean program, but only when it is modified in a Kantian direction by postulating a large store of knowledge of the world contained in the genes that control neural development. This knowledge may remain locked up in those genes if the conditions for their expression do not occur, but of course this consequence of deprivation is not necessarily harmful, for there is no guarantee that the unexpressed genes would have promoted socially beneficial behaviour.

REFERENCES

Atick, J.J. (1992). Could information theory provide an ecological theory of sensory processing? *Network*, **3**, 213–251.

Attneave, F. (1954). Informational aspects of visual perception. *Psychological Review*, **61**, 183–193.

Barlow, H.B. (1959). Sensory mechanisms, the reduction of redundancy, and intelligence. In *The mechanisation of thought processes* (pp. 535–539). London: Her Majesty's Stationery Office.

Barlow, H.B. (1975). Visual experience and cortical development. *Nature*, **258**, 199–204.

Barlow, H.B. (1988). Neuroscience: a new era? *Nature*, **331**, 571.

Barlow, H.B. (2001). Redundancy reduction revisited. *Network: computation in neural systems*, **12**, 241–253.

Blakemore, C. & Vital-Durand, F. (1984). Development of the monkey's geniculo-cortical system. In J. Stone, B. Dreher & D. H. Rapaport (Eds.) *Development of the visual pathways in mammals*. New York: Alan Liss.

Chomsky, N. (1959). Review of Skinner's "Verbal behaviour". *Language*, **35**, 26–58.

Chomsky, N. (1975). *Reflections on language*. New York: Random House.

DeAngelis, G.C., Ohzawa, I. & Freeman, R.D. (1993). Spatio-temporal organisation of simple cell receptive fields in the cat cortex: I, General characteristics and post-natal development. *Journal of Neurophysiology*, **69**, 1091–1117.

Derrington, A.M. (1984). Development of spatial frequency selectivity in striate cortex of vision-deprived cats. *Experimental Brain Research*, **55**, 431–437.

Edelman, G.M. (1987). *Neural Darwinism: The theory of neuronal group selection*. New York: Basic Books Inc.

Elman, J.L., Bates, E.A., Johnson, M.H., Karmeloff-Smith, A., Parisi, D. & Plunkett, K. (1996). *Rethinking innateness: A connectionist perspective on development*. Cambridge, Mass.: MIT Press.

Field, D.J. (1994). What is the goal of sensory coding? *Neural Computation*, **6**, 559–601.

Földiák, P. (1990). Forming sparse representations by local anti-Hebbian learning. *Biological Cybernetics*, **64**(2), 165–170.

Freeman, R.D. & Bradley, A. (1980). Monocularly deprived humans: Non-deprived eye has supernormal vernier acuity. *Journal of Neurophysiology*, **43**, 1645–1653.

Freeman, R.D. & Ohzawa, I. (1992). Development of binocular vision in the kitten's striate cortex. *Journal of Neuroscience*, **12**, 4721–4736.

Guillery, R. (1969). An abnormal retino-geniculate projection in Siamese cats. *Brain Research*, **14**, 739–741.

Hinsley, F.H. & Stripp, A. (1993). *Codebreakers: The inside story of Bletchley Park*. Oxford: Oxford University Press.

Hubel, D.H. & Wiesel, T.N. (1970). The period of susceptibility to the physiological effects of unilateral eye closure in kittens. *Journal of Physiology (London)*, **206**, 419–436.

James, W. (1892). *Psychology*, Chapter 2. New York: Henry Holt.

Kersten, D. (1987). Predictability and redundancy of natural images. *Journal of the Optical Society of America, A*, **4**(12), 2395–2400.

Movshon, J.A. & Van Sluyters, R.C. (1981). Visual neural development. *Annual Review of Psychology*, **32**, 477–522.

Pinker, S. (1994). *The language instinct*. London: Allen Lane.

Pratt, F. (1939). *Secret and urgent: The story of codes and ciphers*. London: Robert Hale Limited.

Ruderman, D. (1994). Statistics of natural images. *Network*, **5**, 517–548.

Shannon, C.E. (1951). Prediction and entropy of printed English. *Bell System Technical Journal*, **30**, 50–64.

Wiesel, T.N. & Hubel, D.H. (1963). Single cell responses in striate cortex of kittens deprived of vision in one eye. *Journal of Neurophysiology*, **26**, 1004–1017.

3

Comparative Overview of Perception of Distal and Proximal Visual Attributes

DEJAN TODOROVIĆ

Toronto, Ontario M3C 1X4, Canada

The theme of this chapter, perception of distal and proximal visual attributes, appears in many guises and variations throughout the psychological and also the philosophical literature on perception. These concepts have relevance for actual experimental setups and tasks set for the subjects in empirical research, as well as for the interpretation of data and theoretical discussions. Furthermore, this distinction is of great importance for the classical issue of perceptual constancies. The commonality of aspects of various constancies has often been noted and discussed in the perception literature. The attempt here is to present these issues in an overall framework and thus to bring them into a sharper focus. The emphasis is on a systematic, terminologically consistent, and unified exposition of main concepts and problems. In this way a number of similarities, differences, and other relations between various phenomena will be stressed, which are not often in the center of attention of researchers of particular effects, but may be helpful for the prospect of increased understanding of the general questions. It is my hope to be able to convey to the reader the feeling that I had many times during the writing of this chapter, that the attempt to present otherwise diverse phenomena from a common viewpoint can be an illuminating and clarifying enterprise, and can help provide insights of a sort that a study of particular phenomena is less likely to do.

I will discuss six visual attributes: size, shape, orientation, direction, and achromatic and chromatic color. In some of these areas these issues are well known, researched and discussed, whereas in others they are only occasionally mentioned. I will first briefly sketch a general account which applies for all six attributes, and will then

Perception and the Physical World: Psychological and Philosophical Issues in perception.
Edited by Dieter Heyer and Rainer Mausfeld. © 2002 John Wiley & Sons, Ltd.

provide more detailed discussions for each one separately. All these discussion will proceed according to the same general outline, stressing the formal similarities of the problems, but also the specificities within individual areas. The final section will provide additional comments.

VISUAL ATTRIBUTES

Visual perception is the optically mediated cognition of the world. Visually relevant properties of external objects can be classified into *geometric* and *photometric* attributes or variables. The geometric attributes concern space and the distribution of matter in it. They can be divided into attributes of *extension* and *position*. Attributes of extension include *size* and *shape*. These attributes, especially for rigid objects, express their intrinsic, constant and defining features. Attributes of position include *location* and *orientation*. These attributes express the current relations of objects with respect to other objects or reference frames and are, especially for mobile objects, generally extrinsic and variable.

Photometric attributes concern light and its interaction with object surfaces. They include *illumination*, that is, the amount and spectral wavelength composition of light arriving at a surface, and *reflectance*, the proportion or percentage of light reflected from a surface at each wavelength. Illumination is accidental and extrinsic, as it depends on the current relation of an object to a light source and its intensity and composition. In contrast, reflectance is generally a constant, intrinsic attribute of object surfaces.

The attributes of external objects noted above are defined without reference to an observer. Observers can, in part, be defined by the geometric characteristics of their visual sensory surface (such as the size, shape, location and orientation of the retina) as well as its photometric characteristics (light absorption features of the receptors). Outside objects are projected upon the retinal surface according to the laws of the external optics of light propagation and the internal optics of the eye imaging apparatus. I will refer to outside objects as *distal objects*, and to their retinal images as *proximal objects*. Similarly, I will refer to properties of distal objects as *distal attributes*, and to properties of proximal objects as the corresponding *proximal attributes*. Thus to the distal size of a distal object there corresponds the proximal size of the corresponding proximal object, which is the size of the retinal image of the distal object. Analogous definitions apply to other proximal attributes, which will be elaborated in appropriate sections below.

It is clear that the values of proximal attributes depend on the values of the corresponding distal attributes. Thus objects with larger distal sizes will have larger corresponding proximal sizes, objects with different distal shapes will have different proximal shapes, etc. However, the distal attribute is not the only variable affecting the proximal attribute. In all cases to be discussed here, there exists at least one additional variable that affects the proximal variable. For example, proximal size depends not only on distal size but also on the distance of the object from the observer, proximal shape does not depend only on distal shape but also on the slant of the object, etc. This

	Variables	Geo / photometry	Equation
Size	*Distal:* size S *Secondary:* distance d *Proximal:* vis. angle α	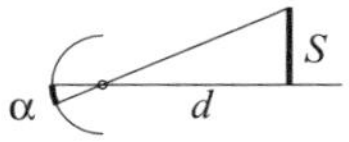	$\alpha = \text{atan}\,(S/d)$
Shape	*Distal:* distal shape E *Secondary:* slant angle s *Proximal:* prox. shape ε	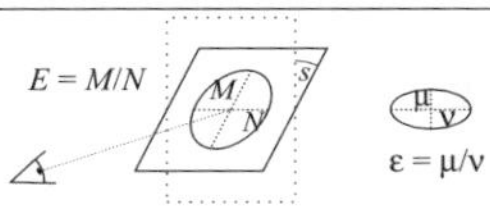 $E = M/N$ $\varepsilon = \mu/v$	$\varepsilon = E \cos s$
Orientation	*Distal:* object orientation O *Secondary:* eye orientation e *Proximal:* prox. orienation ω	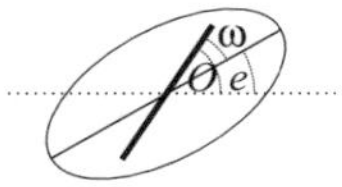	$\omega = O - e$
Direction	*Distal:* object direction D *Secondary:* gaze direction g *Proximal:* retinal location α	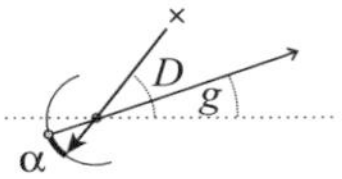	$\alpha = D - g$
Achr. color	*Distal:* reflectance R *Secondary:* illumination i *Proximal:* luminance λ	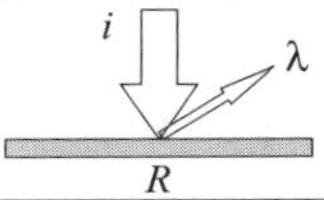	$\lambda = Ri$
Chr. color	*Distal:* reflect. distrib. $R(w)$ *Secondary:* illum. distrib. $i(w)$ *Proximal:* lumin. distrib. $\lambda(w)$	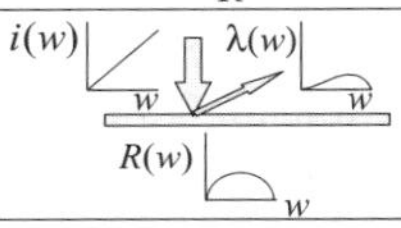	$\lambda(w) = R(w)\,i(w)$

Figure 3.1 Relations of distal, secondary, and proximal variables in six perceptual attributes. For detailed explanations see text.

class of additional variables that affect the proximal variable does not have a commonly accepted general name. Epstein (1973) used the label "orthogonal" variables, presumably to express their independence from the distal variables. I will mainly use the term "secondary" variables, in order to stress that it is the distal variables that are the primary correspondents of the proximal variables, but that the appropriate secondary variables also affect the proximal variables. Another possible label is the "confounding" variables, because these variables confound the effect of the primary, distal variables on the proximal variables.

Figure 3.1 contains a presentation of the basic variables relevant for the six attributes discussed in this chapter. The distal, secondary, and proximal variables are listed in the first column, their relations in some basic cases are depicted geometrically in the second column, and the third column contains an analytic expression of these relations. For consistency, distal variables are always denoted with capital Roman letters, secondary variables with small Roman letters, and proximal variables with small Greek letters. These formulas all have the general form $\pi = f\,(D, s)$, expressing the relation of a dependent variable, π, on two independent variables, D and s, where π denotes the proximal variable, D the distal variable, and s the secondary variable. Note that neither of the three variables is a phenomenal variable. A central aspect of this chapter is that for all discussed attributes both the distal and the proximal variables have a phenomenal counterpart, involving conscious impressions and judgements concerning the distal and the proximal variables. The secondary variables also have a phenomenal counterpart, but this issue will not be addressed here per se. Problems concerning neural representations of phenomenal variables, as well as various theories of visual constancies, are outside of the scope of this chapter.

Each of six visual attributes will be discussed in more detail in a subsequent section. These sections are all structured according to a common format. After an introduction, relations among the three relevant non-phenomenal variables (distal, proximal, and secondary) will be discussed. This is followed by definitions and illustrations of two types of phenomenal variables, one corresponding to the distal variable and the other to the proximal variable. Following that, the tasks and instructions to subjects in experiments designed to record perceptual judgements of the distal and the proximal variables will be discussed. Finally, a brief review of relevant experimental findings will be presented. Detailed reviews of most issues discussed here can be found in Hochberg (1971a, b), Rock (1975), Epstein (1977), Boff et al. (1986), and Walsh and Kulikowski (1998).

The first section involves perception of size. It also serves to introduce some basic notions involving the structure of perceptual matching studies and the types of presentation conditions used in these experiments. These and other more general considerations noted in this section apply for all other attributes, and will not be repeated in detail for each one separately.

PERCEPTION OF SIZE

Size is a relatively simple geometric attribute that can be numerically expressed with a single number. It comprises lengths of linear extents, areas of portions of 2-D surfaces, and volumes of portions of space, but only linear extents will be discussed here. Reviews and discussions of the dependence of perception of size on distance can be found in Baird (1970), Hochberg (1971a), Rock (1975), Sedgwick (1986), Gillam (1995), and McKee and Smallman (1998).

Relations of Non-phenomenal Variables

Row 1 in Figure 3.1 depicts an object of distal size S, oriented perpendicularly to the visual axis (line of regard) and located at a distance d from the so-called nodal point of the eye. The distal object projects an image at the retina, depicted schematically in a semicircular cross-section. The size of the proximal image increases with the increase of distal size and decrease of distance, as expressed by the formula $\alpha = \mathrm{atan}(S/d)$. Thus the value of the proximal variable α, is affected by both the primary, distal variable S, as well as the secondary variable d. For example, an object of distal size $S = 1$ cm at the distance of $d = 57$ cm projects an image of $1°$ visual angle at the retina. This formula does not take into account the effect, on proximal size, of the slant of the distal stimulus, an issue that will be discussed in the section on perception of shape.

Distal size, also called "objective" or "physical" or "bodily" size, can be ascertained by standard means such as measuring tapes, geodesic devices etc. Proximal size, also called "retinal" or "angular" size, is not easily measured directly but it can be calculated by the above or related formulas. Note that proximal size, defined purely as the extent of a retinal region, does not explicitly depend on any particular distal object. However, proximal size can also be attributed as a property of a concrete distal object. This property depends on the vantage point from which the object is observed, and thus the same object can have many different proximal sizes. Just as distal size, proximal size is an objective, non-phenomenal variable, defined by the geometric relation specified above. However, it is a relational, vantage-point dependent property, in contrast to distal size which is an observer-independent and in that sense absolute property.

Phenomenal Attributes

The two different notions of "non-phenomenal size" discussed above correspond to two different notions of "phenomenal size". These two phenomenal attributes will be referred to as "perceived distal size" and "perceived proximal size". Other term pairs used to express this distinction include "visual world size" vs "visual field size" (Gibson, 1950), and "apparent absolute size" vs "apparent angular size" (Joynson, 1949). The first term in each pair refers to conscious impressions and judgements of distal size, and the second term refers to conscious impressions and judgements of proximal size. This distinction will be elaborated in the following paragraphs.

Our judgements of size in everyday life predominantly refer to distal size, and a notion referring to proximal size is rarely met. However, it is not difficult to find situations which exemplify both notions of size and illustrate their difference. For example, such a setup may involve presenting two objects of equal distal size (as well as shape and orientation), such as two persons or two cars, with the main difference that one is located near the observer and the other far, but in visually adjacent directions, so that they can be easily simultaneously compared. Such a display usually induces *size constancy*, that is, the correct impression that the two objects have fairly similar distal sizes. However, it also brings to the attention of the observer the perceptual fact that the two objects are quite different concerning another feature which also involves a kind of size, in respect of which the more distant object is smaller. Expressed in the terminology introduced above, the two objects have similar perceived distal sizes but different perceived proximal sizes. A converse class of examples involves objects of different perceived distal size but similar perceived proximal size. These are cases in which a nearby object, say my thumb, exactly visually covers a distally much greater distant object, such as someone's head, a house, or the moon. Another example that shows the usefulness of the distinction between two kinds of perceived sizes is the case of railroad track ties whose "perceived size" is sometimes confusingly described as both decreasing and remaining constant. This paradox is eliminated by saying that their perceived distal size stays the same but their perceived proximal size diminishes with distance. All these examples involve *partial* phenomenal identities, in the sense that objects that look equal with respect to one type of perceived size look different with respect to the other type. *Totally* phenomenally identical objects, with respect to size, would have to be equal with respect to both types of perceived size.

I wish to emphasize that the notion of "perceived proximal size", and the analogous notions associated with all other visual attributes discussed in the following, are theoretically neutral, and are used here only to point out certain types of perceptual judgements. Such notions are not intended to implicate (or dispute) any theory of how such judgements are performed (such as "direct sensing" of a retinal extent), in the same way as the term "perceived distal size" is not associated with any theoretical account of that type of perceptual judgements (such as "direct pickup" of a distal extent). It is not presupposed here that conscious impressions and judgements of proximal size are exclusively based on objective proximal size, that is, the size of the retinal image. Neither is it assumed that judgements of distal size are computed from representations of proximal size and distance (analogous to solving the above formula for the value of distal size, in the form $S = d \tan \alpha$). Similar considerations apply for all other attributes discussed here.

It is important to note that although perceivers ordinarily may not pay much attention to proximal sizes, the actions of their oculomotor systems are mainly affected by proximal and not by distal size: when I look from one end of an object to the other, the extent of my eye rotation is guided, quite sensibly, by the proximal and not by the distal size of the object. Thus although I may have the correct impression that two objects of equal distal size located at different distances do indeed have equal distal size, my eye excursions inspecting the nearer one will, naturally, be larger.

Tasks and Instructions

Research in size perception, and other attributes dealt with here, often involves *matching procedures*. Such a procedure involves the presentation of a *standard* stimulus and one or more *comparison* stimuli. In size perception research for technical reasons the standard is usually positioned at some farther distance from observer, and the comparison stimuli are nearby; an inverse setup with a nearby standard and distant comparison stimuli is also possible but is more seldom used. The task of the observer is to *identify* the perceptually *matching* comparison stimulus, that is, indicate the one that has the same perceived size as the standard. Two types of such identification procedures are often used in studies of many visual attributes. They are the *adjustment procedure* and the *selection procedure*. In the adjustment procedure, as used in size perception studies, there is a single comparison stimulus which is variable in size, and the task of the subject is to adjust its size until it matches the standard. In the selection procedure, several comparison stimuli of different sizes are presented, and the subject is asked to pick out the one that matches the standard.

Because the notion of "phenomenal size" has two different meanings, properly designed experiments distinguish between the *distal task*, with distally focused instructions, intended to evoke perceptual judgements of distal size, and the *proximal task*, with proximally focused instructions, intended to evoke perceptual judgements of proximal size. These two types of tasks can be used for all visual attributes discussed here.

There are different ways to formulate instructions for subjects in matching studies. These instructions may use different types of *criteria* to convey to subjects the nature of their task. I will provide examples of *distal*, *proximal*, and *phenomenal* criteria. As it will be seen, all three types of criteria may be used both for the distal and the proximal task. Note that these are just examples of possible criteria, which may not all be equally useful in concrete experiments.

Consider first the distal task. According to a distal criterion, the matching comparison stimulus should be such that it could be exactly physically superimposed upon the standard stimulus; or, more conveniently, there should be a third object, such as a portion of a measuring tape, that can be exactly superimposed on both objects. Another, proximal criterion, would be to identify the comparison stimulus that, were it to be located at the same distance as the standard, would project an image of the same size as it. Finally, a phenomenal criterion would be to ask for the identification of the comparison stimulus which, were it to be located at the same distance as the standard, would evoke a totally identical impression of size. Note that the first criterion is based on a distal property (superposition), the second on a proximal property (projected size), and the third on a phenomenal property (impression of size). In normal circumstances all three criteria would pick out the same comparison stimulus as the correct answer in the identification task.

Another set of criteria would apply for the proximal task. A distal criterion would be that if a photograph were made of the standard and comparison stimuli from the vantage point of the subject, the distal size of the *image* of the matching comparison stimulus, as measured on the photograph, would be equal to the distal size of the image of the standard (Gilinsky, 1955). A proximal criterion would be to identify the comparison stimulus whose projected image on the retina has the same size as the proximal image of the standard. A phenomenal criterion would be that the matching comparison stimulus should subtend the same extent of perceived visual space as the standard stimulus; in that case, were it to be positioned in the same direction from the vantage point of the subject, being nearer, it would exactly visually mask the standard.

In the preceding paragraphs I have indicated some possible formulations for distally and proximally focused instructions. However, in some size perception studies instructions were used which are, in a sense, *phenomenally focused*: subjects were asked to produce the match according to the way the sizes of the stimuli "look" or "appear" to them, usually with a stress on "immediate impressions", and without more explicit explanations. The use of such instructions may be motivated by the theoretical attempt to elicit purely phenomenal judgements, free of any dependence on external reality (see Thouless, 1931a). Alternatively, their use may be motivated by the methodological attempt to avoid possible cognitive biases that might be induced by distally or proximally focused instructions. While these considerations may have some merit, the downside of such "apparent" or "look" instructions is that they are likely to be unclear, so that the subjects are in fact left to figure out just what it is that the experimenter asks them to do (see Sedgwick, 1986).

Carlson (1977) discussed several different types of instructions in size perception studies, and claimed that, with the right choice of instructions, within constraints of experimental conditions any degree of size overconstancy and underconstancy (to be defined below) can be obtained, an opinion also shared by Baird and Wagner (1991). He also maintained that "apparent visual size" (perceived proximal size) is in fact an illusory concept that cannot be defined satisfactorily in an instruction. However, as shown above, there are a number of ways in which such instructions can be formulated. This fact agrees with Sedgwick's (1986) assessment that there does not exist a continuum of "perceived sizes", but that there are two different concepts, perceived distal and proximal size, which can be clearly specified with appropriate instructions.Whether a third, phenomenally oriented notion of perceived size can be satisfactorily defined is a matter of debate.

Structures of Experimental Results

Regardless whether the task is distal, proximal, or phenomenal, the results of a matching study yield a set of values of comparison stimuli that, averaging over subjects and trials, are judged to be perceptually equal to corresponding standard stimuli. In case of the distal and the proximal task, one can then assess whether such judgements are *correct* or not. In contrast, in case of the phenomenal task, though one can compare the matching sizes to the corresponding distal and proximal sizes of the standard, the question of correctness is strictly speaking inappropriate, since the task itself does not specify an objective, external criterion.

For both the distal and the proximal task, the potential outcomes of matching studies have the same general structure with respect to correctness: judgements of the subjects may either be *accurate* (or more or less nearly so), or they may be *biased*. Accurate estimates, in which the matching comparison stimulus has the same or similar size as the standard, are said to involve (approximate) *size constancy*. This term is usually used only for judgements of distal size. However, as there are two notions of phenomenal size, it would be terminologically more appropriate to use more precise expressions, and use the term "distal size constancy" for accurate judgements of distal size, and the term "proximal size constancy" for accurate judgements of proximal size.

In case that the judgements of size are biased, there are two possibilities, since the matching comparison stimulus may either be larger or smaller than the standard. The first case, *overestimation* of the size of the standard, is often called "overconstancy of size", and the second case, *underestimation,* is called "underconstancy of size". As in case of accurate judgements, a terminological differentiation of distal and proximal variants of biased judgements may be appropriate.

The outcomes of studies of size perception, as well as of all other attributes discussed here, depend strongly on the conditions under which the stimuli are presented. There are two basic types of conditions, the *full-cue* condition and the *reduced-cue* condition. The full-cue condition involves a more or less everyday viewing situation and a richly structured environment. In size perception studies, such conditions are characterized by a good overview of the visual context of standard and comparison stimuli, allowing their comparison with other objects in the scene, and making available many of the usual cues that provide information about distance, the secondary variable.

With full-cue conditions, in case of the *distal* task, usually more or less accurate size estimates are obtained, except that often some overestimation is found. That is, the distal sizes of the standard stimuli tend to be somewhat overestimated, meaning that the distal sizes of the nearby matching comparison stimuli tend to be somewhat larger that the distal sizes of the faraway standard stimuli (Martius, 1889; Gibson, 1950; Smith, 1953; Gilinsky, 1955; Carlson, 1960; Baird & Biersdorf, 1967). On the other hand, in case of the *proximal* task under full-cue conditions, usually "proximal overconstancy" is found; that is, the proximal sizes of the distant standard stimuli usually tend to be appreciably overestimated. Furthermore, the matching values tend to be more variable than with distally focused instructions (Gilinsky, 1955; Epstein 1963; Carlson & Tassone, 1967; Leibowitz & Harvey, 1967). With phenomenally focused instructions the matching values tend to be intermediate compared to results with distally and proximally focused instructions (Thouless, 1931a; Epstein, 1963). Note that such results may be due to the fact that different subjects understand phenomenal instructions in different ways, some in the distal sense, and others in the proximal sense (Joynson, 1949, 1958a, b; Joynson & Kirk, 1960). Furthermore, the same subject may change the response criterion during the experiment, or may try, within a single trial, to achieve some kind of compromise between the proximal and the distal sense.

A different structure of results is obtained under reduced-cue conditions. These conditions usually consist of very simply structured setups and involve elimination or reduction of various distance cues. Such manipulations include the following: the whole visual field is homogeneous (in order to reduce contextual cues), except for the presented stimuli, which are generally textureless (to reduce slant cues), and have simple geometrical shapes such as lines or disks, for which no particular size is characteristic (to reduce familiarity cues). The stimuli are viewed monocularly (to reduce stereoscopic cues), through an artificial pupil (to reduce accommodation cues), without observer motion (to reduce parallax cues), and for a short time (to reduce cognitive judgement strategies).

The general finding of such studies is that the more such cues are reduced, the more the size judgements of the subjects tend to rely on proximal size. When most of such cues are eliminated, the comparison stimulus that subjects match to the standard stimulus is generally such that its proximal size is fairly close to the proximal size of the standard, regardless of the distal sizes of the two stimuli (Holway & Boring, 1941; Lichten & Lurie, 1950; Hastorf & Way, 1952; Epstein, 1963; Rock & McDermott, 1964). It must be pointed out that in this type of studies the difference between the two senses of perceived size usually was not stressed, but the results appear to hold even with explicit distally focused instructions (Over, 1960). Note that under increasingly reduced-cue conditions, involving decreasing information about the distance of the stimuli, the distinction between the two senses of phenomenal size is likely to get decreasingly salient and eventually break down, with proximal size remaining as the main anchor that subjects can use for matching.

PERCEPTION OF SHAPE

Shape is a relatively complex geometric attribute. I will only consider the shapes of lines and contours of 2-D figures, because such shapes were predominantly used in classical studies of shape constancies. Reviews of shape perception are provided by Epstein and Park (1963) and Sedgwick (1986).

Relations of Non-phenomenal Variables

Row 2 in Figure 3.1 depicts an observer, schematically represented by a side profile of an eye, viewing a stimulus in the shape of an ellipse which is slanted with respect to the visual axis, represented as a dotted line. The slant is indicated by the angle s, subtended by the plane of the ellipse and a plane positioned perpendicularly to the visual axis. Oval figures, including ellipses and circles, are convenient as examples because their shape can be expressed by a single number. This is their "ellipticity", defined here as the ratio E, of the vertical axis M to the horizontal axis N. For circles, both axes have the same length, so that their ellipticity is 1. For vertically elongated ellipses, $E > 1$, and for horizontally elongated ones, $E < 1$.

If the plane of the ellipse is perpendicular to the visual axis, then its retinal image has the same shape, that is, the proximal ellipticity, denoted here as ε, has the same value as the ellipticity of the distal stimulus. If the distance of the ellipse is changed but its orientation is preserved, the proximal size of the image is changed but its shape is preserved. Similarly, the shape is preserved if the ellipse is tilted, that is, rotated about the visual axis (or an axis parallel to it). However, if the ellipse is slanted, that is, rotated about its horizontal axis (or a parallel axis), then the projected length of the horizontal axis, denoted by v in the figure, is preserved, but the projected length of the vertical axis, denoted by μ, is decreased, and so is ellipticity. The dependence of proximal shape on distal shape and slant is given by the formula $\varepsilon = E \cos s$. When the plane of the ellipse is perpendicular to the visual axis, then $s = 0°$, and $\varepsilon = E$, whereas for other angles $\varepsilon < E$. For example, if $s = 60°$ then $\varepsilon = E/2$. For more complicated shapes, more complex formulas are needed. The discussion here applies for planar shapes, and does not include the aspects that arise in the recognition of 3-D figures in various spatial orientations.

In sum, completely analogous to the two different notions of external size, there are two notions of external shape. The distal shape of an object is an observer-independent property, whereas the proximal shape depends on the relative orientation of the object and the retina. The same object may have many corresponding proximal shapes, but both distal and proximal shape are objective, geometrically specified properties.

Phenomenal Attributes

As in the case of size, the duality of the notion of external shape is associated with two notions of phenomenal shape, which may be called "perceived distal shape" and perceived proximal shape". Alternative labels for these notions are "perceived objective shape" vs "perceived projective shape" (see Sedgwick, 1986). These notions will be elaborated below.

Similar to perceived proximal size, the notion of perceived proximal shape is rarely explicitly used in everyday life. However, it can be readily appreciated, especially when comparing objects of equal distal shapes, such as dinner plates or table surfaces, but with very different slants with respect to the visual axis of the observer, and thus involving very different visual angles and retinal projections. In such cases the impression of the equality of the objective, distal shapes of these objects ("shape constancy") is accompanied by the impression that there is another, shape-related aspect, in which they are quite different. Thus these figures have similar perceived distal shapes, but different perceived proximal shapes; converse examples can also be constructed. The classical paradox of the slanted penny which "looks" both round and elliptical is resolved by saying that its perceived distal shape is circular but that its perceived proximal shape is elliptical.

Note that it is not the distal shapes but the proximal shapes that guide oculomotor behavior. For example, when I let my gaze glide along the perimeters of two coins, one oriented vertically with respect to the gaze direction, and the other one slanted, my eye motions will be roughly circular for the vertical coin and roughly elliptical for the slanted one, even though I may perceive their distal shapes to be identical.

Tasks and Instructions

The classical shape perception studies generally used the selection procedure in matching experiments. They involve the presentation of a standard stimulus in one orientation, say a slanted circle, and a set of comparison stimuli in another orientation, such as several vertically oriented oval shapes of different ellipticities. The task of the subject is to identify the comparison stimulus that has the same shape as the standard. A converse setup, with the standard vertical and the comparison stimuli slanted, is also used, but more rarely.

As in the case of phenomenal size, the duality of the concept of phenomenal shape necessitates a corresponding duality of tasks and instructions to subjects in shape perception research. It would be inappropriate to use unfocused instructions that ask subjects to simply match "shapes". Instead, distally and proximally focused instructions must be distinguished, corresponding to the distal and the proximal task. To formulate the appropriate instructions, the same types of criteria (distal, proximal, and phenomenal) may be used as in size perception research.

Consider first the distal task. Here the instructions should clearly indicate that shapes perceived as equal should be objectively equal. For figures of equal distal size, a distal criterion of distal shape equality is that the matching comparison stimulus can be exactly physically superimposed upon the standard. A proximal criterion is that the matching comparison stimulus, were it presented at the same slant as the the standard stimulus, would project the same proximal image. A phenomenal criterion is that in that situation (equal slant of standard and comparison) the two stimuli would provide an identical impression of shape.

In contrast, in the proximal task, proximally focused instructions are appropriate, and should stress the projective equality of the to-be-matched shapes. A distal criterion is that if the stimuli were photographed from the vantage point of the observer, the image of the comparison stimulus, measured as a distal object on the photograph, should have the same shape as the image of the standard. A proximal criterion is that the comparison stimulus should have the same retinal shape as the standard. A phenomenal criterion is that the matching comparison stimulus should cover a same-shaped portion of the visual space as the standard, so that each shape would exactly visually mask the other.

However, as in size perception research, authors of shape perception studies have, instead of distally or proximally oriented criteria, sometimes used *phenomenally* focused "apparent" or "look" instructions, that stress the "immediate appearance" of the shapes of the stimuli, but do not clearly identify the matching criterion.

Structures of Empirical Results

Similar to size perception studies, the outcome of shape perception experiments depends on the type of phenomenal shape that is being studied (distal or proximal), and on presentation conditions (reduced-cue or full-cue). Under reduced-cue conditions, for example when stimuli are presented as luminous outlines in darkness, the matching comparison stimuli usually have a proximal shape which is similar to the proximal shape of the standard (Thouless, 1931a, b; Epstein et al., 1962; Campione, 1977). As in size perception studies, authors of this type of research have not always used focused instructions, but these results appear to hold even with explicitly distal instructions (Beck & Gibson, 1955; Nelson & Bartley, 1956). As in size perception studies, given the presentation conditions, such an outcome is only to be expected.

With full-cue conditions, the task instructions make a difference. With distally focused instructions, approximate distal shape constancy obtains, but it tends not to be perfect, with many studies showing some degree of underconstancy, but others showing overconstancy (see Epstein & Park, 1963; Lichte & Borresen, 1967; Landauer, 1969). In other words, the distal shape of the slanted standard (measured, for example, by its ellipticity) may be both underestimated and overestimated by the distal shape of the vertical matching comparison. In contrast, with proximally focused instructions, generally "proximal overconstancy" obtains, involving overestimation of the proximal shape of the slanted standard. (Epstein et al., 1962; Lichte & Borresen, 1967). Finally, with phenomenally focused instructions, results are obtained which are intermediate between those with proximally and those with distally focused instructions (Lichte & Borresen, 1967; Landauer, 1969). However, as noted, the interpretation of the results of such studies is difficult, much for the same reasons as in size perception studies (Sedgwick, 1986). Experiments by Joynson and Newson (1962) and Lichte and Borresen (1967) indicate that some subjects tend to interpret phenomenally focused instructions as referring to distal shape, and other subjects as referring to proximal shape.

PERCEPTION OF ORIENTATION

Orientation of an object is a relative attribute that refers to a *reference frame* (see Howard, 1982, 1986, 1993). Perceptually relevant reference frames may be *exocentric* (environment-relative), that is, defined with respect to some aspect of the environment, or *egocentric* (observer-relative), that is, based on some aspect of the body of the perceiver. Egocentric reference frames will be discussed in the section on perception of direction. Reviews of perception of orientation and direction can be found in Rock (1975), Ebenholtz (1977), Shebilske (1977), Howard (1982, 1986), and Matin (1986).

One type of exocentric reference frame is *gravity-relative*: the vertical orientation is aligned with the direction of the gravitational force, and the horizontal orientation is perpendicular to it. Another type is *object-relative*. Here orientation is defined with respect to some salient features of environmental objects. For example, the exocentric vertical orientation may be associated with trees or walls, and the horizontal orientation with the level of the water or the ground.

On the retina, the orientation of the projection of an object, such as the image of a straight line, can be defined by the angle it subtends with respect to some retinal meridian (vertical cross-section through the fovea), such as the "horizontal" meridian or the "vertical" meridian. I put quotes on these labels because, although often used, they are in fact only appropriate for such positions of the eye when the head is erect and the observer looks straight ahead. When the head is tilted, a condition which will be discussed below, these meridians change their exocentric orientations, so that the above terms are no longer strictly appropriate, but are still convenient as labels.

Relations of Non-phenomenal Variables

The depiction in row 3 in Figure 3.1 contains a schematic image of the frontal view of the retina of a tilted eye, depicted as an ellipse, whose tilted "horizontal" meridian is depicted with a full line. The shorter, thick line depicts the projection of an external straight line upon the retina. The dotted line represents the exocentric horizontal orientation. The exocentric, distal orientation of the external line is given by the angle O, subtended by the projection of the line in the figure and the horizontal orientation. The proximal orientation of the projected line is given by the angle ω, that it subtends with the "horizontal" meridian. Finally, the exocentric orientation of the retina and the eye itself is given by the angle e, that the "horizontal" meridian subtends with the exocentric horizontal orientation.

Proximal orientation does not depend only on distal orientation but also on a secondary variable, the tilt of the eye. In the presented case, the relation of the three variables is given by a simple formula: $\omega = O - e$. For example, if a distal line is tilted by $O = 30°$ counter-clockwise with respect to the horizontal, and the eye is tilted by $e = 20°$ counter-clockwise, then the projected line is tilted by $\omega = 10°$ counter-clockwise, with respect to the retinal "horizontal" meridian. Note that in these considerations the fact that the retina is a spatially curved projection surface is disregarded.

Phenomenal Attributes

Analogous to phenomenal size and shape, there are, at least in principle, two senses of the notion of "phenomenal orientation". The first, everyday sense, which can be labeled "perceived distal orientation", refers to the conscious impression of orientation of objects as defined with respect to some exocentric reference frame, such as gravity. However, "phenomenal orientation" may also be used in a second sense, as the phenomenal counterpart of proximal orientation. This notion will be referred to as "perceived proximal orientation". Its meaning involves the impression of the orientation of the projection of an object with respect to the retina. However, in everyday conditions this attribute is not at all phenomenally salient. When we tilt our heads, the projected orientations of static distal objects tilt the other way with respect to the retina. But although this fact is easily cognitively appreciated, phenomenally there is little change in the appearance of objects. The phenomenal impression is as if our eyes were holes *through* which we look at the outside world. Tilting the border of such a hole would not affect the image. However, this is of course a completely wrong account of the actual situation, because the image orientations do change with eye tilt. This phenomenal state of affairs appears to be different from the situation in size and shape perception where, as discussed above, large differences in relevant secondary variables (distances and slants) of equal distal objects can readily induce the phenomenal appreciation of the difference of the corresponding proximal variables.

Note that although phenomenally poorly appreciated, proximal orientation must be taken into account by oculomotor mechanisms. If I glide my gaze along a telegraph pole facing me, although in everyday conditions I would perceive it as *vertical*, more or less regardless of the orientation of my head, my eye muscles involved in this action would perform quite different kinds of actions for different head orientations. For example, when my head is erect, and thus the projection of the pole is aligned with the "vertical" meridian, the motion of the gaze direction will be oriented along the jaw-forehead axis, and executed mainly by the so-called vertical as well as oblique eye muscles. In contrast, when my head is tilted by 90°, in which case the projection is aligned with the "horizontal" meridian (that in this case has vertical exocentric orientation), the motion will proceed along the ear-to-ear axis, and will be executed mainly by the so-called horizontal eye muscles.

Tasks and Instructions

Corresponding to the two possible notions of perceived orientation, two different tasks, the distal task and the proximal task, could be used in orientation perception research. However, explicitly proximally focused instructions have apparently not been used in published studies. Reports of perceived proximal orientation could be elicited by instructions to judge orientations of lines with respect to the *eye* rather than with respect to an exocentric reference frame.

In studies of size and shape, the secondary variables (distance and slant) are external, and can be different for two different objects observed at the *same* time. In contrast, eye orientation is an organismic postural variable, and it is not possible for a human observer to simultaneously inspect different objects with different eye tilts. This fact has consequences for the organization of experiments of perception of orientation. One way to design such a study would be to use the same format described above in studies of size and shape, but involving two temporal phases, one for the standard and the other for the comparison. In phase I the standard line is presented at some specified exocentric orientation and observed with some specified eye orientation, and then removed; in phase II a different eye orientation is induced, and the subjects are asked to identify the comparison line that has the same perceived orientation that the standard line had in phase I.

However, most studies in this field have used a different type of design, in which subjects are asked to adjust the orientation of a variable line until it exhibits some *prescribed* orientation, such as horizontal or vertical. This prescribed orientation plays the role of the standard stimulus, and the line with variable orientation plays the role of the comparison stimulus. However, the standard is only described as an *internal perceptual norm* with which the comparison stimulus is to be matched, and is not actually presented to subjects during the matching process.

This type of study format may be called a "single stimulus" or "internal standard" design, in contrast to the described designs in size and shape studies, which could be called "double stimulus" or "external standard" designs. Internal standard designs have the important technical advantage of using only a single stimulus, but they depend on the existence and familiarity of perceptual norms. Such designs can also be used in size and shape perception studies. For example, in a size perception study subjects can be asked to identify the stimulus that has some familiar prescribed size, such as the size of a playing card or a tennis ball; or, in a shape perception study subjects can be asked to pick out the circle from a set of ovals. Norms can also be established through a training process in which subjects learn to reliably recognize a specific size, shape, or some other attribute, prior to the matching phase of the experiment.

Structures of Experimental Results

As noted above, our everyday visual experience informs us that under full-cue conditions in normally structured environments, perceived distal orientations do not change when the head and thus also the eyes are tilted: perceived verticals stay perceptually vertical, perceived horizontals stay horizontal, etc. This is "distal exocentric orientation constancy". However, the perception of purely gravitation-relative orientation is difficult to study experimentally in normal environments, because full-cue conditions usually involve many other vertically or horizontally oriented features, which could be used by subjects as a basis for their judgements of orientation, in the form of visually defined exocentric reference frames.

Such visual cues of orientation are eliminated in experiments under reduced-cue conditions, that is, when stimuli are presented as luminous displays in complete darkness, and the only cues of head tilt are vestibular and kinesthetic. The results of such studies depend on head orientation as the secondary variable. When the head is erect, and thus exocentric and retinal orientation coincide, perceived orientation is quite accurate, and subjects are able to set a variable line within 1° of the gravitationally defined horizontal and vertical (Witkin & Asch, 1948; Mann et al., 1949). However, when the head axis is tilted with respect to vertical for up to 180°, the structure of results is different. In such conditions, perceived orientation is biased, and involves both underconstancy and overconstancy, depending on the angle of tilt (Ebenholtz,

1977; Miller et al., 1965). For angles up to about 50–60°, underconstancy is obtained (known as the *E-effect*), whose amount first increases and then decreases to zero. For example, if the eye is tilted counter-clockwise, then the line that is *perceived* as vertical is objectively also tilted counter-clockwise, though to a much smaller amount than the eye. Consequently, a line that is in fact gravitationally vertical appears to be tilted in the clockwise direction. In other words, whereas the perceived orientation of a line of a given constant distal orientation is rotated *against* the direction of head tilt, the perception of *vertical* is rotated *in* that direction. For angles of head tilt larger than 50–60°, the results are reversed, and orientation overconstancy is obtained (known as the *A-effect*), increasing in amount with increasing angle. Thus in this range perceived *line* orientation is biased *in* the direction of head tilt, whereas the perception of *vertical* is biased *against* this direction. It should be noted that in all such experiments the amount of eye tilt is usually somewhat less than the amount of head tilt because of the effect of *counter-torsion*, a reflex counter-rolling of the eyes about the visual axis in the direction opposite to the head tilt.

PERCEPTION OF DIRECTION

The location of an object, similar to orientation, is determined with respect to some reference frame, which can be exocentric or egocentric. Location can be decomposed into *distance* and *direction*. Here I will only deal with *egocentric direction*, that is, direction of external objects as specified with respect to the observer.

For some purposes the observer can be approximated with a point in space, and then other locations can be specified with reference to that point. However, for other purposes, observers cannot be reduced to a point, and more detailed aspects of their bodies must be taken into account (see Howard, 1982, 1986, 1993). There are different parts of the observer's body with which an egocentric reference frame can be associated, such as the observer's head, eyes, trunk, shoulder, etc. Furthermore, for any given body part, there are different ways in which an egocentric reference frame can be established.

One way to determine a *head-centered* (cephalocentric) reference frame for direction is to define as the reference direction the direction in which the observer is *facing*. All other egocentric directions can then be defined with respect to that direction, which will be referred to as the "straight-ahead axis". This axis can be taken as being roughly perpendicular to the forehead, or the *mid-frontal* plane of the head (the plane that divides the head into the front half and the back half). For binocular perception, this axis may be taken to pass midway between the eyes, whereas for monocular perception, which will be assumed in the following, the axis passes through the center of the eye. The head-centered directions of all objects are defined by their angular relation with respect to the straight-ahead axis.

Note that there are other ways to define the notion of "straight ahead". For example, straight ahead is often taken to refer to external locations in front of the observer corresponding to the *median* plane of the head, which is the plane that divides it into the right half and the left half, imagined to extend indefinitely beyond the head itself.

In this sense, straight ahead refers to locations of all objects that are neither to the left nor to the right of the observer, and does not define a single direction but a family of directions. Similarly, the notion of "eye-level" can be defined to correspond to the eye-level *transverse* plane of the head, which is the plane that passes through both eyes and is perpendicular to the mid-frontal plane. The straight-ahead axis may be defined as the intersection of this plane and the median plane.

A second way to define an egocentric reference frame is to take as the reference direction the direction in which the observer is *looking*. In this way a *gaze-centered* (oculocentric) reference frame is established, with the monocular visual axis (gaze direction) as a reference for all other directions. This axis connects the fovea and the object to which the gaze is turned. The gaze-centered directions of all objects are defined by their angular relation with respect to the visual axis.

Relations of Non-phenomenal Variables

When the observer *looks straight ahead* then the two reference directions coincide, so that the head-centered direction of an object is the same as its gaze-centered direction. However, when the observer does not look where he/she is facing, then the same external object has different directions with respect to the two reference axes. Such a situation is depicted in the sketch in row 4 in Figure 3.1. For simplicity, suppose that the head of the observer, which is not indicated in the sketch, is erect, and that the direction in which the observer is facing is horizontal. The straight-ahead axis, whose exocentric orientation is horizontal, is depicted by the dotted line. It is assumed that the eye is turned upwards, which is indicated by the tilted position of the retina (depicted as a semicircle), as well as by the gaze direction (visual axis), depicted by the out-going arrow whose end is centered at the retina at the small gray disk indicating the fovea. The gaze direction, as measured with respect to the head-centered reference frame, is given by the angle g, which the visual axis subtends with the horizontal straight-ahead axis. An external object is indicated by an "x", and its projection on the retina is depicted by the in-going arrow, the projection ray of the object. The head-centered direction of the object is given by the angle D, that its projection ray subtends with the straight-ahead axis; its gaze-centered direction is given by the angle α that the projection ray subtends with the visual axis. The relation between the three angles in the presented case is given by the formula $\alpha = D - g$. For example, if a distal object is directed at $D = 30°$ away from straight ahead, and the gaze deviates $g = 20°$ from straight ahead in the same direction, then the projection of the object is located at $\alpha = 10°$ from the fovea. This analysis applies to 2-D cross-sections of 3-D space; more complicated formulas would apply for an analysis of direction in full 3-D space.

It is important to note that angle α corresponds to the angular distance of the projection of the object from the fovea. This distance defines the location of the projected image within a *proximal reference frame* centered at the fovea. Thus gaze-centered directions correspond 1-to-1 with proximal locations.

Given a static external object and a fixed straight-ahead axis, when the gaze direction is changed, then the head-centered direction of the object remains the same (because it is defined with respect to the straight-ahead axis), but its gaze-centered direction and proximal location are changed. This situation is formally the same as the analogous relations concerning size, shape, and orientation. A proximal variable (proximal location) depends not only on the corresponding distal variable (head-centered direction) but also on a secondary variable (gaze direction). The only difference is the status of head-centered direction because, being defined with respect to the observer, it is not a true distal variable in the same way as size, shape, or exocentric orientation. However, in the preceding discussions this direction is assumed to be constant so that in that sense it is independent of the observer. On the other hand, when the observer does change the location and orientation of the head, then the external objects, even when they are static with respect to some exocentric reference frame, change their directions with respect to the observer.

Phenomenal Attributes

As it was shown above, the notion of egocentric direction has two senses, one referring to head-centered direction and the other to gaze-centered direction and proximal location. Correspondingly, two meanings of "phenomenal egocentric direction" can be defined. The first meaning, which corresponds to the distal variable (egocentric object direction D), will be referred to as "perceived head-centered (cephalocentric) direction". This phenomenal variable involves the conscious impression and judgement of the direction of external objects with respect to the head and the straight-ahead axis. This meaning is exemplified in descriptions such as "object A lies directly straight ahead of me, object L is off to my left, and object R is off to my right". Recall that head-centered direction depends on the position of the head: in this example, if the head is turned toward object L, then that object comes to lie straight ahead, and object A comes to lie toward right.

The second sense of "perceived direction" corresponds to the proximal variable α, the location of the projection of the external object on the retina, and to the corresponding oculocentric direction. This phenomenal variable may be called "perceived proximal location" or "perceived gaze-centered (oculocentric) direction". Rock (1975) uses the terms "perceived location in the visual field" and "field location". This notion refers to the conscious impression and judgement of the direction of an object within the momentary field of view, relative to gaze direction. Such a notion is relatively rarely used, and will be more elaborated below.

When I look at object A from the previous example (which lies straight ahead), its proximal location is at my fovea, its oculocentric direction coincides with the gaze direction, and its *perceived* oculocentric direction is at the center of my current field of view. The proximal locations of other objects, such as L or R, are away from the fovea, their oculocentric directions are away from my current gaze direction, and their corresponding perceived oculocentric directions are toward the left and right periphery of my current field of view. When I switch my gaze from A to L then, provided that my head (and thus also my straight-ahead axis) remains fixed, the objective, *distal* egocentric directions of these objects do not change: I still face object A, and it remains straight ahead, and object L remains off to my left; the *perceived* distal directions of objects A and L may also not change with change of gaze direction. However, the perceived *proximal* locations and oculocentric directions of these objects do change: object L is now at the center of my field of view, whereas object A lies toward right in the periphery.

Thus with the head fixed and gaze direction variable, perceived head-centered directions usually stay constant but perceived oculocentric directions change. In contrast, with the head mobile and gaze direction fixed, for example, when I tilt my head or pitch it upwards and downwards, but keep looking at the same stationary external spot, the perceived head-centered orientations change, but perceived oculocentric directions stay constant, since the fixated spot remains at the center of view, and the other static objects also keep their oculocentric directions. Finally, when an object moves and my gaze tracks it, with my head fixed, the object changes its perceived head-centered direction but keeps it perceived oculocentric direction at the center of view; however, if my gaze is fixed, then the moving object changes both its perceived directions.

Note that, with the head fixed, it is not head-centric directions but proximal locations and the corresponding oculocentric directions that guide oculomotor behavior. In the preceding example with objects L, A, and R, the head-centered direction of object A remains straight ahead regardless of eye motions. However, in order to move my gaze to the direction of point A, I must move it according to its oculocentric direction: toward right if my gaze is currently directed at point L (and thus the oculocentric direction of point A is toward right), but toward left if my gaze is currently directed at point R (and thus the oculocentric direction of point A is toward left).

Tasks and Instructions

In the section on orientation perception it was pointed out that there are two types of designs of matching studies, one involving external standards, and the other involving internal standards. Both types of design can be used to study the perception of direction. One way to design an external standard study is to use two temporal phases. In phase I, a small target object is exposed as the standard stimulus, in a specified head-centered direction; to control the direction of gaze, a fixation point is provided (which may coincide with the target object). In phase II, the target and the fixation point are removed, and a different fixation point is provided, which induces a change of gaze direction. The task of the subject is to identify the comparison stimulus which has the same perceived direction that the standard stimulus had in phase I. In the distal task perceived direction would refer to head-centered direction. In the proximal task perceived direction would refer to oculocentric direction; however, to my knowledge studies of this type have not been reported.

The internal standard design does not involve the visual presentation of a standard stimulus. Instead, the standard is described verbally in the form of an internal visual norm. Such a norm is a prescribed salient head-centered direction to which the comparison stimulus is to be set. Two such directions have been used: one is "perceived straight ahead" and the other is "perceived eye level". Most experimental studies have used this format. For example, in a study of "perceived straight ahead" the task of the subject is to vary the horizontal position of the target object until it is perceived to lie straight ahead. In studies of "perceived eye level", the subjects are asked to vary the vertical position of the target object (or, alternately, to vary the height of the chair they are sitting on, with the target object staying in a fixed position), until its perceived direction is at the level of their eye height.

Structures of Experimental Results

In order to assess the performance of subjects in studies of egocentric direction perception, it is useful to establish their *accuracy* under conditions of *free* eye movements. Such studies find that for perceived straight ahead there is, on average, no consistent bias toward left or right. In contrast perceived eye level is usually somewhat biased: the point that is perceived to lie at eye height in fact generally lies a few degrees below objective eye height; consequently, a point that is positioned at objective eye height is perceived to lie somewhat above it. This is true for both reduced-cue and full-cue conditions, but the latter settings are somewhat more accurate (Stoper & Cohen, 1986).

In contrast to accuracy studies, in studies of direction constancy the direction of gaze is controlled. For example, in studies of perceived straight ahead, this is done by providing an eccentric, horizontally displaced fixation point. This is analogous to the control of eye tilt in orientation studies, except that in such studies the eye tilt of the subject is mechanically imposed by the experimental setup (except for the effect of counter-torsion), whereas in direction perception studies the subjects retain control over their gaze direction, but are asked to direct the gaze at the fixation point and their compliance is monitored by eye-tracking devices.

Our everyday experience strongly suggests that under full-cue conditions, when we change the direction of gaze the egocentric directions of objects with respect to us appear, correctly, to stay the same, although their retinal locations change. In other words, "egocentric direction constancy" (also called "position constancy") obtains. One reason to expect direction constancy in normal environments is that in such circumstances the information about gaze direction (which in standard theories is supposed to cancel the retinal shift) may not be needed, because the direction of the target object can be specified by *exocentric*, object-relative reference frames, that is, in relation to static objects in the environment.

Under reduced-cue conditions however, when stimuli are presented as single luminous spots in darkness, such exocentric visual cues are eliminated, so that relative spatial relations cannot be used as cues to object direction, and only oculomotor signals remain. Some studies find that, on average, egocentric direction constancy under reduced-cue conditions is relatively accurate (Matin, 1986). However, other studies find some underconstancy: for example, if the gaze is fixated at a point that lies to the *right* of the straight ahead direction, then the comparison stimulus that the subjects identify as being located straight ahead of them is in fact located a few degrees toward *right*. This outcome means that an object that is objectively straight ahead is perceived to lie somewhat to the *left* of straight ahead (Hill, 1972; Morgan, 1978). In other words, the perceived direction of *straight ahead* is displaced *toward* the gaze direction, whereas the perceived direction of a static *point* is displaced *against* this direction.

PERCEPTION OF ACHROMATIC COLOR

Achromatic surfaces reflect approximately the same percentage or proportion of illumination at each wavelength. This proportion is their *reflectance*, which I will refer to as "distal achromatic color". The proximal variable corresponding to reflectance is *luminance* or "proximal achromatic color", which is the amount of light, per unit time and area, that arrives from the surface at the retina. Note that this notion of luminance, as all other proximal variables discussed in this presentation, refers to characteristics of light ray distributions *arriving* at the eye, and is not meant to encompass the subsequent physiological processes. However, it should be noted that this term is often used in a related but different sense, which incorporates the effects of light on retinal receptors in its definition. Reviews of many aspects of achromatic color perception can be found in Rock (1975) and Gilchrist (1994).

Relations of Non-phenomenal Variables

The luminance arriving from a surface is affected not only by reflectance but also by illumination. The relation between the three variables is depicted in row 5 of Figure 3.1. The geometric sketch involves an elongated gray rectangle, representing a surface and its reflectance R, an arrow pointing at the surface, representing the incoming illumination i, and an arrow pointing away from the surface, representing its luminance λ; the latter arrow is thinner than the former, indicating that luminance is a fraction of illumination. Reflectance is the distal variable, luminance is the corresponding proximal variable, and illumination is the secondary variable.

The relation between the three variables in its simplest form is expressed by the formula $\lambda = Ri$. Thus luminance λ is directly proportional to illumination i, with reflectance R as the factor of proportionality. For example, a surface of reflectance $R = 0.5$, illuminated by 100 light units, has a luminance of $\lambda = 50$ light units. This formula presupposes that the direction of illumination is perpendicular to the surface and that the surface is *lambertian*, that is, that it reflects light diffusely and uniformly in all directions. Thus it must be amended to take into account the dependence of luminance on the angle of the incoming light as well as the glossiness and highlights of non-lambertian surfaces.

Phenomenal Variables

Corresponding to two types of external achromatic color, reflectance and luminance, there are two types of phenomenal achromatic colors. The phenomenal counterpart of distal achromatic color (reflectance) can be called "perceived distal achromatic color", or "perceived achromatic reflectance". It involves the conscious impression and judgement of the distal achromatic color of a surface. In contrast to phenomenal geometric variables, this phenomenal photometric variable has a special single-word label, and is generally referred to as *lightness*. In normal viewing conditions the perceived color of achromatic surfaces with reflectance less than about 0.05 is called *black,* and of those with reflectance more than about 0.80 it is called *white,* whereas the intermediate reflectances appear as various shades of *gray.* Older terms for lightness include "quality", "whiteness", and "grayness" (which would perhaps be the most appropriate label).

The phenomenal counterpart of proximal achromatic color (luminance) is "perceived proximal achromatic color", or "perceived achromatic luminance". It also has a single-word label, and is generally referred to as *brightness.* Brightness refers to the conscious impression and judgement of luminance, that is, the amount of light arriving at the eye. It is sometimes described as ranging from *dim* to *bright.* The concept of brightness is referred to in the older literature as "strength", "weight", or "insistence". Discussions and further considerations of appearance of achromatic color have a long history in achromatic color research, and are provided by Hering (1920/1964), Katz (1911/1935), Gelb (1929), Koffka (1935), Evans (1964), Lie (1969), Heggelund (1974, 1992), Arend and Reeves (1986), Whittle (1991), and papers in Gilchrist (1994). "Perceived self-luminosity", a phenomenal attribute of achromatic color that appears in certain luminance conditions, will not be addressed here.

One way to illustrate the difference between lightness and brightness is to compare the appearance of two spatially close surfaces of equal reflectance which receive different amounts of illumination. For example, consider two identical pieces of white paper, one lying in sunshine and the other in a nearby shadow. Such a display usually evokes "lightness constancy", that is, the correct impression that the two papers have equal or similar surface colors. However, in this situation it is not difficult to note that the two papers do differ in another, color-related aspect. This difference can be expressed by saying that the paper receiving higher illumination is *brighter,* that is, sends more light toward the perceiver than the one in shadow. Thus although the papers are similar in lightness, they differ in brightness. A converse example concerns the appearance of two papers of different reflectance, one white and the other black, such that the white paper lies in a shadow and the black paper is exposed to direct light. Such a display ordinarily evokes the correct impression that the two papers have quite different surface colors; however, it may also be accompanied by the impression that the amount of light arriving from the two surfaces is not very different. Thus the two papers are different in lightness but similar in brightness. These examples involve partial phenomenal identities, because objects equal with respect to one type of perceived achromatic color are different with respect to the other type. A total phenomenal identity with respect to achromatic color would involve equality with respect to both lightness and brightness.

Tasks and Instructions

Similar to studies of size and shape, matching studies of achromatic color usually use the external standard design. In classical studies of lightness constancy usually the standard stimulus was a surface subjected to decreased illumination, and the comparison stimuli were well illuminated, although the converse combination could also be used. The differences in illumination of the stimuli were produced in various ways, for example by differences in distance from the light source or orientation with respect to it, but most often by putting the standard in a shadow (Katz, 1911/1935). In more recent research such conditions are often simulated on computer screens. The task of the subject is to identify the comparison stimulus that has the same achromatic color as the standard. Adjustment procedures involve a single, variable comparison stimulus, whose luminance is manipulated by the subject so that it perceptually matches the standard. Selection procedures use graded sets of achromatic comparison stimuli spanning the range from black to white, such as the achromatic Munsell scale.

Corresponding to two senses of "perceived achromatic color" (lightness and brightness), there are two different tasks that can be performed, and two correspondingly different types of instructions. The distal task involves instructions that are distally focused, that is, they stress that it is the reflectances of the two surfaces that are to be compared. A distal criterion of reflectance equality of surfaces is that they are painted with the same shade of paint or cut from the same piece of paper (Arend & Goldstein, 1987). A proximal criterion is that the two surfaces, if put under equal illumination, should reflect the same amount of light. A phenomenal criterion is that if put under equal illumination, the two surfaces would induce a totally identical impression of achromatic color (equality with respect to both lightness and brightness). In contrast, the proximal task involves instructions that are proximally focused, and stress that the judgement concerns the amount of light (luminance) arriving at the eye from the standard and the comparison surface. A distal criterion of luminance equality is that if the two surfaces were photographed, their images on the photographs would have the same reflectance. A proximal criterion is that the two surfaces should reflect the same amount of light into the eye. A phenomenal criterion is that they would induce a totally identical impression, with respect to achromatic color, if observed in isolation on identical backgrounds. Finally, as in size and shape constancy studies, "phenomenally" focused instructions are sometimes used, which stress the immediate, "non-judgemental" color appearance of standard and comparison stimuli.

Structure of Experimental Results

Similar to studies of geometric perception, studies of photometric perception may generally be conducted under two basic types of viewing conditions. In reduced-cue conditions, the two surfaces that are to be matched are observed through two openings in the *reduction screen*: this device, used in classical studies, is usually simply a homogeneous achromatic surface which covers most of the visual field of the observer, except for two openings, which only allow the view of the two relevant surfaces and nothing else in the scene. Such conditions eliminate cues of illumination, the secondary variable, as well as access to the relations of the luminances of the target surfaces and the luminances of other surfaces in the surround (except for the reduction screen). Cues of illumination can also be eliminated without the reduction screen, using specially controlled illumination conditions for isolated regions in the visual field (Gelb, 1929; Kardos, 1934). In contrast, under full-cue conditions the observer has a full, unobstructed view of the experimental setup, including luminance relations and potential illumination cues. The stimuli used in achromatic color research involve various degrees of *complexity*, starting from a patch of light on a zero-luminance background (completely reduced-cue) through stimuli consisting of non-zero surrounds and centers, to stimuli involving many surfaces of different luminances ("mondrians"). More realistic conditions involving 3-D setups, highlights, and various types of shadows are used more rarely.

The results of achromatic perception experiments generally depend on the type of the task (distal or proximal) and on viewing conditions (reduced-cue or full-cue). However, under *reduced-cue* conditions, the type of task does not make much difference: subjects essentially perform a luminance match, that is, they declare as perceptually equal two surfaces with approximately equal luminances, regardless of their differences in reflectance and illumination. Thus a surface under low illumination that is matched with a surface in high illumination has to have a higher reflectance, in order to compensate for the lower illumination it receives.

Under full-cue conditions the type of task strongly affects the results. For the distal task (judgements of lightness), classical studies using standard and comparison stimuli on homogeneous backgrounds have generally reported some degree of underconstancy (Katz, 1911/1935; Jaensch & Mueller, 1920; Helson, 1943). That is, the standard stimulus (presented in decreased illumination) is generally matched by a comparison stimulus (presented under normal illumination), which has somewhat lower reflectance; in short, shaded objects look somewhat darker. However, when the scene presented to the subjects contains many surfaces of many different reflectance levels in addition to the ones being matched, then excellent lightness constancy (reflectance matching) can be obtained (Burzlaff, 1930). That is, surfaces judged to be equal in lightness are indeed about equal in reflectance, despite the difference in luminance induced by the difference in illumination. A similar pattern of results was also found in more recent studies (Arend & Goldstein, 1987; Jacobsen & Gilchrist, 1988; Arend & Špehar, 1993a).

The proximal task (judgements of brightness) was used more rarely with more complex stimuli. Observations by Katz (1911/1935) and Henneman (1935) indicated that in certain conditions subjects have some ability to match surfaces in terms of luminance—a result confirmed by Lie (1969). More recent studies found successful luminance matching only with simple center-surround stimuli whose center had a higher luminance than the surround. However, with centers of lower luminance, and when the standards and comparisons were embedded in more complex displays, brightness judgements were intermediate between luminance matching and reflectance matching; furthermore, the matching values tended to have a larger variability than in the distal task (Arend & Goldstein, 1987; Arend & Špehar, 1993a). Results with *phenomenally* focused instruction are generally intermediate between luminance matching and reflectance matching (Landauer & Rodger, 1964). However, as in case of size and shape perception, such results are not easy to interpret.

PERCEPTION OF CHROMATIC COLOR

Whereas the photometric characteristics of achromatic surfaces can be described with a single number (reflectance), this is not possible for chromatic surfaces, because they reflect different proportions of light at different wavelengths. Thus they must be described with *spectral reflectance distributions*, that is, reflectance must be specified as a *function* of wavelength. The visible light spectrum involves wavelengths approximately within the 400–700 nm range. Strictly speaking, the dependent variable in a real-numbered function is defined by an infinity of numbers. However, if the proportion of reflected light is given, say, for every whole-numbered wavelength, then a reflectance distribution is specified by 300 numbers. In practice, for relatively smooth reflectance distributions exhibited by many natural surfaces, a course sampling at every 10 nm often suffices, and reflectance distributions can be specified with about 30 numbers. Such a reflectance distribution will be referred to as "distal chromatic color" and denoted as $R(w)$. It specifies, for each sampled wavelength w, the proportion of light reflected by that surface at that wavelength.

The light reflected from a chromatic surface and arriving at the eye is also characterized by a spectral distribution. Such *spectral luminance distributions* specify, for each sampled wavelength w, the *amount* of light energy arriving at a retinal locus of unit area in unit time at that wavelength. Such a luminance distribution will be referred to as "proximal chromatic color" and denoted as $\lambda(w)$. Reviews of many aspects of color perception research can be found in Wyszecki and Stiles (1982),Wyszecki (1986), and Pokorny and Smith (1986).

Relations of Non-phenomenal Variables

Proximal chromatic color does not depend only on distal chromatic color but also on a secondary variable, the illumination color, specified by the *spectral illumination distribution*, denoted here as $i(w)$. The relation between the three distributions in the simplest case is the complete functional analogue of the corresponding achromatic case ($\lambda = Ri$), and is given by the equation $\lambda(w) = R(w)i(w)$. Thus for any concrete value of wavelength w, the luminance at that wavelength is given as the product of surface reflectance at that wavelength and illumination at that wavelength.

A geometric representation of this relation is depicted in row 6 of Figure 3.1. This representation uses somewhat artificial, non-realistic examples of spectral distributions. The independent, x-axis variable for all three functions is the wavelength w of light. The spectral distribution of illumination, $i(w)$, is, for simplicity, assumed as linearly rising, that is, the amount of light increases with wavelength. The reflectance spectral distribution, $R(w)$, has the shape of a symmetric, inverted-U (quadratic) function. The resulting luminance spectral distribution, $\lambda(w)$, is also concave, but it is asymmetric within the spectral range and its peak is shifted toward right, due to the effect of the luminance distribution; it is a cubic function, resulting from the multiplication of a quadratic function by a linear function. This situation very roughly corresponds to a greenish surface illuminated by incandescent light, which in this situation reflects more yellowish light than if it were illuminated by daylight.

Phenomenal Attributes

The appearance of chromatic colors is a complex topic; only some selected aspects will be treated here, within the same format as for all other attributes; additional aspects will be addressed in the general discussion section. *Phenomenal colors* are traditionally described as 3-dimensional, the three dimensions being *hue*, *lightness*, and *saturation*. Any color in a standard color appearance system, such as the Munsell system, can be specified with three values, one for each dimension.

In analogy to the achromatic case, two notions of phenomenal chromatic surface colors may be distinguished. The first notion can be called "perceived distal chromatic color" or "perceived chromatic reflectance", and it refers to the conscious impression and judgement of the color of object surfaces. The second notion may be called "perceived proximal chromatic color" or "perceived chromatic luminance", and it refers to the conscious impression and judgement of the color of the light arriving at the retina from some spatial direction. Various authors have proposed related notions. For example, to express a conceptually similar distinction, Evans (1964) used the term pair "object-color perception" and "light-color perception", Arend (1993, 1994) suggested the terms "apparent surface color" and "unattributed color", and Kuriki and Uchikawa (1996) used the terms "surface color" and "apparent color".

One way to illustrate this distinction is by way of an example analogous to the one used for the achromatic case. Consider two identical pieces of red paper, one of which is illuminated by a bluish light source, and the other, lying nearby, by a yellowish source. Such a stimulus may induce distal "chromatic color constancy", that is, the correct impression of two differentially illuminated but objectively equally or similarly colored surfaces. However, the observer might also note that the two papers do differ in a color-related aspect, one paper having a violet tinge, and the other an orange tinge. Thus the two surfaces may be judged to be similar in perceived distal chromatic color but different in perceived proximal chromatic color. Conversely, a yellow surface in reddish illumination next to a red surface in yellowish illumination may be judged to differ in perceived distal color but be similar in perceived proximal color. In these examples, similarities and differences of two types of phenomenal color with respect to hue were stressed. Analogous cases could be described concerning saturation. With respect to the third chromatic color dimension, one could propose that perceived distal color has the dimension of lightness, whereas perceived proximal color has the dimension of brightness. Totally identical color percepts would involve equality in all three dimensions.

Tasks and Instructions

Matching studies in chromatic color perception use designs with both external and internal standards, and usually employ an adjustment procedure. External standard designs involve a standard stimulus presented under one illumination and a comparison stimulus presented under a different illumination. The task of the subject is to adjust the color of the variable comparison stimulus until it matches the standard. Designs using an internal standard do not involve the presentation of a standard stimulus during the adjustment task. Instead, the subjects are asked to adjust the comparison stimulus, presented under different illuminations in different trials, until it matches a prescribed color appearance. The prescribed colors include pure red, pure green, pure blue, pure yellow, as well as achromatic (gray).

The instructions that attempt to elicit perceptual matches associated with the two types of phenomenal attributes introduced above are, in principle, similar to analogous instructions involving achromatic color perception. The distal task, involving distally focused instructions would stress the equality of distal colors. A distal criterion of objective equality of surface colors is that the surfaces are painted with the same pigment or cut from the same piece of material (Arend & Reeves, 1986). A proximal criterion is that the two surfaces would reflect visually equally effective light (see the general discussion section for an explication of this notion) if put under equal illumination. A phenomenal criterion is that the surfaces would look totally color-identical if put under equal illumination. The proximal task, involving proximally focused instructions, would stress the equality of proximal stimuli reaching the eye. A distal criterion of luminance distribution equality is that the images of the two surfaces on a photograph should have the same distal surface color. A proximal criterion is that the two surfaces reflect equally effective light into the eye. A phenomenal criterion is that the two surfaces should look identical if observed in isolation on equal backgrounds.

It should be noted that the distinction between two senses of perceived chromatic color has only relatively recently been explicated in experimental chromatic color research, and was applied only in a handful of experiments. Most color perception studies used unfocused instructions that simply ask subjects to match or adjust "colors". The reason that this distinction has rarely been used may be that the difference between the two types of phenomenal color is phenomenologically less salient than in the achromatic case, or that the conditions used in color perception studies may generally not have been conducive to make it salient. Clearly, further effort is needed by color researchers to resolve these issues.

Structures of Experimental Results

With completely reduced-cue conditions, color matches are performed in terms of luminance distributions. That is, two isolated fields of light are perceived to have equal chromatic color when the compositions of light arriving from them at the retina are equal, regardless of differences in reflectance and illumination distributions.

Everyday observations suggest that when a surface is observed under full-cue conditions, as a part of a more articulated display, its perceived chromatic color in general tends to stay more or less constant, in spite of changes in the composition of illumination, say from daylight to artificial light. Thus approximate "chromatic color constancy" obtains, that is, perceptual matches are made in terms of reflectance distributions. However, experimental studies indicate that, in general, chromatic color constancy is a less stable and dependable phenomenon than achromatic color constancy. Thus whereas constancy may hold very well for some particular stimulus arrangements, for others it may fail drastically (Katz, 1911/1935; Helson et al., 1952; McCann et al., 1976; Blackwell & Buchsbaum, 1988; Valberg & Lange-Malecki, 1990; Brainard & Wandell, 1992; Lucassen & Walraven 1993; Brainard et al., 1997;

Brainard, 1998). Note that the number of potential combinations of surface colors, illumination colors, and surround contexts is huge, so that many experiments have sampled only a portion of the possible stimulus space. Also, because phenomenal color is 3-dimensional, the structure of deviations from constancy is more complex than for 1-dimensional attributes, and the notions of over- and underestimation are not directly applicable. Finally, as noted, in most studies the distinction between two types of phenomenal variables was not drawn, which may have, in some cases, increased the variability of obtained data. Studies in which two types of instructions were explicitly used with equal stimuli (involving the "surface match" or "paper match" vs the "appearance match" or "hue-saturation match") have generally found that constancy of perceived chromatic color is clearly better for perceived distal than for perceived proximal color (Arend & Reeves, 1986; Arend et al., 1991; Cornelissen & Brenner, 1995; Kuriki & Uchikawa, 1996; Bäuml, 1999).

GENERAL DISCUSSION

SUMMARY

The discussions of main aspects of perception of the six perceptual attributes dealt with in this paper have a common formal structure, regardless of the specificities of each attribute. In all cases, a proximal variable is affected both by the corresponding distal variable and by a secondary variable. For each of the two non-phenomenal variables (distal and proximal) there is a corresponding phenomenal variable. In order to sharpen the conceptual distinction between the two phenomenal attributes, illustrative cases were presented involving two objects with similar perceived distal attributes but different perceived proximal attributes, and vice versa. Examples of different definitions of the types of phenomenal attributes were expressed as criteria (distal, proximal, and phenomenal) in instructions to subjects in two types of matching tasks (distal and proximal). Finally, a brief review of results of relevant experimental studies using different design types (external standard vs. internal standard) under different presentation conditions (reduced-cue vs. full-cue) was presented. In general, for intrinsic attributes (size, shape, color) under full-cue conditions perception of the distal attribute is relatively accurate ("distal constancy"), but over- and underconstancy are also often found. Perception of proximal attributes is generally less accurate and more variable. Under reduced-cue conditions matches are increasingly performed in accord with the proximal attribute. For extrinsic attributes (orientation, direction) extensive data on proximal attributes as well as on distal attributes under full-cue conditions are apparently lacking. Under reduced-cue conditions, distal exocentric orientation shows a specific pattern of under- and overconstancy, whereas for distal egocentric direction the result pattern suggests some underconstancy.

Potential Extensions of the Format

The discussions in this paper have avoided issues raised by binocularity, which involves doubling of the proximal stimulus. Also, dynamic aspects of perception were neglected. Note that the distinction between perceived distal and proximal attributes is clearly valid for the perception of motion. Change of location of an external object, as a distal variable, corresponds to the change of location of its retinal image as the proximal variable. However, three types of secondary variables affect retinal image motion, in addition to external object motion. The distance of the moving object affects the speed of retinal motion, eye tilt affects the orientation of the trajectory of retinal motion, and eye motion affects speed, orientation, as well as the shape of the retinal trajectory. Two types of phenomenal motion can in principle be distinguished, "perceived distal motion", referring to the impression of distal motion, and "perceived proximal motion", referring to the impression of proximal motion.

Similarities and Differences

In spite of considerable formal similarities, there are a number of substantial differences between the six perceptual attributes treated here. For example, the extrinsic geometric attributes (direction and orientation) are by definition reference-frame dependent, whereas the intrinsic attributes (size, shape, color) are by definition (though not necessarily in perception) independent from reference frames. Furthermore, direction and orientation share the feature that the secondary variables involved in their perception (gaze direction and eye tilt) are postural, whereas the secondary variables (distance, slant, illumination) involved in the perception of intrinsic attributes are external. Within the intrinsic attributes, one difference is that distance, the secondary variable in size perception, refers to a different portion of space than the object itself, whereas slant and illumination, the secondary variables in shape and color perception, are attributes of the same objects whose distal or proximal attributes (shape or color) are being judged.

Specificity of Chromatic Color

There is an aspect in which chromatic colors are radically different from the other five attributes discussed here. This difference concerns *dimensionality*, that is, the number of independent values needed to specify an attribute. As noted, spectral distributions (for both chromatic reflectances and luminances) need about 30 values for their specification, and thus are, in this sense, 30-dimensional. There is nothing special about number 30; what is important is that a much smaller number of values, say four or five, does not suffice to specify a spectral distribution. In contrast, all other discussed distal attributes were presented as one-dimensional, that is, they could be specified with a single number. Note that sizes and achromatic colors are indeed truly one-dimensional. However, in cases of orientation and direction, the discussion was oversimplified, because to specify these attributes in full 3-D space one angle does not suffice and another one is need, so that these attributes are in fact two-dimensional. As for shape, figures more complex than ellipses would need more numbers for shape specification. But still there remains about an order of magnitude difference in dimensionality between these five attributes and chromatic spectral distributions.

As noted above, perceived chromatic colors (distal and proximal) are usually regarded as three-dimensional. Thus the dimensionality of distal and proximal chromatic colors (roughly 30) greatly exceeds the dimensionality of *perceived* distal and proximal chromatic colors (three). In other words, there is a significant *reduction* of dimensionality in the transformation from the external variables to the phenomenal variables. The dimensional reduction is due to the properties of the visual transduction mechanism. Whatever the complexity of the luminance distribution, a retinal cone can react to it in only one way, by changing its activity level, which is a 1-D variable. Since there are three classes of cones, the large dimensionality of the proximal input is reduced to the three-dimensionality of cone responses. The cone signals are subsequently further transformed, through additive, subtractive, and perhaps more complex combinations, into what are usually called the luminance channel, the red–green channel, and the yellow–blue channel. Such transformations amount to a re-expression of the initial information in different formats, but they cannot increase its dimensionality. A consequence of the reduction of dimensionality is the phenomenon of *metamerism*, the fact that many physically different luminance spectral distributions can induce identical color percepts. This will be the case when they induce identical activities in the three types of cones. This implies that for the purpose of color discrimination the proximal stimulus does not have to be specified as a full 30-D luminance distribution, and thus the *visually effective light* can be defined by only three values. These three numbers can be the cone absorption rates, but many other types of triplets, all interconvertible among each other, are also in practical use (see, e.g., Wyszecki & Stiles, 1982).

The dimensionality of other phenomenal attributes (distal or proximal) is not often discussed, but it is arguable that perceived distal and proximal size and achromatic color are each one-dimensional, and perceived orientation and direction two-dimensional, whereas the dimensionality of phenomenal shape is unclear. Note that the one-dimensionality of, say, both distal and phenomenal size, or both distal and phenomenal achromatic color, means that the information in the conscious impression is *commensurable* with the information contained in the outside object. In this sense, distal size or achromatic color is fully "recovered" in the conscious percept. In contrast, information carried by the external chromatic reflectances and luminances is unrecoverably under-represented in the conscious percept. This is the case independently of the existence of metamerism, which is sometimes regarded as a laboratory phenomenon, not typical for naturally occurring lights and surfaces. However, even if every different surface would evoke a uniquely different color percept, it would still be the case that a lot of information contained in the spectral distribution is not expressed in the corresponding percept. Nevertheless, what does get recovered is probably quite enough for biological purposes.

Status of Perceived Proximal Variables

Although perceived proximal variables are not phenomenally prominent in everyday conditions, their existence can be demonstrated by appropriate examples, and task instructions can be formulated to help subjects focus their attention on that aspect of their percepts. As noted, the distinction between two types of phenomenal variables was not always taken into account in perceptual research concerning the effects of secondary variables. Perceived proximal variables have been explicitly recognized and occasionally studied in the perception of size, shape, and achromatic color. In studies of the perception of direction the status of the perceived proximal variable is indubitable, although it is sometimes regarded more as a nuisance to be overcome than as a topic to which independent study should be devoted. In perception of chromatic color, as noted, the distinction of two variants is currently recognized only by a minority of researchers. Finally, in the perception of orientation, the proximal variant is rarely mentioned, perhaps because it has little phenomenal salience.

Sensation and Perception

A related distinction between two types of phenomenal variables is expressed by the contrast of concepts of *sensation* and *perception* (Hochberg, 1979; Mausfeld, 1996; Atherton, this volume). I have avoided using these terms because they have many connotations, often quite different for different authors, which should not be applied to the notions of perceived distal and perceived proximal variables as used here. For example, sensations are often regarded to be primary mental correspondents of retinal images (usually unnoticed), which are then transformed, through (usually unconscious) processes analogous to reasoning and/or based on acquired knowledge, into full-blown perceptual experiences, corresponding to perceptions. In contrast, the notions of perceived distal and perceived proximal variables as defined here are not linked to this or any other causal account of perceptual processing. As noted earlier, they are only used to point to and differentiate between two types visual conscious impressions (associated with two types of external variables), whose differences should be acknowledged in order to avoid conceptual confusions, regardless of their neural representations, theoretical status, and eventually assigned place in the perceptual causal chain.

Perceptual Attitudes

Another related distinction concerns the difference between perceptual *attitudes* adopted by observers in perceptual tasks and choices of matching values. One type of attitude is the "natural" or "naive" or "everyday" attitude, and it corresponds to perceived distal attributes. The other attitude is "critical" or "analytical" or "painterly", and it corresponds to perceived proximal attributes. The label "painterly" refers to the fact that a "realistic" (photograph-like) representation of a scene in a painting requires that sizes, shapes, and colors of distal objects be depicted in accord with their proximal counterparts. Thus objects of equal distal size but at different distances from the canvas must be represented by images of different physical sizes on the painting, in order to adequately represent objects of equal distal sizes; similar requirements apply for objects of equal shapes but different slants, and objects of equal distal color but in different illumination.

While the distinction of perceptual attitudes may adequately capture the main aspect of the distal–proximal difference, it may overstate its subjective aspect. I have tried in this paper to also stress its objective aspect, that is, that the difference in perception of distal and proximal attributes is based on and refers to an objective difference between attributes of external objects. For example, the distal size of an object and the visual angle it subtends are two objectively defined, different, though related, aspects of the object. They are, in principle, observable simultaneously (like, say, the color and the shape of an object), though perceivers may attend more to one than to the other at any given moment.

Visual Illusions

Perceptual constancies are traditionally characterized by an approximate agreement of objective, distal attributes and corresponding perceived distal attributes, in spite of the discrepancies concerning proximal attributes, induced by secondary variables. For example, objects of equal distal sizes but at different distances are perceived as equal, despite the difference in their proximal sizes. Such issues have always been of interest for perception researchers because of the problems posed by the discrepancies between the relations in the retinal image and the relations in the percept. For example, how can it be that we see objects of equal size when their retinal images are different? Generally and crudely put, the problem is why in such cases we don't see what is on our retinae.

There is another traditional perceptual issue which is also characterized by a discrepancy between phenomenal and proximal attributes. This is the study of *visual illusions*. Examples of such illusions can be found for all six attributes discussed here: two distally equal extents, when appended at their ends by differently oriented lines ("fins") appear different in size (Müller–Lyer size illusion); straight lines appear curved when criss-crossed by other lines (Hering–Wundt shape illusion); a vertical line ("rod"), presented within an oblique frame, appears tilted opposite to the tilt of the frame (rod-and-frame orientation illusion); an object that lies objectively straight ahead presented within an eccentrically positioned frame, appears shifted opposite to the center of the frame (Roelofs direction illusion); surfaces of equal reflectance appear differently colored when surrounded by surfaces of different colors (chromatic and achromatic simultaneous contrast illusion). For reviews of visual illusions, see Robinson (1972) and Coren and Girgus (1978).

Although constancies and illusions share the presence of a discrepancy between relations of proximal and phenomenal attributes, they are different in other respects. For example, in constancies objects with equal distal attributes are perceived to be distally equal, and perception is veridical. In contrast, in illusions objects with equal distal attributes are perceived to be different, and perception is non-veridical. Furthermore, all constancies involve the presence of a secondary variable that affects the value of the proximal variable. Thus distance affects proximal size, slant affects proximal shape, eye tilt affects proximal orientation, gaze direction affects proximal location, and illumination affects luminance. Illusions also involve the presence of an additional, secondary variable, but with the essential difference that this type of secondary variable does not affect the proximal variable, although it does affect the phenomenal variable. In the Müller–Lyer illusion, that secondary variable is the presence of differently oriented fins at line ends, which does not change the projected lengths of the lines but does make them appear differently long. In the Hering–Wundt illusion, the secondary variable also involves the presence of additional lines, which do not change the shapes of the projections of the main lines but change their perceived shapes. In the rod-and-frame effect the secondary variable is the orientation of the tilted frame which does not affect the projected orientation of the rod, but affects its perceived orientation. In the Roelofs effect the secondary variable is the position of the eccentric frame which does not affect the projected location of the object but affects its perceived direction. In simultaneous contrast, surrounding a colored surface with other surfaces does not change its luminance but affects its perceived color. In sum, in constancies there is a discrepancy between distal and proximal attributes but an agreement between distal and phenomenal attributes, whereas in illusions there is an agreement between distal and proximal attributes but a discrepancy between distal and phenomenal attributes.

The difference in the structure of constancies and illusions has consequences for the status of the distinction between distal and proximal variables and their phenomenal counterparts in studies of illusions. The illustrations for this distinction in the case of constancies, as described here for each of the six attributes, were based on examples of situations in which two objects have distally equal but proximally different attributes, or vice versa. However, due to the distal-proximal agreement in illusions, if two objects have distally equal (or unequal) attributes, then they will necessarily also have proximally equal (or unequal) attributes. Note that conceptually the distinction between two types of phenomenal attributes is as valid for illusions as it is for constancies. However, in matching studies of illusions it is of less importance than in matching studies of constancies. For example, in studies of the Müller–Lyer illusion one could ask subjects to match the *distal* sizes of the two lines with differently oriented fins, or one could ask them to match their *proximal* sizes, but the type of the task is not likely to make much of a difference with respect to the structure of results. Because both lines are at the same distance, distally equal (different) lines will also be proximally equal (different). Therefore the distinction between two types of phenomenal size is not very relevant for this type of studies, and the more natural sense, involving distal size, can be assumed as default. Similarly, the distinction of "lightness" and "brightness" for flat, homogeneously illuminated displays, which are also perceived as such, although valid, is not of much consequence, and matches with distal and proximal instructions yield very similar results (Arend & Špehar, 1993b). In such situations a simple, undifferentiated notion of "perceived achromatic color" may suffice.

Note that the loss of the distinction between perceived distal and proximal attributes in illusions has a quite different source than in studies of constancies under reduced-cue conditions. In the former case the distinction is valid, but not very relevant. In contrast, in the latter case, with increasingly reduced cues, the distinction decreases in phenomenal salience.

THEORIES

Discussions of various attempts to *explain* the experimental results briefly summarized in appropriate sections were deliberately left out of scope in this paper. It must be stressed that the common structure of different phenomena, as presented here, does not at all logically implicate a common, single type of explanation for them. Phenomena which are similar according to some criteria might, and sometimes do, have different types explanations, and vice versa. On the other hand, the existence of common structure of a set of phenomena does tend to suggest similarly structured explanations. For example, in one approach, all perceptual constancies are explained by a *taking-into-account mechanism*, in which the perception of the distal variable is based upon the corresponding proximal variable, with the secondary variable being *taken into account* (Epstein, 1973). In contrast, in other approaches constancies are based on relative values of proximal variables of two or more stimuli (Rock, 1975), or on higher-order optical variables (Gibson, 1979). In still another framework perception is heavily based on accumulated experiences of individuals as well as species, in the form of internalizations of external regularities (Shepard, 1984). To what extent these general approaches are successful in the explanations of the phenomena reviewed here can only be decided on the basis of a case by case confrontation of theories with concrete data on concrete phenomena. Out of such confrontations, one or more dependable unifying perceptual explanatory principles might emerge in the end.

ACKNOWLEDGMENTS

I would like to thank Bob Schwartz, Rainer Mausfeld, and Tatjana Seizova-Cajic for useful comments.

REFERENCES

Arend, L.E. (1993). How much does illuminant color affect unattributed colors? *Journal of the Optical Society of America A*, **10**, 2134–2147.

Arend, L.E. (1994). Surface colors, illumination, and surface geometry: intrinsic-image models of human color perception. In A. Gilchrist (Ed.) *Lightness, brightness, and transparency*. Hillsdale: LEA.

Arend, L. & Goldstein, R. (1987). Simultaneous constancy, lightness, and brightness. *Journal of the Optical Society of America A*, **7**, 1929–1936.

Arend, L.E. & Reeves, A. (1986). Simultaneous color constancy. *Journal of the Optical Society of America A*, **3**, 1743–1751.

Arend, L.E., Reeves, A., Schirillo, J. & Goldstein, R. (1991). Simultaneous color constancy: papers with diverse Munsell values. *Journal of the Optical Society of America A*, **8**, 661–672.

Arend, L.E. & Špehar, B. (1993a). Lightness, brightness, and brightness contrast: 1. Illuminance variation. *Perception & Psychophysics*, **54**, 446–456.

Arend, L.E. & Špehar, B. (1993b). Lightness, brightness, and brightness contrast: 1. Reflectance variation. *Perception & Psychophysics*, **54**, 457–468.

Baird, J.C. (1970). *Psychophysical analysis of visual space*. Oxford: Pergamon Press.

Baird, J.C. & Biersdorf, W.R. (1967). Quantitative functions for size and distance judgements. *Perception & Psychophysics*, **2**, 161–166.

Baird, J.C. & Wagner, M. (1991). Transformation theory of size judgement. *Journal of experimental psychology: Human perception and performance*, **17**, 852–864.

Bäuml, K-H. (1999). Simultaneous color constancy: how surface color perception varies with the illuminant. *Vision Research*, **39**, 1531–1550.

Beck, J. & Gibson, J.J. (1955). The relation of apparent shape to apparent slant in the perception of objects. *Journal of Experimental Psychology*, **50**, 125–133.

Blackwell, K.T. & Buchsbaum, G. (1988). Quantitative studies of color constancy. *Journal of the Optical Society of America A*, **5**, 1772–1780.

Boff, K.R., Kaufman, L. & Thomas, J.P. (1986). *Handbook of perception and human performance*, vols. I and II. New York: Wiley.

Borresen, C.R. & Lichte, W.H. (1967). Influence of instructions on degree of shape constancy. *Journal of Experimental Psychology*, **74**, 538–542.

Brainard, D.H. (1998). Color constancy in the nearly natural image. 2. Achromatic loci. *Journal of the Optical Society of America A*, **15**, 307–325.

Brainard, D.H. & Wandell, B. (1992). Asymmetric color matching: how color appearance depends on the illuminant. *Journal of the Optical Society of America A*, **9**, 1433–1448.

Brainard, D.H., Brunt, W.B. & Speigle, J.M. (1997). Color constancy in the nearly natural image. 1. Asymmetric matches. *Journal of the Optical Society of America A*, **14**, 2091–2110.

Burzlaff, W. (1930). Methodologische Beiträge zum Problem der Farbenkonstanz. *Zeitschrift für Psychologie*, **119**, 177–235.

Campione, F. (1977). Shape constancy: a systematic approach. *Perception*, **6**, 97–105.

Carlson, V.R. (1960). Overestimation in size constancy judgments. *American Journal of Psychology*, **73**, 199–213.

Carlson, V.R. (1977). Instructions and perceptual constancy judgements. In W. Epstein (Ed.) *Stability and constancy in visual perception: Mechanisms and processes*. New York: Wiley.

Carlson, V.R. & Tassone, E.P. (1967). Independent size-judgements at different distances. *Journal of Experimental Psychology*, **73**, 491–497.

Coren, S. & Girgus, J.S. (1978). *Seeing is deceiving: The psychology of visual illusions*. Hillsdale, NJ: Erlbaum.

Cornelissen, F.W. & Brenner, E. (1995). Simultaneous colour constancy revisited: an analysis of viewing strategies. *Vision Research*, **35**, 2431–2448.

Ebenholtz, S.M. (1977b). The constancies in object orientation: An algorithmic approach. In W. Epstein (Ed.) *Stability and constancy in visual perception: Mechanisms and processes*. New York: Wiley.

Epstein, W. (1963). Attitude of judgment and the size-distance invariance hypothesis. *Journal of Experimental Psychology*, **66**, 78–83.

Epstein, W. (1973). The process of "taking into account" in visual perception. *Perception*, **2**, 267–285.

Epstein, W. (1977). *Stability and constancy in visual perception: Mechanisms and processes*. New York: Wiley.

Epstein, W., Bontrager, H. & Park, J. (1962). The induction of nonveridical slant and the perception of shape. *Journal of Experimental Psychology*, **63**, 472–479.

Epstein, W. & Landauer, A. (1969). Size and distance judgments under reduced conditions of viewing. *Perception & Psychophysics*, **6**, 269–272.

Epstein, W. & Park, J.K. (1963). Shape constancy: Functional relationships and theoretical formulations. *Psychological Bulletin*, **60**, 265–288.

Evans, R.M. (1964). Variables of perceived color. *Journal of the Optical Society of America*, **54**, 1467–1474.

Gelb, A. (1929). Die "Farbenkonstanz" der Sehdinge. In A. Bethe, G. v. Bergmann, G. Embden & A. Ellinger (Eds.) *Handbuch der normalen und pathologischen Physiologie*, vol. 12/I. Berlin: Springer.

Gibson, J.J. (1950). *The perception of the visual world*. Boston: Houghton Mifflin.
Gibson, J.J. (1979). *The ecological approach to visual perception*. Boston: Houghton Mifflin.
Gilchrist, A. (1994). *Lightness, brightness, and transparency*. Hillsdale, NI: LEA.
Gillam, B. (1995). The perception of spatial layout from static optical information. In W. Epstein & S. Rogers, (Eds.) *Perception of space and motion*. New York: Academic Press.
Gilinsky, A. (1955). The effect of attitude on the perception of size. *American Journal of Psychology*, **68**, 173–192.
Hastorf, A.R. & Way, K.S. (1952). Apparent size with and without distance cues. *Journal of General Psychology*, **47**, 181–188.
Heggelund, P. (1974). Achromatic color vision I: perceptive variables of achromatic colors. *Vision Research*, **14**, 1071–1079.
Heggelund, P. (1992). A bidimensional theory of achromatic color vision. *Vision Research*, **32**, 2107–2119.
Henneman, R.H. (1935). A photometric study of the perception of object color. *Archives of Psychology*, **179**, 5–89.
Hering, E. (1920/1964). *Grundzüge der Lehre vom Lichtsinn*. Translated as *Outlines of a theory of the light sense* (L.M. Hurvich & D. Jameson, Trans.). Cambridge, MA: Harvard University Press.
Helson, H. (1943). Some factors and implications of color constancy. *Journal of the Optical Society of America*, **33**, 555–567.
Helson, H., Judd, D.B., & Warren, M.H. (1952). Object color changes from daylight to incandescent filament illumination. *Illumination Engineering*, **47**, 221–233.
Hill, A.L. (1972). Direction constancy. *Perception & Psychophysics*, **11**, 175–178.
Hochberg, J. (1971a). Perception. I. Color and shape. In J.W. Kling & L.A. Riggs (Eds.), *Woodworth & Schlosberg's Experimental Psychology* (3rd edition). New York: Holt, Rinehart & Winston.
Hochberg, J. (1971b). Perception. II. Space and motion. In J.W. Kling & L.A. Riggs (Eds.) *Woodworth & Schlosberg's Experimental Psychology* (3rd edition). New York: Holt, Rinehart & Winston.
Hochberg, J. (1979). Sensation and perception. In E. Hearst (Ed.) *The first century of experimental psychology*. Hillsdale, NJ: LEA.
Holway, A.H. & Boring, E.G. (1941). Determinants of apparent visual size with distance variant. *American Journal of Psychology*, **54**, 21–37.
Howard, I. (1982). *Human visual orientation*. Chichester: Wiley.
Howard, I. (1986). The perception of posture, self motion, and the visual vertical. In K.R. Boff, L. Kaufman & J.P. Thomas (Eds.) *Handbook of perception and human performance*, vol. I. New York: Wiley.
Howard, I. (1993). Spatial vision within egocentric and exocentric frames of reference. In S.R. Ellis & M.K. Kaiser (Eds.) *Pictorial communication in virtual and real environments* (2nd edition). London: Taylor & Francis.
Jacobsen, A. & Gilchrist, A. (1988). The ratio principle holds over a million-to-one range of illumination. *Perception & Psychophysics*, **43**, 7–14.
Jaensch, E.R. & Müller, E.A. (1920). Über die Wahrnehmumngen farbloser Helligkeiten und den Helligkeitskontrast. *Zeitschrift für Psychologie*, **83**, 266–341.
Joynson, R.B. (1949). The problem of size and distance. *Quarterly Journal of Experimental Psychology*, **1**, 119–135.
Joynson, R.B. (1958a). An experimental synthesis of the Associationist and Gestalt accounts of perception of size. Part I. *Quarterly Journal of Experimental Psychology*, **10**, 65–76.
Joynson, R.B. (1958b). An experimental synthesis of the Associationist and Gestalt accounts of perception of size. Part II. *Quarterly Journal of Experimental Psychology*, **10**, 142–154.

Joynson, R.B. & Kirk, N.S. (1960). An experimental synthesis of the Associationist and Gestalt accounts of perception of size. Part III. *Quarterly Journal of Experimental Psychology*, **12**, 221–230.

Joynson, R.B. & Newson, L.J. (1962). The perception of shape as a function of inclination. *British Journal of Psychology*, **53**, 1–15.

Kardos, L. (1934). Ding und Schatten. *Zeitschrift für Psychologie, Ergänzungsband* **23**.

Katz, D. (1911/1935). Die Erscheinungsweisen der Farben und ihre Beeinflussung durch die individuelle Erfahrung. *Zeitschrift für Psychologie, Ergänzungsband 7*. Second edition translated as *The world of colour* (R.B. MacLeod & C.W. Fox, Trans.). London: Kegan Paul, Trench, Trubner & Co.

Koffka, K. (1935). *Principles of gestalt psychology*. New York: Harcourt Brace.

Kuriki, I. & Uchikawa, K. (1996). Limitations of surface-color and apparent-color constancy. *Journal of the Optical Society of America A*, **13**, 1622–1636.

Landauer, A.A. (1969). Influence of instructions on judgements of unfamiliar shape. *Journal of Experimental Psychology*, **79**, 129–132.

Landauer, A.A. & Rodger, R.S. (1964). Effect of "apparent" instructions on brightness judgements. *Journal of Experimental Psychology*, **68**, 80–84.

Leibowitz, H. & Harvey, L.O. (1967). Size matching as a function of instructions in a naturalistic environment. *Journal of Experimental Psychology*, **74**, 378–382.

Lie, I. (1969a). Psychophysical invariants of achromatic colour vision. I. The multidimensionality of achromatic colour experience. *Scandinavian Journal of Psychology*, **10**, 167–175.

Lie, I. (1969b). Psychophysical invariants of achromatic colour vision. II. Albedo / illumination substitution. *Scandinavian Journal of Psychology*, **10**, 176–184.

Lichte, W.H. & Borresen, C.R. (1967). Influence of instructions on degree of shape constancy. *Journal of Experimental Psychology*, **74**, 538–542.

Lichten, W. & Lurie, S. (1950). A new technique for the study of perceived size. *American Journal of Psychology*, **63**, 281–282.

Lucassen, M. & Walraven, J. (1993). Quantifying color constancy: evidence for nonlinear processing of cone-specific contrast. *Vision Research*, **33**, 739–758.

Mann, C.W., Berthelot-Berry, N.H., & Dauterive, H.J. (1949). The perception of the vertical: I. Visual and non-labyrinthine cues. *Journal of Experimental Psychology*, **39**, 538–547.

Martius, G. (1889). Über die scheinbare Grösse der Gegenstände und ihre Beziehung zur Grösse der Netzhautbilder. *Philosophische Studien*, **5**, 601–617.

Matin, L. (1986). Visual localizations and eye movements. In K.R. Boff, L. Kaufman & J.P. Thomas (Eds.) *Handbook of perception and human performance*, vol. I. New York: Wiley.

Mausfeld, R. (1996). Empfindung vs Wahrnehmung, unbewusste Schlüsse und die Messinstrumentkonzeption der Wahrnehmung: Anmerkungen zur Ideengeschichte der Psychophysik. *Report 35/98*. Bielefeld: ZIF.

McCann, J., McKee, S. & Taylor, T. (1976). Quantitative studies in retinex theory. *Vision Research*, **16**, 445–458.

McKee, S. & Smallman, H.S. (1998). Size and speed constancy. In V. Walsh & J. Kulikowski (Eds.) *Perceptual constancy: Why things look as they do*. Cambridge, UK: Cambridge University Press.

Miller, E.F., Fregly, A.R., van den Brink, G. & Graybiel, A. (1965).*Visual localization of the horizontal as a function of body tilt up to ±90° from gravitational vertical*. (NSAM-942). Pensacola: Naval School of Aviation Medicine.

Morgan, C.T. (1978). Constancy of egocentric visual direction. *Perception & Psychophysics*, **23**, 61–68.

Nelson, T.M. & Bartley, S.H. (1956). The perception of form in an unstructured field. *Journal of General Psychology*, **54**, 57–63.

Over, R. (1960). The effect of instructions on size-judgements under reduction conditions. *American Journal of Psychology*, **73**, 599–602.

Pokorny, J. & Smith, V.C. (1986). Colorimetry and color discrimination. In K.R. Boff, L. Kaufman & J.P. Thomas (Eds.) *Handbook of perception and human performance*, vol. I. New York: Wiley.

Robinson, J.O. (1972). *The psychology of visual illusions*. London: Hutchinson University Library.

Rock, I. & McDermott, W. (1964). The perception of visual angle. *Acta Psychologica*, **22**, 119–134.

Rock, I. (1975). *Introduction to visual perception*. New York: Macmillan.

Sedgwick, H.A. (1986). Space perception. In K.R. Boff, L. Kaufman & J.P. Thomas (Eds.) *Handbook of perception and human performance*, vol. I. New York: Wiley.

Shebilske, W. (1977). Vasomotor coordination in visual direction and position constancies. In W. Epstein (Ed.) *Stability and constancy in visual perception: Mechanisms and processes*. New York: Wiley.

Shepard, R.N. (1984). Ecological constraints in internal representations: Resonant kinematics of perceiving, imagining, thinking, and dreaming. *Psychological Review*, **91**, 417–447.

Smith, W.H. (1953). A methodological study of size distance perception. *Journal of Psychology*, **35**, 143–153.

Stoper, A.L. & Cohen, M.M. (1986). Judgements of eye level in light and darkness. *Perception & Psychophysics*, **40**, 311–316.

Thouless, R.H. (1931a). Phenomenal regression to the real object. Part I. *British Journal of Psychology*, **21**, 339–359.

Thouless, R.H. (1931b). Phenomenal regression to the real object. Part II. *British Journal of Psychology*, **22**, 1–30.

Valberg, A. & Lange-Malecki, B. (1990). "Color constancy" in mondrians patterns: A partial cancellation of physical chromaticity shifts by simultaneous contrast. *Vision Research*, **30**, 371–380.

Walsh, V. & Kulikowski, J. (1998). *Perceptual constancy: Why things look as they do.* Cambridge, UK: Cambridge University Press.

Whittle, P. (1991). Sensory and perceptual processes in seeing brightness and lightness. In A. Valberg & B.B. Lee (Eds.) *From pigments to perception*. New York: Plenum Press.

Witkin, H.A. & Asch, S.E. (1948). Studies in space orientation IV. Further experiments on perception of the upright with displaced visual fields. *Journal of Experimental Psychology*, **38**, 762–782.

Wyszecki, G. (1986). Color appearance. In K.R. Boff, L. Kaufman & J.P. Thomas (Eds.) *Handbook of perception and human performance*, vol. I. New York: Wiley.

Wyszecki, G. & Stiles, W.S. (1982). *Color science. Concepts and methods, quantitative data and formulae.* New York: Wiley.

4

The Physicalistic Trap in Perception Theory

RAINER MAUSFELD

Institut für Psychologie, Christian-Albrechts Universitat, Kiel, Germany

INTRODUCTION

It is a well-known observation from the history of the natural sciences that any field that is not yet mature enough to have a proprietary and sufficiently rich theoretical core of its own has to face the problem of which concepts and notions, and thus which theoretical language, to chose for the segmentation and theoretical organization of relevant phenomena. Perceptual psychology is no exception in this regard. The lack of an appropriate theoretical language of its own results in the temptation to borrow theoretical structure from neighbouring disciplines and to use as a surrogate a theoretical structure that has been developed for different explanatory purposes (and thus is alien to the intrinsic structure of the field in question). In perception theory the fields from which these surrogate structures have been borrowed are sensory physiology and physics. In this essay I will be concerned with what may be called the *physicalistic trap*, namely misconceptions in perception theory that are based on the idea of slicing the nature of perception along the joints of physics and on corresponding ill-conceived "purposes" and "goals" of the perceptual system. Corresponding misconceptions have been disclosed ever since the beginnings of perception theory, in particular by the Gestaltists. Current developments, however, have largely fallen back upon these misconceptions, albeit on levels of considerable technical sophistication. Nevertheless, there is, with respect to the principal points of concern, hardly anything new to say and so I resign myself to assembling a few reminders. My primary concern, however, is not a critique of these misconceptions; rather I intend to delineate, using the physicalistic trap as a background for confrontation, a line of inquiry, inspired by ethology, that helps to focus attention on problems that a genuine theory of perception has to deal with and that seem to me to be largely ignored in current approaches.

Perception and the Physical World: Psychological and Philosophical Issues in Perception.
Edited by Dieter Heyer and Rainer Mausfeld. © 2002 John Wiley & Sons, Ltd.

Perceptual psychology, understood as the endeavour to theoretically understand, within the conceptual framework of the natural sciences, certain aspects of mental activity, has to develop, just as other domains of the natural sciences did, an autonomous theoretical language that appropriately reflects the internal structure of perception and is sufficiently rich to account in an explanatorily satisfactory way for what are considered to be basic principles and phenomena of perception. Perceptual psychology aims at a proper theoretical understanding of the structure of those mental representations that refer to our interacting with the environment. Its theoretical language, therefore, hinges upon how we describe biologically relevant aspects of the environment of the organism—which I will briefly refer to as a description of the "external world"—and how we relate such a description to a theoretical description of the internal structure of perception. That such a description depends on the structure of the sensory system under scrutiny is obvious and almost trivial in cases where we are dealing with sensory receptors and their transduction properties. Different biological species exhibit quite different ways of parsing the physical energy that hits upon the organism into sense modalities and perceptual qualities. Most of the spatio-temporal pattern of this energy is not used for biological purposes (we cannot sense e.g. the direction of magnetic fields). Only some aspects are filtered out for the specific purposes of a perceptual system and transduced into a neural code, whose properties no longer allow the specific physical properties it was caused by to be identified. With respect to transduction properties it is obvious that the choice of concepts that are considered appropriate for a description of properties of the external world (e.g. photons in the case of photo-receptors) is determined by structural properties of the perceptual system. It is less obvious, though indisputable, that an appropriate, i.e. theoretically fruitful, description of the "external world" crucially depends also on more abstract representational properties of the perceptual system. Because we are still far from having a satisfactory theoretical understanding of those abstract properties we can rely only on our best current understanding in choosing appropriate concepts for describing relevant properties of the external world and of the sensory input—a problem of great concern for, e.g., the Gestaltists, Gibson, Marr and Shepard. The development of a conceptual vocabulary for describing, in a theoretically fruitful way, perceptually relevant aspects of the *external* world is a prerequisite of perception theory. However, the structure of perceptual representations does not simply mirror and is not solely moulded by properties of the external world but rather co-determined by internal aspects, such as internal functional constraints or internal architectural constraints. Perceptual representations must not only be adequate with respect to the external world; they must also be functionally adequate, i.e. they have to fit into the entire perceptual architecture including its two fundamental interfaces, viz. the interface with the motor system and that with the cognitive system. These internal aspects have been largely disregarded in current perception theory. Fundamental concepts of perception theory and ideas about internal representations have instead been derived from considerations that are alien to the intrinsic structure of perception. Physics and sensory physiology have served as sources from which core theoretical notions of perception theory have been surreptitiously borrowed. In describing certain lines of thinking as a physicalistic trap, it is not my intention to denigrate their role in perceptual research. It is indisputable that ideas associated with the physicalistic trap are an indispensable part of our ordinary and metatheoretical talk about perception and can, in principle, serve as heuristics in perceptual research. They become a trap, however, when they result in a tendency to dodge an essential task of perceptual research, viz. the identification of the internal conceptual structure of perception. Characteristic theoretical distortions result from using structural elements that serve the explanatory needs of other domains of inquiry as inappropriate surrogates for the yet-to-be discovered structural elements on which explanatory accounts of perceptual representations have to be based. I will illustrate these distortions by discussing six examples in some detail. However, pointing out these distortions is not meant as an end in itself. Rather I intend to use them as whetstones, as it were, to bring out questions and problems that are largely disregarded in current research but that seem to me to be at the core of any genuine theory of perception.

I will only mention in passing, in this introduction, misconceptions based on deriving basic elements of the theoretical structure of perception theory from sensory physiology. Due to the pre-theoretical attribution of certain classes of sensations to sensory organs, it is quite natural from a heuristic point of view that the sense modalities have been considered both as the natural starting point and as the natural units of analyses for perceptual psychology. Thus it was held that they could to a large extent be treated in isolation. However, such a theoretical segmentation according to the classification of sensory input channels almost certainly impedes a deeper theoretical understanding of the intrinsic structure of perception because it distracts the theoretical focus from what can be considered one of the core characteristics of perceptual representations: The internal structure of perception is determined in an essential manner by *transmodal* or amodal representations of the physico-biological environment, and is thus not reducible to the structure of isolated input channels.[1] The ability to free itself from the properties of specific sensory input channels, i.e. from the properties of sensory organs and the neural processes that mediate between the sensory organs and the perceptual representations, is a remarkable achievement of the perceptual system. The sensory input channels only serve as a perceptual medium whose idiosyncratic coding properties have to be discounted by the perceptual system in transmodal representations (in terms of its representational primitives) of the physico-biological environment.

In confusing properties of the transmission medium with internal properties of the perceptual system, variants of the physiologistic trap in perception theory derive alleged "stages of perception" from stages of neurophysiological processing. In this regard the distinction between "high level" vs. "low level" processes has been particularly influential in recent years. This distinction is usually assumed to refer to some kinds of *fixed* and empirically given states of the system under scrutiny. However, without a specific theory about perceptual processes no criteria for such a distinction exist.[2] Even in neurophysiology the high amount of vertical interconnectivity deprives this distinction of any precise meaning (unless we derive its meaning from and relative to a specific model). In perception theory such distinctions, if they can be specified at all, become entirely theory-dependent. Here, absolute high-low level distinctions based on neurophysiological investigations of neural structure erroneously take properties of the medium as theoretical building blocks for explaining perceptual representations. The physiologistic trap thus slices the nature of perception according to the physiological nature of the sense modalities and essentially conceives of perception as consecutive transformations of the sensory input.

The physicalistic trap comes in various guises and is sometimes difficult to disclose. Variants of it have pervaded theoretical attempts to understand the nature of perception ever since the beginnings of systematic inquiries into the nature of perception. Examples can be found under headings as diverse as

- the concept of perceptual illusion
- the idea of a pre-theoretical segregation of phenomena into primary and contextual ones
- the idea that the structure of perception is based on internal correlates of physical scales
- the inverse optics approach of *recovering* properties of the world from image structure
- Bayesian approaches to perception that base their physical description of the sensory *input* on categories of the yet-to-be identified and explained perceptual *output*.

We can distinguish two different varieties of the physicalistic trap: one that derives theoretical descriptions of the structure of perception from descriptions of the sensory input in terms of elementary physical variables,[3] and one that derives them from descriptions of the distal stimulus in terms of concepts from folk physics and physical common sense taxonomies, such as surface, object, illumination, shadow, etc. I will address both in turn and illustrate them by way of examples that seem to me particularly instructive in this respect.

THE PHYSICALISTIC TRAP IN ELEMENTARISTIC APPROACHES TO PERCEPTION

The physicalistic trap in elementaristic approaches to perception looms up most clearly in what may be called the *measurement device conception of perception*. This is an influential though highly misleading heuristics that comes in many guises and is rarely spelled out explicitly. It is based on the metaphor of conceiving the perceptual system as some kind of measurement device that has to inform us about elementary physical quantities. Being a legacy of the way we have separated physical and psychological aspects in the philosophical history of the field since the time of the pre-Socratics this metaphor has governed our thinking in the study of perception ever since. Along with this conception comes the idea that there are atoms of perception, as it were, that are strongly tied to these elementary physical variables: namely the sensations from which perceptions—as something referring to the distal external world—are constructed. According to this view the energy pattern from the external world that affects the senses is evaluated by the perceptual system locally, as it were, and leads to "sensations" out of which "higher level perceptions" are constructed. Elementary physical variables, like energy of sound, intensity and wavelength of light, are regarded as the basis for fundamental perceptual variables, like loudness, brightness and colour.[4]

The measurement device conception considers those perceptual phenomena for which a stable correspondence between local properties of the physical stimulus and the perceptual appearance or neural reaction can be observed to be the basic and fundamental ones. "Normal perception", then, can be disturbed or biased, by so-called "context effects". The price that had to be paid for this way of slicing up the space of phenomena into "basic" and "secondary" ones was that one had to classify phenomena that are fundamental with respect to the representational primitives of the system inappropriately as "context effects", "perceptual illusions", "constancy phenomena", or "higher order phenomena". The problem of colour constancy may serve to illustrate the ensuing theoretical distortions.

EXAMPLE I: THE PROBLEM OF COLOUR CONSTANCY

The measurement device misconception has a long tradition in the field of colour perception.[5] It is disguised here in the idea that there are some kinds of "raw colours" or "primordinal colours" that are given by the receptor excitations elicited by the local incoming light stimulus and that are transformed and modified in subsequent stages of processing in order to fulfil certain requirements, such as sensitivity regulations, optimal and efficient coding or invariance requirements. In the wake of these approaches it became a matter of course to conceive decontextualized small colour patches (that virtually have no localization or orientation)—such as the ones underlying CIE colour space—as the building blocks of colour perceptions, as raw and pure colour sensations or unanalysable instantiations of colour qualia. The local connection between these "primordinal colours" and colour appearances, as expressed for example in CIE space, is considered as the "normal case" and thus the so-called constancy phenomena are regarded as more surprising and in greater need of explanation than the "normal case". Perceptual representations of, say surface colours, are, on this view, built up in a locally-atomistic way from these raw colours, i.e. the perceptual bases of colour perception are the primary colour codes that arise from the transduction of physical energy into neural codes and that are transformed by "secondary" and "higher" processes into representations of, say, surface colours. In other words, the "primary elements" of colour perception are constituted on the level on which a stable correspondence between local properties of the sensory input and the neural reaction can be observed, and are then further processed and transformed, modified, or supplemented by "secondary", "higher order" processes to yield perceptual achievements or appearances. By focusing on transformations and "secondary" operations of primary colour codes the elementaristic perspectives in colour research divorced colour from its intrinsic anchorage within the perceptual architecture. The theoretical treatment of simultaneous contrast phenomena in centre-surround situation provides an interesting case in point of how classifications based on a distinction between elementaristic primary colour codes and "context effects" can produce taxonomic artefacts that veil core structural principles underlying colour perception. Many classic writers realized that phenomena associated with geometrical configuration of small and sharply demarcated infields in large surrounds cannot appropriately be accounted for by simple transformations of elementary colour codes but require explanations based on the internal concepts of "surface colour" and "illumination colour". For instance, Bühler (1922, p. 131) interpreted the phenomenon of simultaneous contrast in such situations as a degenerate marginal phenomenon attesting to the visual system's capability of preserving colours under changes of illumination. The perceptually relevant aspect of such situations is the figure-ground segmentation that they give rise to. Rubin (1921, p. 56), for instance, observed that transformations in the direction of colour constancy are stronger when a certain area is perceived as figure rather than as ground. Empirical and theoretical evidence (cf. Mausfeld, & Niederée, 1993; Mausfeld, 1998) suggests regarding centre-surround type configurations as "minimal" stimuli, as it were, for triggering, albeit in rudimentary form, representations that are based on the representational primitives "object colour" and "illumination colour".

Though the elementaristic perspective has proved to be fruitful for the neurophysiological purposes of understanding the nature of transduction and peripheral coding, it is at a cost for perceptual psychology, of which both Helmholtz and Hering were well aware. They realized that concepts from sensory physiology alone do not constitute an appropriately rich theoretical language for dealing with perception but that a richer set of concepts, including "unconscious inferences" in the case of Helmholtz, and "memory colours" in the case of Hering, is required for appropriate explanatory frameworks. It is not the specific nature of such concepts themselves that is of interest here, but rather the unequivocal elucidation that an additional level of analysis beyond the neurophysiological one—and correspondingly a different theoretical language— is needed for a successful theoretical account of perception.[6] Though introducing "psychological" concepts as an additional level of analysis increased the explanatory power of the theoretical language it accentuated and deepened inappropriate classifications of perceptual phenomena into "basic" and "secondary" ones.

The problem of colour constancy is the legacy of the way the structure of perception has been divided into foundational building blocks of "raw sensations" that exhibit a stable correspondence to their local physical causes, on the one hand, and "higher order", "psychological" effects that connect these "raw sensations" with biologically meaningful distal objects, on the other hand. The field of colour perception, more than other fields of perception, is dominated by variants of the measurement device misconception.[7] The problem of colour constancy came to be regarded as a problem confined to "pure" colour perception, where transformations of some "raw colours" result in a discounting of the illuminant. As a result of this way of trivializing the problem of the internal representational structure of colour perception and of idealizing away the perception of the illumination the problem of colour constancy became misidealized and misrepresented.[8] Gelb (1929) was the first to arrive at a clear understanding of the structure of the problem of colour constancy. He considered the distinction between "physiological" and "psychological" levels as "wrong" and regarded, in Gelb (1932), any such "dualisms of explanatory principles" as inappropriate and misleading. He convincingly argued "that the problem of colour constancy, rather than being a problem of an alleged discrepancy between 'stimulus' and 'perceived colour', has to do with the general problem of the constitution and structure of our perceptual visual world. The phenomenal segregation into illumination and illuminated object (i.e. the correlate of the percept 'object colour') reveals a propensity of our sensorium and is nothing but the expression of a certain structural form of our perceptual visual world" (Gelb, 1929, p. 672). In the same vein, Cassirer (1929, p. 155) considers the phenomena relating to a dual account of an "object colour" and an "illumination colour" attached to it not to be a result of some additional processing, but rather as an expression of the *"very primordial format of organization"*. Such insights into the structural role of colour within perceptual representations were far from being mere speculations, but rather were, even at that time, strongly suggested by the theoretical and empirical evidence available. Yet they have been almost completely ignored in subsequent approaches. I will return to these issues below in the discussion of computational treatments of colour constancy.

EXAMPLE II: ARE THERE PERCEPTUAL ERRORS AND ILLUSIONS?

Since the time of the pre-Socratics, who were the first to deal with the "fallibility" of the senses, there has been a long history of wrestling with the concept of perceptual errors, both in epistemology and in perceptual psychology. Historically, the enterprise of physics began when in pre-Socratic times a distrust in the senses showed up, which basically stemmed from the observation that different senses can lead us to different beliefs about the world (think of a rod half dipped in water). The attempt to accomplish a picture of the "real world" behind the "unreliable picture" that our senses convey to us is the starting point of physics. Since then we have a split between the world as experienced and the world as pictured by physics. We began to take physics as a reference system for the veridicality of our perceptions and to speak of perceptual illusions when we became aware of a discrepancy between the physical description and our perception.

There are many intricate philosophical issues connected with this issue. Fortunately, however, most of these have no bearing on the usage of the concept of "error" in visual psychophysics, which I will address here. Particularly, I can leave aside all issues centring around the (legitimate) concept of "error of perceptual judgement" (which every-day usages refer to).

At the root of the idea of perceptual errors—again: in the sense of "errors of perceptual mechanisms", not as errors of perceptual judgement—is the conviction that the goal of the visual apparatus is something like a veridical seeing of the true physical situation. But what is the "true physical situation"? What is the reference frame for the beliefs and expectations that give rise to a distinction between "normal" and "illusionary" perception?

Most often, our expectations derive from folk physics: perception is called veridical if it conforms to a folk-physics description of what is out there. There is, of course, no good reason why such expectations should be relevant for guiding perceptual research (though, they served historically as heuristic starting-points that brought basic problems of perceptual research to our attention). A perceptual phenomenon is not just therefore in need of explanation because it does not conform to some pre-theoretical expectations. Folk-physical descriptions, however, often receive a higher epistemological dignity, as it were, and when there is a conflict between two levels of description of what is out there—including conflicts between descriptions provided by different sense modalities like touch and sight, or vision and static sense—perception is considered as illusionary. Often such expectations about the alleged correct output of visual mechanisms go hand in hand with the idea that the goal of the perceptual system is to "inform" us about the true physical situation as measured by elementary physical devices, i.e. with the *measurement device conception* of perception.[9]

Once we retreat from folk physics as a reference frame guiding our expectations about perception, our expectations about what has to be considered as accidental or essential, as proper or improper, as normal or deviant can only be derived from specific theoretical ideas about the perceptual system. If we had a complete understanding of the visual system, we would certainly cease to call certain responses "errors". Of course, we can speak of non-optimality of design in terms of an adaptational coupling, or malfunctioning in the clinical sense, but these are different concepts.

The locution, however, that the perceptual system is susceptible to illusions under ecologically atypical conditions requires us to go beyond perception theory proper and to state what function the system is serving and what the proper function of the system is. Take the example of the frog's "fly detector", i.e. that part of the frog's visual system whose proper function, according to the frog's specific evolutionary history, is the detection of flies. This mechanism will still perform its adaptive function in an environment in which no flies exist but instead a species "pellies", which are nutritious small dark moving pellets. In that case the frog's visual system does not refer to flies any longer and thus fails to perform its proper function. A generation of scientists unaware of this change of environment would characterize this visual submechanism as a pellies-detector.[10] This may illustrate why, among other reasons, I prefer to restrict the domain of a formal theory of perception to an explanatory account of the perceptual system of a given organism in terms of its internal functioning, and to shift talk about evolutionary history and proper function to a metatheoretical level. Notions like "perceptual error", "veridicality", "reference" or "proper function" do not figure in a formal theory of perception. They only come into play if we, in ordinary discourse or as scientists from a metatheoretical viewpoint, make a conjecture about the "proper" object of perception and the "true" antecedents of the sensory information, among the infinite set of potential causal antecedents. No such notions can enter our descriptions of the functioning of perceptual subsystems of the mind. The visual system simply does what it does. There are no "errors" with respect to its representational primitives, an idea already lucidly expressed by Helmholtz (1855, p. 100): "The senses cannot deceive us, they work according to their established immutable laws and cannot do otherwise. It is us who are mistaken in our apprehension of the sensory perception."

EXAMPLE III: THE PREOCCUPATION WITH LINEAR PERSPECTIVE IN THEORIES OF PICTURE PERCEPTION

Pictures and pictorial representations can, from a naive point of view, also be regarded as a kind of illusion because they evoke perceptual impressions of objects, spatial relations or events in us that are actually not there. Above all because of this, phenomena that can be encountered in picture perception (cf. Hochberg, 1980; Gombrich, 1982; see also Schwartz, this volume) have often been regarded as particularly challenging for theories of visual perception. This is surprising because picture perception hardly constitutes a natural domain for exploring core structural elements of perception. Like all perceptual tasks that involve human artefacts, it rests on and exploits the complex interactions of given perceptual structures and interpretative faculties, whose properties are presently only poorly understood. Artefacts depend on human intentions and their use therefore is subject to interpretation; this holds for TV screens, microscopes, books or pictures. They exploit given capacities, but one has to understand what they were designed for. From the perspective of the cognitive sciences, picture perception does not constitute a domain of phenomena that is bound together by some specific set of explanatory principles. Nonetheless, picture perception has become a field of inquiry within perceptual psychology that has brought forth its own lines and frameworks of inquiry and its own specific problems. A dominant theme in the field of picture perception have been issues centring around notions of perceptual space and the extent to which corresponding percepts can be evoked by features of pictorial representations, notably by linear perspective (cf. Haber, 1980; Rogers, 1995).

Linear Perspective as an Artist's Means to Achieve "Visual Truth" in Paintings

The interest in techniques of linear perspective arose during the Renaissance and was motivated by the artists' desires to imitate nature and to achieve "visual truth" in their paintings. This gave rise to corresponding inquiries into artistic techniques for the evocation of space and in particular into techniques how to create on a canvas geometrically correct two-dimensional pictorial representations of the three-dimensional layout of the pictured scene. In these investigations, as Kemp (1990, p. 165) has observed, "the eye figures little, the mind features even less". Rather what was to be accomplished was "the demonstration of an internally consistent system of the spatial elements in a picture and, above all, a proof that the system rested upon non-arbitrary foundations" (ibid., p. 11). The canvas was regarded as a window, often referred to today as *Alberti window*, through which the painter views the world and which intersects his visual cone (Lindberg, 1976). This gave rise to the idea that a realistic appearance of depth and space can be achieved in pictures by mimicking the exact geometrical relations in the structure of light that reaches the eye from a three-dimensional scene.

Correspondingly, a system of construction rules gained prominence in Renaissance art as an artistic engineering technique for the purpose of creating on a flat canvas pictorial representations that induce a strong appearance of depth in the observer. Though these artistic techniques later joined with ideas on geometrical processes of image formation in the eye, their use and development were primarily shaped by considerations internal to the complex variety of cultural purposes underlying artistic productions. For the endeavour to imitate nature and to achieve visual truth in two-dimensional representations of the world the importance of rules for linear perspective is, however, on a par with those for simulating the effect of lights and the interaction of light and objects by using spatial pigment patterns on a flat surface (Schöne, 1954). It is a historically contingent development of art history that linear perspective rather than other aspects first gained prominence in this context.

With respect to linear perspective as well as other pictorial concepts like shadows or light, two different kinds of inquiries have to be distinguished. The one inquiry, pertaining to artistic craftsmanship, concerns the physical generation process by which a three-dimensional scene can be mapped in a perceptually adequate and satisfactory way to a two-dimensional representational medium. The other inquiry, pertaining to perceptual psychology, concerns the way the visual system exploits the sensory input in terms of its primitives.

The techniques for generating pictures that imitate nature with respect to its spatial appearance do not touch upon, and actually had at their origin been thought of as independent of how the perceptual process, beyond its geometrical aspects, has to be conceived of. If we are interested in the principles underlying perception rather than in the simulation aspect, i.e. in the second kind of inquiry, we have to ask how the visual system exploits the Alberti window (understood as a physico-geometrical description of the sensory input), independently of how it was physically generated. This may lead to the heuristics to understand certain rules of linear perspective as belonging to the set of rules and principles *internal* to the visual system by which it exploits the sensory input in terms of its primitives. To derive, however, from the geometrical importance that rules of linear perspective have for relating a three-dimensional scene to its two-dimensional representation a distinguished status for these rules within perception theory would amount to succumbing to the physicalistic trap. I will shortly address two ways in which the physicalistic trap may be disguised, one pertaining to the so-called robustness of perspective, and one related to the notion of a perceptual space.

The "Robustness" of Perspective under Changes of Vantage Point

The term "robustness of perspective" refers to the phenomenon that in viewing a picture a displacement of vantage point usually does not result in strong perceptual distortions, such as expansion, compression or shearing, of the "virtual space", as would be expected by geometrical considerations on the bases of the original vantage point from which the picture was geometrically constructed. Like in other cases of so-called constancy phenomena, this way of formulating the problem is based on a pre-theoretical segregation of phenomena into "normal" ones, and ones that are in need of particular explanation. The "normal" case, viz. the perceptual appearance that is evoked by viewing the picture from the "true" vantage point, is considered to be basically explained by referring to linear perspective. It is then noticed that this "explanation" cannot explain what happens when we view the picture from a point that considerably differs from the vantage point underlying its geometrical construction. Therefore the need arises to invoke additional mechanisms subserving robustness of perspective. This pattern of explanation is based on the presumption that the task of the visual system is to invert the geometrical process and to calculate backwards from the image the true three-dimensional layout of objects in a scene. With respect to the "true" vantage point this does not constitute a particular problem and thus corresponding phenomena are considered to be not in need of a particular explanation.[11] This is basically the *inverse optics perspective* (Poggio, 1990) according to which it is the task of the visual system to recover the structure of scene characteristics from characteristics of the sensory image by physico-geometrical computations. Ideas like this can be regarded as a complex variant of the measurement device misconception of perception. Though they can, in specific cases, provide interesting heuristics for the identification of internal rules, there is no evidence supporting the idea that internal spatial representations are based on inverting linear perspective. The "true" vantage point is of no particular relevance for what has to be explained. Rather, what has to be achieved is an explanation that accounts for the structure of the percept elicited by a specific sensory input and its stability over certain variations of the input.

The Notion of Phenomenal Space

The idea that the organism has to recover projective or metric aspects of physical space and derive an internal representation of this space that is adaptively transformed for its biological purposes is strongly rooted in a measurement device misconception of perception. There is a long tradition in the psychology of spatial perception—based on what Koenderink and van Doorn (1998, p. 297) describe as the "weird notion that we don't really see the world but only some deformed copy of it in our head"—to investigate the quantitative and metrical aspects of a presumedly homogeneous and uniform "perceptual space".[12] This notion of a coherent visual space is so seductive that arguments pointing out that it is conceptually misguided and empirically inadequate (MacLeod & Willen, 1995; Koenderink, 1998) have scarcely undermined its impact.

Internal spatial representations have a rich but up to now poorly understood internal structure. They seem to be subserved by a rich structure of subsystems, pertaining to aspects such as occlusion, motion, shading, perspective, texture and stereo disparity. A sketch of a few lines, or patterns that give rise to the impression of one object partly occluding another or of an attached or cast shadow, patterns of texture, etc., they all can elicit forms of internal spatial representations. Such representations seem to be part of the data format of perception, "the innate three-dimensional organization of visual appearances" (von Szily, 1921, p. 971). Though they are barely understood presently, the evidence available suggests that rather than being based on some fixed and homogeneous space in the sense of geometry these representations have a dynamic situation-dependent nature involving topological, projective and metrical aspects with a complex structure of parameters and interactions with other primitives.

The Dual Character of Pictures

Ideas underlying the physicalistic trap in picture perception not only tend to generate pseudo-problems that result in a distorted theoretical picture of the nature of perceptual representations. They also increase the danger of concealing important structural properties of perception. An interesting case in point are phenomena that are discussed under the heading of the *dual character of pictures*. This term refers to the observation that pictures can generate an in-depth spatial representation of the scene depicted while at the same time appearing as flat two-dimensional surfaces hanging on a wall (cf. Michotte, 1948). From a physicalistic perspective they refer to a kind of discrepancy between what is physically there, viz. a flat surface, and the perceptual impression evoked. Postulating such a discrepancy, however, rests on conflating the level of the physical generation process of the sensory input with the level referring to perceptual processes by which this sensory input is exploited.

Rather than being a problem of a discrepancy between what is physically there and the percept, the observation that we can simultaneously handle in perception both the flatness aspect of the canvas and the spatial depth of the depicted scene seems to point to a pervading property of the cognitive system, which we can also encounter in various other domains, namely the ability of the system to handle what may be called *conjoint representations over the same input* (Mausfeld, in press-b). Corresponding phenomena in picture perception show that two representations are not independent but interlocked, and that we can phenomenally accentuate one or the other aspect and switch back and forth in an effortless way (though such switches are correlated with depth aspects, they actually pertain to the entire perceptual or-ganization of the visual field). The "realities" of pictures as objects and depicted objects bear different amounts of internal computational relevance and phenomeno-logical vividness. Similar observations can be made in many other domains, such as pretence play (a special case of *acting as if*, where the pretender correctly per-ceives the actual situation), in perspective taking (the ability to consider how objects, events or mental states are perceived from the point of view of another person and to simultaneously handle the egocentric and an allocentric perspective), or in lan-guage (where we can by some expression refer to something that is simultaneously abstract and concrete, cf. Chomsky, 2000). These cases appear to have interesting features in common and seem to point to an important property of highly complex perceptual and cognitive systems. Such systems have to subserve simultaneously a great variety of tasks and thus must internally have the outputs of many sub-modules available for purposes of stable higher-order representations, which naturally gives rise to conjoint representations over the same input. The internal handling of conjoint representations and their transformational structures can phenomenally be either im-perceptible or it can be mirrored in multistability, perceptual vagueness, or a kind of book-keeping by double entry, as it were (see Mausfeld, in press-b, for a more detailed account).

THE PHYSICALISTIC TRAP IN FUNCTIONALIST AND COMPUTATIONAL APPROACHES TO PERCEPTION

Within an elementaristic approach to perception, as exemplified by classical psychophysics, perceptual representations were investigated with respect to elementary physical variables that putatively had to be "properly" perceived by the visual system. To the extent that it came to be recognized that the achievements of the perceptual system cannot be understood by using isolated elementary physical variables as a reference frame an important and influential conceptual shift in perception theory took place. The stage for these developments had been predominantly set by the Gestalt psychologists, by Bühler, Brunswik, Michotte, and Gibson, and they culminated in the computational approach as pioneered by Marr. In functionalist and computational approaches perception theory has to start with an analysis and description of a specific perceptual achievement and then try to relate it, by a computational theory, to a suitable description of the available sensory input. Such computational approaches made it obvious that the perceptual system must have some *primitives* built in from the start (most investigations, however, exhibit a preference for a thin set of physically rather elementary primitives). Physical descriptions of the sensory input are then given in terms of these primitives and in terms of the biologically and perceptually relevant categories that are internally built up from these primitives.

In this respect, it is important to notice an essential difference between perception theory and machine vision: In machine vision the internal data structure and the physical properties and invariants, which are the basis of the system's achievements, are already determined *in advance*, i.e. machine vision deals with a categorically fixed and predetermined world. The contrary holds for perception theory: Its task is to *identify* what in machine vision is given by a fixed theoretical language, namely the internal data structure and the invariants in the sensory input that elicit the visual system's output, and thus to provide an explanatory theory of how perceptual concepts such as "object", "surface", "event", "illumination", "transparency", "shadows", etc., come about. Interestingly, it is precisely this problem that not only the elementaristic perspective, which is based on ideas from signal processing and communication engineering, has bracketed, but surprisingly also the functionalist-computational one.

In order to succesfully deal with this problem one has to construct a conceptual framework for physically describing the relevant aspects of the world that is suitable for perceptual purposes, a framework that ties the physical description as closely as possible to the description of the perceptual mechanisms under scrutiny. This is what ecological physics is about. The development of the conceptual apparatus for describing the perceptually relevant physical aspects and of the one for describing the perceptual achievement have to go hand in hand, resembling the hermeneutic cycle in interpretative arts. Their "natural kinds" cannot, of course, for principled reasons, coincide. However, a more suitable conceptual framework for ecological physics will greatly facilitate the development of successful explanatory theories of perception. It is still a major task of perceptual psychology to develop such a conceptual framework for describing perceptually relevant aspects of the physical world and thus of the sensory input.

Folk physics, though it is the necessary starting point for developing such a framework (cf. Smith & Casati, 1994), is an inapt guide in this respect. Using physical categories from common-sense taxonomies often results in the temptation to regard them as independent descriptions of the physical world that allegedly need to be "recovered" from the sensory input in the process of perception. This, however, would amount to misconceiving the role of ecological physics and to by-passing the core problem of perception theory to identify the internal primitives and the categorial structure they give rise to. Nevertheless, corresponding ideas can be encountered in many current computational approaches that take the perceptual classification of the environment as pre-given and describe the external world by using concepts from folk physics, like objects, shapes, shadows, surfaces, or lights (mostly in refined forms as provided by ecological physics). However, these concepts themselves are formed by perceptual processes, and consequently cannot be viewed independently from them. Thus corresponding approaches are prone to surreptitiously using categories belonging to the yet-to-be explained perceptual categories for a description of the physical input while investigating how these categories can be "recovered" from the sensory input. Hence, the question of what primitives are underlying those perceptual processes by which the physical world is parsed into perceptual categories, such as objects and events, is almost trivialized.

The case of apparent motion provides a simple example of the fact that perceptual and physical categories do not coincide. Furthermore, the existence of physical objects is not only not sufficient, but not even necessary for the corresponding percept (think of an object on a CRT screen or in a virtual reality setting). To lump together concepts of perceptual and physical categories and to "explain" the former as a computational recovery of the latter is again an example of the *physicalistic trap*. Particularly the idea, already mentioned above, to conceive of "vision as inverse optics" (Poggio, 1990, p. 143) can be considered a legacy of the measurement device conception of perception (notwithstanding its merits for purposes of machine vision).

The relations between properties of the external world that causally give rise to the physico-geometrical structure of the sensory input on the one hand, and between properties of the sensory input and internal outputs of the visual system on the other hand are, as mentioned above, two utterly separate problems that need to be distinguished and dealt with separately (Gibson emphasized the first part, Gestalt psychology only dealt with the second part). The only physics of the external world that figures in a formal theory of visual perception is the physico-geometric properties of the incoming light array. Within such theories the level of analysis that vicariously represents the physical world is the *Alberti window*, understood as an abstract mathematical entity. An Alberti window is, intuitively speaking, a two-dimensional array orthogonal to a possible line of view of an observer.[13] It is characterized by a spatio-temporal energy pattern caused by some physical processes. For reasons indicated before, notions like "veridicality" do not figure in formal theories of perception. They only arise in (indispensable) ordinary or metatheoretical discourse when we, as researchers, make a guess about the most plausible physical causes of an Alberti window. Though formal theories of perception refer to properties of the mental structure of the observer only and have no place for notions such as "reference to the external world" or "veridicality", we cannot, in the development of such theories, dispense of heuristics derived from ecological physics.

EXAMPLE IV: BAYESIAN APPROACHES TO PERCEPTION

There is a long tradition in perception theory, stretching from Alhazen through Helmholtz to Marr, that considers visual perception as essentially an inference-like process by which certain conclusions about the external world can be drawn from the premises given by the information in the retinal image. In recent years important conceptual clarifications of these intuitions have been achieved and comprehensive mathematical frameworks have been developed (Bennett et al., 1989; Knill & Richards, 1996; Kersten & Schrater, this volume) that make these notions precise and allow their theoretical and empirical fruitfulness to be explored. The basic idea of these approaches can be described by reference to the Bayesian formula of inverting conditional probabilities: Vision is considered as being based on inferences by which scene properties are estimated from image properties. Since an estimation of scene properties is highly underdetermined by image properties, the goal of the visual system is, on this view, to derive the probability of various scene interpretations for a given sensory image and to base an appropriate decision on this information. The probability of a world scene given the image (*posterior distribution*) is basically given by the product of the probability of the image given the scene (*likelihood function*) and the apriori probability of the scene (*prior distribution*). The form of the prior distribution models prior knowledge that the visual system has available about the probability of different features of the world (which helps to substantially narrow down the degree of non-uniqueness of scenes that could have given rise to the image). A decision scheme that operates on the posterior distribution allows a unique interpretation of the image in terms of a scene to be derived. This decision scheme incorporates, for example, consequences of misclassifications, preferences for certain interpretations, or different accuracy requirements for different kinds of parameters. Using Bayesian decision theory for modelling inference processes in perception yields more general schemes than inverse optics (and corresponding regularization schemes) because a Bayesian framework can incorporate decision aspects as well as a greater variety of constraints.

Bayesian frameworks stress that the inference process must be couched in terms of "world properties" (understood as perceptual concepts) rather than in terms of image properties,[14] and thus direct our attention to the problem of how to describe corresponding physical world properties in a theoretically fruitful way. They resemble the Gibsonian approach—rather than traditional psychophysics—with respect to the chosen level of physical description in that they tie the physical description to the macroscopic scale of environmentally and perceptually relevant categories. They, thus, do not refer to those concepts that have proved explanatorily useful for physical theory as such, but rather to a kind of relational or ecological physics that deals with physical descriptions of the categories that an organism employs in perceptually segmenting its environment.

Bayesian approaches, however, do not explicitly address and are neutral with respect to a core problem that we are faced with in the context of perception theory, namely the question of which conceptual vocabulary to use to describe in a theoretically fruitful way relevant properties of the image and relevant properties of the world. Shall we describe the image in terms of pixels, or geometrical entities, or natural objects, and thus base the inference process on luminous flux, on edges, or on meaningful objects, respectively? The vocabulary we use for the description of the input has to be as close as possible to the "semantic" distinctions that the visual system makes, because computational operations on the incoming light array cannot result in a unique set of new meaningful perceptual categories, unless these categories are already built-in as primitives.[15] What holds for the description of the image also holds for the description of the scene or the external world. In what terms can we formulate an explicit model of world structure? Apparently innocent locutions such as "The world we live in is a very structured place" veil the problem that what we have to refer to in models of world structure are not propositions about the physical world as such but about the world as structured by the yet-to-be-explained perceptual system of an observer. In which way, then, can we, without trivializing the problem of perceptual structure, make use of categories that describe the *output* of the visual system for a physical description of the input? Only if we assume that the categories for linking image events to world events, and thus the categorical structure of the priors itself, are given from the start and are built into the system.[16] It is the structure of the internal representations that relates image structure to world structure (a relation that can be contingent from the point of physics or geometry).

This problem of chosing an appropriate set of internal primitives also extends to the specification of priors. The priors not only capture statistical dependencies between physical properties of the environment but also crucially refer to the conceptual perceptual structure of the observer. The primitives that define the data format of internal processing and the structure of internal representations will dictate a core set of priors.

Current Bayesian approaches, instead of making this problem explicit, refer to the indefinite commendation to use "higher level descriptions" of image and scene. They focus on the probabilistic inference structure linking image properties and world properties while sidestepping the problem of identifying the concepts and primitives that these processes operate upon. The general approach is succinctly described by Hoffman (1996, p. 220): "What we in fact do is to fabricate those priors (and likelihoods) which best square with our posteriors." Though this is necessary in order to make the Bayesian apparatus work, it conceals a core problem of perception theory that has to be tackled on its own. Richards (1996, p. 228) legitimately deplores that aspects of "design and the creation of meaningful cognitive structures" receive little discussion in these developments. Rather, current Bayesian approaches sidestep such aspects by trading upon an equivocation of terms such as surface, object, event surface colour, illumination colour, etc. which denote both physical categories for describing the input as well as perceptual categories for describing the output of the visual system (as revealed by using the same variable "scene" in the posteriors and in the likelihood function). Because of this, current Bayesian approaches are strongly imbued with ideas from the inverse optics perspective and measurement device misconceptions, as is revealingly illustrated in typical phrases such as "the visual system attempts to estimate properties of the scene".[17]

However, once we have achieved a better understanding, beyond physical common sense taxonomies, of the internal categorial structure that gives rise to the posteriors, the general framework offered by Bayesian approaches has the attractive feature of jointly dealing within a common mathematical framework both with the internal structure of perceptual representations and with descriptions by ecological physics of relevant aspects of the external world. The Bayesian framework provides an inductive logic for describing the way in which the exploitation of given perceptual capacities and a given conceptual structure of perception varies with variations of the sensory input. It cannot, however, teach us anything about what the conceptual structure of perception is nor, in particular, derive it from physical descriptions of the sensory input.

EXAMPLE V: COLOUR CONSTANCY FROM
A COMPUTATIONAL POINT OF VIEW

According to elementaristic approaches to colour perception the alleged goal of the visual system is "to estimate the spectral shape of the incoming colour stimulus". Elementaristic approaches tie colour representations to the physical nature of the sensory input. In order to account for phenomena of approximate colour constancy of objects under varying illumination secondary "compensation mechanisms" have to be invoked. This way of carving the problem of colour perception had already been criticized by Hering (1920, p. 13): "Vision is not a matter of perceiving light rays as such, but the ability to see external objects by means of these rays; the eye's task is not to inform us about the respective intensity or quality of the light that comes from the external objects, but to inform us about the objects themselves." Bühler, Heider, Brunswik, Kardos and others have since then pursued similar functionalist perspectives on perception, which culminated when they merged with a computational approach, as pioneered by Marr. A functionalist-computational approach regards it as crucial for attempts to understand the structure of internal representations to start with an appropriate conjecture about the purpose for which they are used. Such ideas together with corresponding distinctions of levels of analysis constitute an important conceptual step in the development of the field. Since we are, however, far away from understanding the purposes of the various components of the visual system, we encounter immense problems when we try to substantiate these ideas in concrete cases. In such situations it is seductive to derive, by mis-idealizing the perceptual achievement, purported goals from physical considerations. This is what had happened with respect to colour perception, as exemplified by the assertion that basically "the goal of colour vision is to recover the invariant spectral reflectance of objects (surfaces)" (Poggio, 1990, p. 147). The idea that the structure of internal colour representations

is determined by the computational goal of recovering from the sensory input a function that depends only on certain physical properties of objects, viz. characteristics of
surface reflectance, though, of course, not without heuristic value, is patently a distal variant of the measurement device misconception of perception. Corresponding
approaches are encumbered with both empirical and theoretical problems.

Concerning their empirical adequacy they impute to the visual system a goal that
is not consonant with its actual achievements. What is achieved is not an estimation
of spectral reflectance functions, but rather an abstractive categorial description of
the "colour of a perceived object", which is more stable than can be expected on the
basis of the local sensory input, i.e. the wavelength composition of the light coming
from the object to the eye. In this sense, the percept "colour of an object" seems to
be more strongly tied to the spectral reflectance characteristics of the object than to
the wavelength composition of the local sensory input. There is, however, no colour
constancy in the strict sense that two locations of the same spectral reflectance "look
the same" under two different illuminations. One can see the "same colour" but
yet have a different colour experience by seeing it under a different illumination. The
phenomena concerning the interplay of surfaces and illumination in colour perception,
e.g. Helmholtz's observation that "colours that can be seen *at the same location* of
the visual field one behind the other", point to much deeper principles of the visual
system than those of some re-normalizing of the local colour code or the visual
system's alleged propensity to keep its colour equivalence classes congruent with
the physical structure of "reflectances of surfaces" (cf. Mausfeld, 1998). In the early
literature several promising attempts were made to identify these structural principles,
e.g. by Bühler (1922), Gelb (1929), Koffka (1932), MacLeod (1932) or Kardos (1934),
attempts that have almost been completely forgotten under the influence of the sensory
data processing approaches that since then have become the dominant paradigm in
colour perception, be they neurophysiologically oriented in the sense of neural data
processing or computationally oriented in the sense of sensory image processing
guided by some functional goal. Corresponding theoretical distortions have been
facilitated by our lack of a suitable theoretical language for the phenomenal description
of the percepts associated with the interplay of perceived illumination and perceived
objects, since such a description has to deal with aspects of, for instance, vagueness,
abstraction and categorization.

From a theoretical point of view the computational approaches to colour perception
mentioned throw together two different levels of analysis. It is one question to ask
what properties of the environment give rise to perceptually relevant properties of the
Alberti window (or to study what, from an evolutionary point of view, is the "normal
explanation" for the structure of the Alberti window), and a completely different
problem to investigate how structural properties of Alberti windows are exploited by
the visual system in terms of its primitives.

The same characteristics of a light array reaching the eye can be physically produced in many different ways. With respect to the percept "surface under chromatic
illumination" the same spatio-temporal light pattern that is caused by a certain interaction of physical surfaces and light sources and that elicits corresponding percepts
can be produced by light sources alone (using, for example, a slide or a CRT screen).

The visual system cannot distinguish these cases, it simply doesn't know whether the causal chain giving rise to this pattern arises from surfaces and light, or lights alone. A goal of perceptual psychology is to identify the equivalence classes of input patterns that give rise to the same internal outputs and thus to provide an abstract explanatory framework for the structure of perceptual representations. A description of such equivalence classes in the language of physics will very likely lead to very abstract mathematical entities that are quite unnatural from the point of both theoretical physics and folk physics. This again highlights the futility of attempting to provide a description of the equivalence classes of colour codes in terms of their possible physical causes; colours do not constitute a well-formed physical kind. The internal structure of colour perception is given by the structure of representational primitives in which parameters for "colour" figure. These primitives determine the structure of internal colour codes, and thus by the kind and structure of equivalence classes of input codes that result in corresponding output codes. Because the equivalence classes are "held together" by the structure of our perceptual system, rather than by the structure of the physical environment itself, any reference to the potential distal causes of the Alberti window is extrinsic to a formal theory of colour perception. Again, notions of representational content or reference to the environment do not figure in formal theories that provide explanatory frameworks for our understanding of the internal structure of colour. The question of whether colours "represent" what they normally stem from in our environment is of no relevance for our formal theories of perception, though corresponding considerations are, of course, an indispensable part of our *metatheoretical* talk about colours.

The structure of internal representations cannot be revealed by referring to physical properties like surface reflectance characteristics from the outset because there are no such things in the Alberti window. They cannot even be assumed to be necessary causes for the corresponding categories. Internal concepts, such as "surface colours", are not constituted by the corresponding categories of physics or tied to them, e.g. in the sense of the latter being necessary and sufficient conditions for the former. Rather they are constituted by biologically relevant features of the environment as well as by internal constraints and requirements of the entire perceptual architecture. Not much is known today about the "internal semantics" (as a purely syntactically-defined feature) of the visual system, but there are good reasons to assume that basic "semantic" units of perception are predetermined and tied to certain spatio-temporal characteristics of the incoming energy.

Experimental and theoretical evidence strongly suggests, however, that the segregation into "surface colour" and "illumination colour" is not something that is derived from an analysis of the "physical scene" but rather a primordial format of organization of representational primitives in which "colour" figures as parameter. The perceptual system exploits the incoming light array in terms of its representational primitives. For instance, what can be described as an "inference" whether a chromatic deviation of the space-averaged colour codes from some neutral point is due to a "non-normal", i.e. chromatic, illumination or due to an imbalanced spectral reflectance composition of the scene has to be achieved by a specific activation of representational primitives by signs that the sensory system provides on the basis of relevant reliable regularities of the incoming light array. We found evidence that second-order statistics of chromatic codes of the incoming light array differentially modulate, by a specific class of parameterized transformations, the relation of the two kinds of representational primitives involved (Mausfeld & Andres, in press).

EXAMPLE VI: EVOLUTIONARY INTERNALIZED REGULARITIES OF THE PHYSICAL WORLD

There are many other cases in which the physicalistic trap imbues the way problems of perception theory are formulated. As a final example I will briefly address an approach of current interest that comes under the heading "evolutionary internalized regularities" (see also Bennett & Hoffman, this volume) and has been prominently advanced by Shepard (e.g. 1987, 1994). This approach connects inquiries into the internal structure of perceptual representations with conjectures about physical regularities that may have phylogenetically become mirrored in perceptual structure. Such regularities may refer to "the fact that space is three-dimensional, that objects have six degrees of freedom of global motion, that light and dark alternate with a fixed period, and that sets of objects having the same significant consequences tend to form a compact region in an appropriate parameter space" (Shepard, 1987, p. 269). We can distinguish various types of relevant regularities, such as general physical regularities (like gravitation or the three-dimensionality of local space), physico-geometrical regularities resulting from a specific relation between observer and environment (like perspective geometry), physically contingent global regularities (like the spectral composition of sunlight), and local niche-specific regularities. The urge to look for internalized physical regularities arose from the observation that there is a huge discrepancy between the sensory input and the perceptual achievement and that the structure of perceptual representations cannot simply be accounted for by the information available in the sensory input. It is thus occasioned by the same fundamental insight that resulted in the invocation of concepts like "unconscious inference", "higher order" processes, Gestalt principles, or "internalized knowledge,"[18] an insight that time after time has been obstructed and disowned by empiristic ideology. One can hardly overestimate the strength and longevity of the behaviouristic and empiristic tradition.[19] Its core element, viz. the disregard for mental structure, still provides, in various modern disguises, the basis for much of current thinking about perception. Hence, referring to mental structure and concepts in perception theories is still considered by many as anathema. In contrast, Shepard clearly recognized the explanatoric vacuum caused by the prevailing disregard for the internal structure of mental representations and emphasizes the need for exploring the properties of the rich internal structure of the perceptual system. Taking serious the idea that we need to postulate, within explanatory theories of perception, a rich internal structure which the perceptual system is endowed with will have radical consequences for the kind of questions asked in perception theory. Shepard, who has reinvigorated psychological inquiries into the structural form of mental representations, seems to eschew these radical consequences and resorts to the idea that the rich structure is imprinted on the mind of the perceiver almost entirely from without by the evolutionary internalization of external physical regularities.

As a research strategy heuristics pertaining to evolutionary internalized physical regularities have, of course, much to offer. They exhibit again the explanatory gap between the meagre sensory input and the exceedingly rich perceptual output, and generate theoretical speculations that can enrich, in concrete cases, our knowledge about the internal structure of perception. Corresponding endeavours bear a close resemblance to and extend inquiries into ecological physics.

Notwithstanding the potential fruitfulness of such heuristics, we have, with respect to perception theory, to distinguish the level of analysis that pertains to the individual organisms in a specific context (or to a submechanism subserving a specific function) from the one that pertains to the corresponding evolutionary history. The first level of analysis aims at an explanatory account of the structure of perceptual representations for a given organism. The second level pertains to the question, whether the structure of internal representations can be related to specific physical regularities of the environment that have been internally encoded in evolutionary history and are used for or constrain internal computations.[20] In an successful explanatory theory of perception, based on an appropriately rich set of internal primitives, no need arises to refer to some internalization of physical regularities. Here, as elsewhere in biology, a satisfactoy *ahistorical* account for a functional structure does not ipso facto suffer from some kind of explanatory deficit. Furthermore, evolutionary speculations about cognitive structure are encumbered with well-known problems (e.g. Lewontin, 1998); presently we know next to nothing about the specific evolutionary mechanisms and about the physical or functional constraints that are responsible for the development of the internal structure of perception nor about the features, the selection for or of which has shaped the structure of internal representations. Obviously, the organism *as an entirety* has been adapted to the specific circumstances and properties of the environment in which it has evolved; from this it does not follow, however, that the structure and the properties of specific perceptual *subsystems* are primarily determined by and "optimally" adapted to specific features of the environment.

Regarding evolutionary aspects as external to an explanatory account of the nature of perception and as belonging to metatheoretical discourse, does not, of course, amount to denying any dependencies. The question is not, how in reality things are related to each other; perception is related to and dependent on various aspects of reality like phylogenetic development, metabolism, the immune system or the physics of the brain. The question rather is what constitutes an appropriate level of idealization for successful explanatory frameworks of perception.

Furthermore, it is not clear what is meant by the notions of "physical regularity" and "internalization". Shepard (1987, p. 269) has been arguing "that to the extent that the principles of the mind are not merely arbitrary, their most likely ultimate sources are the abiding regularities of the world". Of course, understood in the wider sense that principles of the mind have evolved within the regularities of the world and are ultimately themselves part of the regularities of the world, this assertion is true, but of no theoretical interest. In a more specific sense it can be understood as the assertion that the structure of internal representations is determined first of all by regularities of the external physical world, whereas no essential explanatory importance is attached to factors such as behavioral regularities of conspecifies, to internal physical and architectural constraints or to idiosyncratic properties of the cognitive architecture. It is indubitable that we can, in many cases, find some external regularities to which properties of internal coding "conform" but nothing about internalization is implied by that. But it is Shepard's main point that regularities of internal representations are due to an internalization of external physical regularities, and that the most abiding regularities under which the system has evolved are good candidates for regularities that have become internalized. Even if we would accept, despite the lack of corresponding empirical evidence, the assertion that, in general, principles of internal representations are determined by external regularities, we are faced with an intrinsic indeterminateness of the set of potential "candidates for regularities that have become internalized". We can formulate literally infinitely many physical regularities, i.e. relations on sets of physico-mathematical entities that remain invariant under certain sets of transformations, of any degree of "unnaturalness", under which the perceptual system has evolved. What the intuition behind the notion of regularities seems to be aiming at, however, is something like "natural" physical regularities that can be related to but are, in principle, independent of the specific perceptual design of the observer. These are understood as providing constraints that have been phylogenetically internalized by the perceptual system and determine the structure of its internal representation. There is, however, no a priori notion of organism-relevant physical regularities. What is a regularity depends on the structure of the organism under scrutiny, such as its size, the spatial and temporal integration properties of receptors and other neural structure, the properties of its memory and its representational capacities. The structure of the organism determines which regions of the parameter space of the physical world are regarded as an environment. Concepts such as "regularities", or Barlow's "redundancies" and "suspicious coincidences" can, in the context of perception theory, only be defined relative to given representational capacities of the respective organism. Corresponding considerations inevitably lead back to the core problem of perception theory, viz. to understand the internal conceptual structure of perception, a problem that cannot be dodged by referring to physico-geometrical or statistical regularities of the physical world.

It is noteworthy that Shepard's primary motivation for postulating an internalization of features of the physical world is not to enable the system to solve an otherwise highly underdetermined task. His major thrust rather is to provide an explanation for the specific structural form of internal representations. In doing so he refers to principles that "reflect quite abstract features of the world, based as much (or possibly more) in geometry, probability, and group theory as in specific, physical facts about concrete material objects" (Shepard, 1994, p. 26), and ties the internalization process to the evolutionary advantage that "genes that have internalized these pervasive and enduring facts about the world" (ibid., p. 2) ultimately have. His approach thus extends the approach of ecological physics to more abstract mathematical descriptions of regularities of the world, which can be used then as heuristics for exploring the structure of internal representations. Still, the critical ambiguity about the internal role of external regularities that can be found in standard functionalist-computational approaches translates into his approach. The perceptual system can take advantage of a physical regularity in the sense that the way internal mechanisms work is based on the existence of specific physical regularities. In this sense we can say that the regularity is mirrored in the design of the system, as in the case of "the hawk and the ground squirrel (who) have internalized the period of the terrestrial circadian cycle" (ibid., p. 2). Being based on or taking in evolutionary history advantage of a physical regularity does not imply, however, that the system has internalized the regularity in the sense that it is explicitly encoded or used in some internal computations.

Approaches based on the notion of internalized physical regularities rightly acknowledge that we have to assume a rich internal structure of the perceptual system in order to account for its output. They thus draw our attention to a core problem of perception theory, viz. to understand the structural form of internal representations. They claim, however, that the structure required can be borrowed from, possibly highly abstract, external regularities. The danger, again, is that one uses physical regularities of the external world not just as an important heuristics about the structure of internal representations but rather projects them, as it were, into the perceptual system as a surrogate for internal structure.

PERCEPTION THEORY BEYOND THE PHYSICALISTIC TRAP

Still, the only reasonable way, it seems, to embark on investigations about perceptual representations, is to venture ideas about the aspects of the physical world that are internally represented by the perceptual system. After all, the perceptual system subserves the function of coupling the organism in an adaptively appropriate way to the external world. Therefore, internal perceptual representations thus cannot be "inconsistent" with biologically important physical regularities of the world. Thinking along the lines of physical descriptions of the external world then is, one might argue, the only means to understand the nature of perceptual representations, rather than being a trap. How else could we, according to this claim, arrive at a theoretical understanding of perception than by trying to identify the physical regularities to which the system is tied and which are internally mirrored in its machinery? In a very general sense, this is, of course, true; it simply rephrases, however, the general definition of perception. Also, it is indisputable that considerations both from phenomenology and from folk physics, including ideas about veridicality, are an indispensable part of our metatheoretical discourse about perception. The trouble arises when we try to derive more specific formulations from this idea. Even if we simply restrict our attention to the physical side of perception, i.e. to perceptually appropriate physical descriptions of the external world, the general idea that the function of perception is a coupling to the external world does not provide a clue to which set of physical concepts, from infinitely many, we use for a description of the external world and of physical regularities. Should we couch a description of biologically relevant aspects of the physical world in terms of, for example, quanta, light rays, spectral energy distributions, optical flow, surfaces, or physical descriptions of semantic categories, like "edible things"? Any (conjectural) decision has to be based on arguments provided by perception theory. Neither descriptions based on elementary physical variables nor those based on common-sense classifications as underlying folk physics are exempted from such a justification. The physicalistic trap amounts to assigning such descriptions a higher degree of plausibility and using them in a somewhat a priori way not only for describing allegedly relevant physical aspects but also for theoretically segmenting perceptual structure. However, any successful explanatory account of perception has to be based on a physical description of the external world that is tied as closely as possible to the (yet-to-be identified) conceptual structure of the perceptual system.

A problem of much greater concern for perception theory is that the structure of perceptual representations cannot be understood if we restrict our attention to the physical side of perception, however appropriately we have chosen our vocabulary for describing the external world. The structure of internal representations is shaped not only by regularities of the external physical world, but also by biological regularities (e.g. the behaviour of conspecifies) that are contingent with respect to physics, by internal and architectural constraints, and by contingent properties of internal coding. As mentioned in the beginning, it is not sufficient for perceptual representations to be adequate with respect to the external world, they must also be functionally adequate, in the sense that they have to fit into the entire perceptual architecture including its interfaces with the sensory system, the motor system and the higher cognitive system, where meanings are assigned in terms of "external world" properties. It is a characteristic feature of the physicalistic trap that it ignores these aspects and overlooks the extent to which perceptual representations are structured by internal constraints. Presently we know much less about these other constraints than we know about aspects of ecological physics.[21]

Many early writers, notably the Gestaltists, Michotte, and ethologists, were aware of this and rightly emphasized the rich internal structure of perceptual representations by which the organism imposes a structure on the sensory input that cannot be derived from an analysis of the physical input alone. They did not, however, have the rich conceptual tools made available today by ecological physics and computational approaches to put these insights to work. Due to the prevailing empiristic presuppostions most of these insights have been forgotten or even ostracized. Therefore, approaches that tend to regard the perception process as being based on the information, with regard to external environmental contraints, available in the sensory input (plus some "generalized learning mechanisms") still dominate the field. These approaches typically share an extremely empiricist point of view with respect to mental structure.

In contrast, ethologists, such as v. Uexküll, Lorenz and Tinbergen, have marshalled—taking the entire organism as the level of analysis—an impressive array of observations in support of innate and phylogenetically shaped building blocks of behaviour. With respect to perception we can find approaches similar to or inspired by ethology in perceptual psychology (e.g. Heider, 1930; Tolman & Brunswik, 1935), in neuroethology (e.g. Barlow, 1961) and in computational neuroethology (e.g. Hassenstein & Reichardt, 1956; Gallistel, 1998). Ethological investigations have suggested a theoretical picture according to which perception cannot be understood as the "recovery" of physical world structure from sensory structure by input-based computational processes. Rather, the sensory input serves a dual function: firstly, it provides triggering cues for which representational primitives are to be activated, and thus selects among potential data formats in terms of which input properties are to be exploited. Secondly, it triggers processes that result in a specification of the values of the free parameters of the activated representational primitive. (Thus, even "highly impoverished" sensory inputs can trigger perceptual representations whose "complexity" far exceeds that of the triggering stimulus and whose relation to the sensory input can be contingent from the point of physics or geometry.)

The tension between intuitions that regard visual perception as essentially being based on inverse optics-like computations and those that regard it as being based on a rich structure of given primitives and internal computations that are triggered by the sensory input can be traced back to the beginnings of perception theory (see Appendix). It is important to note that intuitions about a triggering of perceptual representations must not be understood as being based on the idea that the mind is a repository of prefigured and innate ideas and that the sensory stimulus elicits something from this internal storehouse of ideas. Rather they refer to the observation that while the sensory input is a causally necessary requirement for perceptual representations, the perceptual computations triggered are under the control of an internal programme based on a set of representational primitives.[22] Perceptual computations are thus representation-driven rather than stimulus-driven. They mirror the way perceptual representations *as an entirety* are organized, rather than being locally tied to the physical variables that causally gave rise to the sensory input.

There is hardly any disagreement among theoretical perspectives on perception that our visual system must be based on some representational primitives that are built-in from the start; however, different theoretical approaches strongly disagree about the question, how rich and complex—in relation to physical descriptions of the sensory input—these primitives have to be assumed to be. Though we are far from having a clear theoretical picture about the structure of primitives underlying perceptual representations, available theoretical and empirical evidence strongly suggests that primitives such as "surface", "object", or "event" are among the pillars on which the structure of perceptual representations rests.[23]

A wealth of observations, stretching from Gestaltists' observations on figure-ground segmentation, to Gibson's ideas, to computational approaches indicate that among the representational primitives of the perceptual system "surface" plays a distinguished role (see Nakayama et al., 1995, for a more recent account). Perceptual representations are organized in terms of "surfaces" among which certain ones can play special roles, notably the ground plane (Sedgwick, 1986). As representational primitives, "surfaces" have a variety of perceptual attributes, such as depth, orientation, colour, brightness, texture, etc. (understood as *internal* concepts), that have to be specified by the incoming sensory information. The formats of these attributes are determined by the internal architecture; they are, in line with Müller's law of specific nerve energies, given by design. Their concrete values, however, are dependent on the specific sensory input and on the perceptual representations to which they are attached. We can conceive of them as free parameters attached to certain primitives and as part of the representational format of these primitives. For example, in the case of colour we have, accordingly, to distinguish different types of colour parameters, depending on the particular primitive to which they belong. "Colours" that are attached to an internal representation of the transmission medium subserve a different function and exhibit different coding properties than "colours" attached to the internal concept "surface". Which parameters are specified in which way and which associated classes of transformations are activated (pertaining, e.g., to the idealized functional goals of "scene invariance" or "illumination invariance") is then determined by specific physico-geometrical properties of the sensory input (Mausfeld & Andres, in press; Mausfeld, in press-a).

On the basis of currently available evidence successful explanatory accounts of perception not only have to be based on postulating a sufficiently rich set of structural primitives such as "object" or "event" of various types—which specify the internal data format, as it were—but also on domain-specific relational and transformational primitives pertaining to, for example, similarity, identity, continuity, coherence, to a variety of spatial and temporal relations, to topological properties, or to the requirement of guaranteeing smooth transitions between internal representations. Prominent examples of relational primitives are "causality" in the case of physical entities (Michotte, 1946; Scholl & Tremoulet, 2000), and "intention" in the case of mental entitites (Premack & Premack, 1995).

While the theoretical picture of the basic principles underlying perception that is emerging is still very skeletal and of necessity has to be based on considerable theoretical speculation, it receives support also from more recent study of the newborn and young children in developmental psychology. Corresponding studies provide convincing evidence that our mental apparatus is, as part of our biological endowment, equipped with a rich internal structure pertaining to, for example, structural knowledge about properties of the physical world, to distinguishing between physical and biological objects, or to imputing mental states to oneself and to others.[24]

Our perceptual apparatus serves to couple the organism to biologically relevant aspects of the external world. For an organism with a mental structure as rich as ours the relevant aspects of the "external world" do not only pertain to physical and biological aspects but also to the mental states of others. We perceive not only colour, shape, depth, and physical relations as causality, but also emotional states and intentions of others. With respect to the architecture and functioning of the perceptual system there is no fundamental difference between perceiving physical aspects of the external world or aspects of the mental states of others. In both cases the sensory input serves as a sign for biologically relevant aspects of the external world that elicits internal representations on the basis of given representational primitives. Though we are still far from understanding the structure of perceptual representations and their role within mental architecture, there are good reasons to assume that perceiving physical aspects like shape, colour or depth is not more direct or immediate than perceiving mental states of others. Once we recognize that both rely on the selfsame basic principles we are able to ask novel and promising questions about the internal representational structure of perception.

APPENDIX

HISTORICAL ANNOTATIONS ON THE NOTIONS OF SENSORY DATA-BASED COMPUTATION VS. TRIGGERING IN PERCEPTION THEORY

The tension between intuitions about sensory image-based computation-like processes in perception (i.e. transformations based on the same theoretical vocabulary) and triggering theories of perception (i.e. transformations based on different sets of primitives) goes back to the earliest conceptual developments in the history of perception.[25]

According to ancient conceptions of perception things imprint themselves (*influxus physicus*) as entire objects into the soul by some forms (*species sensibiles*) which emanated from physical objects. Thus, no distinction between sensation and perception could have been made. However, similars can only be perceived by similars (*similia similibus percipiuntur*). Therefore some *tertium quid* must exist—as in *eidola* conceptions—that mediates between the dissimilar instances of soul and material objects. Building on these ideas, Alhazen and Kepler assumed that the senses transmit images of objects to the mind and that consequently perception is the mental correlate of the retinal image.

Alhazen was aware, however, that the process of visual perception cannot solely be understood on the basis of the geometrical processes involved. Rather, he assumed that non-geometrical mental operations have to be involved. It is interesting to note that the assumption of inference-like mental operations opens the way for an entirely new conception of perception, namely perception as mediated by signs. Alhazen noted that properties of objects like shape, position, size or movement can be perceived "only by inference and signs" (*Optics*, Bk. I, 6, 60). For Alhazen a sign is, as Sabra (1989, p. 80) put it, "a distinctive mark or feature or property of an object which serves as an index or clue of the object's identity". Perception by signs is possible because "the forms of all familiar objects and species, and of all common properties, have been established in the soul and shaped in the imagination and are present in memory". Perception of such properties therefore can be achieved "by means of signs and prior knowledge" (*Optics*, Bk. II, 4, 22). It is important to note that visual inferences based on signs can refer to cues that are *not* supplied by the optical images themselves. Though Alhazen's idea of inferences based on signs differs from the much more radical (but very different) conceptions of a sign or symbol theory of perception proposed later by, say, Arnauld Cudworth, Reid or Helmholtz, his distinction between *two* kinds of inference, one based on signs (*comprehensio per signum*; *Optics*, Bk. II., ch. 3, 24, 25, ch. 4, 20–25), the other on a thorough inference performed by the "faculty of judgement" (*per aliquam modorum ratiocinationis, Optics*, Bk. II, ch.3, 20) was an important conceptual step that paved the way for later developments.

A corresponding distinction of two such different processes can also be gathered from Descartes' writings. For Descartes the material object does not cause a physiological copy which then serves as the immediate object of perception. Rather the mechanistic physiological process is only a *means* of perception that arouses certain ideas in the mind. Thus, the movements of the nerves only act as *signs* that—mediated by movements of the pineal gland—stimulate certain mental ideas (which corresponds to Descartes' second grade of sensation). (As Atherton, this volume, states, "part of his project is to argue that the retinal image qua image plays no role in sensation".) These movements do not resemble what they represent. As a kind of blending of bodily and mental states (*confusi quidam cogitandi modi, Meditationes* VI, 13), the sensations which were aroused in the pineal gland do not resemble external objects, in the same way that words do not resemble the objects that they denote. This has the important consequence that not even sensory concepts can be derived from experience.[26] Also form or size are abstract ideas that cannot directly be derived from the senses. Rather some "raw ideas" of size, form, etc., are triggered by certain excitations of the senses. The structural relationship between these ideas is assumed to resemble the structural relationship between the corresponding external qualities. In this sense, Descartes seems to assume that the "real" properties of the external world are completely divorced from the corresponding ideas in the mind. On the other hand, however, he holds that there are processes (which do not operate on the retinal image, but within the domain of abstract ideas) that allow us to achieve (partly and imperfectly) access to properties of external objects. In the wake of Alhazen, Descartes postulated calculation-like processes based on natural geometry, by which we can achieve judgements of a higher degree of reliability of the corresponding properties of the external objects. (Cf. Hatfield's account, this volume, of the corresponding ideas of Alhazen and Descartes.) The caginess and even incoherence of Descartes' corresponding writings indicate that he was loath to varnish over the huge complexities that he identified in his attempts to provide a new explanatory framework for the relationship of the mental and the physical. Malebranche was more willing to sacrifice part of the complexity for consistency and gave a perfectly straightforward inverse optics account according to which, as Atherton (this volume) shows in detail, "the visual world is the result of a calculation in which the retinal image serves as a step in the calculation".

Cudworth, in his account of perception, followed Descartes very closely. Nevertheless some aspects of both his emphasis and his framing of the problem are of interest in the present context. He was, in his more general perspective, strongly opposed to Descartes' sharp distinction between the human mind and animal mechanisms.

> On Cudworth's view, anything is incorporeal which has a force of its own, anything which is not merely the passive recipient of pushes and pulls. Not everything which is incorporeal is mental, and not everything which is mental is conscious. . . . The essential division, as Cudworth sees it, is that between the mechanical and the teleological, not between the unthinking and the thinking. He rejects the Cartesian view that animals

are mechanisms, and with it the sharp Cartesian contrast between the animal and the human. What links the human with the animal are instincts: these, Cudworth maintains, are certainly not mechanical, for they have ends, which no mechanism can have, and since they are not mechanical, they cannot be corporeal. . . . To Descartes there is simply the dualism of mind and matter; but, as we saw, Cudworth's division of reality comes at a different point, as a dualism of the active and the passive. (Passmore, 1951, p. 23/24)

Cudworth clearly noted that "sense, which either lies in the same level with that particular material object which is perceived, or rather under it and beneath it, cannot emerge to any knowledge or truth concerning it" (1731, p. 95). He therefore argued for a rich "innate cognoscitive power" (ibid., p. 131), by which the mind "is enabled as occasion serves and outward objects invite, gradually and successively to unfold and display it self in a vital manner, by framing intelligible ideas or conceptions within it self of whatsoever hath any entity or cogitability" (ibid., p. 135). Sensible ideas and conceptions of the mind were not passively presented or imprinted by the senses, but rather, "according to nature's instinct, (the mind) hath several seemings or appearances begotten in it of those resisting objects without it at a distance, in respect of colour, magnitude, figure and local motion" (ibid., p. 152). Sensible ideas "are excited and awakened occasionally from the appulse of outward objects knocking at the doors of our senses" (ibid., p. 150). "Sense is but the offering and presenting of some object to the mind, to give it an occasion to exercise its own inward activity upon" (ibid., p. 94). The connection between the "local motions" that the external world exerts on the senses and the ideas and conceptions that were triggered by them in the mind is established "by Nature's law . . . though there be no similitude at all betwixt them" (ibid., p. 216). For Cudworth, as for Descartes, sense can be compared to speech by which "Nature as it were talking to us in the sensible objects without, by certain motions as signs from thence communicated to the brain" (ibid., p. 215). As speech is a medium only whose idiosyncratic physical properties bear no direct interest for what is conveyed by it, so the mind,

as by a certain secret instinct, understanding Nature's language, as soon as these local motions are made in the brain, doth not fix its attention immediately upon those motions themselves, as we do not use to do in discourse upon meer speech, but presently exerts such sensible ideas, phantasms and cogitations, as Nature hath them to be signs of, whereby it perceives and takes cognizance of many other things both in its own body, and without it, at a distance from it, in order to the good and conservation of it.

(Ibid., pp. 216–17).

Similar ideas were expressed by Arnauld (1683/1990) and Charles Bonnet (see Yolton, 1984, p. 29). In our attempts to "better understand how far the passion of the sense reaches, and where the activity of the mind begins", we have to avoid a misconception that still prevails among many perception scientists: "these men not distinguishing betwixt the outward occassion or invitation of those cogitations, and the immediate active or productive cause of them, impute them therefore alike, as well these intelligible, as the other sensible ideas, or phantasms, to the efficiency or activity of the outward objects upon us" (Cudworth, 1731, p. 150).

Cudworth clearly recognized that we have to assume a rich internal structure of the mind in order to account for its active "cognoscitive power"; because of this he played a prominent role in the research programme for cognitive science that Chomsky (1966) set out along historical lines in his *Cartesian Linguistics*. Cudworth maintained that we cannot understand the active forces of the mind but by assuming "that there are some ideas of the mind which were not stamped or imprinted upon it from the sensible objects without, and therefore must needs arise from the innate vigor and activity of the mind it self" (ibid., p. 148), among which he included ideas as contingency, possibility, genus and species, knowledge, justice, verity, equity, obligation, honesty, volition and cogitation, as well as sense itself (ibid., pp. 140/149). Furthermore, "there are many relative notions and ideas, attributed as well to corporeal as incorporeal things that proceed wholly from the activity of the mind comparing one thing with another" (ibid., p. 149): The mind "raises and excites within it self the intelligible ideas of cause, effect, means, end, priority and posteriority, equality and inequality, order and proportion, symmetry and asymmetry, aptitude and ineptitude, sign and thing signified, whole and part" (ibid., p. 155).

Reid, whose conception of the perceptual process shared certain elements with the conceptions of Descartes and Berkeley (as to Berkeley, see Hatfield, this volume), emphasized the distinction between "sensations" and "perceptions".[27] Reid completely divorced "sensations" that accompany physiological impressions from "perceptions". For him *perceptions* are not mental transformations, supplements or interpretations of sensations. They are rather a completely different kind of mental states, which are characterized by a "strong and irresistable conviction and belief" in the external existence of objects. This belief is "not the effect of reasoning" but part of our biological endowment. "The belief which is implied in it, is the effect of instinct" (*An Inquiry into the Human Mind*, ch. VI, §XX). Reid further distinguished "original perceptions" from "acquired perceptions". The "original perceptions" serve as "signs", which elicit "acquired perceptions". The ability to interpret these "signs" was considered by Reid to be innate. By completely cutting any rational relation between sensation and perception, Reid rejected previous ideas of calculation-like processes in perception. Reid thus proposed an extreme version of a sign theory of perception. In his conception the relation between sensations and perceptions cannot be rationally explained; it is simply due to a law of nature. It may be tempting to speculate that Reid would have filled this essential blank in his system if he had been acquainted with evolutionary theory.

Taine, although hardly of interest on his own rights in the present context, did give a pithy characterization of how to conceive of perception along such lines (even if he was in general at odds with core ideas of Reid). Taine argued in his framework of naturalistic psychology "that external perception, even when accurate, is an hallucination":

A sensation, and notably a tactile or visual sensation, engenders, by its presence alone, an internal phantom which appears an external object.... It matters little whether the sensation be purely cerebral and arise spontaneously, without preliminary excitation of the peripheral extremity of the nerve, in the absence of the objects which usually produce the excitation. As soon as ever the sensation is present, the rest follows; the prologue entails the drama. . . . If its existence be established by its antecedents, it is confirmed by its consequents. (Taine, 1875, pp. 1/2)

An elaborated account of a sign theory of perception that is accompanied by an explicit mechanism for explaining how sensations and perceptions are bound together can be found in the work of Helmholtz (e.g. 1878, 1894), who with his sign theory incorporated Kantian elements in his otherwise empiristic stance. According to Helmholtz, there is no similarity between our percepts and the structure of the physical environment. The senses provide only *signs* for our cognitive system, which have to be interpreted according to (ontogenetic or phylogenetic) learning and experience. Unlike pictures, signs do not resemble the object they refer to; however, they mirror lawful relations in the world. However, one has to presuppose a unique functional relation—governed by causal dependencies—between a system of signs and the objects they refer to, i.e. operations on signs correspond to operations on objects. "Innumerable mistakes and incorrect theories in perceptual research were caused by not distinguishing clearly between the concept of a sign and that of a picture." ("Dass man den Begriff des Zeichens und des Bildes bisher in der Lehre von den Wahrnehmungen nicht sorgfältig genug getrennt hat, scheint mir der Grund unzähliger Irrungen und falscher Theorien gewesen zu sein.") (Helmholtz, 1868, p. 319). Associative connections mediated by experience allow us to interpret in a correct, i.e. adaptively useful, way the signs which result from the impingement of the outer world on the senses.

The sense impressions are thus "signs which we have learnt to read; they are a language bestowed upon us by our organization, in which the outer world speaks to us. But we have to learn this language by training and experience, just like our mother language." (Die Sinnesempfindungen sind also "Zeichen, welche wir lesen gelernt haben, sie sind eine durch unsere Organisation uns mitgegebene Sprache, in der die Außendinge zu uns reden; aber diese Sprache müssen wir durch Uebung und Erfahrung verstehen lernen, eben so gut wie unsere Muttersprache" (Helmholtz, 1869, p. 393). "The character of these signs is imposed on me by the nature of my sense organs and of my mind; this distinguishes the sign language of perception from the arbitrarily chosen sign of speech and writing." (Die Art der Zeichen ist "mir durch die Natur meiner Sinnesorgane und meines Geistes aufgedrungen. Dadurch unterscheidet sich diese Zeichensprache unserer Vorstellungen von den willkürlich gewählten Laut- und Buchstabenzeichen unserer Rede und Schrift" (Helmholtz, 1867, p. 446). What we can infer from the external world by this sign language can only be symbolic in character since there is no *tertium comperationis*. We call our ideas of the external world true when they provide us with sufficient evidence concerning the consequences of our action and when they allow us to infer expected changes correctly (Helmholtz, 1867, p. 443).

For Helmholtz the signs themselves exhibit a rich internal structure of operations that mirror corresponding operation on external objects (cf. Hatfield, 1990, pp. 208ff.). These ideas provided the foundations for what can be considered an important theoretical insight into the nature of perception, namely the structural or transformational

theories of perception. According to these ideas, which are based more or less explicitly on group theoretic concepts, the proper objects of perception are abstract
higher-order objects, namely transformational structures. A specific sensory input
triggers in sufficiently rich situations an entire transformational structure, which constitutes a "frame of reference" with respect to which classes of visual "objects"
were defined. The segmentation of the sensory input into "objects" and "events"
thus depends on the kind of transformational structure that it triggers. Although corresponding intuitions in various forms pervade theoretical ideas on perception since
Helmholtz, they were first discussed under the perspective of group theory by Cassirer
(1944) and more recently taken up by Shepard (e.g. 1994).

While the insight that the perceptual system imposes a structure on the sensory input that cannot be derived a priori from an analysis of the physical input alone, as well
as corresponding notions of triggering, became crucial in ethology (and also in earlier
ethology-inspired computational approaches), they have been almost completely ignored within current empiricist accounts, such as sensory data-based computational
approaches or data processing models of perception guided by ideas from signal
processing and communication engineering. Corresponding insights and intuitions,
however, are at the core of the general research programme that has been set out for
the study of cognition by Chomsky (e.g. 1966, 1996, 2000) and have led, in the domain of language, to real advances in our attempts to develop successful explanatory
accounts of the structure of mental representations.

ACKNOWLEDGEMENT

I wish to express my gratitude to Margaret Atherton, Andrea van Doorn, Franz Faul, Don
Hoffman and Gary Hatfield for valuable comments on a first draft of this paper.

NOTES

1. Interesting new kinds of relevant evidence come from experiments with babies and very
   young children (e.g. Streri et al., 1993).
2. Of course, in anatomy we can speak—though in a theoretically not very interesting way—of
   "low levels" or "high levels" of the visual system, as we can in machine vision, where these
   levels mirror the way we have designed a system.
3. The physicalistic trap bears some relation to what, in classical psychophysics, Titchener
   called the "stimulus error", by which he meant problems that result from confusing mental
   aspects with aspects of the stimuli that give rise to them (see Boring, 1921).
4. This perspective is most explicit in the research programme of classical psychophysics.
   Stevens based his approach on a reference to elementary variables of physics, like length,
   weight, light intensity, or frequency of sound waves, and tried to construct for each of
   these variables a transformation that characterizes its subjective analogue. The perceptual
   system is conceived as some kind of measuring device for the textbook variables of physics.
   A theoretically more sophisticated form is the research perspective of R.D. Luce, who tried
   to establish a structure of interrelated subjective scales that allow a reduction to a simple
   pattern of units and simple connections with the scales of physics: an internal analogue of
   the dimensional structure of physics.

5. A variant of the measurement device concept is what Gilchrist called, with respect to brightness perception, the *photometer metaphor* (Gilchrist, 1994).

6. These insights, as right and important as they were, have encumbered further developments with an unfortunate and misleading cleavage of perception into "physiological" and "psychological" processes.

7. This may be exemplified by Buchsbaum and Gottschalk's (1983, p. 92) remark that *"The visual system is concerned with estimating the spectral functional shape of the incoming colour stimulus."*

8. It was in this form that it was taken up as the computational problem of arriving, on the basis of the sensory input, at colour designators of a scene that are invariant under different illumination (see Example V on p. 91f.). Though great conceptual advances and insights with respect to the development of an ecological physics have been brought forth by corresponding investigations, they also contributed to veiling the proper structure of the perceptual problem involved.

9. Whether we call a phenomenon an illusion depends on how sophisticated our ideas about the properties of internal coding are. The poorer the theoretical structure the greater the tendency is to guide expectations by a *measurement device conception* of perception. This can be illustrated by comparing the Müller–Lyer demonstration with Wallach's brightness demonstrations that underly the formulation of his ratio principle. The Wallach demonstrations refer to a situation that has, with respect to brightness, the same logical structure that the Müller–Lyer demonstration has with respect to length. While the Müller–Lyer demonstration is called an illusion, no one would, however, refer to the Wallach demonstration as a brightness illusion, which is rather considered as demonstrating a relational coding property of brightness.

10. Dretske's (1986) discussion of certain magnetotactic marine bacteria is also instructive in this respect. These bacteria use a physically contingent relation between geomagnetic north and oxygen-free water that holds in the northern hemisphere to orient themselves away from deadly oxygen-rich surface water (Blakemore & Frankel, 1981). Transplanting this kind of bacterium to the southern hemisphere results in a deadly "perceptual error", though "the magnetotactic system functions as it is supposed to function, as it was (presumably) evolved to function".

11. For each image there is, however, an infinity of potential physical processes that causally may have given rise to it. These are, as Koenderink et al. (2000, p. 183) expressed it, "related by some group of 'ambiguity transformations'. What this implies is that the orbit of the fiducial scene under the group of ambiguity transformations is a 'metamer' of the fiducial scene. (. . .) Thus all metameric scenes have an equal claim on the epithet 'veridical'!" Whence they rightly state, "It is the 'veridicality' question that makes no sense." There is, thus, no notion of a "true" vantage point that can figure in a formal theory of perception.

12. The idea of a "personal phenomenal space", i.e. a joint coherent spatial representation underlying judgments of distance, movement or orientation, has been called *The Tidy Mother model*—"a place for everything, and everything in its place"—by MacLeod. MacLeod and Willen (1995, p. 59) conclude from various empirical findings that "the notion of visual space, natural though it is, may not capture important realities of visual space perception".

13. The concept of the Alberti window is a purely physical one and does not refer—as the concept of a proximal stimulus does—to any properties of the observer. For the present purposes of conceptual clarification I can ignore problems that arise from the restriction to passive aspects of a merely visual input only, whereas in fact the internal data format is to a large extent transmodal and also reflects properties of an active observer.

14. Bayesian approaches also make clear that objects, 3-D shape, texture, shading, motion or stereo depth are not the input but rather the *output* of the visual system. "In short, the table, and all properties of it that I experience, are my conclusions. What holds for tables also holds for forks, suns, brains, and neurons. These are the products of perception, not the

antecedents. In perception, as a Bayesian would put it, we perceive only our posteriors" (Hoffman, 1996, pp. 219–220).

15. This is essentially Fodor's (1975, p. 80f.) argument that one cannot, by some mechanism of inductive inference, acquire "a conceptual system richer than the conceptual system that one starts with", i.e. a conceptual structure "whose predicates express extensions not expressible by predicates of the representational system" whose employment mediates the acquisition.

16. Even an extreme version of empiricism would have to assume that there is a set of given representational primitives; it would, however, assume that this set is exhausted by concepts used for the physical description of the sensory input.

17. The Bayesian framework as such, however, does not suggest these interpretations and is, in fact, perfectly compatible with sign theories of visual perception. In particular, an *internalist* version of the Bayesian framework can be formulated, which specifies computational procedures that mediate the relation between the sensory system (which deals with the transduction of physical energy into neural codes and their subsequent transformations into codes that are "readable" by and fulfil the needs of the perceptual system) and the perceptual system (which contains, as part of our biological endowment, the rich perceptual vocabulary—which extends far beyond physical aspects of the external world—in terms of which we perceive the "external world").

18. Rock (1983, p. 326).

19. The empiristic stance that pervades current inquiries into perception and other kinds of mental activity and which emphasizes plasticity and variations due to individual and cultural learning history seems to be a natural element of our common-sense reasoning about mental activity that we illegitimately transfer to scientific inquiry (cf. Chomsky, 2000, p. 163).

20. Cf. note 13.

21. An intriguing example of an internal functional constraint is the principle of genericity, which favours non-accidental interpretations over accidental ones (cf. Albert & Hoffman, 1995).

22. A felicitous description is, with respect to the mental entity "pictorial relief", given by Koenderink et al. (2000, p. 184): "The picture acts as a 'constraint' on the beholder's creativity." Koenderink et al. speak of a "true creative force and not simply a bag of tricks. (. . .) It is much as with 'Gestalt laws' of 'early vision': They are spontaneously acting (creative) forces rather than simple 'filters'." Three hundred years earlier, Cudworth (see Appendix) expressed basically the same thought: "Sense is but the offering and presenting of some object to the mind, to give it an occasion to exercise its own inward activity upon." In perceptual psychology similar ideas have been express time after time; they have suggested themselves first and foremost by the observation of the "wide gulf between sensory stimulus and percept" (von Szily, 1921, p. 971). The task of perceptual psychology then is to develop an explanatory framework to account for the "creative forces" (ibid., p. 971) of the perceptual system that mediate between sensory input and percept.

23. Among representational primitives pertaining to "objects" are, as corresponding evidence suggests, not only those that pertain to "physical objects" of various types but also a great variety of specific types that pertain to categories such as "intentional physical objects" "potential actors" "self", or "other person". Representational primitives pertaining to "events" can be expected to exhibit, as temporal analogs to "objects", a corresponding variety of different types.

24. From the extensive set of investigations that are of relevance in the present context I will only mention Landau et al. (1984), Carey & Spelke (1994), Spelke (1995), Meltzoff (1995), and Trevarthen (1998).

25. See Atherton's (this volume) historical analysis of the distinction between vision based on natural geometry and calculation-like processes vs. perception by signs, and Hatfield

(this volume) for a critical discussion of approaches that attribute sophisticated physical concepts to the visual system.

26. This view of Descartes was shared by Leibniz, who also argued, in his *New Essay Concerning Human Understanding,* "that our ideas, even those of sensible things, come from within our own soul".

27. This distinction became a very influential one in perceptual psychology, where it was used, e.g. by Spencer, James, Lotze, Wundt or Helmholtz, in the sense of referring to an alleged hierarchy of processing stages. According to James, for example, sensations and perception "shade gradually into each other, being one and all products of the same psychological machinery of association" (*Principles of Psychology,* ch. XIX).

REFERENCES

Albert, M.C. & Hoffman, D. (1995). Genericity in spatial vision. In R.D. Luce, M.D'Zmura, D. Hoffman, G.J. Iverson & A.K. Romney (Eds.) *Geometrical representations of perceptual phenomena* (pp. 95–112). Mahwah, NJ: Lawrence Erlbaum.

Arnauld, A. (1683/1990). On true and false ideas. New York: Edwin Mellen Press.

Barlow, H. (1961). Possible principles underlying the coding of sensory messages (pp. 217–234). In W. Rosenblith (Ed.) *Sensory communication.* Cambridge, Mass.: MIT Press.

Bennett, B.M., Hoffman, D.D. & Prakash, C. (1989). *Observer mechanics. A formal theory of perception.* San Diego: Academic Press.

Blakemore, R.P. & Frankel, R.B. (1981). Magnetic navigation in bacteria. *Scientific American,* **245**, 42–49.

Boring, E.G. (1921). The stimulus error. *The American Journal of Psychology,* **32**, 449–471.

Buchsbaum, G. & Gottschalk, A. (1993). Trichromacy, opponent colours coding and optimum colour information transmission in the retina. *Proceedings of the Royal Society London,* **B220**, 89–113.

Bühler, K. (1922). Die Erscheinungsweisen der Farben. In K. Bühler (Ed.) *Handbuch der Psychologie. I. Teil. Die Struktur der Wahrnehmungen* (pp. 1–201). Jena: Fischer.

Carey, S. & Spelke, E.S. (1994). Domain-specific knowledge and conceptual change. In L.A. Hirschfeld & S.A. Gelman (Eds.) *Mapping the mind. Domain specificity in cognition and culture* (pp.169–200). Cambridge: Cambridge University Press.

Cassirer, E. (1929). *Philosophie der symbolischen Formen. Dritter Teil: Phänomenologie der Erkenntnis.* Berlin: Bruno Cassirer.

Cassirer, E. (1944). The concept of group and the theory of perception. *Philosophy and Phenomenological Research,* **5**, 1–35.

Chomsky, N. (1966). *Cartesian linguistics. A chapter in the history of rationalist thought.* New York: Harper & Row.

Chomsky, N. (1996). *Power and prospect. Reflections on human nature and the social order.* London: Pluto Press.

Chomsky, N. (2000). *New horizons in the study of language and mind.* Cambridge: Cambridge University Press.

Cudworth, R. (1731). *A treatise concerning eternal and immutable morality.* London: James and John Knapton (reprinted 1976 by Garland, New York).

Dretske, F. (1986) Misrepresentation. In R.J. Bogdan (Ed.) *Belief: Form, Content, and Function* (pp.17–36). Oxford: Oxford University Press.

Fodor, J.A. (1975). *The language of thought.* Cambridge, Mass.: Harvard University Press.

Gallistel, C.R. (1998). Symbolic processes in the brain: the case of insect navigation. In D. Scarborough & S. Sternberg (Eds.) *Methods, models and conceptual issues. An invitation to cognitive science* (vol. 4, pp. 1–15). Cambridge, Mass.: MIT Press.

Gelb, A. (1929). Die "Farbenkonstanz" der Sehdinge. In A. Bethe, G.v. Bergmann, G. Embden & A. Ellinger (Eds.) *Handbuch der normalen und pathologischen Physiologie*. Bd. 12, 1. Hälfte. Receptionsorgane II (pp. 594–678). Berlin: Springer.

Gelb, A. (1932). Die Erscheinungen des simultanen Kontrastes und der Eindruck der Feldbeleuchtung. *Zeitschrift für Psychologie*, **127**, 42–59.

Gilchrist, A.L. (1994). Theories of lightness perception. In A.L. Gilchrist (Ed.) *Lightness, brightness, and transparency* (pp. 1–34). Hillsdale, NJ: Lawrence Erlbaum.

Gombrich, E.H. (1982). *The image and the eye*. Oxford: Phaidon Press.

Hassenstein, B. & Reichardt, W. (1956). Systemtheoretische Analyse der Zeit, Reihenfolge und Vorzeichenauswertung bei der Bewegungsperzeption des Rüsselkäfers Chlorophanus. *Zeitschrift für Naturforschung*, **11b**, 513–524.

Hatfield, G. (1990). *The natural and the normative. Theories of spatial perception from Kant to Helmholtz*. Cambridge, Mass.: MIT Press.

Heider, F. (1930). Die Leistungen des Wahrnehmungssystems. *Zeitschrift für Psychologie*, **114**, 371–394.

Helmholtz, H. v. (1855). Über das Sehen des Menschen. In *Vorträge und Reden*, 4. Aufl., Bd.1, 1896. Braunschweig: Vieweg.

Helmholtz, H. v. (1867). *Handbuch der Physiologischen Optik*. Hamburg: Voss.

Helmholtz, H. v. (1868). Die neueren Fortschritte in der Theorie des Sehens. In *Vorträge und Reden*, 4. Aufl., Bd. 1, 1896. Braunschweig: Vieweg.

Helmholtz, H. v. (1869). Ueber das Ziel und die Fortschritte der Naturwissenschaft. In *Vorträge und Reden*, 4. Aufl., Bd. 1, 1896. Braunschweig: Vieweg.

Helmholtz, H. v. (1878). Die Thatsachen in der Wahrnehmung. In *Vorträge und Reden*, 4. Aufl., Bd. 2, 1896. Braunschweig: Vieweg.

Helmholtz, H. v. (1894). Ueber den Ursprung der richtigen Deutung unserer Sinneseindrücke. *Zeitschrift für Psychologie und Physiologie der Sinnesorgane*, **7**, 81–96.

Hering, E. (1920). *Grundzüge der Lehre vom Lichtsinn*. Berlin: Springer.

Hochberg, J. (1980). Pictorial function and perceptual structure. In M.A. Hagen (Ed.) *The perception of pictures* (vol. II, pp. 47–93). New York: Academic Press.

Hoffman, D.D. (1996). What do we mean by "Structure of the World"? In D.C. Knill & W. Richards (Eds.) *Perception as Bayesian inference* (pp. 219–221). New York: Cambridge University Press.

Kardos, L. (1934). *Ding und Schatten. Eine experimentelle Untersuchung über die Grundlagen des Farbensehens*. Leipzig: Barth.

Knill, D.C., Kersten D. & Mamassian, P. (1996). Implications of a Bayesian formulation of visual information for processing for psychophysics. In D.C. Knill & W. Richards (Eds.) *Perception as Bayesian inference* (pp. 239–286). New York: Cambridge University Press.

Knill, D.C. & Richards W. (Eds.) (1996). *Perception as Bayesian inference*. New York: Cambridge University Press.

Kemp, M. (1990). *The Science of Art. Optical Themes in Western Art from Brunelleschi to Seurat*. New Haven, CT: Yale University Press.

Koenderink, J.J. (1998). Pictorial relief. *Philosophical Transactions of the Royal Society London*, **A356**, 1071–1086.

Koenderink, J.J. & van Doorn, A.J. (1998). Exocentric pointing. In L.R. Harris & M. Jenkin (Eds.) *Vision and action* (pp. 295–313). Cambridge: Cambridge University Press.

Koenderink, J.J., van Doorn, A.J. & Kappers, A. (2000). Surfaces in the mind's eye. In R. Cipolla & R. Martin (Eds.) *The Mathematics of Surfaces IX* (pp. 180–193). London: Springer.

Koffka, K. (1932). Some remarks on the theory of colour constancy. *Psychologische Forschung*, **16**, 329–354.

Landau, B., Spelke, E.S. & Gleitman H. (1984). Spatial knowledge in a young blind child. *Cognition*, **16**, 225–260.

Lewontin, R.C. (1998). The evolution of cognition: Questions we will never answer. In D. Scarborough & S. Sternberg (Eds.) *An invitation to cognitive science: Methods, models, and conceptual Issues* (pp. 107–132). Cambridge, Mass.: MIT Press.

Lindberg, D.C. (1976). *Theories of vision form Al-Kindi to Kepler.* Chicago: University of Chicago Press.

MacLeod, R.B. (1932). An experimental investigation of brightness constancy. *Archives of Psychology*, **135**, 5–102.

MacLeod, D.I.A. & Willen, J.D. (1995). Is there a visual space? In R.D. Luce, M. D'Zmura, D. Hoffman, G.J. Iverson & A.K. Romney (Eds.) *Geometrical representations of perceptual phenomena* (pp. 47–60). Mahwah, NJ: Lawrence Erlbaum.

Mausfeld, R. (1998). Color perception: From Grassmann codes to a dual code for object and illumination colors. In W. Backhaus, R. Kliegl & J. Werner (Eds.) *Color Vision* (pp. 219–250). Berlin/New York: De Gruyter.

Mausfeld, R. (in press-a). The dual coding of colour: "Surface colour" and "Illumination colour" as constituents of the representational format of perceptual primitives. In R. Mausfeld & D. Heyer (Eds.) *Colour perception: From light to object.* Oxford: Oxford University Press.

Mausfeld, R. (in press-b). Cojoint representations and the mental capacity for multiple simultaneous perspectives. In H. Hecht, R. Schwartz & M. Atherton (Eds.) (in press) *Looking into pictures: An interdisciplinary approach to pictorial space.* Cambridge, Mass.: MIT Press.

Mausfeld, R. & Andres, J. (2002). Second order statistics of colour codes modulate transformations that effective varying degrees of scene invariance and illumination invariance. *Perception*, **31**, 209–224.

Mausfeld, R. & Niederée, R. (1993). Inquiries into relational concepts of colour based on an incremental principle of colour coding for minimal relational stimuli. *Perception*, **22**, 427–462.

Meltzoff, A.N. (1995). Understanding the intentions of others: Re-enactment of intended acts by 18-month-old children. *Developmental Psychology*, **31**, 838–850.

Michotte, A. (1946). *La perception de la causalité.* Louvain: Fondation Universitaire de Belgique.

Michotte, A. (1948). L'énigma psychologique de la perspective dans le dessin linéaire. *Bulletin de la Classe des Lettres de l'Académie Royale de Belgique*, **34**, 268–288.

Nakayama, K., He, Z.J. & Shimojo, S. (1995). Visual surface representation: A critical link between lower-level and higher-level vision. In S.M. Kosslyn & D.N. Osherson (Eds.) *Visual cognition. An invitation to cognitive sciences* (vol. 2, pp. 1–70). Cambridge, Mass.: MIT Press.

Passmore, J.A. (1951). *Ralph Cudworth: An interpretation.* Cambridge: Cambridge University Press.

Poggio, T. (1990). Vision: The "other" face of AI. In K.A. Mohyeldin Said, W.H. Newton-Smith, R. Viale & K.V. Wilkes (Eds.) *Modelling the mind* (pp.139–154). Oxford: Clarendon Press.

Premack, D. & Premack, A.J. (1995). Intention as psychological cause. In D. Sperber, D. Premack & A.J. Premack (Eds.) *Causal cognition* (pp. 185–199). Oxford: Clarendon.

Richards, W. (1996). Priors by design. In D.C. Knill & W. Richards (Eds.) *Perception as Bayesian inference* (pp. 225–228). New York: Cambridge University Press.

Rock, I. (1983). *The logic of perception.* Cambridge, Mass.: MIT Press.

Rodgers, S. (1995). Perceiving pictorial space. In W. Epstein & S. Rogers (Eds.) *Perception of space and motion* (pp. 119–163). San Diego: Academic Press.

Rubin, E. (1921). *Visuell wahrgenommene Figuren.* Kopenhagen: Gyldendalske Boghandel.

Sabra, A.I. (1989). The optics of Ibn Al-Haytham, Books I–III. On direct vision. Translation and commentary, 2 vols. London: The Warburg Institute.

Scholl, B.J. & Tremoulet, P.D. (2000). Perceptual causality and animacy. *Trends in Cognitive Science*, **4**, 299–309.

Schöne, W. (1954). *Über das Licht in der Malerei*. Berlin: Gebr. Mann.

Sedgwick, H.A. (1986). Space perception. In K.R. Boff, L. Kaufman & J.P. Thomas (Eds.) *Handbook of perception and human performance, vol. I. Sensory processes and perception*. New York: Wiley.

Shepard, R.N. (1987). Evolution of a mesh between principles of the world and regularities of the world. In J. Dupré (Ed.) *The latest on the best. Essays on evolution and optimality* (pp. 251–275), Cambridge, Mass.: Bradford.

Shepard, R.N. (1994). Perceptual-cognitive universals as reflections of the world. *Psychonomic Bulletin & Review*, **1**, 2–28.

Smith, B. & Casati, R. (1994). Naive physics. *Philosophical Psychology*, **7**, 227–247.

Spelke, E.S. (1995). Initial knowledge: Six suggestions. In J. Mehler & S. Franck (Eds.) *Cognition on cognition* (pp. 433–447). Cambridge, Mass.: MIT Press.

Streri, A., Spelke, E.S. & Rameix, E. (1993). Modality-specific and amodal aspects of object perception in infancy: The case of active touch. *Cognition*, **47**, 251–279.

Taine, H. (1875). *On Intelligence,* (Vol. II. New York: Henry Holt.

Tolman, E.C. & Brunswik, E. (1935). The organism and the causal texture of the environment. *Psychological Review*, **42**, 43–77.

Trevarthen, C. (1998). The concept and foundations of infant intersubjectivity. In S. Bråten (Ed.) *Intersubjective communication and emotion in early ontogeny* (pp. 15–46). Cambridge: Cambridge University Press.

von Szily, A. (1921). Stereoskopische Versuche mit Schattenrissen. *Gräfes Archiv für Ophtalmologie*, **105**, 964–972.

Yolton, J.W. (1984). *Perceptual acquaintance from Descartes to Reid*. Minneapolis: University of Minnesota Press.

Part II

Unconscious Inferences
and Bayesian Approaches

5

Perception as Unconscious Inference

GARY HATFIELD

Department of Philosophy, University of Pennsylvania, USA

Consider for a moment the spatial and chromatic dimensions of your visual experience. Suppose that as you gaze about the room you see a table, some books, and papers. Ignore for now the fact that you immediately recognize these objects to be a table with books and papers on it. Concentrate on how the table looks to you: its top spreads out in front of you, stopping at edges beyond which lies unfilled space, leading to more or less distant chairs, shelves, or expanses of floor. The books and paper on the table top create shaped visual boundaries between areas of different color, within which there may be further variation of color or visual texture. Propelled by a slight breeze, a sheet of paper slides across the table, and you experience its smooth motion before it floats out of sight.

The aspects of visual perception to which I've drawn your attention are objects of study in contemporary perceptual psychology, which considers the perception of size, shape, distance, motion, and color. These phenomenal aspects of vision are sometimes contrasted with other, more typically cognitive aspects of perception, including our recognition that the objects in front of us include the table, books, and paper, our seeing that the table is old and well crafted, and our identifying the sheets of paper as the draft of an article in progress. All of these elements of our visual experience, whether characterized here as phenomenal or cognitive,[1] seem to arise effortlessly as we direct our gaze here and there. Yet we know that the cognitive aspects must depend on previously attained knowledge. We are not born recognizing books and tables, but we learn to categorize these artifacts and to determine at a glance that a table is an old one of good quality. What about the phenomenal aspects?

A persistent theme in the history of visual theory has been that the phenomenal aspects of visual perception are produced by inferences or judgments, which are

Perception and the Physical World: Psychological and Philosophical Issues in Perception.
Edited by Dieter Heyer and Rainer Mausfeld. © 2002 John Wiley & Sons, Ltd.

unnoticed or unconscious. The persistence of this theme is interesting because, unlike our capacity to recognize a book or to identify something as the draft we have been working on, simply having a phenomenal experience of surfaces arranged in space and varying in color does not obviously require prior knowledge (even though describing such experience does). Nor does such experience seem on the face of it to be the product of reasoning or inference, such as we might employ in reasoning from the fact that our friend's books are lying open on the table to the conclusion that she is about. Nonetheless, from ancient times theorists have accounted for visual perception of the size, shape, distance, motion, and (sometimes) color of objects in terms of judgment and inference.

Hermann Helmholtz (1867/1910) provided the paradigm modern statement of the theory that visual perception is mediated by unconscious inferences. His name is frequently invoked by recent advocates of the theory (Barlow, 1990; Gregory, 1997, p. 5; Hochberg, 1981; Rock, 1983, p. 16; Wandell, 1995, pp. 7, 336). Helmholtz maintained that perception draws on the same cognitive mechanisms as do ordinary reasoning and scientific inference (1867/1910, 3: 28–29), and some theorists make similar comparisons (Barlow, 1974; Gregory, 1997, pp. 9–13). Others in the twentieth century have argued that perception is not literally inferential but is "like inference" or "ratiomorphic" (Brunswik, 1956, pp. 141–146), while still others postulate special-purpose inferential mechanisms in perception, isolated from ordinary reasoning and knowledge (Gregory, 1974, pp. 205, 210; Nakayama et al., 1995, p. 2; Rock, 1983, ch. 11).

In this chapter I examine past and recent theories of unconscious inference. Most theorists have ascribed inferences to perception literally, not analogically, and I focus on the literal approach. I examine three problems faced by such theories if their commitment to unconscious inferences is taken seriously. Two problems concern the cognitive resources that must be available to the visual system (or a more central system) to support the inferences in question. The third problem focuses on how the conclusions of inferences are supposed to explain the phenomenal aspects of visual experience, the looks of things. Finally, in comparing past and recent responses to these problems, I provide an assessment of the current prospects for inferential theories.

UNCONSCIOUS INFERENCES
IN THEORIES OF PERCEPTION

The idea that unnoticed judgments underlie perception has been in the literature of visual science at least since the *Optics* of Ptolemy (ca. 160; see Ptolemy, 1989, 1996). In the past millennium, Alhazen (ca. 1030; 1989), Helmholtz (1867/1910), and Rock (1983) have offered explicit versions of the theory that perception results from unconscious inferences, in the form of (respectively) syllogisms, inductive inferences, and deductions in predicate logic. I will sometimes apply the term "unconscious inference" to all such theories, despite the fact that this technical term was introduced by Helmholtz (in a German equivalent), and despite variations in theorists' characterizations of such inferences, which are noted as needed. To give some sense of the range of theories, I begin by briefly examining two areas: size and distance perception, and color constancy.

PERCEPTION OF SIZE AT A DISTANCE

Prior to the development of new conceptions of optical information by Gibson (1966) and their extension by Marr (1982), theories of the perception of size relied on a common analysis of the stimulus for vision. One element of this analysis was contributed by Euclid (fourth century B.C.; 1945), who equated apparent size with the visual angle subtended at the eye. Five centuries later, Ptolemy argued that the perception of an object's size depends on both visual angle and perception or knowledge of the object's distance (1989, 1996, II.56). Surviving versions of his work illustrate the problem, as in Figure 5.1. The eye at E sees objects AB and GD under the same visual angle. If size were determined by visual angle alone, the two objects would appear to have the same size. But, Ptolemy says, when the difference in distance is detectable, such objects do not appear to be of the same size, but are seen with their real sizes (if our apprehension of the distance is accurate). Ptolemy was an extramission theorist who held that the crystalline humor (now known as the lens) is the sensitive element in the eye; he argued that the eye sends something out into the air, which allows the eye to feel the length of visual rays such as EA or EG (Ptolemy, 1989, 1996, II.26). Leaving aside the direct apprehension of distance, his position on the relation between visual angle and distance in size perception was accepted by subsequent authors, whether extramissionists or intromissionists, and whether they believed the crystalline or the retina is the sensitive element. Indeed, the geometrical analysis of the perception of size-at-a-distance was unaffected by Kepler's discovery that the lens causes inverted images to be formed on the retinas (see Hatfield & Epstein, 1979).

Ptolemy made only brief allusion to the judgments he posited for combining visual angle and distance in size perception. Nearly a millennium later, Alhazen (Ibn al-Haytham) developed an extended analysis of such judgments (Alhazen, 1989). According to Alhazen, the sense of sight perceives only light and color through "pure sensation" (1989, II.3.25). Alhazen was an intromission theorist, who held that the

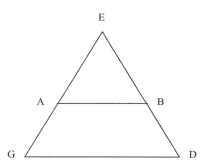

Figure 5.1

eye receives and transmits into the brain a cross-section of the visual pyramid, which constitutes a two-dimensional, point-for-point ordered record of the field of view (1989, I.6.22–32). In receiving this cross-section, the sense of sight also registers the direction from which the light and color comes (1989, II.3.97), and so has available the visual angle subtended by an object. The faculty of judgment then combines visual angle and distance information, through an "inference and judgment" that has become habitual, rapid, and unnoticed, to yield a perception of the size of an object that takes distance into account (1989, II.3.145–148).

Although the Euclidean equation of apparent size with visual angle was sometimes rehearsed in subsequent literature (e.g., Chambers, 1738, vol. 1, "Apparent magnitude"; Smith, 1738, 1: 31–32), Alhazen's view that size perception depends on rapid, unnoticed judgments that combine perceived distance with visual angle became standard doctrine. The judgmental account of size perception was repeated in diverse works, including those of Descartes (1637/1984–85, pt. 6), Rohault (1735, 1: 254), Porterfield (1759, 2: 377–380), Le Cat (1767, 2: 441–484, especially 471–484), and Gehler (1787–96, 2: 537–542). Berkeley (1709) rejected the judgmental account, arguing that the perceptual processes leading to size and distance perception are mediated by association, not by judgment or inference. Helmholtz combined aspects of the judgmental and associative accounts by proposing that size perception results from unconscious inference while giving an associative analysis of the process of inference itself (1867/1910, 3: 24, 236–237, 242, 434, 439). More recently, neo-Helmholtzians have used the language of inference without association (Gregory, 1997; Rock, 1983), and so in fact are in the tradition of Ptolemy and Alhazen. Others have developed a subjectivist probabilistic analysis of perceptual inference (Bennett et al., 1989).

COLOR CONSTANCY

The tendency of observers to perceive objects as having a constant size at various distances despite variations in the visual angle they subtend at the eye was dubbed "size constancy" in the twentieth century. A similar constancy occurs in the case of color. We typically see objects as having the same color (e.g., as being the same shade of blue) under varying conditions of illumination (e.g., in sunlight and under artificial lighting). There is, within limits, constancy of perceived color under variations in the intensity and color of the ambient light.

Alhazen produced an early description of color constancy. He observed that light reflected by an object is modified by the color of the object. As he put it, the quality of the light and of the object are "mingled" in the light that reaches the eye. Through a cognitive act, the perceiver is able to separate light and color:

> from perceiving the variations of lights falling upon visible objects, and from perceiving that objects are sometimes luminous and sometimes not, the faculty of judgement perceives that the colours in these objects are not the same as the lights that supervene upon them. Then, as this notion is repeated, it is established in the soul, as a universal, that colours in coloured objects are not the same as their lights. (Alhazen, 1989, II.3.48)

Alhazen indicated that through experience the faculty of judgment learns the characteristics of various forms of illumination (1989, II.3.50). He presumably held that it then is able to separate the color of the object from the quality of the illumination.

Unlike size and shape constancy, color constancy did not become standard fare in the early modern literature and was prominently discussed starting only in the nineteenth century.[2] Twentieth-century theorists have been fascinated by color constancy and achromatic brightness constancy, and some hold that the fundamental task of color perception is to extract information about the reflectance properties of objects from the light reaching the eyes. Specifically, many investigators formulate the task of the visual system in color constancy as that of recovering the spectral reflectance distribution of surfaces. A spectral reflectance distribution describes the percentage of ambient light of differing wavelengths reflected by a surface. It thus gives a precise physical description of the property of objects that gives them color: the disposition to absorb and reflect differing amounts of light as a function of wavelength. If we represent this distribution by R, let I stand for the spectral composition of the illuminant and L for that of the light reaching the eyes, then $L = I*R$. The problem for the visual system is to disambiguate I and R, which requires additional information or background assumptions.

Maloney and Wandell formulate the problem of color constancy as that of "estimating the surface reflectance functions of objects in a scene with incomplete knowledge of the spectral power distribution of the ambient light" (1986, p. 29). They show that approximate color constancy is possible if the visual system uses the fact that many natural surfaces can be modeled as linear combinations of a small number of "basis functions" (spectral reflectance functions), and if the range of ambient light is also describable as a linear combination of a small number of basis functions. That is, they suggest that the visual system makes limiting assumptions about the composition of natural illuminants and the shapes of surface reflection functions, which allow it to make nearly accurate estimates of distal surface reflectance distributions on the basis of the incoming light. On this view, the goal of color constancy is to generate a physical description of the spectrophotometric properties of distal surfaces. In a recent theoretical survey of linear models and other computational approaches to color constancy, Hurlbert (1998) endorsed this conception of the aim of color constancy, arguing that since "spectral reflectance is an invariant property of surfaces," it is therefore "plausible, if not perfectly logical, to assume that color constancy results from the attempt to recover spectral reflectance in the more general pursuit of object recognition" (1998, p. 283).

PROBLEMS FOR UNCONSCIOUS INFERENCE THEORIES

In order to count as a psychological or perceptual *theory*, a description of visual perception as involving unconscious inferences must do more than simply compare perceptual processes to the making of inferences. It must do such things as the following: describe the premises of such inferences, say how the premises come to be instantiated, account for the process of inference from premises to conclusions, describe the conclusions, and say how arrival at the conclusion constitutes or explains perception.

My own reflections on theories of unconscious perceptual inference indicate that they face (at least) three challenging problems. First, since they attribute unconscious inferences to the perceptual system, they must account for the cognitive resources needed to carry them out. Are the unconscious inferences posited to explain size perception and color constancy carried out by the same cognitive mechanisms that account for conscious and deliberate inferences, or does the visual system have its own inferential machinery? In either case, what is the structure of the posited mechanisms? This is the *cognitive machinery problem*. Second, how shall we describe the content of the premises and conclusions? For instance, in size perception it might be that the premises include values for visual angle and perceived distance, along with a representation of the algorithm relating the two. Or in color constancy, the conclusion might describe a spectral reflectance distribution. But shall we literally attribute concepts of visual angle and wavelength to the visual system? This is the *sophisticated content problem*. Third, to be fully explanatory, unconscious inference theories of perception must explain how the conclusion of an inference about size and distance leads to the experience of an object as having a certain size and being at a certain distance, or how a conclusion about a spectral reflectance distribution yields the experience of a specific hue. In other words, the theories need to explain how the conclusion to an inference, perhaps conceived linguistically, can be or can cause visual experience, with its imagistic quality.[3] This is the *phenomenal experience problem*.

COGNITIVE MACHINERY

Inferential theories typically posit an early sensory representation that differs from ordinary perception in its portrayal of various properties of objects. This original sensory representation, or sensation, might represent the shape of an object as a two-dimensional projection, so that a circle tilted away from the observer would be represented as an ellipse. Judgment or inference would then be called upon to mediate the change in representation from sensation to perception—in this case, to the perception of the true (circular) shape. The means for carrying out such inferences need to be specified, and the long history of inferential theories has seen various conceptions of the psychological processes thought to be involved.[4]

Although Ptolemy assigned a role to judgment in the apprehension of size, he provided little analysis of such judgments, simply referring them to a "governing faculty" or "discerning power" (1989, 1996, II.22–23, 76). Alhazen, by contrast, carefully analyzed the role of judgment in perception (1989, II.3.1–42). He contended that any perceptual act beyond the passive apprehension of light and color requires judgment or inference. Such acts include recognition of color categories (as opposed to mere sensations of color), perception of similarity or dissimilarity between objects, and perception of distance. Further, the judgments or inferences in question typically require comparison with previous instances (in the case of acts of recognition), or depend on previous learning (as when the known size of an object is used together with visual angle to judge distance). But since on his view the senses themselves do not judge, compare, or learn from previous instances (1989, II.3.17–25), the faculty of judgment must enter into perception.

Judgmental theories are faced with the fact that if perception relies on judgments, the judgments go unnoticed. In providing an explanation of this fact, Alhazen gave his fullest description of the judgments themselves. He began by contrasting the unnoticed judgments of perception with the visual theorist's careful and deliberate judgment that perception is judgmental (1989, II.3.26, 30, 36). The former judgments are rapid and habitual, the latter slow and reflective. In ordinary acts of perceiving we do not usually undertake the slow and reflective act of determining that, say, the perception of size requires a judgment. We therefore remain unaware that a rapid and habitual judgment has occurred. Alhazen nonetheless argued that unnoticed perceptual judgments are carried out by the same "faculty of judgment" involved in all judgments, including conscious ones. He further contended that perceptual judgments are equivalent to syllogistic inferences (1989, II.3.27–42). This identification of the process of perception with logical inference required further explanation, since perception is on the face of it not linguistic, whereas syllogisms apparently are.

Alhazen explained away this apparent dissimilarity between perception and inference by arguing that ordinary syllogistic inferences need not be properly linguistic, either. He contended that syllogistic inferences of the sort that can be expressed by a verbal syllogism need not be and typically are not actually produced in explicit linguistic form. He compared the rapid inferences of perception to cases in which we reach a conclusion rapidly, without consciously entertaining any logical steps. In one of his examples, upon hearing someone exclaim "How effective this sword is!" the listener immediately understands that the sword is sharp. She does so on the basis of the universal premise "Every effective sword is sharp". But the conclusion is achieved "without the need for words or for repeating and ordering the premises, or the need for repeating and ordering the words" (1989, II.3.28). As Alhazen explained, in neither perception nor in the sword example (where one premise is given verbally) does the faculty of judgment need to formulate an explicit syllogism using words in order for it to carry out an inference. Rather, from the moment it understands the content of the particular premise, given that it remembers the content of the universal, it immediately understands the conclusion (1989, II.3.29). Alhazen would seem to suggest that in both sorts of case the faculty of judgment operates from a non-linguistic grasp of the content of premises and conclusions. Accordingly, he could claim that the same judgmental capacity which underlies our rapid understanding of everyday events serves as the cognitive machinery for perception. It carries out its operations by grasping content directly, and does not require linguistic form.

Five centuries later the philosopher and mathematician René Descartes, who wrote in an optical tradition continuous with Alhazen, appealed to unnoticed processes of reasoning in explaining size, shape, and distance perception.[5] In his *Optics* Descartes explained that the size of objects is judged "by the knowledge or opinion we have of their distance, compared with the size of the images they imprint on the back of the eye—and not simply by the size of these images" (1637/1984–85, 1: 172).

In the sixth set of Replies to Objections to the *Meditations*, he explained that these judgments, though rapid and habitual, are made "in exactly the same way as those we make now" (1641/1984–85, 2: 295). Descartes held that sensation yields an image whose elements vary (at least) in size, shape, and color. As infants, we gain habits for judging the size, shape, distance, and color of distant objects on the basis of such images. Apprehension of shapes, size, and color in the images, as well as other relevant information (such as eye position), provide the content of the minor premises of our perceptual inferences. The major premises are rules such as the one relating size, visual angle, and distance. Through repetition the transition from visual angle and distance information to the experience of an object's size becomes habitual and so is no longer recognized as being judgmentally based. Nonetheless, Descartes affirmed that both the unnoticed judgments of perception and the reflective judgments of the mature thinker are carried out by the same cognitive mechanism, which he described as the faculty of intellect.

The fact that Descartes and Alhazen (and many others) proffered a faculty analysis of mind has been seen as an embarrassment. Such analyses were later ridiculed in the manner of Molière's famous jest in which a doctor says that opium makes people sleepy because it has a dormitive virtue (Molière, 1673/1965, p. 143). Such jokes, and the easy dismissal of faculty psychology, fail to distinguish two potential aims of faculty theories, only one of which is sometimes laughable. Molière's joke plays on the idea that a physician has sought to *explain* how opium puts people to sleep by appealing to its dormitive virtue, rather than simply to *describe* its power to do so. Now it may well be that some of those ascribing "faculties" or "powers" to things understood this to be an inherently explanatory act, as it may be in some circumstances (see Hutchison, 1991). But in other cases talk of powers is descriptive and taxonomic, and amounts to a nontrivial parsing of the real capacities of things. In the case of Alhazen's and Descartes' appeal to the intellectual faculty, Molière's joke would apply to them only if they tried to explain how the mind reasons by saying it has a faculty of reason. Instead I see their efforts as part of an attempt to analyze the mind into a set of primitive capacities that are then used to explain particular abilities. So, in the case of size perception, a seemingly pure sensory ability is explained by appealing to an interaction between the capacity for rational inference and the passive reception of sensory information. The mind's capacity for rational inference is invoked to explain how sensations are transformed or supplanted to yield perceptions of shape. The judgmental capacity itself is not explained.

One might expect that since Descartes argued that the same intellectual faculty is involved in perception and other reasoning he would hold that perceptual judgments are subject to modification and correction in relation to consciously entertained knowledge. But he (in effect) admitted the opposite. In the familiar illusion of the straight stick that appears bent when half submerged in water, Descartes held that the appearance results from unnoticed judgments (habits of judging visual position) learned in childhood (1641/1984–85, 2: 295–296). When an adult suffers the illusion, the intellect operates by habit, without forming a new judgment for the occasion. At the same time, the intellect is able, by reflecting on its tactual experience, to know that the stick is really straight. Descartes wrote with full appreciation of the fact that this judgment does not affect the appearance of the stick. In general, the unnoticed judgments he posited to explain perception were not open to conscious revision. Later, Immanuel Kant drew explicit attention to the fact that the moon illusion is impervious to knowledge, presumably because the judgments that underlie it are habitual and unnoticed and so not open to scrutiny or correction (Kant, 1787/1998, pp. 384, 386; see Hatfield, 1990, pp. 105–106).

Berkeley introduced a new position into the psychology of visual perception when he sought to replace the accepted judgmental account of the processes underlying perception with an associational account. Motivated in part by a desire to support his immaterialist metaphysics (Atherton, 1990, ch. 12), Berkeley rethought visual theory from the ground up, focusing on the psychology of vision. He began from a point that was shared by intromission theorists, that distance is not "immediately sensed" (as Ptolemy, an extramissionist, had held), but must be perceived via other cues or sources of information, whether contained in the optical pattern or received collaterally (as in feelings from the ocular musculature). In Berkeley's terms, since distance is not directly perceived, it must be perceived "by means of some other idea" (1709, sec. 11). From there, he mounted a frontal assault on the widely shared theory that distance is perceived via "lines and angles", as when distance is allegedly perceived by reasoning using the angle–side–angle relation of a triangle and the perceived convergence of the eyes, or using the known size of the object together with perceived visual angle. Berkeley's argument unfolded in two steps. First, he maintained that "no idea which is not itself perceived can be the means for perceiving any other idea" (1709, sec. 10). Second, he denied that we are ever aware of "lines and angles" in visual perception: "In vain shall all the mathematicians in the world tell me that I perceive certain lines and angles which introduce into my mind the various ideas of distance so long as I myself am conscious of no such thing" (1709, sec. 12). He explained the perception of distance by means of several cues, including: (1) the interposition of numerous objects between the viewer and the target object (1709, sec. 3; 1733, sec. 62); (2) faintness of the target (1709, sec. 3; 1733, sec. 62); (3) visible magnitude in relation to known size (1733, sec. 62); (4) height in visual field (objects further off are typically higher in the field of vision but below the horizon; 1733, sec. 62); and (5) the muscular sensation accompanying the rotation of the eyes during convergence (1709, sec. 16; 1733, sec. 66).

Counterparts to each of these five cues were in the optical literature. Berkeley departed from previous accounts in contending that in none of the cases is there a "rational" or "necessary" connection between cue and perceived distance. The various factors listed in (1) to (5) serve, in his view, as so many arbitrary visual signs, whose meanings with respect to tactually perceived distance must be learned. For example, for angle–side–angle reasoning in distance perception he substituted an acquired association between ocular muscle feelings and tactually perceived distance (1709, secs. 12–20). Such associations, or connections of "suggestion", are formed between two ideas that regularly co-occur. They are not the result of a cognitive connection judged to exist between the perceived contents of the ideas, but arise solely from repeated co-occurrence. But, Berkeley argued, connections made through blind habit are distinct from (content-sensitive) inferences (1733, sec. 42). His process of habitual connection or suggestion is equivalent to what became more widely known as the association of ideas.

Berkeley is the originator of the associationist account of distance perception. He also made famous the position that we "learn to see" objects in depth at a distance. In the 150 years after he wrote, various judgmental or associationist accounts of perception were proposed. Some authors took the analysis of perceptual experience into sensational ingredients even further than Berkeley, and attempted to show how spatial representations could be derived form aspatial or punctiform elementary sensations via association (Steinbuch, 1811) or via a combination of reasoning and association (Brown, 1824, lecs. 22–24, 28–29). Others adopted the radical analysis of spatial perception into aspatial elements, but posited innate laws of sensibility (distinct from judgment and inference) to govern the construction of spatial representations (Tourtual, 1827). In each case, the authors supposed that each nerve fiber in the optic nerve produces a single sensation, varying only in quality and intensity. Meanwhile, the textbooks repeated the older account that size perception starts from an innately given two-dimensional representation and proceeds via unnoticed judgments (see Hatfield, 1990, ch. 4).

In the latter half of the nineteenth century, Helmholtz formulated the classical statement of the theory that spatial perception results from unconscious inferences. The primary statement of the theory occurred in section 26 of his *Handbuch der physiologischen Optik* (1867/1910). Helmholtz combined the associative and inferential accounts by giving an associational account of inference. He compared the inferences of perception to syllogisms in which the major premise has been established inductively. He adopted the radical punctiform analysis of visual sensation. In his account, stimulation of any given retinal nerve fiber initially yields a sensation that varies in only three ways: hue, intensity, and "local sign". A local sign is a qualitative marker peculiar to each nerve fiber (Helmholtz 1867/1910, 3: 130, 435–436). These signs originally carry no spatial meaning, but through coordination with bodily motion and sensations of touch (which are assumed to have spatial meaning) the observer acquires the ability (unconsciously) to localize sensations on the basis of local signs. For example, the observer might acquire a universal premise that light hitting the right side of the retina comes from the left (1867/1910, 3: 24). Helmholtz described the process of learning the spatial meaning of local signs in terms of active testing, and compared it to hypothesis testing in science. But in both cases he conceived the psychological processes that yield inductive conclusions from testing as associative. In the case of learning the meaning of local signs via touch, Helmholtz maintained that "while in these cases no actual conscious inference is present, yet the essential and original office of an inference has been performed" (1867/1910, 3: 24).[6] The inference is achieved "simply, of course, by the unconscious processes of the association of ideas going on in the dark background of our memory" (1867/1910, 3: 24). In this way, Helmholtz assimilated inference to association.[7]

The most explicit recent analysis of unconscious inferences in perception is due to Irvin Rock (1983). Rock identified four sorts of cognitive operations at work in perception: (1) unconscious description, in the case of form perception (1983, ch. 3); (2) problem solving and inference to the best explanation, in the case of stimulus ambiguity or stimulus features that would yield unexplained coincidences if interpreted literally (1983, chs. 4–7); (3) relational determination of percepts, such as those involved in perceiving lightness and relational motion through the interpretation of relational stimulus information in accordance with certain assumptions (1983, ch. 8); and (4) deductive inference from a universal major premise and an unconsciously given minor premise, used to explain the constancies (1983, ch. 9). All four operations posit unnoticed acts of cognition. The first operation is not inferential, since it merely involves description; but it illustrates Rock's view that the cognitive operations of perception are based upon internal descriptions in an (unknown) language of thought (1983, p. 99). Rock's formulations are cautious: he says perception is "like" problem-solving and deductive inference (1983, pp. 1, 100, 239, 272, 341). But his account is not merely ratiomorphic. In the end, he held that perception does involve unconscious reasoning, including both inductive formation of rules (1983, pp. 310–311) and deductive inference from rules. The cognitive machinery for such inferences operates in a linguistic medium and follows the rules of predicate logic (1983, pp. 99, 272–273). The rules governing perceptual inference may be either learned or innate—Rock rejected Helmholtz's emphasis on learning (1983, pp. 312–316).

Rock's cautious formulations reflect the fact that he recognized a sharp divide between the processes of perception and the processes that underlie conscious describing, problem solving, rule-based calculations, and deductive inference. Some separation of this kind is demanded by the fact known to Descartes, Kant, and others: that the perceptual process often is impervious to knowledge, as when visual illusions persist despite being detected. It is a seeming paradox for cognitive accounts of perceptual processing that perception is isolated from and inflexible in the face of other cognitive factors, such as the conscious knowledge that the lines are the same length in the Mueller–Lyer illusion (Rock, 1983, pp. 336–337). Rock responded by proposing a strict separation between ordinary cognition and the cognitive processes underlying perception. He separated the knowledge relevant to perception into two divisions: immediate stimulus-based information, and unconscious descriptions, concepts, and rules (1983, p. 302). The unconscious processes typically take into account only such information about particular stimulus as is available in current stimulation; he called this the condition of "stimulus support" (1983, p. 303). Achromatic color illusions, such as the Gelb effect—in which a black circle appears white if it alone is illuminated by a spotlight in an otherwise dark room—disappear when a white contrast paper is moved into the light, but reappear as soon as the stimulus support provided by the white paper is removed. Apparently the perceptual system is caught up in the moment! Rock further postulated that the concepts and rules used in the unconscious cognitive operations of perception are isolated from central cognitive processes of description, categorization, and hypothesis formation (1983, pp. 306, 310, 313, 315). He in effect posited a special-purpose domain of concepts, rules, and reasoning to support the processes of perception.

Rock supported his comparisons of perception to problem solving and inference with an extensive program of empirical research. Others, pursuing general theories of mind in the fields of artificial intelligence and cognitive science, have used perception as an example of a mental process that fits their general model. Such theoreticians have of necessity been explicit about the cognitive machinery. They have sought to provide an explanation of the cognitive capacities that were used as explanatory primitives by earlier theorists.

Fodor (1975) was an early and articulate advocate of the theory that the mind is importantly similar to a general-purpose digital computer and that its cognitive operations are carried out in an internal language of thought. He compared the language of thought to the machine language in a computer (1975, pp. 65–68). Just as a computer is "built to use" its machine language, and so need not acquire it, the brain comes with its own built-in language. This language then serves as the medium in which perceptual hypotheses are framed and tested. Although I agree with Crane (1992, p. 148) that it remains an open question whether one absolutely must posit an internal language in order to account for the inferential abilities of humans and other cognitive agents, Fodor's posit of a language of thought does provide a powerful model for unconscious inferences. The inferential machinery of perception is a full-scale language, with syntactically based inference rules for drawing conclusions from premises.

Fodor (1983) took into account the same fact that we have found in Rock (1983), that perceptual inferences are relatively insulated from the consciously available knowledge of the perceiver. Largely in response to this fact, Fodor adopted the position that perceptual processes take place in cognitively insulated modules. Although Fodor (1983) did not describe precise structures for his innate machine language, he gave no reason to suppose that the language-of-thought of the various perceptual modules is the same as that of other cognitive modules. Theory would dictate that the output of such modules must be usable by subsequent processes. But there is no necessity for the postulated linguistic medium that underlies the processes of shape perception to have precise analogues of the shape vocabulary of the central cognitive processes of shape identification. The modularity thesis and its counterpart in Rock (1983) undermine the assumption that perceptual inferences are one with ordinary thought.

Acceptance of the modularity thesis forsakes the (perhaps implausible) parsimony of traditional inferential accounts. From Alhazen (ca. 1030/1989) to Helmholtz (1867/1910), theorists had posited a unity between the mechanisms underlying perception and those underlying thought more generally. The notion of cognitively isolated (Rock, 1983) or insulated (Fodor, 1983) modules replaces this simple unity with distinct cognitive mechanisms and processes for the postulated inferences of perception and the inferences of conscious thought. This separation of processes places a new burden on contemporary inferential theories, for now they must account for the cognitive resources employed in perception independently of the general cognitive resources of perceivers.

SOPHISTICATED CONTENT

Theorists who posit that perception occurs via inferences from sensory premises to perceptual conclusion take on a commitment to the psychological reality of the premises and conclusions. This in turn requires a commitment that the visual system, governing agency, faculty of judgment, or the intellect has the resources to think the premises and conclusions. If perceptual processes are indeed unnoticed judgments, then the cognitive faculty that carries them out must be able to comprehend the content of such judgments. In more modern terms, if unconscious processes are posited that involve descriptions, then the perceptual system or its auxiliary must have the conceptual resources to express the content found in the descriptions.[8]

Early theorists recognized the need for supplying conceptual resources to the visual system by bringing the faculty of judgment or the intellect into perception. Thus, when Alhazen argued that one and the same intellectual faculty operates in everyday cognition and in the unnoticed judgments of perception, he presumably assumed that the faculty has the same conceptual resources available in both cases. Alhazen held that over the course of a lifetime, we learn to recognize instantaneously all of the visible properties of things, without being aware of the acts of recognition or judgment involved (1989, II.3.42). He thus believed that the perceiver's full range of concepts is available for perception.

Descartes also maintained that sensory perception relies on habitual judgments of the intellect. Because he attributed innate ideas to the perceiver, one would expect him also to believe that the intellect has all its concepts available for perceptual inference. Nonetheless, he recognized a *de facto* limitation on the conceptual vocabulary expressed in unnoticed perceptual judgments. He suggested that we are unable to revise our habitual judgment, formed in childhood, that objects contain something "wholly resembling" the color we experience (1644/1984–85, I.70–72). Because the childhood judgments have become frozen as unnoticed habits, we are unable to use the concepts of the true physics, discovered through mature intellectual reflection, to revise our early judgments about resemblance. As befits the infantile formation of unnoticed perceptual judgments, their conceptual content is restricted by comparison with the sophisticated concepts of the metaphysician and natural philosopher.

By contrast, Berkeley's associationist account avoided any need for the unnoticed processes of perception to use sophisticated conceptual content, because the processes he described make no use of conceptualized content of any sort. In his account of size perception, visual ideas corresponding to visual angle give rise to perceptions of size as a result of acquired associations among visible magnitudes (visual angle), visual cues for distance, and tactual perceptions of distance. The elements to be associated are related to one another as arbitrary signs. In his view, there is no intelligible connection between cues such as ocular muscle feelings and tactual distance. The mind does not perceive distance because it understands that certain muscle feelings result from accommodations of the lens that vary with distance; rather, the perceiver is simply trained by experience to associate specific muscle feelings with specific tactual distances.

Berkeley contrasted his account with that of Descartes, in which a perceiver might make use of intelligible relations among ideas, as in angle–side–angle reasoning about distance.[9] He challenged the proposal that perceivers make use of geometrical lines and angles in everyday perception by asserting that most people do not possess the requisite notions. He denied that lines and angles are "ever thought of by those unskillful in optics" (Berkeley, 1709, sec. 12). Ordinary perceivers therefore cannot bring the technical concepts of optics to bear in unconscious or unnoticed descriptions of the objects vision. He further argued that since perceivers (whether geometrically sophisticated or not) are not conscious of reasoning from lines and angles, they do not reason from them. On the face of it this argument seems weak, for Berkeley himself posited unnoticed processes of suggestion (or association). But he might argue that it is plausible for at least some noncognitive habits to remain unnoticed throughout both their formation and operation, while sophisticated geometrical inferences could not. Some noncognitive motor habits are surely formed without our even knowing we have them (e.g., habits of gait). By contrast, we are all familiar with the ways in which we at first have to pay attention to new cognitive tasks, before they become habitual. But the adherents of unconscious inference posit inferential acts of which we seem never to have been aware. Hence Berkeley might be proposing that the sort of sophisticated mathematical reasoning ascribed by the "natural geometry" argument is not the sort of thing that could become habitual if it had not first been part of a conscious reasoning process. By contrast, his unnoticed processes are habits formed through blind acts of association, which serve to connect ideas to one another simply as a result of their temporal co-occurrence.

Early nineteenth-century theorists, such as Steinbuch (1811) and Tourtual (1827), developed an extensive analysis of visual perception which described its initial content as phenomenal and unconceptualized. They described the sensational elements of visual perception as unspatialized punctiform sensations varying in hue and intensity, and then gave a detailed account of how psychological operations create spatial representations from this nonspatial sensory core (see Hatfield, 1990, ch. 4). Both theorists posited noncognitive operations, distinct from the judgment and intellect, that order sensations by quality and intensity. Steinbuch posited learned associations among muscle sensations, built up slowly, starting *in utero*, to create a mapping from retinal fibers to two-dimensional representation (allegedly) on the basis solely of phenomenal similarity and temporal contiguity.[10] Tourtual posited innate laws of sensibility, also operating on the qualitative character of elemental sensations. In each case, there was no question of sophisticated conceptual content doing the ordering, since the operations were conceived as preconceptual.

We have seen that Helmholtz also posited aspatial elemental sensations, but that he characterized the transformative processes as at once associational and inferential. His contention that unconscious inferences could be explained psychologically as resulting from associational processes meant that his analysis of the psychology of perception could focus on the phenomenal character of sensations, since association operates on phenomenally characterized sensations. His description of the resultant perceptual images as the conclusions of inferences introduced a certain tension into his account, because of the apparent difference between perceptual images and the linguistic conclusions of logical inferences. But Helmholtz held that there is "only a superficial difference between the inferences of logicians and those inductive inferences whose results we recognize in the intuitions of the outer world we attain through our sensations". (By "intuition" he means a perceptual image.) He continued: "The chief difference is that the former are capable of expression in words, while the latter are not, because instead of words they deal only with sensations and memory images of sensations" (1896, 1:358; 1995, p. 198). So the content of perceptual premises and conclusions are sensations and images.[11] What about the major premises, the universal rules for localizing sensations in space? These are associations among sensations, forged through relations of contiguity and resemblance. They operate over the phenomenal properties of sensations, including, for vision, punctiform sensations varying in hue, intensity, and local sign, and feelings of innervation of the ocular (and bodily) musculature. Helmholtz's associationist account of unconscious inference allowed him to restrict the content and operation of perceptual inferences to the phenomenal properties of sensations and phenomenal relations among sensations, operated upon by conceptually blind laws of association. There is no need to attribute sophisticated content to Helmholtzian perceptual inferences.

In the twentieth century, appeal to laws of association operating over aspatial sensations characterized by phenomenal qualities has fallen out of favor.[12] The most developed of today's inferential accounts posit underlying language-like representations to mediate the inferential connections. As we have seen, theorists such as Rock (1983) and Fodor (1983) posit special cognitive subsystems for perception. This allows them to restrict the range of concepts attributed to the subsystem. Rock's isolated cognitive domain requires only a comparatively modest conceptual vocabulary for describing sensory aspects of objects, such as form and other spatial characteristics. His problem-solving and inference-formation operations work on these perceptual features. A typical Rockian inference might combine information about the egocentric tilt of line with information about head-tilt to yield a perception of real-world orientation, or combine visual angle and distance information to yield a perception of size (Rock, 1983, 273–274). The descriptive vocabulary here is impoverished relative to general cognition, focusing as it does on spatial properties in egocentric and environmental frames of reference (1983, 331–332). Fodor's (1983, pp. 86–97) point about the conceptually "shallow" outputs of perceptual modules provides a more general framework for attributing special-purpose, modest conceptual vocabularies to the visual system.

Other computational accounts of vision strain the bounds of plausibility in ascribing perceptual inferences with sophisticated content. Difficulties arise especially for certain computational models of color constancy. We have seen that Maloney and Wandell describe the task of the visual system in color constancy as that of "estimating the surface reflectance functions of objects in a scene with incomplete knowledge of the spectral power distribution of the ambient light" (1986, p. 29). If one takes these authors at their word, they attribute a rich conceptual vocabulary to the visual system, including sophisticated physical concepts such as surface reflective function (spectral reflectance distribution). It seems implausible to attribute such content to encapsulated processes of early vision. The human species came upon these physical concepts only late in its development, after the time of Newton. Yet the species developed trichromatic color vision hundreds of thousands of years earlier (Goldsmith, 1991). So the mechanisms and processes that yield our trichromatic color vision, whether viewed as occurring in a language of thought or via nonlinguistic processing mechanisms, could not have had access to sophisticated physical concepts. And if they are encapsulated, as seems certain, then these processes still would not have access to such concepts (even if the perceiver has "central system" knowledge of physics). Consequently, the output of the color system does not conceptually encode such notions.

There is an alternative way of construing the statements of Maloney and Wandell (1986), which would make sense of their saying that the visual system contains information about spectral reflectance distributions, but which would cut against inclusion of their color constancy model in the family of "unconscious inference" theories. The mathematical notion of information—developed by Shannon (1948) and others and brought into perceptual theory in the 1950s by Attneave (1954)— provides a way of describing the information contained in a signal (or a perceptual state) without needing to attribute knowledge of or access to that information to the containing system. Dretske (1981) has provided a thorough analysis of the use of this notion of information to describe perceptual content. On this way of viewing things, if perception of a particular hue is strictly correlated (under appropriate environmental background or "channel" conditions) with a particular reflectance distribution in the stimulus, then perception of that hue carries the information that the reflectance distribution is present (but see Hatfield, 1992a). It can do so without the perceiver even knowing what a reflectance distribution is—for, as Dretske explains (1981, ch. 9), this notion of information is distinct from conceptual meaning. But, if so, then any supposition that the visual system "estimates" the physical properties of the distal stimulus from its "knowledge" of retinal values is thereby undercut. Inference and estimation are cognitive acts. Our best philosophical and psychological accounts of such acts suggest that they occur through operations over premises that encode knowledge conceptually (Crane, 1992, pp. 142–149; Smith, 1995). But the color constancy models mentioned above make no provision for that sort of cognitive act. Hence, they would appear to be better classed as cases of the metaphorical application of an inferential model to perception. The computational aspects of color vision would then be understood as cases of informational combination and transformation via noncognitive mechanisms.

PHENOMENAL EXPERIENCE

The aim of much visual theory has been to explain the contents of phenomenal experience, the "way things look". This has been the case in central areas of perceptual theory, such as the perception of spatial and chromatic aspects of things. To meet this explanatory aim an unconscious inference theory of perception must provide some explanation of how inferences yield phenomenal experience. A complete explanation of the production of phenomenal experience would presuppose a solution to the mind–body problem. It would require explaining how perceptual processes in the brain produce phenomenal experience, which is a difficult problem. But less ambitious explanatory agendas are available. One might, for instance, posit psychophysical linking propositions (Teller & Pugh, 1983), or psychoneural linking hypotheses (Hatfield & Pugh, unpublished), to bridge the gap between the brain states and experience, without thereby seeking to explain the ontology of such links. Similarly, one might treat the conclusions of inferences as a certain kind of data array (Marr, 1982, ch. 4; Tye, 1991, ch. 5), and use the representational content of the data array to explain imagistic experience.

Alhazen sought to explain the looks of things, as is apparent in his distinction between size as a function of visual angle and (phenomenally) perceived size. I think he would have had little problem explaining the looks of things via judgment, since on his view the judgments of perception are not linguistic and they operate directly on phenomenally given materials. He was not, however, explicit on how inferences operate on sensations to produce the ultimate looks of things. Two possibilities suggest themselves: inferences operate either to transform the representation of spatial properties in sensation into a representation of perceived spatial properties, or inferences operate to create a new representation exhibiting the perceived properties. Leaving aside metaphysical difficulties about the status of phenomenal experience itself—which are common to all theories and remain unresolved—no special problem of phenomenal experience arises for Alhazen.

As we have seen in the previous section, perceptual theory from Descartes to Helmholtz retained phenomenally-defined theoretical primitives. Descartes followed Alhazen and the optical tradition in conceiving the premises of perceptual inferences as graspings of phenomenally given sensations, and the conclusions of such inferences as phenomenal experiences. The associationist tradition developed a finer analysis of the processes by which the spatial representations of perceptual experience are constructed from sensory elements. Aspatial sensory elements are conjoined associatively to yield phenomenal representations of a three-dimensional visual world. Although Helmholtz adopted an inferential account of perception, he offered a phenomenalist account of the conclusions of perceptual inferences. Since he considered the conclusions of such inferences to be images, he left no gap between conclusion and experience.

The notion that perceptual psychology attempts to explain the "looks of things" was fundamental to the work of the Gestalt psychologists (Köhler, 1929, ch. 1; Koffka, 1935, ch. 1 and pp. 73–76), who used a principle of spatial isomorphism to explain how brain states are related to experience. They argued that experience of voluminous shaped regions is produced by (or identical with) three-dimensional isomorphically shaped areas in the brain, so that the experience of a sphere is caused by a spherical region of brain activity. Although the Gestaltists' brain theory has been rejected, many investigators hold that phenomenal experience is a primary explanatory object for perceptual theory (Cutting, 1986, p. 4, ch. 15; Gibson, 1971, p. 4; Goldstein, 1996, pp. 15, 29; Natsoulas, 1991), though some disagree (for instance Kauffman, 1974,

p. 16). Despite this explanatory goal, no detailed explanations of how the processes posited in perceptual theory yield the phenomenal aspects of sense perception are yet extant. The strategy of Helmholtz and his predecessors, of maintaining that perceptual experience is constructed from phenomenally characterized sensations, is no longer accepted. But no generally accepted model of how brain events are related to phenomenal experience has arisen to replace the one-fiber, one-sensation doctrine. Explaining phenomenal experience itself remains an unrealized goal of modern perceptual (and cognitive) theory.

Some proposals have been made. Wandell has offered the intriguing suggestion that phenomenal color, or color appearance, "is a mental explanation of why an object causes relatively more absorptions in one cone type than another object" (1995, p. 289). Although providing a detailed theory of how information about surface reflectance might be recovered (1995, ch. 9), he does not offer anything further on the problem of how an estimation of a surface reflectance's relative effect on a cone type yields the experience of color.

Others have suggested that percepts are generated from early representations in the processing stream via cognitive, language-mediated processes. In his 1975 book, Fodor conjectured that perceptual processes are initially carried out as operations on sentence-like objects, with images subsequently being constructed from symbolic descriptions. He speculated that this construction might be likened to a "digital to analog" conversion (1975, p. 193, n. 26), but said nothing further about how this might occur.

Rock (1975, ch. 11) was acutely aware of the need for and difficulty of explaining perceptual experience. He considered percepts themselves to be "analogic, picturelike, and concrete" (1983, p. 52), by contrast with descriptions of percepts framed in the language of thought. He clearly stated (1983, p. 272) that the outcome of perceptual inference "is a percept rather than a conclusion" (by which he meant a linguistically-expressed conclusion). But he did not say how such percepts are generated from the unconscious descriptions found in perceptual inferences.

Michael Tye (1995, ch. 5) has most fully elaborated a conception of how a language-like symbolist view of perceptual and imagistic representations might explain phenomenal experience. Drawing on Marr (1982, ch. 4), he proposed that imagistic representations be conceived as symbol-filled arrays. Such arrays are formed from a matrix of cells that represent distal surface locations in two dimensions. The individual cells (matrix units) are addressed by the relative positions they represent, corresponding to columns and rows. The physical locations of the cells in the brain is irrelevant on Tye's view; rather, the arrays are treated as having imagistic content in part because the processes operating over them treat the cells with numerically adjacent column and row addresses as if they were adjacent (1995, p. 94). Further imagistic content is provided by symbols within the cells, which represent the depth, color, intensity, and surface texture of a distal point (small area). Full image content arises only when the arrays are associated with a sentential interpretation, such as "this represents a pig". Our imagistic experience arises from the fact that we have symbolic representations of spatial, chromatic, and categorial aspects of things, which we access by symbol-reading processes that treat the areas represented in cells which have contiguous addresses as being distally contiguous. An image is constituted by thousands of words, containing labels for spatial location attached to descriptions of depth and color. The matrix arrays are not analog, but they do represent spatial relations of small areas that may be treated as forming a continuous surface.

Tye's view has the advantage that it can draw on ongoing work seeking to explain the production of the symbol-filled array, including Marr's (1982) explanations of the production of the "$2\frac{1}{2}$-D sketch" (which was a model for Tye's symbol-filled array). But there remains a question of why Tye believes the postulated symbol-filled array explains phenomenal experience. It is the array's representational or informational content that does the work for Tye (1991, pp. 136, 142), and not any relation to neural states or to nonsymbolic mental states. Specifically, Tye posits that phenomenal experience arises when we have symbolic-matrix representations of distal states that are ready to be taken up cognitively (e.g., brought under description). As a description of the role that phenomenal experience itself might play in perception and cognition, as providing representations for further cognitive response, this strikes me as a good description. But Tye intends it to explain our (apparent) phenomenal experience itself. In the case of color vision, he says that phenomenal blue simply arises when we have symbolic states that represent distal blue things (1991, p. 133; 1995, pp. 145–147). He rejects sensations, qualia, or other mental items that might present phenomenal blue (1991, ch. 7). The phenomenal blue, he explains, is not in the head, but is on the surfaces of things. He is aware that the property possessed by some distal things, which makes them blue, is the physical property of having a spectral reflectance distribution that falls within a certain class of such distributions. It is his view that a nonconceptual representation of this property in the visual system at a stage ready for conceptual description just is the perception of the distal blue surface in a phenomenally blue manner (1995, pp. 137–143). No further explanation of the phenomenal content is given.

Kosslyn (1995) surveyed the literature on visual imagery and proposed that there are two sorts of symbolic systems in the head: propositional and depictive. Propositional representations consist of discrete symbols of various classes (signifying entities, relations, properties, and logical relations), with rules for combining them. The spatial relations among the symbols have only an arbitrary significance. Property symbols may always be written to the right of the entity symbols to which they apply, but this does not mean that they are on the right hand side of the entity! By contrast, spatial relations of symbols in the depictive style of representation have that sort of nonarbitrary spatial meaning. The depictive style of representation involves only two classes of symbols, points (small punctiform areas) and empty spaces. The combination rules are merely that the symbols must be put in spatial relation to one another, and any relation is allowed (Kosslyn 1995, pp. 280–282).

It is misleading for Kosslyn to label the points that compose his depictive representations "symbols", since no operations are defined which respond to the points based on variation in their form, as happens in classical symbol-processing models (Fodor, 1975, ch. 2; Pylyshyn, 1984, ch. 3). Indeed, Kosslyn seems to assume that noncognitive processes yield the depictive structure of the basic parts of images. At least, in Kosslyn's mature theory there is no discernible commitment to positing cognitive or inferential processes to generate the spatial relations internal to image parts.[13] Interpretive processes then operate over spatial relations found in the image, which is composed of points in spatial arrangement (Kosslyn, 1995, pp. 273–275). The images are spatially concrete. The potentially continuously varying spatial relations among points give them their content. Because continuous variation in spatial relations is permitted, the medium is analog.

Originally, Kosslyn (1983, p. 23) understood the spatial relations found in images to be a functional space consisting of paths of access among address labels for represented points as read by processing mechanisms (a conception similar to Tye's symbol-filled array). Neuroscientific findings led him to suggest that these functional relations may indeed be realized by real spatial relations in the cerebral cortex (Kosslyn, 1995, pp. 290–292). Although Kosslyn does not explicitly say so, he appears to suggest that the spatial relations experienced in images result from isomorphic spatial relations in the brain, presumably in accordance with a linking proposition (Teller & Pugh, 1983). This proposal is similar to the Gestalt psychologists' earlier postulation of a spatial isomorphism between brain events and the structure of perceptual experience (Köhler, 1929, pp. 61–66, 142–147; Koffka, 1935, pp. 56–67; see also Scheerer, 1994). An extension of Kosslyn's theory in this direction would yield a noncognitive principle of explanation for the spatial structure in phenomenal experience via spatially isomorphic patterns of activity in the brain. If we treat linking propositions as hypothesized laws of nature, then the existence of spatially organized phenomenal experience is explained as the lawful product of the spatial properties of activity in certain areas of the brain.

Stepping back, it would seem that the most promising route for inferential theories to explain the spatial structure of perception is the postulation of language-like inferential processes that produce analog or depictive representations. If we give due regard to Rock's and Fodor's point about encapsulation, then these inferential processes would take place in a conceptually impoverished vocabulary, perhaps limited to spatial and chromatic properties and focusing on the production of a representation of the spatially articulated surfaces of objects via a symbol-filled array.

At present there is no worked out account of how an encapsulated inferential process would produce either a genuinely analog representation or one of Marr's arrays. Moreover, there are rival accounts of processing mechanisms that could yield analog representations without relying on a language-like or inferential medium. Historically, the Gestalt theory of self-organizing dynamical systems in the brain provided a noncognitive basis for generating perceptual results (Hatfield & Epstein, 1985, pp. 178–179). In more recent times, connectionist models provide a conception of perceptual processing in which perceptual information can be combined in regular ways to yield analog representations, without positing cognitive operations such as inference (Hatfield, 1988, 1991a, b). To the extent that these rival accounts provide a means for modeling the production of analog representations, they go further than inferential accounts in addressing the production of the spatial structure of phenomenal experience.

CONCLUSION

Highly articulated theories of unconscious inference in perception have been extant for 1000 years (since Alhazen, ca. 1030), and have been widespread for nearly 400 years (following Descartes, 1637). The structure of the theories has varied, as can be seen by reviewing their various theoretical primitives, that is, what is taken as given as opposed to what needs an explanation. Prior to the nineteenth century, the inferential machinery required to make unconscious inferences was taken as a given: it was the intellect, or the faculty of judgment. Subsequently, various proposals were made to explain this machinery: via association in the case of Helmholtz, via an unconscious language of thought in the case of Fodor and Rock. Prior to the late twentieth century, it was assumed that the same concepts are employed in unconscious inferences and conscious thought. In recent decades, the fact that perception is often impervious to consciously entertained knowledge has led investigators to posit a separate, encapsulated domain of perceptual processing, which must then be supplied with its own cognitive resources. Finally, prior to the twentieth century the primitive elements posited in perceptual theories were sensations with phenomenal properties. Processes were then posited to augment or transform those properties, for example, by ordering the sensations spatially. In the twentieth century such sensational primitives have been rejected. For contemporary unconscious inference theories, the problem then arises of explaining how linguistic inferential processes can yield the phenomenal aspects of perceptual experience.

The literature of artificial intelligence and computational accounts of vision is replete with talk of "descriptions" and "inferences". In some cases, such as Marr (1982, pp. 342–344), the approach has been allied with a Fodorean conception of symbolic computation. But in many cases no real support is given for such talk. It is as if causal transitions among information-bearing states of a system that occur according to rules and that lead to appropriate outcomes should be counted as inferences on the face of it, without supplying cognitive machinery or making provision to explain the conceptual content found in the inferences. As we found with the work on color constancy discussed above, such discussions are best classed as metaphorical uses of the concepts of inference and description. They are not inferential theories of perception, but theories of information transformation in perception.[14] The problem with taking these positions as literal inference theories is that they make no provision for the cognitive resources that would be needed to sustain unconscious inferences.

Literal theories of perceptual inference that do posit cognitive resources, in the manner of Fodor (1983) and Rock (1983), have the opposite problem. They need to defend their invocation of cognitive apparatus to carry out rule-based transformations on information-bearing states in perception. Recall that our discussion has been limited to the phenomenal aspects of sense perception, that is, to the generation of imagistic perceptual representations. Rock argues that the outcomes of perception are clever enough to require truly intelligent (or at least genuinely cognitive) mechanisms in their production. The question of whether "smart mechanisms" must simply be engineered smartly (or evolved "smartly"), or must contain genuinely cognitive apparatus, is of great interest (Runeson, 1977). More generally, it would be interesting to contemplate similarities and differences among the various processes by which sensory information is encoded, perceptions are formed and brought under concepts, words are applied to perceptions, and meanings of words are altered on empirical (inductive) grounds (Barlow, 1974, p. 132). But for present purposes it will be enough to consider briefly an alternative means for conceiving perceptual processes noncognitively.

One of the reasons that unconscious inference models are attractive is that perception is mental and involves transformations of information in accordance with rules. It has seemed reasonable or even necessary that the rules would be represented and applied by a cognitive apparatus. But the development of connectionist computational architectures provides a means of conceiving of rules for information transformation that are instantiated in neural nets, without being cognitively represented and accessed. Connectionist models can treat information processing in perception as the outcome of stimulus-driven inputs to nodes in a connectionist net and the subsequent settling down of that net (or one downstream) into a stable state. Spatial information might be carried in such nets by adjacency relations within a retinotopic projection (Bienenstock & Doursat, 1991). By organizing a pyramid of nets that respond to the spatial properties of represented images at many different scales, local computations can respond to global features of images in a reasonable number of steps (Rosenfeld, 1990). Within the connectionist framework it is possible to think of networks of nodes as instantiating processing rules (Hatfield, 1991a) without representing those rules in explicit symbolic form or operating upon them via language-like inferential apparatus. Because such nets process information in accordance with rules without the necessity that the stimulus be described internally in a conceptual vocabulary (however modest), such models are noncognitive (Hatfield, 1988). For basic sensory processes, evolutionary engineering presumably has shaped the instantiated rules. Marr's (1982) theory of early vision, long a bastion of symbolist and inferential conceptions of psychological processes, admits of a nonsymbolic, noncognitive connectionist interpretation (Hatfield, 1991b; Kosslyn & Hatfield, 1984).

Noncognitive models of sense perception face (counterparts to) only two of the three problems discussed herein. As the complement of the cognitive machinery problem, they must provide computational machinery to explain transformations among perceptual representations. As the complement to the phenomenal experience problem, they must explain how the phenomenal aspects of sensory perception arise from noncognitive processes and operations. They are not faced with the sophisticated content problem in relation to sense perception, since they do not posit cognitive operations that represent conceptual content (sophisticated or no) in their explanations. Connectionist versions of noncognitive theories do, of course, face the problem of sophisticated content in framing explanations of cognitive achievements such as object recognition. They will in that case need to provide their own models of conceptual content and object recognition (on which, see Quinlan, 1991, pp. 120–131).

The previous hegemony of inferential models of the psychological processes underlying sense perception (by contrast with cognitive or meaningful perception) has fallen subject to challenge (Epstein, 1993; Hatfield, 1988; Kanizsa, 1979, ch. 1, 1985). The fate of inferential models will be decided in the longer course of empirical research and theoretical assessment. It is clear that the mere presence of specified processing rules or of "clever" perceptual outcomes cannot support the theory that sense perception results from inference, to the exclusion of noncognitive theories. Although seeing usually leads to believing, it remains an open question whether simple seeing results from belief-like inferences. The slow movement of theory is toward thinking it does not.

ACKNOWLEDGMENTS

An earlier version of this paper was given to the Perception and Evolution group at the Center for Interdisciplinary Research in Bielefeld, June, 1997. The author thanks Jacob Beck, Allison Crapo, and Susan Peppers for helpful comments on later drafts.

NOTES

1. In using "phenomenal" and "cognitive" as contrastive qualifiers of "perception" and related terms, I do not mean to imply that our recognition of the table as a table is not a part of our visual experience, or is not as phenomenally immediate as the experience of the shape or color of the table. I need contrastive terms that signal the seemingly noncognitive aspect of shape or color perception (here distinguished from shape or color recognition, classification, and identification), as opposed to decidedly cognitive achievements such as object recognition or identification. For a statement of the distinction between perceptual and cognitive aspects of vision, see Rock (1975, ch. 1, especially p. 24). For a statement of the division from a computational and neurophysiological perspective, see Arbib and Hanson (1987, especially pp. 4–5). For a philosophical statement of the contrast, see Dretske (1995, especially pp. 332–335). The present contrast concerns aspects of perceptual experience itself, and does not describe the processes that produce these aspects, which may themselves be cognitive or noncognitive. In this chapter I focus on cognitive theories of the processes that produce the phenomenal aspects of experience, though I will mention noncognitive theories as well. I am not concerned with epistemological aspects of the theories; on epistemological aspects of inferential theories, see Schwartz (1994, pp. 104–110). Finally, other characterizations of the objects of study in contemporary visual perceptual psychology can be substituted for the traditional list given above (size, shape, etc.), including: the spatial and chromatic layout and changes within it, or the spatial and chromatic structure of surfaces and its changes.
2. Phenomenal color constancy was mentioned by Thomas Young (1807, 1: 456), using the example of white paper under varying intensities and colors of illumination. It was brought into prominence by Helmholtz (1867/1910, 2: 110, 243–244) and Ewald Hering (1875, pp. 335–338; 1920, pp. 13–17), who discussed the constancy of object colors in addition to white.
3. Dennett (1991, ch. 12) would contest this way of posing the third problem, since he denies the reality of imagistic phenomenal experience; but a theorist who subscribed to his views would still be faced with the problem of explaining how an inferential conclusion can *seem* to be the experience of a specific hue, or whatever.
4. My formulation of the cognitive machinery problem is distinct from *a priori* arguments that conclude, on conceptual grounds, that unconscious inference theories must be false, as when Ludwig (1996) argues that the very concept of an unconscious inference is

incoherent. Among Ludwig's other arguments, only one overlaps with my three problems. He requires (1996, pp. 398–399) that the concepts expressed in perceptual inferences be attributed to perceivers (my sophisticated content problem), and argues that the visual system could not have them (on conceptual grounds), and that children and animals do not have them (a common-sense empirical argument). None of my three problems is purely conceptual or *a priori*; the first two concern the empirical plausibility of needed explanatory apparatus, and the third concerns the explanatory adequacy of theories as developed thus far. The question of the attribution of subpersonal cognitive states has generated discussion (see Davies, 1995). On this score I agree with Fodor (1975, pp. 52–53). Although there are various moral, legal, and cultural reasons for wanting, in many contexts, to use the language of "inference" and "belief" to describe only acts of (whole) persons, for the purposes of psychological theory there are not adequate grounds *a priori* to preclude ascriptions of cognitive states to subsystems of persons, including the psychological mechanisms underlying vision. There may of course be theoretical or empirical grounds for such a preclusion.

5. Descartes also gave a purely psychophysical account of distance perception, according to which the brain states that control accommodation and convergence directly cause a corresponding idea of distance (Descartes, 1664/1972, p. 94; 1637/1984–85, 1: 170; see Hatfield, 1992b, p. 357).

6. The translations are mine. The third German edition of 1910 reprinted the text of the first edition of 1867 and added a great deal of useful apparatus and commentary by the editors, and it was translated by J. P. C. Southall as Helmholtz 1924–25. Southall conveniently provided the corresponding page numbers for the third German edition at the top of each page, which makes it easy to coordinate my citations of the German with his translation. Southall's translation, while useful for many purposes, is misleading on numerous occasions, especially concerning Helmholtz's psychological theory.

7. Helmholtz (1867/1910, 3: 23) cited John Stuart Mill in support of his associationist account of inductive inference, and in fact in his *Logic* of 1843 Mill endorsed an associational account; but in the 1851 edition he qualified this endorsement (Mill, 1974, p. 664). For additional problems with Helmholtz's associative account of inference, see Hatfield (1990, pp. 204–208).

8. As is explained at the end of this section, I am assuming that genuine inferences are couched in representations that express their content in such a way that it is available to the subsystem performing the inference. Systems that merely transform and transmit information without sensitivity to its content, such as a computer keyboard system (which transforms physical pressure into internal symbols, and may do so conditionally, as with the "shift" key), do not count as performing inferences. By contrast, in a conceptual encoding, having a concept requires its being connected to other concepts (Crane, 1992, pp. 142–149; Smith, 1995). Philosophers have, of course, been interested in the question of how there could be systems in which conceptual content is expressed (e.g., Dretske 1988). Further, it has been thought that inferential operations might take place solely in virtue of the syntax of internal inscriptions; but even in such cases the syntactic entities will have to be related to other syntactic entities in sufficiently complex ways to treat some of them as predicates corresponding to concepts (Fodor, 1975, ch. 2).

9. Although Descartes provided a purely psychophysical (and so noncognitive) account of distance perception via convergence, in some cases he attributed unnoticed geometrical reasoning to the perceiver, as in the perception of distance from known size and visual angle (see Hatfield, 1992b, p. 357).

10. Although Alhazen (1989, II.13.22) treated similarity as something to be detected intellectually, the associationist tradition in the nineteenth century posited laws as operating blindly over one-dimensional similarities (as among sensations within a single modality, or along a single dimension within a modality, such as hue).

11. Helmholtz believed that an image can contain the content of a judgment: "it is clearly possible, using the sensible images of memory instead of words, to produce the same kind of combination which, when expressed in words, would be called a proposition or judgment" (1896, 1: 358; 1995, p. 199). Indeed, Helmholtz considered concepts of objects to be resolvable into a series of images of the objects, comprising both perspectival and cross-sectional images (1882–95, 3: 545; 1971, p. 507). As Fodor (1975, pp. 174–184) has observed, any theory that attempts to equate propositions with images faces problems of ambiguity. For example, does a picture of a man walking on a slope and facing upwards express the content that he is walking up, or walking down backwards? One cannot avoid introducing an active mental element of grasping or connecting the "relevant" aspects of an image with other images to express a propositional content. The continuation of the passage quoted in this note suggests that Helmholtz was sensitive to this point and believed that associative connections would suffice.

12. Connectionism is often regarded as carrying on the associationist tradition (Quinlan, 1991, pp. 2–3). Further, some connectionist models provide a noncognitive basis for detecting similarities among patterns (Quinlan, 1991, pp. 49–56). The patterns are matched via the activation of patterns of input nodes, not by unreduced phenomenal qualities of hue and intensity. Still, in cases in which the input nodes are feature detectors, these accounts bear an analogy to a dephenomenologized Helmholtzian account, with the important exception that they probably are not aptly characterized as inferential accounts (on which, more below).

13. To put the point in Kosslyn's technical vocabulary, there is no discernible commitment that the operations by which compressed images (1994, pp. 118–119) are used to reconstruct depictive representations are cognitive, though of course the decompression process may be initiated cognitively.

14. It is possible to read this literature as implicitly proposing that all inference should be treated as information transformation, without worrying about the system's sensitivity to the content of the information. More generally, it seems clear that Horace Barlow (1974, 1990) adopts the attitude that mechanisms of information transformation, from the bacterium to the human, are best treated as lying on a continuum, with no in-principle dividing line separating the processes and marking off what I have called concept-mediated inferences from the "inferences" of the bacterium. This line of thought is of great interest. At the same time, without further articulation and defense of its claims about continuity, it would seem to slip into panmentalism; for it equates thought content with information transformations of any kind, and so does not account for the internal structure of conceptual thought (see Dretske, 1981) that distinguishes cognitive beings from computer keyboards.

REFERENCES

Alhazen, A. (1989). In A.I. Sabra (Ed.) *The Optics of Ibn al-Haytham*, Books I–III, 2 vol. (ca. 1030). London: Warburg Institute.

Arbib, M.A. & Hanson, A.R. (1987). Vision, brain, and cooperative computation: An overview. In M.A. Arbib & A.R. Hanson (Eds.) *Vision, brain, and cooperative computation* (pp. 1–83). Cambridge: MIT Press.

Atherton, M. (1990). *Berkeley's revolution in vision*. Ithaca: Cornell University Press.

Attneave, F. (1954). Some informational aspects of visual perception. *Psychological Review*, **61**, 183–193.

Barlow, H.B. (1974). Inductive inference, coding, perception, and language. *Perception*, **3**, 123–134.

Barlow, H.B. (1990). Conditions for versatile learning, Helmholtz's unconscious inference, and the task of perception. *Vision Research*, **30**, 1561–1571.

Bennett, B.M., Hoffman, D.D. & Prakash, C. (1989). *Observer mechanics: A formal theory of perception.* San Diego: Academic Press.

Berkeley, G. (1709). *An essay towards a new theory of vision.* Dublin: Rhames & Papyat.

Berkeley, G. (1733). *The theory of vision or visual language.* London: J. Tonson.

Bienenstock, E. & Doursat, R. (1991). Issues of representation in neural networks. In A. Gorea (Ed.) *Representations of vision: Trends and tacit assumptions in vision research* (pp. 47–67). Cambridge: Cambridge University Press.

Brown, T. (1824). *Lectures on the philosophy of the human mind* (2nd edn., 4 vols.). Edinburgh: Tait.

Brunswik, E. (1956). *Perception and the representative design of psychological experiments* (2nd edn.). Berkeley: University of California Press.

Chambers, E. (1738). *Cyclopaedia, or, An universal dictionary of arts and sciences* (2nd edn., 2 vols.). London: D. Midwinter and others.

Crane, T. (1992). The nonconceptual content of experience. In T. Crane (Ed.) *The contents of experience* (pp. 136–157). Cambridge: Cambridge University Press.

Cutting, J. (1986). *Perception with an eye for motion.* Cambridge: MIT Press.

Davies, M. (1995). Tacit knowledge and subdoxastic states. In C. Macdonald & G. Macdonald (Eds.) *Philosophy of psychology: Debates on psychological explanation* (Vol. 1, pp. 309–330). Oxford: Blackwell.

Dennett, D.C. (1991). *Consciousness explained.* Boston: Little, Brown & Company.

Descartes, R. (1637/1984–85). Optics (selections). In J. Cottingham, R. Stoothoff & D. Murdoch (Eds.) *Philosophical writings of Descartes* (2 vols., 1: 152–175). Cambridge: Cambridge University Press.

Descartes, R. (1641/1984–85). Meditations on first philosophy. In J. Cottingham, R. Stoothoff & D. Murdoch (Eds.) *Philosophical writings of Descartes* (2 vols., 2: 3–301). Cambridge: Cambridge University Press.

Descartes, R. (1644/1984–85). Principles of philosophy (selections). In J. Cottingham, R. Stoothoff & D. Murdoch (Eds.) *Philosophical writings of Descartes* (2 vols., 1: 179–291). Cambridge: Cambridge University Press.

Descartes, R. (1664/1972). In T. S. Hall (Ed.) *Treatise of man.* Cambridge: Harvard University Press.

Dretske, F.I. (1981). *Knowledge and the flow of information.* Cambridge: MIT Press.

Dretske, F.I. (1988). *Explaining behavior: Reasons in a world of causes.* Cambridge: MIT Press.

Dretske, F.I. (1995). Meaningful perception. In S.M. Kosslyn & D.N. Osherson (Eds.) *Visual Cognition: An invitation to cognitive science* (vol. 2, 2nd edn., pp. 331–352). Cambridge: MIT Press.

Epstein, W. (1993). On seeing that thinking is separate and thinking that seeing is the same. *Giornale Italiano di Psicologia, 20*, 731–747.

Euclid (1945). The *Optics* of Euclid, translated by H. E. Burton. *Journal of the Optical Society of America, 35*, 357–372.

Fodor, J.A. (1975). *Language of thought.* New York: Crowell.

Fodor, J.A. (1983). *Modularity of mind: An essay on faculty psychology.* Cambridge: MIT Press.

Gehler, J.S.T. (1787–96). *Physikalisches Wörterbuch, oder Versuch einer Erklärung der vornehmsten Begriffe und Kunstwörter der Naturlehre,* 6 vols. Leipzig: Schwickert.

Gibson, J.J. (1966). *The senses considered as perceptual systems.* Boston: Houghton Mifflin.

Gibson, J.J. (1971). The legacies of Koffka's *Principles. Journal of the History of the Behavioral Sciences, 7*, 3–9.

Goldsmith, T.H. (1991). Optimization, constraint, and history in the evolution of eyes. *Quarterly Review of Biology, 65*, 281–322.

Goldstein, E.B. (1996). *Sensation and perception* (4th edn.). Pacific Grove, Calif.: Brooks/Cole Publishing Company.

Gregory, R.L. (1974). Perceptions as hypotheses. In S.C. Brown (Ed.) *Philosophy of psychology* (pp. 195–210). London: Macmillan.

Gregory, R.L. (1997). *Eye and brain: The psychology of seeing* (5th edn.). Princeton: Princeton University Press.

Hatfield, G. (1988). Representation and content in some (actual) theories of perception. *Studies in History and Philosophy of Science*, **19**, 175–214.

Hatfield, G. (1990). *The natural and the normative: Theories of spatial perception from Kant to Helmholtz*. Cambridge: MIT Press.

Hatfield, G. (1991a). Representation and rule-instantiation in connectionist systems. In T. Horgan & J. Tienson (Eds.) *Connectionism and the philosophy of mind* (pp. 90–112). Boston: Kluwer.

Hatfield, G. (1991b). Representation in perception and cognition: Connectionist affordances. In W. Ramsey, D. Rumelhart & S. Stich (Eds.) *Philosophy and connectionist theory* (pp. 163–195). Hillsdale, NJ: Lawrence Erlbaum.

Hatfield, G. (1992a). Color perception and neural encoding: Does metameric matching entail a loss of information? In D. Hull & M. Forbes (Eds.) *PSA 1992* (2 vols., 1: 492–504). East Lansing, Mich.: Philosophy of Science Association.

Hatfield, G. (1992b). Descartes's physiology and its relation to his psychology. In J. Cottingham (Ed.) *Cambridge companion to Descartes* (pp. 335–370). Cambridge: Cambridge University Press.

Hatfield, G. & Epstein, W. (1979). The sensory core and the medieval foundations of early modern perceptual theory. *Isis*, **70**, 363–384.

Hatfield, G. & Epstein, W. (1985). The status of the minimum principle in the theoretical analysis of vision. *Psychological Bulletin*, **97**, 155–186.

Hatfield, G. & Pugh, E.N. (unpublished). Psychophysical laws, qualia, and psycho-neural linking hypotheses.

Helmholtz, H.L. (1867/1910). *Handbuch der physiologischen Optik*. Leipzig: L. Voss. Reprinted, with extensive commentary, in A. Gullstrand, J. von Kries & W. Nagel (Eds.) *Handbuch der physiologischen Optik* (3rd edn.). Hamburg and Leipzig: L. Voss.

Helmholtz, H.L. (1882–95). *Wissenschaftliche Abhandlungen* (3 vols.). Leipzig: Barth.

Helmholtz, H.L. (1896). *Vorträge und Reden* (4th edn., 2 vols.). Braunschweig: Vieweg.

Helmholtz, H.L. (1924–25). In J.P.C. Southall (Ed.) *Helmholtz's treatise on physiological optics*, translated from the 3rd German edition. Rochester, NY: Optical Society of America.

Helmholtz, H.L. (1971). In R. Kahl (Ed.) *Selected writings of Hermann von Helmholtz*. Middletown, Conn.: Wesleyan University Press.

Helmholtz, H.L. (1995). In D. Cahan (Ed.) *Science and culture: Popular and philosophical essays by Hermann von Helmholtz*. Chicago: University of Chicago Press.

Hering, E. (1875). Zur Lehre von der Beziehung zwischen Leib und Seele. I. Mitteilung. Ueber Fechner's psychophysisches Gesetz. *Sitzungsberichte der Kaiserlichen Akademie der Wissenschaften zu Wien. Mathematisch- Naturwissenschaftliche Classe*, **72**, Pt. 3, pp. 310–48.

Hering, E. (1920). *Grundzüge der Lehre vom Lichtsinn*. Leipzig: W. Engelmann.

Hochberg, J.E. (1981). Levels of perceptual organization. In M. Kubovy & J.R. Pomeranz (Eds.) *Perceptual organization* (pp. 255–278). Hillsdale, NJ: Erlbaum.

Hurlbert, A.C. (1998). Computation models of color constancy. In V. Walsh & J. Kulikowski (Eds.) *Perceptual constancy: Why things look as they do* (pp. 283–322). Cambridge: Cambridge University Press.

Hutchison, K. (1991). Dormitive virtues, scholastic qualities, and the new philosophies. *History of Science*, **29**, 245–278.

Kanizsa, G. (1979). *Organization in vision: Essays on Gestalt perception.* New York: Praeger.

Kanizsa, G. (1985). Seeing and thinking. *Acta Psychologica,* **59**, 23–33.

Kant, I. (1787/1998). In P. Guyer & A. Wood (Eds.) *Critique of pure reason* (2nd edn.). Cambridge: Cambridge University Press.

Kauffman, L. (1974). *Sight and mind: An introduction to visual perception.* New York: Oxford University Press.

Koffka, K. (1935). *Principles of Gestalt psychology.* New York: Harcourt, Brace.

Köhler, W. (1929). *Gestalt psychology.* New York: Liveright.

Kosslyn, S.M. (1983). *Ghosts in the mind's machine: Creating and using images in the brain.* New York: Norton.

Kosslyn, S.M. (1994). *Image and brain: The resolution of the imagery debate.* Cambridge: MIT Press.

Kosslyn, S.M. (1995). Mental imagery. In S.M. Kosslyn & D.N. Osherson (Eds.) *Visual Cognition: An invitation to cognitive science* (vol. 2, 2nd edn., pp. 267–296). Cambridge: MIT Press.

Kosslyn, S.M. & Hatfield, G. (1984). Representation without symbol systems. *Social Research,* **51**, 1019–1045.

Le Cat, Claude-Nicolas (1767). *Traité des sensations et des passions en général, et des sens en particulier* (2 vols.). Paris: Vallat-La-Chapelle.

Ludwig, K. (1996). Explaining why things look the way they do. In K. Akins (Ed.) *Perception* (pp. 18–60). New York: Oxford University Press.

Maloney, L.T. & Wandell, B.A. (1986). Color constancy: A method for recovering surface spectral reflectance. *Journal of the Optical Society of America, A* **1**, 29–33.

Marr, D. (1982). *Vision: A computational investigation into the human representation and processing of visual information.* San Francisco: W. H. Freeman.

Mill, J.S. (1974). *System of logic, ratiocinative and inductive,* 2 vols. London: Routledge & Kegan Paul.

Molière, J. (1673/1965). In P.H. Nurse (Ed.) *Le Malade imaginaire.* Oxford: Oxford University Press.

Nakayama, K., He, Z.J. & Shimojo, S. (1995). Visual surface recognition: A critical link between lower-level and higher-level vision. In S.M. Kosslyn & D.N. Osherson (Eds.) *Visual cognition: An invitation to cognitive science* (vol. 2, 2nd edn., pp. 1–70). Cambridge: MIT Press.

Natsoulas, T. (1991). "Why do things look as they do?": Some Gibsonian answers to Koffka's question. *Philosophical Psychology,* **4**, 183–202.

Porterfield, W. (1759). *A treatise on the eye: The manner and phaenomena of vision,* 2 vols. Edinburgh: J. Balfour.

Ptolemy, C. (1989). In A. Lejeune (Ed.) *L'Optique de Claude Ptolémée, dans la version latine d'après l'arabe de l'émir Eugène de Sicile.* Leiden and New York: E. J. Brill.

Ptolemy, C. (1996). In A.M. Smith (Ed.) *Ptolemy's theory of visual perception: An English translation of the Optics.* Philadelphia: American Philosophical Society.

Pylyshyn, Z. (1984). *Computation and cognition: Toward a foundation for cognitive science.* Cambridge: MIT Press.

Quinlan, P.T. (1991). *Connectionism and psychology: A psychological perspective on new connectionist research.* Chicago: University of Chicago Press.

Rock, I. (1975). *Introduction to perception.* New York: Macmillan Publishing Co.

Rock, I. (1983). *Logic of perception.* Cambridge: MIT Press.

Rohault, P. (1735). *System of natural philosophy,* translated by J. Clarke (3rd edn., 2 vols.). London: James, John and Paul Knapton.

Rosenfeld, A. (1990). Pyramid algorithms for efficient vision. In C. Blakemore (Ed.) *Vision: Coding and efficiency* (pp. 423–430). Cambridge: Cambridge University Press.

Runeson, S. (1977). On the possibility of smart perceptual mechanisms. *Scandinavian Journal of Psychology*, **18**, 172–179.

Scheerer, E. (1994). Psychoneural isomorphism: Historical background and contemporary relevance. *Philosophical Psychology*, **7**, 183–210.

Schwartz, R. (1994). *Vision: Variations on some Berkeleian themes*. Oxford: Basil Blackwell.

Shannon, C.E. (1948). A mathematical theory of communication. *Bell System Technical Journal*, **27**, 379–423, 623–656.

Smith, E.E. (1995). Concepts and categorization. In E.E. Smith & D.N. Osherson (Eds.) *Thinking: An invitation to cognitive science* (vol. 3, 2nd edn., pp. 3–33). Cambridge: MIT Press.

Smith, R. (1738). *Compleat system of opticks*, 2 vols. Cambridge: Printed for the author.

Steinbuch, J.G. (1811). *Beytrag zur Physiologie der Sinne*. Nurnberg: J.L. Schragg.

Teller, D.Y. & Pugh, E.N. (1983). In J.D. Mollon & L.T. Sharpe (Eds.) *Colour vision: Physiology and psychophysics* (pp. 577–589). London: Academic Press.

Tourtual, C.T. (1827). *Die Sinne des Menschen in den wechselseitigen Beziehungen ihres psychischen und organischen Lebens: Ein Beitrag zur physiologischen Aesthetick*. Münster: Coppenrath.

Tye, M. (1991). *The imagery debate*. Cambridge: MIT Press.

Tye, M. (1995). *Ten problems of consciousness: A representational theory of the phenomenal mind*. Cambridge: MIT Press.

Wandell, B.A. (1995). *Foundations of vision*. Sunderland, Mass.: Sinauer Associates.

Young, T. (1807). *Course of lectures on natural philosophy and the mechanical arts*, 2 vols. London: Joseph Johnson.

6

Statistical Decision Theory and Biological Vision

LAURENCE T. MALONEY

Institut für Biophysik, Freiburg, Germany

I know of only one case in mathematics of a doctrine which has been accepted and developed by the most eminent men of their time ... which at the same has appeared to a succession of sound writers to be fundamentally false and devoid of foundation. Yet this is quite exactly the position in respect of inverse probability [an estimation method based on Bayes' theorem].

R.A. Fisher (1930) *Inverse Probability*

Statistical Decision Theory (SDT) emerged in essentially its final form with the 1954 publication of Blackwell and Girshick's *Theory of Games and Statistical Decisions*. The elements out of which it developed antedate it, in some cases by centuries, and, as the title indicates, an immediate stimulus to its development was the publication of *Theory of Games and Economic Behavior* by von Neumann and Morgenstern (1944/1953). Like Game Theory, SDT is normative, a set of principles that tell us how to act so as to maximize gain and minimize loss.[1]

The basic metaphor of SDT is that of a game between an Observer and the World. The Observer has imperfect information about the state of the World, analogous to sensory information, and must choose an action from among a limited repertoire of possible actions. This action, together with the true state of the World, determines its gain or loss: whether it has stumbled off a cliff in the dark, avoided an unwelcome invitation to (be) lunch, or—most important of all—correctly responded in a psychophysical task. SDT prescribes how the Observer should choose among possible actions, given what information it has, so as to maximize its expected gain.

Bayesian Decision Theory (BDT) is a special case of SDT, but one of particular relevance to a vision scientist. Recently, a number of authors (see, in particular, Knill et al., 1996; Knill & Richards, 1996; Kersten & Schrater, this volume) have argued that BDT and related Bayesian-inspired techniques form a particularly congenial "language"

Perception and the Physical World: Psychological and Philosophical Issues in Perception.
Edited by Dieter Heyer and Rainer Mausfeld. © 2002 John Wiley & Sons, Ltd.

for modeling aspects of biological vision. We are, in effect, invited to believe that increased familiarity with this *"language"* (its concepts, terminology, and theory) will eventually lead to a deeper understanding of biological vision through better models, better hypotheses and better experiments. To evaluate a claim of this sort is very different from testing a specific hypothesis concerning visual processing. The prudent, critical, or eager among vision scientists need to master the language of SDT/BDT before evaluating, disparaging, or applying it as a framework for modeling biological vision.

Yet the presentation of SDT and BDT in research articles is typically brief. Standard texts concerning BDT and Bayesian methods are directed to statisticians and statistical problems. Consequently, it is difficult for the reader to separate important assumptions underlying applications of BDT to biological vision from the computational details; it is precisely these assumptions that need to be understood and tested experimentally. Accordingly, this chapter is intended as an introduction for those working in biological vision to the elements of SDT and to their intelligent application in the development of models of visual processing. It is divided into an introduction, four "sections", and a conclusion.

In the first of the four sections, I present the basic framework of SDT, including BDT. This framework is remarkably simple; I have chosen to present it in a way that emphasizes its visual or geometric aspects, although the equations are there as well. As the opening quote from Fisher hints, certain Bayesian practices remain controversial. The controversy centers on the representation of belief in human judgment and decision making, and the "updating" of belief in response to evidence. In the initial presentation of the elements of SDT and BDT in the next section, I will avoid controversy by considering only decisions made at a single instant of time (*"instantaneous BDT"*), where the observer has complete information.

SDT comprises a "mathematical toolbox" of techniques, and anyone using it to model decision making in biological vision must, of course, decide how to assemble the elements into a biologically-pertinent model: SDT itself is no more a model of visual processing than is the computer language Matlab®. The second section of the article contains a discussion of the elements of SDT, how they might be combined into biological models, and the difficulties likely to be encountered Shimojo and Nakayama (1992), among others, have argued that optimal Bayesian computations require more "data" about the world than any organism could possibly learn or store. Their argument seems conclusive. If organisms are to have accurate estimates of relevant probabilities in moderately complex visual tasks, then they must have the capability to assign probabilities to events they have never encountered, and to estimate gains for actions they have never taken. The implications of this claim are discussed.

The third section comprises two "challenges" to the Bayesian approach, the first concerning the status of the visual representation in BDT-derived models. To date, essentially all applications of BDT to biological vision have been attempts to model the process of arriving at internal estimates of depth, color, shape, etc., with little consideration of the real consequences of errors in estimation. A typical "default" goal is to minimize the least-square error of the estimate. But the consequences of errors in, for example, depth estimation depend on the specific visual task that the organism is engaged in—leaping a chasm, say, versus tossing a stone at a target. BDT is in essence a way to choose among actions given knowledge of their consequences: it is equally applicable to leaping chasms, and to tossing stones. What is not obvious is how BDT can be used to compute internal estimates when the real consequences of error are not known. This discussion is evidently relevant to issues concerning perception and action raised by Milner and Goodale (1996) and others.

The second challenge concerns vision across time and what I will call the *updating problem*. Instantaneous BDT assumes that, in each instant of time, the environment is essentially stochastic. Given full knowledge of the distributions of the possible outcomes, instantaneous BDT prescribes how to choose the optimal action. Across time, however, the distributional information may itself change, and change deterministically. The amount of light available outdoors in terrestrial environments varies stochastically from day to day but also cycles deterministically over every 24-hour period. I describe a class of *Augmented Bayes Observers* that can anticipate such patterned change and make use of it.

A recurring criticism of Bayesian biological vision is that is computationally implausible. Given that we know essentially nothing about the computational resources of the brain, this sort of criticism is premature. Nevertheless, it is instructive to consider possible implementations of BDT, and the fourth section of the article discusses what might be called "Bayesian computation" and its computational complexity.

Blackwell and Girshick's *Theory of Games and Statistical Decisions* appeared just 300 years after the 1654 correspondence of Pascal and Fermat in which they developed the modern concepts of expectation and decision making guided by expectation maximization (reported in Huygens, 1657; Arnauld 1662/1964; see Ramsey, 1931a). It appeared obvious to Pascal, Fermat, Arnauld and their successors that any reasonable and reasonably intelligent person would act so as to maximize gain. It is a peculiar fact that all of the ideas underlying SDT and BDT (probabilistic representation of evidence, expectation maximization, etc.) were originally intended to serve as both normative *and* descriptive models of human judgment and decision making. Many advocates of a "Bayesian framework" for biological vision find it equally evident that perceptual processing can be construed as maximizing an expected gain (Knill et al., 1986; Kersten & Schrater, this volume).

It is therefore important to recognize that, as a model of *conscious* human judgment and decision making, BDT has proven to be fundamentally wrong (Green & Swets, 1966/1974; Edwards, 1968; Tversky & Kahneman, 1971, 1973, 1970; Kahneman & Tversky, 1972; see also Kahneman & Slovic, 1982; Nisbett & Ross, 1982). People's use of probabilities and information concerning possible gains deviates in many respects from normative use as prescribed by SDT/BDT and the axioms of probability theory. The observed deviations are large and patterned, suggesting that, in making decisions consciously, human observers are following rules other than those prescribed by SDT/BDT.

Therefore, those who argue that the Bayesian approach is a "necessary", "obvious" or "natural" framework for perceptual processing (Knill et al., 1996; Kersten & Schrater, this volume) should perhaps explain why the same framework fails as a model of human conscious judgment, for which it was developed. It would be interesting to systematically compare "cognitive" failures in reasoning about probability, gain, and expectation to performance in analogous visually-guided tasks. I will return to this point in the final discussion.

A companion article in this volume (Kersten & Schrater, this volume) contains a review of recent work in Bayesian biological vision, and a second companion article (von der Twer, Heyer & Mausfeld, this volume) contains a spirited critique. Knill and Richards (1996) is a good starting point for the reader interested in past work. Williams (1954) is still a delightful introduction to Game Theory, a component of SDT. Ferguson (1967) is an advanced mathematical presentation of SDT and BDT, while Berger (1985) and O'Hagan (1994) are excellent, modern presentations with emphasis on statistical issues.

AN OUTLINE OF STATISTICAL DECISION THEORY

> *... to judge what one ought to do to obtain a good or avoid an evil, one must not only consider the good and evil in itself, but also the probability that it will or will not happen; and view geometrically[2] the proportion that all these things have together ....*
> A. Arnauld (1662/1964) Logic, or the Art of Thinking

ELEMENTS

As mentioned above, Statistical Decision Theory (Blackwell & Girshick, 1954) developed out of Game Theory (von Neumann & Morgenstern, 1944/1953), and the basic ideas underlying it are still most easily explained in the context of a game with two players, to whom I'll refer as the *Observer* and the *World*.

In any particular application of Statistical Decision Theory (SDT) in biological vision, the Observer and the World take on specific identities. The possible states of the World may comprise a list of distances to surfaces in all directions away from the Observer, while the Observer is a depth estimation algorithm. Alternatively, the World may have only two possible states (SIGNAL and NO-SIGNAL) and the Observer judges the state of the World. As these examples suggest, the same organism may employ different choices of "Observer", "World", and the other elements of BDT in carrying out different visual tasks via different visual "modules".

In both of these examples, the Observer's task is to *estimate* the state of the World. SDT and the subset of it known as Bayesian Decision Theory (BDT) are typically used to model estimation tasks within biological vision: "the World is in an unknown state; estimate the unknown state". Recent textbooks tend to emphasize estimation, and vision scientists do tend to view early visual processing as fundamentally an estimation task (Marr, 1982; Wandell, 1995; Knill & Richards, 1996).

Yet SDT itself has potentially broader applications: earlier presentations (Blackwell & Girshick, 1954; Ferguson, 1967) emphasized that SDT is fundamentally a theory of preferable actions, with estimation regarded as only one particular kind of action. Rather than estimate the distance to a nearby object, the Observer can decide whether it is desirable to throw something at it, or to run away, or both, or neither. And, rather than assess whether a SIGNAL is or is not present, the Observer may concentrate on what to tell the experimenter in a signal detection task, so as to maximize his reward. In both cases the emphasis is on the consequences of the Observer's actions, and the Observer's "accuracy" in estimating the state of the World is of only secondary concern, if it is of any concern at all.

What is constant in all applications of SDT is that (1) the Observer has imperfect information about the World through a process analogous to sensation, that (2) the Observer acts upon the World, and that (3) the Observer is rewarded as a function of the state of the World and its own actions. I'll begin by describing the elements of SDT (and eventually BDT) at *a single instant of time*. We are not yet concerned with past or future but only with selecting the best action at one point in time that I'll refer to as a *turn*.

On each turn, the World is in one of several possible states,

$$\Theta = \{\theta_1, \theta_2, \ldots, \theta_m\}, \tag{6.1}$$

and the current state of the World is denoted θ_*. Each of the states of the World can be a vector (a list of numbers) and need not be just a single number. In any modeling application, the World need only include the information needed to determine the consequences of the Observer's possible actions.

On each turn, the Observer's selects one of its possible *actions,*

$$A = \{\alpha_1, \alpha_2, \ldots, \alpha_n\}. \tag{6.2}$$

Each action can be a vector (a list of actions). An action might, for example, specify a sequence of motor commands to be issued. The chosen action is denoted α_*. The current state of the World and the Observer's choice of action together determine the Observer's *gain*. The *gain function*, $G(\alpha, \theta)$, is simply a tabulation of the gain corresponding to any combination of World state and action.

If the current state of the world, θ_*, were known, it would be a very simple matter to find an action α_* that maximized $G(\alpha_*, \theta_*)$, the gain to the Observer (there may be several actions that each maximize gain). We will assume that the Observer does not have direct knowledge of the current state of the World and must select an action without knowing precisely what gain will result. The framework developed so far is that of Game Theory, and any text on Game Theory contains descriptions of strategies to employ when we have no information about the current state of the World (for example, Williams, 1954).

Within the framework of Statistical Decision Theory, the Observer has additional, imperfect information about the current state of the World, in the form of a random variable, X, whose distribution depends upon it. The random variable, X, which serves to model sensory input, can only take on values[3] in a set of *sensory states*,

$$X = \{\chi_1, \chi_2, \ldots, \chi_p\}. \tag{6.3}$$

Again, each of the sensory states can be a vector. For example, the current sensory state could comprise the instantaneous excitations of all of the retinal photoreceptors of an organism. The probability of taking on any particular value χ_* during the current turn depends, at least formally, on the current state of the world, θ_*. The *likelihood function*,

$$\lambda(\theta_i, \chi_j) = P[X = \chi_j \mid \theta_* = \theta_i], \tag{6.4}$$

serves as a summary of these conditional probabilities. I will refer to the current value of X on the current turn as the Observer's *current sensory state*, denoted χ_*.

On a single turn, the only useful information available to the Observer about the current state of the World is the sensory state, the value of the random variable X. I will assume, for now, that his choice of action, α_*, is completely determined by this current sensory state, χ_*. We can then write,

$$\alpha_* = \delta(\chi_*), \tag{6.5}$$

a *(deterministic) decision rule*.[4] Since χ_* is a random variable, so is α_*, and so is the gain, $G(\delta(\chi_*), \theta_*)$.

There are n^p possible, distinct decision rules (each of the p sensory states can be mapped to any one of n possible actions). Because there are only a finite number of possible World states, possible Sensory states, possible Actions, and possible decision rules, I will be able to present SDT in a very straightforward and intuitive manner. In the section titled "*The continuous case*" (p. 158), I'll describe how the basic mathematical results of the theory change once we abandon the assumption of finiteness.

For any given choice of rule, we can compute the *expected gain* (EG)[5] for any particular state of the World, θ,

$$EG(\delta, \theta) = \sum_{j=1,2,\ldots,p} \lambda(\theta, \chi_j) G(\delta(\chi_j), \theta). \tag{6.6}$$

The expected gain depends upon both the decision rule, δ, and the unknown state of the World, θ. SDT assumes that all preferences among rules are determined by the expected gains. Statistical Decision Theory is the study of how to choose a good decision rule, δ. Its elements are summarized in Figure 6.1. We next consider criteria that help us decide which rules are "better" than others.

DOMINANCE AND ADMISSIBILITY

For now, let's assume that there are only two possible World states, θ_1 and θ_2. Each of the points in Figure 6.2 corresponds to a decision rule. For each rule, δ, the expected gain $EG(\delta, \theta_1)$ in World state θ_1 is plotted on the horizontal axis versus the expected gain $EG(\delta, \theta_2)$ in World state θ_2. I'll refer to this point as the *gains point* corresponding to the rule. Of course, two rules may share a single gains point if they result in identical expected gain in each World state. I'll sometimes refer to "the rules corresponding to a particular gains point" or "a rule corresponding to a particular gains point". If there were more than two World states we would add dimensions to this *gains plot*, but each decision rule would still map to a single point in this higher dimensional space.

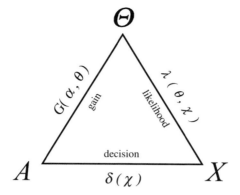

Figure 6.1 *The elements of Statistical Decision Theory.* The three sets at the vertices are Θ, the possible *states of the World*, X, the possible *sensory states*, and A, the available *actions*. The three edges correspond to the gain function, G, the likelihood function, λ, and the decision rule, δ.

Next, consider the expected gains obtainable from each of the three rules labeled δ_1, δ_2, and δ_3. Expected gain increases as we go up or to the right in the graph in Figure 6.2. Examining the rules, it is clear that some of them have higher gain than others, independent of the state of the World. Rule δ_3, in particular, is a sad creature. No matter what the state of the World, rule δ_1 has a higher expected gain than rule δ_3. Rule δ_1 is said to *dominate* rule δ_3 and it is evident that rule δ_3 should never be employed if rule δ_1 is available. The exact definition of dominance is slightly more complicated: one rule is said to dominate a second if its expected gain is never less than that of the second rule for any state of the World, and is strictly greater for at

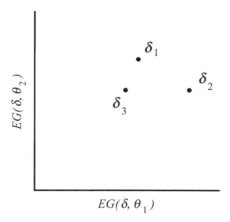

Figure 6.2 *A gains plot.* For any decision rule δ, we plot its expected gain in the first World state, $EG(\delta, \theta_1)$, on the first axis, its expected gain in the second World state, $EG(\delta, \theta_2)$, on the second, etc. The resulting *gains points* for three rules are shown, labeled δ_1, δ_2, and δ_3. The plot shown is two-dimensional and, consequently, can only correspond to a World with two states. If there are m World states the gains plot will be m-dimensional.

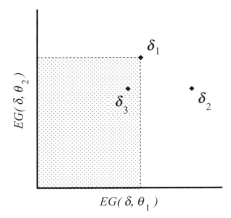

Figure 6.3 *Dominance.* Examples of a *dominated* rule, δ_3, and two *admissible* rules δ_1 and δ_2 in a gains plot are shown. The rule δ_3 is dominated by the rule δ_1 since the latter has a higher expected gain in both World states. It is also dominated by the rule δ_2 since the latter has the same expected gain in one World state and a strictly higher expected gain in the other. The *dominance shadow* of δ_1, enclosing δ_3, is shown. A rule whose gains points fall in this region (including the edges but *not* the Northeast vertex) is dominated by rule δ_1.

least one state of the World. By this definition, rule δ_2 dominates rule δ_3, even though the two rules have the same expected gain in World state 2. The dotted lines in the gains plot in Figure 6.3 sketch out the "dominance shadows" of one of the rules. Any rule falling in the dominance shadow of a second is dominated by it.

Rule δ_2 does not dominate rule δ_1 in Figure 6.2, nor does rule δ_1 dominate rule δ_2. Rules that are dominated by no other rule are *admissible rules* (Ferguson, 1967). The wise decision maker, in choosing a rule, confines his attention to the admissible rules.

MIXTURE RULES

Given two rules, δ_1 and δ_2, we can create a new rule d by *mixing* them as follows: "Given the current sensory state χ_*, take action $\delta_1(\chi_*)$ with probability q, otherwise take action $\delta_2(\chi_*)$." The new rule is an example of a *randomized decision rule* or *mixture rule*. We will use the letter d to denote such rules. From now on I'll refer to the original, non-randomized decision rules as *deterministic rules*. While there are only finitely many deterministic rules, the mixture of any two of them results in infinitely many randomized decision rules, one for each value of q. The application of a mixture rule to the current sensory state is, accordingly, denoted $d(\chi_*)$.

When the mixture probability q is 1, the resulting mixture rule is identical to the deterministic rule $\delta_1(\chi_*)$, so we can regard all of the deterministic rules as mixture rules as well. The expected gain of a mixture rule is easily computed,

$$EG(d, \theta_*) = q EG(\delta_1, \theta_*) + (1 - q)EG(\delta_2, \theta_*) \qquad (6.7)$$

that is, one may expect to receive the expected gain associated with rule δ_1 with

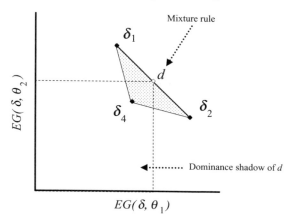

Figure 6.4 *Mixture rules.* The upper-right edge of the shaded triangle contains the gains points for all the randomized decision rules resulting from probabilistic mixtures of the deterministic rules, δ_1 and δ_2. The triangle contains the gains points of all randomized rules resulting from probabilistic mixtures of δ_1, δ_2, and δ_4. The rule δ_4 is dominated by several of the rules resulting from mixtures of δ_1 and δ_2, and one dominance shadow containing δ_4 is shown. Note that δ_4 is dominated by a mixture of δ_1 and δ_2 but not by either δ_1 or δ_2 alone.

probability q, and otherwise, with probability $1-q$, the expected gain associated with rule δ_2. Further, it is permissible to mix mixture rules to get new mixture rules.

The graphical representation of mixture rules is very simple: as q is varied between 1 and 0, the gain points corresponding to the new mixture rules fall on the line segment joining the points corresponding to δ_1 and δ_2 (see Figure 6.4). If we mix the new mixture rules corresponding to points along this line segment with the point labeled δ_4, the resulting points fill a triangle with vertices labeled δ_1, δ_2, and δ_4. These are precisely the expected gains in the two World states that can be achieved, given the three deterministic rules and all their mixtures. Note that δ_4 is not dominated by either of the deterministic rules δ_1 or δ_2 but is dominated by a mixture of the two. The dominance shadow of one of the mixtures that dominates δ_4 is shown in Figure 6.4.

The shaded area in any gains plot (the *region of achievable gains*) will always be convex,[6] and the admissible rules will correspond to points along its upper-right frontier. The admissible rules in the gains plot in Figure 6.4 are precisely the mixtures of δ_1 and δ_2, including, of course, the two deterministic rules themselves.

From now on, the term "rule" will be used to refer to both mixture rules and deterministic rules considered as special cases of mixture rules. The letter used to denote a rule will typically be d.

EXAMPLE: THE THEORY OF SIGNAL DETECTABILITY

Consider a very simple perceptual task: The World is in one of two states,

$$\Theta = \{\text{SIGNAL}, \text{NO-SIGNAL}\} \tag{6.8}$$

and the Observer has two possible actions,

$$A = \{\text{SAY-YES, SAY-NO}\} \qquad (6.9)$$

The sensory information X available to the Observer has different distributions, depending on the state of the World, known in the Theory of Signal Detectability (TSD)[7] as the *signal + noise distribution* and the *noise distribution*. These two distributions, taken together, determine the likelihood function introduced above. Much work in TSD theory begins with an explicit assumption concerning the parametric form of the signal + noise and noise distributions (Green & Swets 1966/1974; Egan, 1975) but the particular choice of distributions is not relevant to this example.

TSD can be treated as an application of SDT (Statistical Decision Theory) to the simple problem just outlined (Green & Swets, 1966/1974; Egan, 1975).[8] We can define the gain function as follows: one unit of gain results if the state of the World is SIGNAL and the action selected is SAY-YES or if the state of the world is NO-SIGNAL and the action selected is SAY-NO. Otherwise the gain is 0. The expected gain is easily computed: when the state of the World is SIGNAL, it is the probability of SAY-YES, when the state of the World is NO-SIGNAL, it is the probability of SAY-NO. In the standard terminology of TSD, these two probabilities are referred to as the HIT rate, denoted H, and the CORRECT-REJECTION rate, denoted CR. Figure 6.5 is the gains plot for this version of TSD. The convex shaded area corresponds to the gains

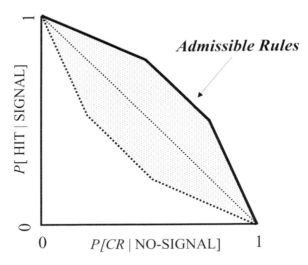

Figure 6.5 *A gains plot for a version of the Theory of Signal Detectability.* The two possible World states are SIGNAL and NO-SIGNAL, and the expected gains are the probability of saying YES when the World state is SIGNAL (a "Hit" in the terminology of TSD) and the probability of saying NO when it is NO-SIGNAL (a "Correct Rejection"). The gains points corresponding to admissible rules (bold solid contour) form the "ROC curve" of TSD, reflected around the vertical axis (in TSD it is customary to plot the False Alarm rate on the horizontal axis, not the Correct Rejection rate). The shape of the ROC curve depends on the choice of the underlying distributions and it may be smooth or polygonal as shown here (Egan, 1975).

achievable by any possible rule. The admissible rules fall on the darkened edge facing up and to the right, as shown.

Of course, the set of admissible rules is precisely the Receiver Operating Characteristic (ROC) curve[9] of TSD, slightly disguised. We plotted *CR* as the measure of gain along the horizontal axis where the World-state is NO-SIGNAL. In TSD, it is customary to use the FALSE-ALARM rate, denoted *FA*, which is just 1-*CR*. The net effect of this is simply to flip the normal TSD plot around the vertical axis. Viewed in a mirror, the locus of admissible rules takes on the appearance of the familiar ROC curve.

The shaded area represents all the possible observable performances for the Observer. Even if the Observer attempts to do as badly as possible in the task, for example, by replying YES when NO is dictated by an admissible rule, his performance will just fall on the mirror of the ROC curve, the locus of optimally-perverse performance. Even if he switches from rule to rule at random, his averaged performance will fall somewhere within the shaded area.

ORDERING THE RULES

The reader familiar with TSD may have remarked that we neglected to include some of the familiar components of TSD, notably the *prior probability* that a signal will occur. We will introduce such prior distributions in the next section, remedying the omission. However, it is important to realize that Statistical Decision Theory (SDT) is not limited to the case where we know the prior probability that the World is in any one of its states. It is applicable even when the World state cannot reasonably be modeled as a random variable, as, for example, when the World is another creature capable of anticipating any strategy we develop and dedicated to defeating us. It is important to understand what is gained through knowing this prior distribution and what is lost by acting as if it were known when in fact, it is not.

Note that SDT, as developed so far, cannot, in general, tell us which of two rules to choose. Only in the special case where one rule dominates the other, is it clear that the dominated rule can only lead to reduced expected gain. Although SDT cannot tell us which rule is the best, we can assume that the best rule will be an admissible rule.

We seek an ordering criterion that allows us to order the rules unambiguously, and to select the best among them. The Bayes criterion, presented in the next section, is such a criterion.

[*An aside*: The literature concerning Bayesian approaches to biological vision is almost entirely concerned with rules judged to be optimal by the Bayes criterion. The Bayes criterion can also be used to order rules (and visual systems) that are distinctly sub-optimal. We'll return to this point in later sections.]

There are plausible criteria for ordering the rules other than Bayes. The remainder of this section concerns a second ordering criterion, the Maximin criterion. The Maximin criterion of Game Theory (von Neumann & Morgenstern, 1944/1953) assigns to each rule its "worst case" gain: for any rule δ, the *Maximin gain* is,

$$\text{Mm}(\delta) = \min_{\theta \in \Theta} EG(\delta, \theta). \tag{6.10}$$

The expected gain for rule δ can be no less than $\text{Mm}(\delta)$, no matter what the state

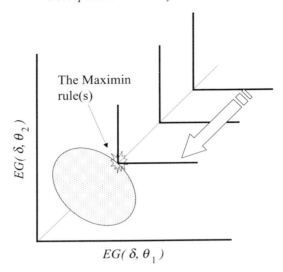

The Maximin
rule(s)

$EG(\delta, \theta_2)$

$EG(\delta, \theta_1)$

Figure 6.6 *Graphical computation of the gains point corresponding to the Maximin rule.* The "wedge" slides along the 45-degree line from upper-right to lower-left until it just touches the convex area at the point surrounded by a "blast". Any rule with this gains point is a Maximin rule.

of the World. The rules are now ordered by their Maximin gains, and the rule with largest Maximin gain is a *Maximin rule* (whose Maximin gain is the *max*imum of the *min*ima of the gains of all the rules).

The gains plot in Figure 6.6 serves to illustrate how a Maximin rule can be defined graphically. The right-angled wedge "slides down" the 45 degree line until it first touches the convex set of gains. Any rule corresponding to this point (there may be several) is a Maximin rule. If you compare the gains for a Maximin rule to that for any of the other possible rules, you will find that in at least one World state, the second rule would do worse.

The Maximin criterion is particularly appropriate when the Observer faces an implacable, omniscient World, capable of anticipating the strategic options of the Observer and taking advantage of any error. The Maximin Observer is guaranteed the Maximin gain no matter what the World chooses to do. Should the World prove to be a bit dim, indifferent, or even benevolent, the Maximin Observer can only do better.

The Maximin criterion can, of course, be used to order any two rules, admissible or not. Graphically defined, the better rule is the one whose gain point in the gains plot (Figure 6.6) first[10] touches the sliding wedge as it goes from upper-right to lower-left.

Savage (1954) criticizes the use of the Maximin criterion, notably its excessive pessimism. In particular, the Maximin Observer makes no use of any non-sensory information he may have about the state of the World. Of course, this in itself is not unreasonable. If, for example, the World is an intelligent opponent, there is reason for him to act "improbably" precisely so as to gain an advantage. Little Red Riding Hood had an accurate prior belief that wolves were not often present in Grandmother's house, and certainly not in Grandmother's bed. The Wolf took advantage of her prior belief.

PRIOR DISTRIBUTION AND BAYES' GAIN

Like Maximin Theory, Bayesian Decision Theory (BDT) provides a criterion for imposing a complete ordering on all rules, specifying when two rules are *Bayes-equivalent*, and otherwise which of the two is the better. It can also tell us which, of all the rules, is the best. In making the transition to Bayesian theory, we must first assume that the current state of the World is drawn at random from among the possible states of the World, Θ: the Intelligent, Malevolent World of Game Theory has been reduced to a set of dice. The probability that state θ is picked is denoted $\pi(\theta)$ and the probability mass function $\pi(\theta)$ is referred to as the *prior distribution* or simply the *prior* on the states of the World.

The ordering principle inherent in BDT is based on the *expected Bayes' gain* of each rule d, defined as,

$$EBG(\delta) = \sum_{\theta \in \Theta} \pi(\theta) EG(\delta, \theta), \qquad (6.11)$$

The expected Bayes' gain is the "Expected Expected Gain", averaging across the states of the World. According to the Bayes criterion, one rule is better than a second if its *EBG* is greater. Any rule with the maximum *EBG* is a *Bayes' rule*.

The graphical definition of the Bayes' rule is particularly pleasing. Consider, in Figure 6.7, the solid line that passes through the points $(0, 0)$ and $(\pi(\theta_1), (\pi(\theta_2))$, the *prior line*. The dashed lines are perpendicular to the prior, and the points on each of these dashed lines satisfy,

$$EBG(\delta) = \pi(\theta_1) EG(\delta, \theta_1) + \pi(\theta_2) EG(\delta, \theta_2) = \text{constant} \qquad (6.12)$$

These are the *lines of constant (expected) Bayes' gain*[11]; any two rules that fall on a single line of constant Bayes' gain have the same Bayes' gain: they are *Bayes-equivalent*. Bayes' gain increases as we travel up or to the right, and the optimal rules, according to the Bayes criterion, correspond to the point or points lying on the dashed line that just "touches" the upper-right frontier of the convex set of possible gains (marked in Figure 6.7). The ordering of the rules is the ordering of the lines of constant Bayes' gain.

If one accepts the assumptions of SDT and the additional assumption that there is a known prior on the (randomly-selected) states of the World, *and* if one seeks to maximize Bayes' gain, any Bayes' rule is the optimal decision rule. Please re-read the previous sentence.

The consequences of having the wrong prior distribution are very easy to visualize. In Figure 6.8 the dashed lines of constant Bayes' gain correspond to an incorrect choice of prior distribution. The solid line corresponds to the correct one. The incorrect and correct maximum gains points are highlighted and a double-arrow line shows the amount of Bayes gain lost by choosing the incorrect prior.

It is also interesting to consider the relation between the ordering of rules induced by the Maximin criterion and the ordering of rules induced by the Bayes criterion for a given prior. Is there a prior distribution such that the gains point corresponding to

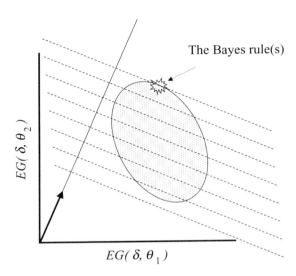

Figure 6.7 *A graphical computation of the gains point corresponding to a Bayes' rule for a given prior.* (a) The bold vector has, as coordinates, the prior probabilities of the World states: $(\pi(\theta_1), \pi(\theta_2))'$. The dashed lines are all perpendicular to the prior vector: they are the *lines of equivalent Bayes' gain.* All rules whose gains points fall on the same line of equivalent Bayes' gain have the same Bayes' gain. The Bayes' gain for these lines increases as the line is further to the North and East. The gain point with the highest Bayes' gain is marked with a "blast". The rules corresponding to this gain point are the Bayes rules for this prior. (b) The same plot, but for a different choice of prior. Note that the gain point of the Bayes rules has changed.

the Maximin rule is among the gains points corresponding to the Bayes' rule? The answer is yes: there is always[12] a choice of prior such that the gains point for any admissible rule is among the gains points of the Bayes' rule for that prior (Ferguson, 1967). As the Maximin rule is admissible, there must be a choice of prior that results in a Bayes point that has the same gains point as the Maximin rule.

This prior is sometimes, but not always, the *maximally-uninformative or uniform prior* that assigns equal probability to every World state, but it need not be. Figure 6.9 contains three diagrams, the first illustrating a case where it is, and two where it is not.

[*A caution:* When there are more than two World states, the geometric version of the Bayesian approach remains valid. The *prior line* remains a line, but the perpendicular lines of constant Bayes' gain become planes or hyper-planes. The ordering of these planes along the prior line induces the ordering of the rules.]

THE CONTINUOUS CASE

I've presented SDT and BDT in the special case where the number of possible World states, possible Sensory states, and possible actions are all finite. So soon as this finiteness assumption is abandoned, both the derivation and presentation of the basic results of the theory become difficult. Remarkably, the basic geometric intuitions

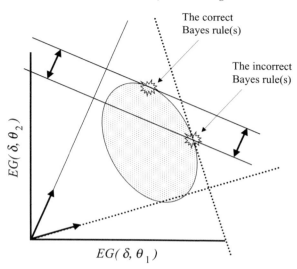

Figure 6.8 *Consequences of selecting an incorrect prior.* The dotted lines mark the location of the gain point of the Bayes rules for a prior distribution that is incorrect. The lines of equivalent Bayes' gain for the true prior are shown as solid line. Note that the Bayes rules for the incorrect prior share a Bayes' gain strictly inferior to the Bayes' gain for the *true* Bayes' rules. The double-headed arrow marks the cost of having incorrect prior information.

remain more or less intact, even when the gains plot becomes infinite-dimensional. The corresponding proofs become difficult and non-intuitive, and center on issues of existence. Is there always one or more admissible rules, a Maximin rule, a Bayes' rule for every prior? ("No", "No", "No".) Even when a Bayes' rule does not exist, we can typically find rules that, although they are not admissible, come as close as we like to the performance of the non-existent Bayes' rule. Ferguson (1967) presents this difficult material very clearly with constant reliance on geometric intuition accumulated in consideration of the finite case.

To translate from the finite case to what I will refer to as the continuous case, we need only change the notation above slightly. Recall that θ, χ, and α were potentially vectors above, something we made no use of (and will make no use of). The sets Θ, A, and X are subsets of real vector spaces of possibly different dimensions, the gain function $G(\alpha, \theta)$ is defined as before, and the likelihood function $\lambda(\theta, \chi)$ is a probability density function on χ for any choice of the world state θ (it is a parametric family of probability density functions with parameter θ). The summation signs in the finite case are replaced by integrals. Expected gain (Equation 6.6) becomes (replacing the notation for a deterministic decision rule δ by that for a randomized rule d),

$$EG(d, \theta) = \int \lambda(\theta, \chi) G(d(\chi), \theta) d\chi, \qquad (6.13)$$

a multidimensional integral if X is a subset of a multidimensional real space.

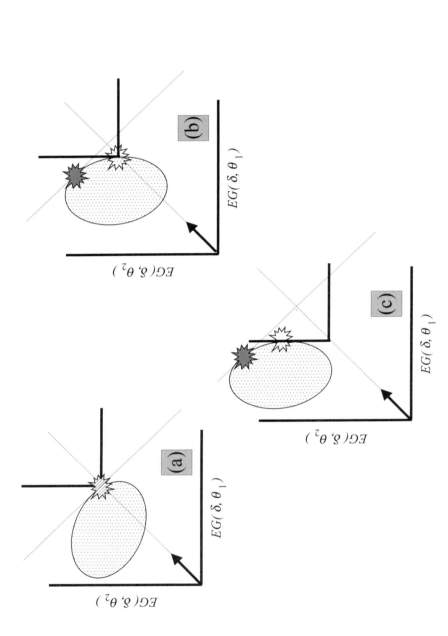

Figure 6.9 *Maximin and Bayes.* The Maximin rule has the same gains point (marked with a starburst) as the Bayes' rule with a uniform (*maximally-uniformative*) prior. (b) and (c). The prior of the Bayes' rule corresponding to the Maximin rule is not uniform. The gains point corresponding to the Maximin rule is marked with a white starburst, the gains point corresponding to the Bayes' rule with uniform prior is marked with a shaded starburst.

Expected Bayes' gain (Equation (6.11)) becomes,

$$EBG(\delta) = \int \pi(\theta) EG(d, \theta) d\theta, \tag{6.14}$$

which is a multidimensional integral if θ is multidimensional. Substituting Equation (6.13) into Equation (6.14), we find that

$$EBG(\delta) = \iint \pi(\theta) \lambda(\theta, \chi) G(d(\chi), \theta) \, d\chi d\theta. \tag{6.15}$$

If, for a given prior, there is a rule whose expected Bayes' gain, computed by the previous equation, is greater than or equal to that of all other rules, then it is a Bayes' rule.

BAYES' THEOREM AND THE POSTERIOR DISTRIBUTION

A vision scientist familiar with the usual presentation of BDT in the vision literature may feel that something is missing. We have developed Bayesian Decision Theory without mentioning Bayes' Theorem! A version of Bayes' Theorem[13] is often the first equation to appear in a vision article concerned with Bayesian approaches. In fact, Bayes' Theorem plays a very minor role in BDT, serving only to help us develop a clever way to compute optimal rules based on Equation (6.11) or (6.14). Bayes' Theorem lets us develop a simple method for computing the rule d that maximizes,

$$EBG(\delta) = \iint \pi(\theta) \lambda(\theta, \chi) G(d(\chi), \theta) d\chi d\theta. \tag{6.16}$$

In this section, I'll first describe how Bayes' Theorem allows us to simplify Equation (6.16). Of course, were we ignorant of Bayes' Theorem, we could still maximize Equation (6.16) numerically by choice of d (see O'Hagan, 1994, Ch. 8).

First note that the likelihood function $\lambda(\theta, \chi)$ is, within the framework of BDT, a conditional distribution $f(\chi \mid \theta)$ of the random variable χ on the random variable θ and, by a variant of Bayes' Theorem,[14] we can find probability density functions g and h such that,

$$f(\chi \mid \theta) \pi(\theta) = g(\theta \mid \chi) h(\chi) \tag{6.17}$$

Substituting the right-hand side of Equation (6.17) into Equation (6.16), and reversing the order of integration by Fubini's Theorem (Buck, 1978), we have,

$$EBG(\delta) = \int \left[\int g(\theta \mid \chi) G(d(\chi), \theta) d\theta \right] h(\chi) d\chi \tag{6.18}$$

The probability density function $h(\chi)$ is non-negative: to maximize the outer integral, it suffices to maximize the inner integral separately for each choice of χ, plausibly a simpler computation than the maximization of the original integral.

This method of computation, made possible by an application of Bayes' Theorem, has a straightforward interpretation. Once the Observer, following a Bayes' rule, has learned the current Sensory state χ_*, he effectively forgets that there were ever alternative outcomes for the Sensory state and chooses his action α so to maximize,

$$\int g(\theta \mid \chi_*)G(\alpha, \theta)d\theta \qquad (6.19)$$

the expected gain with respect to the *posterior distribution* $g(\theta \mid \chi_*)$ on θ. At this point, the current sensory state (or rather, its realization) χ_* is known, non-stochastic. We can interpret the posterior distribution as an updated prior distribution and, arguably, the Observer should use it, rather than the prior on a subsequent turn, all else being equal. This use of the posterior as the new prior is a controversial aspect of Bayesian theory, and I'll return to it in the third section.

SDT AS A MODEL OF BIOLOGICAL VISUAL PROCESSING

This model will be a simplification and an idealization, and consequently, a falsification. It is to be hoped that the features retained for discussion are those of greatest importance in the present state of knowledge.
A.M. Turing (1952) *The Chemical Basis of Morphogenesis*

Let us distinguish two possible applications of instantaneous BDT to biological vision. We could, first of all, use SDT/BDT to model the instantaneous visual environment of an Observer, making no claims about how the Observer processes visual information. Most psychophysical experiments are instantiations of instantaneous *Bayesian environments* designed by an Experimenter: there is a well-defined and typically small set of possible world states with specific prior probabilities and a limited set of actions available to the Observer, etc. The Experimenter takes care that the state of the World on any trial is a random variable, independent of the state of the World on other trials. We could apply the results of the previous section to compute the expected Bayes gain of an Ideal Bayesian Observer in such an experiment and compare ideal performance to the Observer's performance. This sort of application of BDT is important (Geisler, 1989; Wandell, 1995) but neither new nor controversial.

Alternatively, we could develop a model of human visual processing as a *Bayesian Observer* which,[15] given sensory information, employs BDT to maximize its expected Bayes' gain. If this Bayesian Observer had perfect information concerning the likelihood function, gain function, prior, and so forth, then it is simply the Ideal Observer just discussed. When human performance in a visual task falls short of ideal, as is typical (Geisler, 1989), the Ideal Observer is evidently an inappropriate model for human visual processing.

In this section, I consider, as candidate models of human visual processing, Bayesian Observers that have less than perfect information concerning the gain function and prior probabilities. (We could also consider Bayesian Observers that have less than perfect information concerning the other elements of SDT/BDT such as the likelihood function, but we will not do so here.)

In the previous section we saw that the Bayes criterion not only allows us to determine which rules are optimal (the Bayes rules) but also how to order all rules, optimal or not. In Figure 6.8 we saw how an incorrect choice of prior affects the expected Bayes' gain of an otherwise optimal Bayesian Observer, and we can similarly evaluate the consequences of choosing an incorrect gain function. In brief, within the framework described in the previous section, we can analyze and compare the performances of all Bayesian Observers from bad to (nearly) ideal. Such *Non-ideal Bayesian Observers* would seem to be the obvious candidate models of biological visual processing that could properly be called "Bayesian". This section comprises an analysis of the components of *Bayesian Observers*, ideal and non-ideal.

NON-IDEAL BAYESIAN OBSERVERS

The drop over the edge at the top is fatal but the views are splendid.
R. Maqsood (1996) *Petra: A Traveler's Guide*

Hesitating a few steps away from Maqsood's cliff, bordering the High Place of Sacrifice,[16] straining to see over the edge, even the sworn Bayesian may be allowed to doubt whether he has correct estimates of the instantaneous gain function and the prior distribution on friction coefficients of sandstone. He may also feel that, however much he trusts the prior distribution and gain function that allow him to navigate the streets of a city, the current situation requires something else.

Bayesian Observers choose actions by Bayesian methods, specifically by maximizing expected Bayes' gain given information about the environment encoded as priors, gain functions, etc. The Observer's environment is assumed to be a Bayesian environment with a well-defined set of World states, possible actions, and so forth. The prior distribution and the gains function, in particular, are objective, measurable parts of this environment just as much as the intensity of illumination. In this section, as in the previous section, I'll consider only a single instant of time and the action to be chosen at that instant of time.

The Ideal Bayesian Observer is assumed to have the correct values of all of the elements of SDT in Figure 6.1 and, in addition, the correct prior. In this section, we consider Bayesian Observers whose information about the prior distribution and the gains function may not be the true prior or gain function of the Environment. To raise this issue, requires a small change in notation. In addition to the objectively correct components of SDT (Figure 6.1) and the prior of BDT, which accurately describe the Bayesian environment, we have the corresponding elements available to the *Bayesian Observer*: a gain function $\tilde{G}(\theta, \alpha)$, and a prior distribution, $\tilde{\pi}(\theta)$. The tilde over each symbol indicates that the element belongs to the Observer and need not be the same as the corresponding Environmental element.

THE PRIOR FUNCTION AS "PROBABILITY ENGINE"

A recurring criticism of Bayesian approaches to modeling biological vision is that, in even very simple visual tasks, the number of possible states of the world is large, and

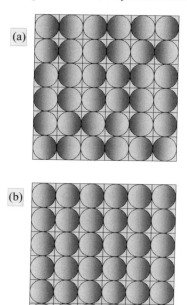

Figure 6.10 *Patterns and probabilities.* A Bayesian Observer, designed to model pattern vision, must assign probabilities to very large numbers of patterns including the "checkerboard patterns" illustrated here. The sheer number of such patterns guarantees that almost all of them have never been seen by a human observer before. The demands of the Bayesian formalism insist that a non-zero probability be assigned to such a pattern if it is to be seen at all.

it is difficult to imagine how a biological organism comes to associate the correct prior probability with each state. The states of the world in a visual task might correspond to all possible arrangements of surfaces in a scene, and is difficult to see how a visual system could acquire or encode all of these prior probabilities (Shimojo & Nakayama, 1992). Of course, we are considering non-ideal as well as ideal Bayesian Observers and we need not demand that the organism arrive at exactly the correct prior probability for each state.

   Even for relatively simple visual tasks, the number of possible World states can be very large. Consider, for example, stimuli like the one in Figure 6.10(a), $N \times N$ checkerboards, with a single "item" placed in each square and where each "item" has only one of two possible states. There are 2^{N^2} possible states in this very simple World and it would be easy to envision using such stimuli in psychophysical experiments. Yet the number of "states" in this simple world (with $N = 6$) is about 69 billion. For comparison, the number of seconds in the nominal 70-year life span is about 2.2 billion. It would take about two millennia, viewing these patterns at the rate of one per second, to encounter them all just once. It is implausible that a prior probability distribution on such patterns could be based on frequency counts of the occurrences of such patterns.

Yet these patterns form a very small proportion of the patterns that a prior distribution for a "pattern vision" Bayesian Observer should encompass. The checkerboards have an evident interpretation as "shape-from-shading" stimuli, and thus all of these stimuli fall within the domain of a Bayesian Observer model devoted to "shape from shading." Yet how could these probabilities even be stored in a nervous system? If the checkerboard is expanded to 8×8, there are more than 10^{19} patterns possible, a number larger by far than either the number of neurons or the number of synapses in the human brain. We might also wish to save a bit of brain for something besides storage of checkerboard pattern priors.

So long as we continue to think in terms of explicit storage of learned estimates of prior probabilities, the objection of Shimojo and Nakayama is unanswerable. There are too many things we *might* see, and every evaluation of expected Bayes' gain (Equation (6.11) or Equation (6.15)) involves the prior probability of every one of them. Even if we somehow decided to ignore most of the patterns in evaluating Equation (6.11) (or its continuous version, Equation (6.15)), we certainly must include the prior probability for the pattern we in fact see in Figure 6.10(a). Yet that pattern could have been any one of the 2^{N^2} possible patterns.

In the fourth section, I address the apparently overwhelming computational demands of Equations (6.11) and (6.15) and suggest that they are illusory. Yet it seems inescapable that a Bayesian Observer, even one that is specialized to be a model of just pattern vision, must be able to assign probabilities to very large numbers of possible visual outcomes, almost all of which it has never seen and almost certainly will never see.

It seems an inescapable implication of the Bayesian approach that the visual system assign probabilities to large numbers of possible scenes (or components of scenes) and that these probabilities affect visual processing. The mechanism of assignment of probabilities to scenes I'll refer to as a *Probability Engine*, for concreteness. The Probability Engine of a Bayesian Observer corresponds to $\bar{\pi}(\theta)$ in the mathematical formulation.

Consideration of the analogous problem in human judgment and decision making is instructive. Given a sentence that describes a state of affairs in the world such as (A) "Boris Yeltsin is roller-blading in Red Square", can you assign a probability to it? You may feel that, although you have a consistent assignment of probabilities to events including the one just described, you cannot come up with a number that you could write down or say out loud. You may be capable of reasoning with such probabilities, but are unable to turn them into numerical estimates on demand. Even so, there are several alternative ways for me to test whether you can coherently assign probabilities to events.

Suppose that you agree that you can order events according to their probabilities: given any two events, you can tell me which of the two is more probable. Given two sentences, the one above, and the alternative, (B) "Boris Yeltsin is asleep", you can order them by probability. Given only your ordering responses, I cannot reconstruct the probabilities you assign to these events, but I can test whether you are assigning probabilities in a way that is consistent with probability theory. Consider a third event, (C) "Boris Yeltsin is secretly married to Madonna". You assert that B is more probable than C and that C is more probable than A. Next I ask you to compare B and A. If you respond that A is more probable than B, then your pattern of responses is inconsistent. If P[B] > P[C] and P[C] > P[A], then it is not possible that P[B] > P[A]. I have tested, and rejected, the hypothesis that your orderings are consistent with any pattern of underlying probabilities assigned to events.

The probabilities assigned by the Probability Engine of any Bayesian Observer must also conform to the axioms of probability theory. This constraint can provide the basis for the sort of empirical test just outlined. If we can design experiments that plausibly allow us to infer which of any pair of patterns drawn from the class of patterns illustrated in Figure 6.10(a) is assigned a higher probability by the visual system, then we can test the transitivity property just discussed (For any three events, A, B, and C, P[A] > P[B] and P[B] > P[C] implies that P[A] > P[C]).

We can test other implications of probability theory. To return to the case of human conscious judgment and decision making, the sentence "Boris Yeltsin is roller-blading somewhere" must *not* be ranked as less probable than the sentence "Boris Yeltsin is roller-blading in Red Square". The former event, includes the latter and, by elementary properties of probability, cannot be less probable. Yet previous research suggests that, for at least some pairs of events, human judges fail precisely this kind of test (Tversky & Kahneman, 1980; see also Nisbett & Ross, 1982). It is certainly of interest, given an experimental situation where perceptual prior probabilities can be ordered, to determine whether this essential Bayesian assumption holds up.

If we can develop experimental methods that allow us to estimate not only the ordering but also the difference or ratio between pairs of events, then we can develop correspondingly more powerful tests of the claim that visual modules combine evidence according to the axioms of probability theory (Edwards, 1968; Krantz et al., 1971).

A "pattern vision" Bayesian Observer, then, must assign coherent probabilities to Figure 6.10(a) and also to the highly-regular Figure 6.10(b). If the Bayesian approach to biological vision is taken seriously, then it becomes of some importance to understand how these probabilities are generated, and it is plausible that the presence or absence of subjective patterns may influence the assignment of probabilities.

Research concerning human conscious judgment of the probabilities of patterns is perhaps relevant. In reasoning about sequences arising from independent tosses of a "fair coin" ($P[H] = P[T] = 1/2$), human judges consistently judge the sequence HHHHHH to be less probable than the sequence HHTHTH (Kahneman & Tversky, 1972; Nisbett & Ross, 1982). Of course, for a fair coin, any sequence of six tosses is as likely as any other and the human judges have gotten it wrong once again. It is plausible that the judges are responding to patterns (or the absence of patterns) in the coin toss sequences, assigning lower probability to patterned outcomes. If this were so, then it suggests that a mechanism for assigning probabilities to visual patterns is not completely unreasonable.

It would certainly be of interest to determine whether the prior probabilities assigned by a pattern vision Bayesian Observer to the patterns in Figure 6.10(a) and (b) and other patterns of this sort and try to understand how a Probability Engine assigns probabilities to never-before-encountered stimuli.

The ability to reason and judge the possible sequences resulting from successive, independent tosses of a "fair coin" itself presupposes something like a Probability Engine in cognition. It is unlikely that you have ever encountered a "fair coin": "... whenever refined statistical methods have been used to check on actual coin tossing, the result has been invariably that head and tail are not equally likely" (Feller, 1968, p. 19). Feller argues that a "fair coin" is a model, an idealization: "... we preserve the model not merely for its logical simplicity, but essentially for its usefulness and applicability. In many applications it is sufficiently accurate to describe reality." (Feller, 1968, p. 19). Just as the mathematical idealization called a "fair coin" can assign probabilities to never-before encountered coin-toss sequences, so a Probability Engine assigns probabilities to scenes. They need not be precisely correct, only useful.

THE LIKELIHOOD FUNCTION AND THE LIKELIHOOD PRINCIPLE

The likelihood function serves two roles in SDT and BDT. First of all it summarizes what we need to know about the operating characteristics of the sensors that provide information about the state of the World. Second of all, once the current sensory state χ_* is known, the likelihood function $\lambda(\theta, \chi_*)$, as a function of θ, is precisely what the Bayesian Observer knows about the state of the World. At first glance, it might seem that we would be better off retaining the actual sensory data χ_* rather than running the risk of losing information by discarding it and retaining only the likelihood function. Or perhaps it would be better to supplement the likelihood function with additional measures derived from the data.

It turns out that we lose *no* information about the state of the World when we replace the raw sensory data by the likelihood function, a remarkable result known in statistics as the *Likelihood Principle*: "All of the information about θ obtainable from an experiment is contained in the likelihood function for θ given X" (Berger & Wolpert, 1988, p. 19).

Probably every psychophysicist who collects psychometric data by an adaptive psychophysical procedure such as a "staircase" method has wondered whether it could really be correct to fit the resulting data exactly the same as if it had been collected by method of constant stimuli. After all, using an adaptive procedure, the specific intensities presented to the observer depended on the observer's performance on previous trials. Yet the fitting procedure is exactly the same as if the experiment had chosen precisely those intensities before the start of the experiment and presented them to the Observer in some other, randomized order. The justification for computing the same maximum-likelihood estimate of a psychometric function in both cases is the *Likelihood Principle*.

The likelihood function is an example of a *sufficient statistic,* a transformation of the data that retains all of the information concerning the parameters that gave rise to the data (the World state, θ, for our purposes). Any additional information in the data that is lost, is not relevant to θ.

Suppose, for example, that we have a sample, $X_1, X_2, \ldots, X_N$, of size N from a Gaussian distribution with unknown mean μ and unknown variance σ^2. We compute the maximum likelihood estimates[17] of the unknown parameters:

$$\overline{X} = \sum_{i=1}^{N} X_i / N \quad \text{and} \quad S^2 = \sum_{i=1}^{N} (X_i - \overline{X})^2 / N,$$

and consider the joint statistic $(\overline{X}, S^2)$. Given $(\overline{X}, S^2)$, how much *additional* information about μ and σ^2 is contained in the raw data, $X_1, X_2, \ldots, X_N$? The answer is: *none*. The joint statistic $(\overline{X}, S^2)$ is an example of a sufficient statistic that captures all of the information relevant to estimating the unknown parameters. Put another way, the N numbers in the original data set have been compressed to only 2 without loss of information concerning the unknown parameters. Note that we have lost information. Given $(\overline{X}, S^2)$, we cannot reconstruct the raw data when $N > 2$. We cannot even determine the order in which the data occurred. Permuting the data does not affect $(\overline{X}, S^2)$ at all and consequently no order information is preserved. What is the case is that the conditional probability distribution of $X_1, X_2, \ldots, X_N$ *given* $(\overline{X}, S^2)$ does not depend on μ or σ^2: this property is essentially the definition of a jointly sufficient statistic. Further discussions of likelihood and sufficiency can be found in Edwards (1972) and Berger and Wolpert (1988).

A visual system which retains the likelihood function, then, can do no better. Helmholtz, and especially Barlow, emphasized that neural processing concerns the representation and processing of likelihood (von Helmholtz, 1909; Barlow, 1972, 1995), a viewpoint buttressed by the Likelihood Principle.

If sensory data from multiple sources are independent, likelihood information can be readily combined across the sources. In our terminology, if the sensory data $\chi = (\chi^1, \ldots, \chi^p)$ is itself a vector, representing sensory information from p independent sensors, then the overall likelihood function is just the product of the likelihood functions based on the individual sensory data:

$$\lambda(\theta, \chi) = \prod_{k=1}^{p} \lambda(\theta, \chi^k). \tag{6.20}$$

Barlow has suggested that one of the organizing principles of neural processing is to transform sensory data so that the resulting encoding comprises many independent channels, each signaling likelihood (Barlow 1972, 1995).

GAIN FUNCTION

The choice of a gain function is, of course, important, and a non-ideal Bayesian Observer may have less than perfect information concerning the true gain function in the environment it inhabits. Freeman and Brainard (1995; Brainard and Freeman, 1997) analyze different candidate gain functions, comparing them against one another. The intent of their research is laudable, but there is a fundamental incoherence in their

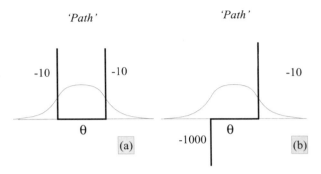

Figure 6.11 *Biases introduced by gain functions.* The figures correspond to two versions of the same visual task. The visual information is the same in both cases: a single Gaussian variable X drawn from a Gaussian distribution with mean θ. The distribution is sketched for both cases. (a) In the first the Observer must choose where to step in a path given imperfect visual information. The gain associated with going to far to right or left ("bumping into a wall") is symmetric and, across many trials the Observer's choice of step point will be symmetric about the midpoint of the path. (b) In the second version, the cost of deviations toward the left ("a sheer drop") is much greater than the cost of deviations to the right ("bumping into a wall"). The Observer's choice of step point is (correctly) biased to the right.

approach. An evident criterion for choice of a gain function is whether it reflects the true gains to the Observer: and comparing different formal gains functions to one another to see which one produces the "best" performance, judged intuitively, cannot be correct.

One possible approach would be to develop psychophysical methods that allow us to estimate the gain function of a human Observer in a particular task (just as we might estimate a contrast sensitivity function). Consideration of such empirical gain functions would give us some insight into the rewards and penalties embodied in visual processing.

The possible effect of the gain function on performance can be illustrated by a simple thought example (Figure 6.11). The visual task is to choose a location to place one's foot on a rather narrow path. There is considerable visual uncertainty concerning the location of the center of the path (perhaps it is night time) but the width of the path is known: 20 cm. The sensory data is a single random variable X, drawn from a Gaussian distribution whose mean is the center of the path, θ, and whose standard deviation is half the width of the path: 10 cm. The likelihood function is, as a consequence, a Gaussian of the same width and mean X. The maximum likelihood estimate of θ is just X, but the task is not to estimate θ: the task is to decide where to place one's foot. To make the example easier to follow, let's assume that there is no "motor" uncertainty. The foot will land wherever it is aimed. The only uncertainty in the thought example is due to the visual uncertainty surrounding the location of the center of the path.

To decide where to place the foot, we must next consider the gain function. In Figure 6.11(a), there are symmetric penalties involved in running into the two walls beside the path (-10 for running into either wall). If the likelihood function is unimodal, symmetric about its center, then a simple argument from symmetry suggests that the

Observer will place his foot in the middle of the current likelihood function, i.e. he will step on the point marked by X.

In Figure 6.11(b), however, the gain function is highly asymmetric: there is a cliff face to the right (-10 for collision) and a sheer drop (-1000) to the left. The Bayesian choice of foot placement, taking into account this asymmetry in gain, will be skewed to the right, away from the sheer drop, toward the cliff face. Again the visual information is symmetric and the bias in the response is solely due to the asymmetric gain function. I'll return to this discussion in the next section.

EXPERIMENTAL APPROACHES

The gain function $\tilde{G}(\theta, \alpha)$ and the prior $\tilde{\pi}(\theta)$ of the non-ideal Bayesian Observer are estimable psychophysical parameters, no different in kind than spectral sensitivities or contrast sensitivity. Unfortunately, we do not yet know how to design experiments so that it is possible to obtain estimates of $\tilde{G}(\theta, \alpha)$ and $\tilde{\pi}(\theta)$, directly from the data. Ramsey (1931b), von Neumann and Morgenstern (1944/1953), and Savage (1954) all developed methods that permitted estimation of subjective probability and/or subjective utility based on human performance in preference tasks. In the simple case of the Theory of Signal Delectability, prior odds and gains could, in part, be estimated from the Observer's performance once the experimenter assumed specific parametric forms for the noise and signal + noise distributions (Green & Swets, 1966/1974). The conclusions drawn were hostage to the parametric assumptions made, but it was in principle possible to separately test and verify the distributional assumptions, e.g. by consideration of the precise shape of the ROC curve (Green & Swets, 1966/1974; Egan, 1975).

Mamassian and Landy (1996; see also Mamassian et al., in press), for example, consider simple shape-from-shading stimuli where prior distributions on both the direction of illumination and on contour cues are varied independently. They are able to estimate both distributions from Observers' data with parametric assumptions on the possible priors. This sort of estimation of the components of Bayesian Decision Theory from the data would seem to be a very promising and important result of the use of BDT as a modeling framework. Of course this is only possible with strong assumptions on the possible distributions, functions, etc., that must also be independently tested.

CHALLENGES

Unfortunately, Bayes's rule has been somewhat discredited by metaphysical applica-tions . . . William Feller (1968) *An Introduction to Probability Theory*

The first part of this section contains a discussion of the status of the visual representation in an instantaneous Bayesian Observer. Simply put, most work in Bayesian vision is directed to modeling the estimation of internal representations of visual information: depth, shape, and so on. Yet SDT and BDT are theories of *preferred action*, not theories of representation, and the basis for preferring one action to another are the consequences of the actions. It is not obvious what consequences an internal visual estimate of depth can have. In this first section, I will discuss possible links between the actions of a Bayesian observer and claims about its internal visual representation, and describe how observed inconsistencies in representation inferred from different kinds of actions (Milner & Goodale, 1996) may be illusory, a simple consequence of the form of the gain function.

In the second part of this section, I will discuss the problems encountered in modeling optimal (or even "good") performance in environments where the true prior distributions and gain functions change deterministically across time, as they do in almost any environment outside the psychophysicist's laboratory.

ACTION AND REPRESENTATION

"How many fingers, Winston?"
"Four! Four! What else can I say? Four!" ....
"How many fingers, Winston?"
"Four. I suppose there are four. I would see five if I could. I am trying to see five."
"What do you wish: to persuade me that you see five, or really to see them?"
"Really to see them." George Orwell (1983) *1984*

SDT and BDT are theories of preferable actions, not representations. A moment's consideration of Winston's horrific situation, at the mercy of O'Brien in the Ministry of Love, serves to emphasize the distinction. O'Brien's goal is that Winston see five fingers when O'Brien holds up four, and his means of persuasion are most painful for Winston. It is not enough that Winston "see" four and respond five. He must "see" five, something he claims he really wants to do. The gain function here is clear, as are the possible actions, etc. If Winston were a good Bayesian Observer he would "see" five rather quickly, with a minimum of pain, something that, in the course of the novel he apparently manages to do, but only at great personal cost.

Applications of BDT to date are overwhelmingly models of internal estimates of depth, color, etc. To focus on a particular problem, let's suppose we want to estimate the distance to the edge of Maqsood's cliff. The possible answer are a range of (I would hope non-negative) real numbers, the possible states of our World. The available sensory data is the posterior distribution including the prior. We combine this posterior with a fixed gain function (I'll refer to this combination of posterior distribution and gain function as *Bayesian resolution*). Perhaps we choose a gains function that results in a least-squares estimate.

We are about to take a step and we know that errors that lead us beyond the edge of the cliff lead to very different consequences than the same magnitude of error that falls short of the edge of the cliff. The gain function we would like to combine with the posterior distribution should be highly asymmetric. Unfortunately, if we have access only to the distance representation, we have lost the posterior distribution and it is too late to compute the correct stepping distance using all of the available sensory information. The sequence of computations involved is summarized in Figure 6.12(a). The Bayesian resolution occurs before the representation, and makes use of a fixed gain function that is inappropriate to the current situation.

Perception and the Physical World

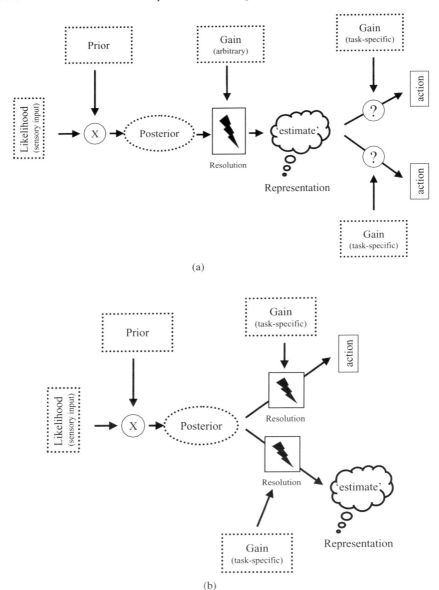

(a)

(b)

Figure 6.12 *Bayesian resolution and visual represent.* (a) Bayesian resolution occurs before the visual representation employing a fixed nominal gain function. The resulting point estimates of visual quantities such as depth must then be combined with realistic gains functions, appropriate to the current situation. The rule of combination cannot be Bayesian as the distributional information (the posterior distribution) is no longer available. (b) The visual representation is viewed as one among many different visual tasks, each of which may have a distinct gain function. (c) The visual representation is identified with the posterior distribution.

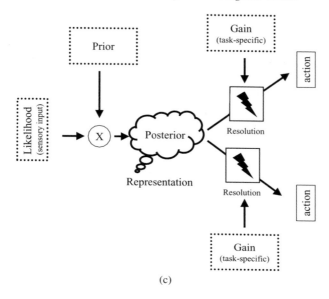

(c)

Figure 6.12 (*continued*)

A second possibility (Figure 6.12(b)) is that we combine a realistic gain function with the sensory information. If we use different realistic gain functions for determining the visual representation and for deciding how close to the edge to step, then we may exhibit an apparent dissociation between vision and action. The edge, judged psychophysically and by a stepping task, are estimated to be in different locations. It is not at all obvious what a "realistic gain function" for the representation would be: representation has no direct consequences.

Figure 6.12(c) suggests a third alternative, that what we should think of as the representation is itself the posterior distribution, or at least includes the posterior distribution. The advantage is obvious: we postpone the Bayesian resolution until after the representation and we can now use a more flexible gain function, possibly one that represents gain near the edge of a cliff or in the hands of O'Brien. There is however a marked disadvantage. What does it mean to perceive a distribution rather than a point estimate of depth?

One possible solution is to assume that conscious access to the sensory representation is itself a kind of act, one that we can model as a Bayesian resolution, but with a fixed choice of gain function specific to that sort of act (Figure 6.12(b)). Given another class of actions, such as stepping toward the cliff, we, in effect, use a different gain function.[18] If we are told to point to the edge of the cliff, or to say how far the edge of the cliff is from our feet, or to step to the edge of the cliff, the associated gain functions may lead to actions that can be interpreted as inconsistent estimates of the location of the edge.

Milner and Goodale (1996) describe the apparent discrepancies in inferred location and shape of objects based on different tasks and classes of actions. I wish to point out here that this is to be expected under BDT given Figure 6.12(c) and the discussion of bias introduced by the choice of gain function in the previous section (Figure 6.11). Recall that we examined how the structure of the gain function affected where a Bayesian Observer might choose to step on a difficult-to-see path. When the gain function is asymmetric, the Bayesian Observer's aim point is biased away from the greater source of danger (the sheer drop to the left) and toward the wall. If we were to change the class of action from step-point selection to throwing a projectile down the path, then the gain function in Figure 6.11(b) is plausibly no longer asymmetric. It makes little difference (I'll assume) whether the projectile vanishes off the path into the chasm to the left, or hits the wall to the right and stops. The Bayesian Observer for stepping and for projectile throwing would "aim" for different places on the path, given exactly the same visual information. It is no great leap to the idea that different biases are associated with different classes of actions.

Again, if it were possible to measure experimentally the gains function and prior for different tasks in the same scene, we could determine whether a verbal estimate, or pointing has the same gain function as an estimate based on a different task.

PATTERNS ACROSS TIME

We may imagine Chance and Design to be, as it were, in Competition with each other, for the production of some sort of Events . . . .
                          Abraham de Moivre (1718/1967), *The Doctrine of Chances*

Updating Priors, Updating Gain Functions

The discussion in the previous section touched on the obvious idea that both objective priors on the states of the world may change, as may objective gain functions.[19] The idea of a *probability engine* was introduced to make it clear that even very simple Bayesian Observers, specialized to depth or pattern vision, say, must be able to assign probabilities to states of the World never before encountered and that perhaps will never be encountered. In this section I consider a closely related problem. It is plausible (and will prove to be true) that an Observer who correctly updates his own subjective prior distribution and gains function can outperform an Observer with a fixed prior and a fixed gain function, across many successive turns. For this to be possible, information from the past must be preserved and used in selecting the new prior.

[*An aside:* BDT provides an obvious candidate for an updating rule, known as *Bayesian updating.* We encountered it before: at the end of each turn, we need only substitute the current posterior distribution (incorporating the sensory information) for the previous prior. The use of Bayesian updating in judgment and decision making is one of the more controversial aspects of the theory in human judgment and decision making. Even confirmed Bayesians such as Jeffrey argue that Bayesian updating is inappropriate (Jeffrey, 1983). These criticisms and potential problems are not directly relevant to the point made here, which is simply the following: Bayesian updating is a method for updating when the prior is stationary (not changing across time). It is tempting to consider using it on slowly-changing or even rapidly-changing priors in the hope that it will "track" the prior across time. The following example illustrates why Bayesian updating is not very suitable for tracking changing priors.]

Night and Day

This example concerns Bayesian updating when the objective prior does in fact change. There are two states of the World, *Day* and *Night*. *Day* endures for 40 turns followed by *Night* for 40 turns. The sensory states of the Observer are *Light* and *Dark*. The initial prior on the state of the World is uniform: the probability of *Day* and of *Night* are both 0.5. The likelihood of *Light* during the *Day* is 0.75, of *Dark*, is 0.25. During the *Night*, the likelihood of *Light* is 0.25, that of *Dark* is 0.75. We will follow the Observer's prior through a full *Day* and *Night*. Of course, the prior distribution is a distribution and we need only follow *P[Day]*, as *P[Night]* is $1 - P[Day]$.

Following "dawn", the Bayesian updating procedure rapidly moves the prior probability that it is *Day* toward 1.[20] After 10 turns, the prior is 0.9959, that it is *Day*. The problem arises at "dusk", where the state of the World turns deterministically to *Night*: the Observer's prior only slowly migrates away from 1. Indeed, three-quarters of the way through the night, the prior probability that it is *Day* is still 0.9959 despite the evidence to the contrary in the most recent 30 trials. Even at the end of the night, the probability that it is *Night* is only 0.5: the 40 turns of *Day* and of *Night* have canceled out, returning the prior to indifference just as "dawn" breaks.

The defect exhibited here is not superficial. The essential problem is that Bayesian updating gives exactly the same weight to evidence from recent turns and from turns that occurred much earlier. It has no mechanism for discarding a prior that is in serious disagreement with (recent) sensory data. As a consequence, it will tend to be very insensitive to changes in the prior distribution of states of the World, both sudden and gradual. Note that this example is in no way a criticism of Bayesian updating, but rather a criticism of attempts to use it to track a prior that changes over time.

The Bayesian Observer in *Night-and-Day* needs an alarm clock that tells it when to discard the current posterior and adapt a better estimate of the prior. Or perhaps it needs a small program that detects temporal edges in the *Light/Dark* sensory states, and resets its prior, something an instantaneous Bayesian Observer cannot do.

Augmented Bayes Observers

Suppose that we address the updating problem directly. Let's first of all concentrate on Environments where the prior distribution on the states of the World, $\pi(\theta)$, changes deterministically, according to a specific algorithm. We can imagine that, on the τth turn, a *Prior Demon* selects a new prior, $\pi_\tau(\theta)$, for the World. In the *Night-and Day* example, the Prior Demon need do little more than count to 40, switch from the *Night* prior to the *Day* prior, or vice versa, reset the counter to 0 and start over again.

The true priors on (*Day, Night*) on any turn are, of course, degenerate: $\pi(Day)$ is 1 and $\pi(Night)$ is 0 during the first 40 of each group of 80 successive turns; $\pi(Day)$ is 0 and $\pi(Night)$ is 1 during the second 40. The choice of the uniform prior $(^1/_2, ^1/_2)$ for $\tilde{\pi}(\theta)$ is a compromise imposed upon the instantaneous Bayesian Observer, essentially due to its ignorance of the deterministic pattern in the successive choices of state of the World, its inability to make use of this pattern. If the state of the World were in fact drawn at random on every trial with the uniform prior, the instantaneous Bayesian Observer is, of course, optimal. An instantaneous Bayesian Observer, then, is poorly equipped to act in a World where the prior distribution on states of the World changes algorithmically. The lack of a mechanism for updating $\tilde{\pi}(\theta)$ to "follow" a deterministically-changing $\pi(\theta)$ is its essential weakness.

Several initiatives in Bayesian vision can be viewed as attempts to augment the instantaneous Bayesian Observer to permit it to deduce from sensory input a plausible, instantaneous choice of $\tilde{\pi}(\theta)$. For example, the competitive priors of Yuille and Bülthoff (1996) provide a simple method for "prior switching" in response to sensory data. Kersten and Schrater (this volume) describe various alternative approaches to tracking changing priors across time.

The challenge proposed here can be treated as a search for an algorithm that, given sensory data across multiple turns, $X_1, X_2, \ldots, X_t$, can provide estimates of a prior that evolves in time taking on the value $\pi_t(\theta)$ at time t. Formally, we seek operators $T_t(X_1, X_2, \ldots, X_t)$ that estimate $\pi_t(\theta)$ given the sensory data so far available. This estimate at each point of time serves as the prior of the instantaneous Bayesian Observer. The resulting *Augmented Bayes Observer* has the potential to outperform an instantaneous Bayes Observer with a fixed prior when the environmental prior changes deterministically[21] and it is possible to estimate the current prior given only sensory data.

Cat-and-Mouse

Suppose that, as you are reading this section in your comfortable office with the doors and windows closed. You suddenly see a mouse scurry across the floor. Your instantaneous prior on mice in your surroundings $T_1(X_1)$ given this sensory event, X_1, is likely going to change. If you aren't the owner of a pet mouse, it has likely increased from the small value T_0 which was your prior before you saw the mouse.

The mouse has vanished but it is reasonable to assume it is still in your (sealed) office. How does your prior estimate $T_t(X_1, X_2, \ldots, X_t)$ evolve across time, in the absence of further sightings of the mouse? What will it be a day later, after you've left the office and returned (perhaps the janitor let the mouse escape)? How does the temporally evolving prior affect your perception of any sudden motion in the periphery? When does it return to its initial value (if ever)?

Your intuition concerning the time-evolution of the prior in this thought example likely reflect considerable knowledge about deterministic aspects of the environment. Mice, like most objects, do not vanish, and do not leave rooms unless there is an exit of some sort. They may be able to gnaw an exit, but that would take some time. If alive, they will likely be seen from time to time. Of course, they may die in your bookcase, changing the modality of the problem from visual to olfactory. The issue then, is whether the visual system makes use of earlier sensory data from a few minutes ago or even days ago in selecting its current prior.

Designing intelligent Augmented Bayes Observers, then, is the challenge proposed here. As noted at the beginning of this section, human observers are typically evaluated in experiments that perversely mimic instantaneous Bayesian environments. To understand how human observers update prior and gain function across time (if, in fact, they do), new kinds of experiments are needed.

BAYESIAN COMPUTATION AND COMPUTATIONAL COMPLEXITY

If you, dear reader, are weary with this tiresome method of computation, have pity on me,
who had to go through it at least seventy times, with an immense expenditure of time.
Johannes Kepler (1609) *Astronomica Nova*

Bayesian Computation

Let's consider the computational demands implicit in Bayesian Decision Theory in the evaluation of Equations (6.11) or (6.15). If we could dissect a Bayesian Observer, what characteristic computational resources would we find? Alternatively, if we were to dissect an arbitrary Observer, what about its computational resources would convince us it was, in fact, a Bayesian Observer? SDT and BDT do not prescribe any particular kind of processing despite the formulas included. We have already seen that the "difficult" computation implicit in Equation (6.15) is reduced to a "simpler" computation in Equation (6.19) by an application of Bayes' Theorem. A particular Bayesian Observer is characterized by its decision rule, d, a mapping from sensory states to actions. BDT imposes an ordering on all decision rules but does not require that any particular decision rule be computed in any particular fashion. In this section I will explore possible "Bayesian architectures" and develop computational algebras that allow use to replace operations on full distributions by induced operations on a finite number of parameters. Anyone who has translated a multiplication (hard) into an addition (easy) by means of logarithms has done something similar.

This section is somewhat more mathematical than the remainder of the chapter, and the reader uninterested in the details can skip to the *Discussion* where the main points of this section are summarized.

Multiplication–Normalization

Only two computational operations are really needed in evaluating Equation (6.15). The first is the multiplication of two distributions[22] $f(\theta)$ and $g(\theta)$. The second computational operation needed is the maximization of Equation (6.19) by choice of action for any particular gain function and posterior distribution. In this section, I'll confine attention to the first operation. At any point prior to the choice of an action, this is the single operation presupposed by BDT.

The product of the two distributions is typically scaled so that it is also a distribution. The computation of the posterior distribution from the prior and the likelihood function is an example of this operation. When the likelihood function is the product of likelihood functions for independent sources of sensory information, it can also be computed by the same multiplication–normalization. If we let $\otimes$ denote this

A step-function family

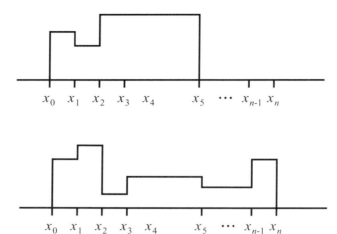

Figure 6.13 *A family of probability density functions that are step-functions.* The step regions, defined by the $n + 1$ points $x_0, x_1, \ldots, x_n$, are fixed, part of the definition of the family. The members of the family differ in the non-negative values $(v_1, v_2, \ldots, v_n)$, each has on the n intervals delimited by $x_0, x_1, \ldots, x_n$. Each step function is 0 outside these intervals and the area under each step function must be 1. Multiplication of two members of the same step-function family $v = (v_1, v_2, \ldots, v_n)$ and $v' = (v'_1, v'_2, \ldots, v'_n)$ is equivalent to component-wise multiplication of the entries of the two vectors followed by a scaling of all the entries.

multiplication–normalization operation, then it is defined as,

$$(f \otimes g)(\theta) = \frac{f(\theta)g(\theta)}{\int f(\theta)g(\theta)d\theta} \tag{6.21}$$

when the denominator is non-zero. The denominator can only be zero if the product of the two distributions is the zero-function. It will prove to be convenient to introduce the zero-function $0(\theta) = 0$, as an "honorary" distribution. With this convention, I define $f \otimes g$ to be $0(\theta)$ when the denominator in Equation (6.21) is 0.

Suppose that the choice of possible distributions is restricted to a parametric family Ξ indexed by a finite number of parameters $\xi = (\xi^1, \ldots, \xi^\nu)$. The reader is very likely familiar with a number of parametric families with a finite number of parameters: the Gaussian, the Exponential, etc. A less familiar example of such a parametric family is constructed as follows. First, we assume that θ is a real number, not a vector of real numbers, and we select ν intervals on the real line. The values $\xi = (\xi^1, \ldots, \xi^\nu)$ are interpreted as the values of a step-function (Figure 6.13), which has constant value ξ^i on the ith interval and is otherwise 0. In order to be a distribution each of the values ξ^i must be non-negative, and the area under the step function must be 1; we assume that these conditions are met. This finite-parameter "Step Function" family is one we might employ in approximating Equation 6.15 numerically.

Closed Parametric Families

Let us confine attention to parametric families Ξ that are *closed* under the multiplication–normalization operation: whenever f and g are in Ξ, then $f \otimes g$ is also in Ξ. If a likelihood function and a prior distribution are both members of a closed family, then so is the resulting posterior distribution. Put another way, if likelihood and prior share a common finite-parameter representation in a closed family, then the posterior can be expressed in terms of the same parameters. The same can be said of a likelihood function produced as a product of likelihood functions: if a series of likelihood functions are all members of a closed family, then so is their product which then has the same parametric representation as its factors.

What are examples of closed parametric families? The step-function family of Figure 6.13 is almost 1. The product of any two step functions with the same interval boundaries is also a step function with those interval boundaries. The problem is that the resulting step function may be uniformly 0: $\xi = (0, 0, \dots, 0)$; we need only add the zero function to the family to solve the problem.

The Gaussian Family

A second example of a closed parametric family is the Gaussian,

$$f(\theta; \mu, \sigma) = \frac{1}{\sqrt{2\pi}\sigma} e^{-[(\theta-\mu)^2/2\sigma^2]} \tag{6.22}$$

with parameters $\xi = (\mu, \sigma)$. Of course, any one-to-one transformation of the parameters can equally well serve as a parameterization. If we use the parameterization, $\xi = (\mu, r)$, where $r = 1/\sigma^2$, then Equation (6.22) becomes

$$f(\theta; \mu, r) = \sqrt{\frac{r}{2\pi}} e^{-[r(\theta-\mu)^2/2]} \tag{6.22'}$$

With this new parameterization, we can compute the outcome of a multiplication–normalization very easily. If the two Gaussian distributions have parameterizations $\xi_1 = (\mu_1, r_1)$ and $\xi_2 = (\mu_2, r_2)$, then the result of multiplication–normalization is a Gaussian distribution with parameters $(\bar{r}_1 \mu_1 + \bar{r}_2 \mu_2, r_1 + r_2)$, where $\bar{r}_i = r_i/(r_1 + r_2), i = 1, 2$.

The multiplication–normalization operation of Equation (6.21), restricted to a closed parametric family, induces an operation on the parameters themselves. We can unambiguously write, for the Gaussian case,

$$(\bar{r}_1 \mu_1 + \bar{r}_2 \mu_2, r_1 + r_2) = (\mu_1, r_1) \otimes (\mu_2, r_2) \tag{6.23}$$

knowing that this operation on the parameters mirrors the operation on the distributions defined by Equation (6.21). To give a formal definition, if one distribution has parameters ξ_a, and a second has parameters ξ_b, then the parameters of the distribution resulting from the multiplication–normalization of the two distributions are, by definition, $\xi_a \otimes \xi_b$. Of course, we are now using the symbol $\otimes$ in two distinct ways, as an operator on distributions and as an operator on their parameters, but this should lead to no confusion.

The Gaussian family

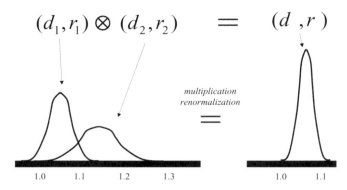

$$(d_1, r_1) \otimes (d_2, r_2) \qquad = \qquad (d\ ,r\ )$$

multiplication renormalization

Figure 6.14 *Operations on parameters induced by multiplication–normalization of probability density functions.* Multiplication–normalization of members of the Gaussian family induce operations on the parameters of the family.

Figure 6.14 may help to clarify this induced operation. We represent a distribution by its parameters and represent operations on distributions by induced operations on the parameters, and vice versa.[23]

Looking back at the simple Gaussian example, we see that a simple weighted average and an addition (Equation (6.23)) is equivalent to a multiplication-renormalization operation on Gaussian distributions: visual processing confined to humble weighted averages and sums, is, in fact, equivalent to Bayesian resolution on certain corresponding distributions.

The Uniform Family

A third, and final, example of a parametric family closed under multiplication–normalization is the family of all uniform distributions (on open intervals). Figure 6.15 illustrates a few members. The product of any two of them is either the zero distribution or, after normalization, another member of the family. Accordingly, we once again include the zero function as a member of the family. If we parameterize each such distribution by its endpoints, (a, b), then the multiplication–normalization of (a_1, b_1) and (a_2, b_2) induces the following operation on the parameters,

$$(\max\{a_1, a_2\}, \quad \min\{b_1, b_2\}) = (a_2, b_2) \otimes (a_2, b_2) \tag{6.24}$$

with the convention that (a, b) with $a > b$ denotes the 0-function.

Combining Families

We can take any two parametric families Ξ and Ξ' and construct a new one, denoted[24] $\Xi \otimes \Xi'$ as follows: the distributions in the new family are the normalized products of

The uniform family

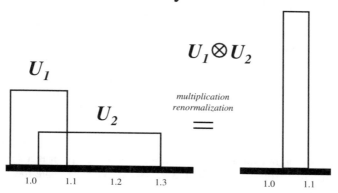

Figure 6.15 *Some members of the Uniform family.* Multiplication–normalization of members of the Uniform family induces operations on the parameters of the family.

pairs of distributions, one from the first family and one from the second:

$$\Xi'' = \Xi \otimes \Xi' = \{f \otimes g \mid f \in \Xi \text{ and } g \in \Xi'\} \tag{6.25}$$

The parameter list for each $f \otimes g$ parameter list is the concatenation of the lists for f and the list for g. There is a natural choice of a parameter list for the product of two families: it is the concatenation of the parameters lists of the two families. For the Gaussian–uniform family the new parameter list is a 4-tuple,

$$(\mu, r, a, b) = (\mu, r) \oplus (a, b), \tag{6.26}$$

where the symbol $\oplus$ denotes concatenation. The operation induced by multiplication–normalization on the product family is definable in terms of the induced operations on the two original families,

$$(\mu_1, r_1, a_1, b_1) \otimes (\mu_2, r_2, a_2, b_2) = [(\mu_1, r_1) \otimes (\mu_2, r_2)]$$
$$\oplus [(a_1, b_1) \otimes (a_2, b_2)]. \tag{6.27}$$

There are infinitely many closed parametric families, and, as we have just seen, we can construct new ones from old. Further, we can re-parameterize the parameters of a family by any one-to-one transformation as we did for the Gaussian, replacing (μ, σ) by (μ, r). There is a well-defined operation induced on the new parameters as well.

Equivalent Data Principle

Once we choose some specific finite-parameter family, the corresponding parameter lists $\xi = (\xi^1, \ldots, \xi^\nu)$ represent *evidence*. Sensory data and prior distribution are represented in the same format and, consequently, the prior distribution at any instant is precisely equivalent to a piece of sensory data that never occurred. Suppose, for example, that there is one source of sensory information and that, for convenience, the Gaussian family with the $\xi = (\mu, r)$ is appropriate. Let $\xi_d = (\mu_d, r_d)$ be the sensory data and $\xi_p = (\mu_p, r_p)$ the instantaneous prior distribution. The first quantity μ in each 2-tuple is the estimate of the quantity of interest, the second, an estimate of its reliability as described above. The resulting estimate will have a bias in the direction of μ_p, but the magnitude of the bias depends on the relative reliability of the prior and the sensory data. If r_d is 0 (the data are worthless), the resulting estimate will be the prior estimate μ_p. If $r_d \gg r_p$, then the prior "data" will be (almost) ignored.

Edward's Challenge

A standard criticism of the Bayesian approach (Edwards, 1972) is the following: If μ_p is not very different from μ_d, the effect of including the prior is not very great. If μ_p *is* very different from μ_d, why would you want to contaminate the sensory data with a prior that almost contradicts it? The preceding example discloses a new role for a prior, as a default mechanism, that ceases to enter into visual processing so soon as reasonable sensory data is available, and it would suggest in agreement with Edwards argument, that the effect of the prior is only noticeable when the sensory data is of poor quality or ambiguous in some respect, that prior information is, in effect, only used when little or no sensory information is available.

Implications

The implications for the complexity issues is straightforward: *there is no characteristic form of Bayesian computation:* two observers with very different computational resources and sequences of computations may be equivalent as Bayesian Observers. The only invariant across these finite-parameter Observers is the number of independent parameters. Further the computational demands of Bayesian resolution need not be very great if Bayesian Observers are constrained to closed, finite-parameter distributional families and carry out computations by induced operations on parameters.

CONCLUSION

"Yes, I suppose what I am saying does sound very general," said Malta Kano. "But after all, Mr. Okada, when one is speaking of the essence of things, it often happens that one can only speak in generalities."
H. Murakami (1998) *The Wind-up Bird Chronicles*

The first section of this chapter included an introduction to the elements and basic results concerning Statistical Decision Theory (SDT) and Bayesian Decision Theory (BDT). In the second section I introduced a family of finite-parameter Bayesian Observers that all share the same descriptions of the states of the World, possible actions, possible sensory states, and likelihood functions. They differ in their assumed gain functions and prior distributions. The Bayesian Observer whose gain function and prior distribution matches the true gain function and prior distribution of the environment is the Ideal Bayesian Observer, but the other, *Non-ideal Bayesian Observers* were more plausible choices as BDT-derived models of biological visual processing.

A simple counting argument was used to motivate the claim that prior distributions and gain functions could not be learned by repeated exposure to all possible states of the World. A BDT-derived model of biological visual processing must have the ability to compute the prior probability of World states never before encountered and the likely consequences of particular actions never before taken.

Consideration of the *updating problem* and *vision across time* led to a similar conclusion: the Bayesian Observer's prior distribution and gain function need to change as the true prior distribution and gain function change. The change can be deterministic or nearly so, and BDT is an awkward language to describe deterministic change. An instantaneous BDT Observer can be woefully inferior to a hybrid Augmented Bayes Observer that incorporates a small amount of additional computational capacity.

On page 77ff we considered the computational demands of BDT. These need not be great, at least if we can confine our modeling to some closed parametric family of distributions and compute by means of induced operations on the parameters of the family. Whether this is possible is simply a statement about the form of the priors that occur in environment, the choice of visual sensors, and the choice of early transformations in the visual system to enhance computability (Barlow, 1972, 1995).

The discussion of Bayesian computation leads from a different starting point to the conclusion that non-optimal Bayesian Observers are the Bayesian Observers of interest in modeling biological vision. Yet, if all distributions employed by a Bayesian Observer are constrained to a specific closed, finite-parameter family of distributions, it is implausible that the true environmental prior would happen to be a member of the family. If the Bayesian Observer cannot represent the true prior, it will be sub-optimal. A similar discussion of the representation of gain functions (not considered) leads to the same conclusion: the Bayesian Observers of interest to biological vision are not the ideal Bayesian Observers.

Last of all, estimation models of visual representation were discussed and, as it turns out, they are somewhat difficult to justify within the Bayesian framework. In a World of changing gains functions, it is not clear why one would reduce the available sensory information to a representation using a fixed gain function before deciding on the task at hand and the particular dangers and opportunities available in the current scene. In short, there is some confusion in current applications of BDT to biological vision as to the point in visual processing where prior and gain are combined to select actions.

How could we decide that the Bayesian approach to modeling biological vision is worthwhile? What sorts of experimental results would suggest that it is in serious trouble? As I noted at the beginning, the Bayesian approach is not a specific falsifiable hypothesis but rather a (mathematical) language that allows us to describe the structure of the environment and the flow of visual processing. It is a powerful language and therein lies a difficulty. After the data are collected it is not very difficult to develop a Bayesian model that accounts for it. Indeed, almost all of the applications of Bayesian tools to vision are post-hoc fitting exercises.[25] If Bayesian models are to be judged useful, they must also permit prediction of experimental outcomes, quantitatively as well as qualitatively.

The prior distributions of a Bayesian observer are readily interpreted as claims about the environment. In the discussion of the sub-optimal Bayesian observer, I argued that it was reasonable to expect the prior embodied in a biological observer to be discrepant from the true objective prior and consequently, an observed discrepancy between the prior on X estimated from experimental data and the true prior on X in the world is not conclusive evidence against the Bayesian approach. However, if we find ourselves estimating the same prior on X in two different experiments, and find that the two estimates are discrepant, then there are serious grounds to question the entire Bayesian enterprise.

Am I a Bayesian? Not yet, though the temptation is there. The concepts underlying Bayesian Decision Theory are both evident and profound. I do think that a careful program of experimentation devoted to evaluating the Bayesian approach will lead to a much deeper understanding of how the visual system represents and combines evidence—whether or not the Bayesian approach survives the program.

To conclude, it is interesting to compare the current status of Bayesian models in cognition and in perception.

Bayesian models of (cognitive) decision making are controversial and inconsistent with experimental results. The controversies concern *belief*: whether our beliefs can be represented as probability distributions on the states of the World, whether our beliefs follow the axioms of probability, or even whether they should. The sharpest attacks on the Bayesian position concentrate on alternative representations of belief (Fisher, 1936; Edwards, 1972; Shafer, 1976). The Bayesian counterattack (Ramsey, 1931b; Savage, 1954; see Berger, 1985) is equally vigorous.

There is considerable evidence suggesting that our beliefs are not consistent with probability theory (Edwards, 1968; Green & Swets, 1966/1974; Kahneman & Tversky, 1972; Tversky & Kahneman, 1971, 1973; Kahneman & Slovic, 1982; Nisbett & Ross, 1982). Consider, for example, the following problem (adapted from Edwards (1968), illustrated in Figure 6.16):

> There are two urns. The "Black Urn" contains two-thirds black balls and one-third white. The "White Urn" contains two-thirds white balls and one-third black. One of the two urns is selected at random by tossing a fair coin. You'd most likely accept that the probability that the "Unknown Urn" is the "Black Urn" is one-half, that it is the "White Urn" is one-half. Your prior distribution on the two Urns is (0.5, 0.5). Now let's take a sample from the "Unknown Urn". We sample (with replacement) from the Unknown Urn 17 times. There are 11 black balls and 6 white. You'll likely consider that to be evidence in favor of the claim that the Unknown Urn is in fact the "Black Urn". But what exactly is the probability now, after seeing the data, that the "Unknown Urn" is the "Black Urn"?

Please look at Figure 6.16 and make an estimate before reading further.

Most people, given the problem above, estimate that the posterior probability that the "Unknown Urn" is the "Black Urn" to be about 0.75 (Edwards, 1968). The posterior probability distribution on the two Urns is then (0.75, 0.25), about 3:1 odds in favor of the "Black Urn". The correct answer is (0.97, 0.03), or odds of 32:1, in favor of the

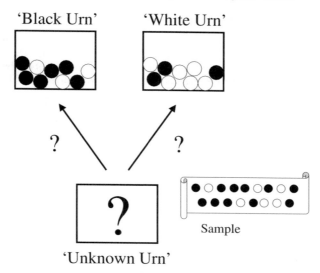

Figure 6.16 *"Conservatism"*. The "Unknown Urn" is either the "Black Urn" or the "White Urn" and the prior odds that it is the one or the other is ($1/2$, $1/2$). A sample of size 17 is drawn from the "Unknown Urn" and the results are shown. What is the probability, now that you have seen the sample, that the "Unknown Urn" is the "Black Urn"? The correct answer is given in the text.

"Black Urn". The discrepancy between the intuitive estimate of human observers and the correct odds is an example of *Conservatism*, a pervasive error in human reasoning with probabilities: Humans estimate odds that are roughly the cube root of the correct odds (3:1 instead of 32:1).

Conservatism is observed not only in word problems such as the problem above but also in human performance in the Theory of Signal Detectability: whatever the prior odds of SIGNAL + NOISE and NOISE, human observers respond as if (roughly) the cube root of the prior odds were, in fact, the true prior odds (Green & Swets, 1966/1974). Conservatism, the "cognitive illusions" of Kahneman and Tversky (Kahneman & Slovic, 1982) and other documented failures of human probabilistic reasoning are difficult to explain away as minor deviations from probability theory.

What if advocates of a Bayesian approach to biological vision turn out to be correct? What if BDT-derived models do not break down as completely as their cognitive counterparts, exhibiting analogous failures? What if a consensus develops that such models mirror visual processing in important respects? In sum, what if Bayesian Decision Theory turns out to be the natural "language" for developing accurate models of visual processing? If that all came to pass, we could certainly draw solace from the idea that, although we don't seem able to judge or reason very well, at least something in our skull, our visual system, can.

ACKNOWLEDGMENTS

Preparation of this chapter was supported by grant EY08266 from the National Institute of Health, National Eye Institute, and a research grant from the Human Frontiers Science Program. The author is also grateful to the Institute for Biophysics at the University of Freiburg for support as a guest professor while preparing this chapter. He is particularly grateful to Dr. Lothar Spillmann for his encouragement and help.

Several people were kind enough to comment on earlier drafts or to sit through presentations and discussions of the topics discussed here: Bart Anderson, Donald Hoffman, Dan Kersten, Michael Landy, Paul Schrater, and the complement of the Rochester Symposium on Environmental Statistical Constraints, University of Rochester, Rochester, New York, June, 1998. I am especially grateful to Pascal Mamassian for his willingness to discuss Bayesian ideas while waiting for the stimuli to dry.

NOTES

1. I will use the terms *gain*, *expected gain*, etc., throughout and avoid the terms loss, expected loss (= risk), etc. Any loss can, of course, be described as a negative gain. This translation can produce occasional odd constructions as when we seek to "maximize negative least-squares'. You win some, you negative-win some.
2. The phrase "view geometrically the proportion" describes what we would now call "compute the expected value."
3. A reader of an earlier version of this chapter wondered whether the term "random variable", most often encountered in phrases such as "Gaussian random variable" or "uniform random variable", is applicable to a process where there are only finitely many possible outcomes. It is. The set of possible values of random variables can be finite and can even contain non-numeric values such as "HEADS" or "TAILS".
4. The term *strategy* can also be used. We will encounter *randomized decision rules* in a later section.
5. Not to be confused with *Expected Bayes' Gain*, defined further on. *Expected Gain* depends on the state of the World, *Expected Bayes' Gain* does not.
6. A set of points is convex if the line segment joining any two points in the set is also in the set. An "hourglass" is an example of a non-convex set.
7. The Theory of Signal Detectability (TSD) is better known as Signal Detection Theory, whose abbreviation (SDT) is identical to that of Statistical Decision Theory. To avoid confusion, I will use TSD throughout in referring to the Theory of Signal Detectability / Signal Detection Theory.
8. TSD also takes into account rewards and penalties associated with different kinds of errors. The current discussion illustrates only one way to model TSD within SDT.
9. The reader may be surprised that the "ROC curve" in the figure consists of a series of line segments instead of the usual smooth curve see in text books. The region of achievable gains is always a convex polygon if the set of sensory states and the set of possible actions are both finite, as we are currently assuming they are. The particular shape of the ROC curve is of no importance to the example.
10. If more than one gain point touches the sliding wedge at the same time, then the Maximin rules correspond to the gain point that is furthest up or to the right among the simultaneously touching points.
11. For the reader familiar with vector notation: Equations (6.11) and (6.12) are inner products of the prior vector with gains points and Equation (6.12) is just the usual formula for the lines perpendicular to a given vector.
12. I emphasize: in the finite-dimensional case.
13. Bayes' Theorem is (Equation 6.17) below. It can be found in almost any probability or statistics text (e.g. O'Hagan, 1994, Ch. 1).

14. Both sides of Equation (6.17) are equal to the joint probability density function $l(\theta, x)$ of the random state of the world θ and the random sensory state χ. The two sides are just the two possible ways to define conditional probabilities of θ on χ and vice versa. Bayes's signal contribution was to correctly define conditional probability. His "theorem" is an obvious consequence of his definition of conditional probability.

15. I emphasize that a Bayesian Observer is a piece of mathematics intended to describe some component of visual processing. While the language of probability and gain may prove useful in describing this component, there is no assumption that the human observer is consciously aware of these probabilities or gains or that his own beliefs concerning probability or gain influence visual processing.

16. On the peak of Jabal al-Najar in Petra, Jordan.

17. Note that the maximum likelihood estimate of the variance has N, not $N - 1$, in the denominator.

18. I will speak of different gain functions for different actions but, of course, only one gain function is needed, one that we partition according to the different kinds of actions.

19. Of course, all the elements of SDT and BDT may change from moment to moment, but we will be mainly concerned with priors and gain functions here.

20. The posterior distributions (the successive prior distributions) are themselves random variables that depend on the exact sequence of *Light* and *Dark*. For simplicity, in this example, I have compute the priors that would result from the mean number of *Lights* and *Darks* after a given number of turns. That is, after 12 turns of *Day*, I assume that *Light* has occurred exactly 9 times (0.75×12). The probabilities reported, then, are not the probabilities to be expected in any single "run" of a simulation of the prior updating process nor need it be the mean of the probabilities across many runs. The essential points, that Bayesian updating responds slowly to change and that it gives the same weight to recent and long-past information are, however, correct.

21. The argument is readily extended to the case where the choice of prior on each turn is partly deterministic and partly stochastic. Many of these considerations could as readily be applied to the gains function as to the prior.

22. For a continuous random variable, the term "probability density function" should be used here. For a discrete random variable, the term "probability mass function" is appropriate. I'll refer to both by the term "distribution" in this section.

23. The relation between the closed family of distributions and the parameters is an example of an isomorphism.

24. We are implicitly assigning a third meaning to the symbol $\otimes$ in defining this product of families.

25. Also known as "death by a thousand parameters."

REFERENCES

Arnauld, A. (1662/1964). *Logic, or the art of thinking ("The Port-Royal Logic")*. Bobbs-Merrill.

Barlow, H.B. (1972). Single units and sensation: A neuron doctrine for perceptual psychology? *Perception*, **1**, 371–394.

Barlow, H.B. (1995). The neuron doctrine in perception. In M. Gazzaniga (Ed.) *The cognitive neurosciences* (Ch. 26, pp. 415–435). Cambridge, MA: MIT Press.

Berger, J.O. (1985). *Statistical decision theory and Bayesian analysis*. New York: Springer.

Berger, J.O. & Wolpert, R.L. (1988). *The Likelihood Principle: A review, generalizations, and statistical implications* (2nd edn.). Lecture Notes—Monograph Series, Vol. 6. Hayward, CA: Institute of Mathematical Statistics.

Blackwell, D. & Girshick, M.A. (1954). *Theory of games and statistical decisions*. New York: Wiley.

Brainard, D.H. & Freeman, W.T. (1997). Bayesian color constancy. *Journal of the Optical Society of America, A,* **14**, 1393–1411.

Buck, R.C. (1978). *Advanced calculus*, McGraw-Hill.

de Moivre, A. (1718/1967). *The doctrine of chances.* Reprint: New York: Chelsea (reprint).

Edwards, A.W.F. (1972). *Likelihood.* Cambridge University Press.

Edwards, W. (1968). Conservatism in human information processing. In B. Kleinmuntz (Ed.) *Formal representation of human judgment.* New York: Wiley.

Egan, J.P. (1975). *Signal Detection Theory and ROC Analysis.* Academic Press.

Feller, W. (1968). *An introduction to probability Theory and its applications* (Vol. I, 3rd edn.). New York: Wiley.

Ferguson, T. (1967). *Mathematical statistics: A decision theoretic approach.* Academic Press.

Fisher, R.A. (1930). Inverse probability. *Proceedings of the Cambridge Philosophical Society,* **26**, 528–535.

Fisher, R.A. (1936). Uncertain inference. *Proceedings of the American Academy of Arts and Sciences,* **71**, 245–258.

Freeman, W.T. & Brainard, D.H. (1995). Bayesian decision theory, the maximum local mass estimate, and color constancy. *Proceedings of the Fifth International Conference on Computer Vision* (pp. 210–217).

Geisler, W. (1989), Sequential ideal-observer analysis of visual discrimination. *Psychological Review,* **96**, 267–314.

Green, D.M. & Swets, J.A. (1966/1974). *Signal Detection Theory and Psychophysics.* New York: Wiley. Reprinted 1974, New York: Krieger.

von Helmholtz, H. (1909). *Handbuch der physiologischen Optik.* Hamburg: Voss.

Huygens, C. (1657). *De Rationicii in Aleae Ludo* (*On calculating in games of luck*). Reprinted in Huygens, C. (1920) *Oeuvres Completes.* The Hague: Martinus Nijhoff.

Jeffrey, R. (1983). Bayesianism with a human face. In J. Earma (Ed.) *Testing scientific theories.* University of Minnesota Press.

Kahneman, D. & Slovic, P. (1982). *Judgment under uncertainty.* Cambridge, UK: Cambridge University Press.

Kahneman, D. & Tversky, A. (1972). Subjective probability: A judgment of representativeness. *Cognitive Psychology,* **3**, 430–454.

Kepler, J. (1609). *Astronomica Nova.* Translated as Kepler, J. (1992) *New Astronomy.* Donahue, W.H. (trans.), Cambridge, UK: Cambridge University Press.

Knill, D.C., Kersten, D. & Yuille, A.L. (1996). Introduction. In D.C. Knill & W. Richards (Eds.) *Perception as Bayesian inference* (pp. 1–221). Cambridge University Press.

Knill, D.C. & Richards, W. (Eds.) (1996). *Perception as Bayesian inference.* Cambridge University Press.

Krantz, D.H., Luce, R.D., Suppes, P. & Tversky, A. (1971). *Foundations of measurement* (Vol. 1): *Additive and Polynomial Representation.* Academic Press.

Maqsood, R. (1996). *Petra: A Traveler's Guide, New Edition.* Garnet.

Mamassian, P. & Landy, M.S. (1996). Cooperation of priors for the perception of shaded line drawings. *Perception,* **25**, Suppl., 21.

Mamassian, P., Landy, M.S. & Maloney, L.T. (in press). A primer of Bayesian modeling for visual psychophysics. In R. Rao, B. Olshausen & M. Lewicki (Eds.) *Statistical theories of the brain.* Cambridge, MA: MIT Press.

Marr, D. (1982). *Vision: A Computational Investigation into the Human Representation and Processing of Visual Information.* San Francisco: Freeman.

Milner, A.D. & Goodale, M.A. (1996). *The visual brain in action.* Oxford: Oxford University Press.

Murakami, H. (1998), *The wind-up bird chronicles.* J. Rubin (Translator), New York: Vintage.

von Neumann, J. & Morgenstern, O. (1944/1953). *Theory of games and economic behavior* (3rd edn.). Princeton University Press.

Nisbett, R.E. & Ross, L. (1982). *Human Inference: Strategies and Shortcomings of Social Judgment.* Englewood Cliffs, NJ: Prentice Hall.

O'Hagan, A. (1994). *Kendall's Advanced Theory of Statistics; Vol. 2B; Bayesian Inference.* New York: Halsted Press (Wiley).

Orwell, G. (1983). *1984.* New York: Vintage.

Ramsey, F.P. (1931a). Truth and probability. In *The foundations of mathematics and other logical essays.* London: Routledge & Kegan Paul.

Ramsey, F.P. (1931b). *The foundations of mathematics and other logical essays.* London: Routledge & Kegan Paul.

Savage, L.J. (1954). *The foundations of statistics.* New York: Wiley.

Shafer, G. (1976). *A mathematical theory of evidence.* Princeton, NJ: Princeton.

Shimojo, S. & Nakayama, K. (1992). Experiencing and perceiving visual surfaces. *Science,* **257**, 1357–1363.

Turing, A.M. (1952). The chemical basis of morphogenesis. *Philosophical Transactions of the Royal Society,* **B237**, 37–72.

Tversky, A. & Kahneman, D. (1971). Belief in the law of small numbers. *Psychological Bulletin,* **2**, 105–110.

Tversky, A. & Kahneman, D. (1973). Availability: A heuristic for judging frequency and probability. *Cognitive Psychology,* **4**, 207–232.

Tversky, A. & Kahneman, D. (1982). Judgments of and by representativeness. In D. Kahneman & P. Slovic (Eds.) *Judgment under uncertainty* (pp. 84–98). Cambridge, UK: Cambridge University Press,

Wandell, B.A. (1995). *Foundations of vision.* Sinauer.

Williams, J.D. (1954). *The compleat strategyst.* New York: McGraw-Hill.

Yuille, A.L. & Bülthoff, H.H. (1996) Bayesian decision theory and psychophysics. In D.C. Knill & W. Richards (Eds.) *Perception as Bayesian inference* (pp. 123–162). Cambridge: Cambridge University Press.

7

Pattern Inference Theory: A Probabilistic Approach to Vision

DANIEL KERSTEN AND PAUL SCHRATER

Department of Psychology, University of Minnesota, USA

PERCEPTION IS PATTERN DECODING

Few would dispute the view that visual perception is the brain's process for arriving at useful information about the world from images. Divergent opinions, however, have been expressed over how to describe the computations (or lack thereof) underlying visual behavior. Visual perception has been described as unconscious inference (Helmholtz & Southall, 1924; Gregory, 1980), reconstruction (Craik, 1943), resonance (Gibson, 1966), problem solving (Rock, 1983), computation (Marr, 1982), and more recently as Bayesian inference (Knill & Richards, 1996). In part, the debate gets muddled due to lack of a well-specified explanatory goal and level of abstraction. To clarify, we see the grand challenge to be the development of testable, quantitative theories of visual performance that take into account the complexities of natural images and the richness of visual behavior. But here the level of explanation is crucial: if our theories are too abstract, we lose the specificity of quantitative predictions; if the theories are too fine-grained, the model mechanisms for natural pattern processing will be too complex to test.

Our proposed strategy follows that of statistical mechanics. Few physicists doubt that the large-scale properties of physical systems rest on the lawful function of individual molecules, just as few brain scientists doubt that an organism's behavior depends on the lawful function of neurons. Physicists would agree that the modeling level has to be appropriate to the measurements and phenomena of large-scale systems; thus statistical mechanics links molecular kinetics to thermodynamics. Although the

Perception and the Physical World: Psychological and Philosophical Issues in Perception.
Edited by Dieter Heyer and Rainer Mausfeld. © 2002 John Wiley & Sons, Ltd.

bridge between neurons and system behavior has yet to be built, the language of Bayesian statistics provides the level of description analogous to thermodynamics.[1] For vision, theories at this level are testable at the level of visual information and perceptual constraints,[2] and are less committal about representations, algorithms, or mechanisms.

The purpose of this chapter is to describe the fundamental principles of value in addressing the grand challenge. These principles constitute what we will refer to as *pattern inference theory*. The basic elements of pattern inference theory are not new and have their mathematical roots in communication and information theory (Shannon & Weaver 1949), Bayesian decision theory (Berger, 1985), pattern theory (Grenander 1996), and Bayes nets (Pearl, 1988). The refinement of the principles are derived from a history of applications to human vision in the domains of signal detection theory (Green & Swets 1974), ideal observer analysis (Geisler, 1989; Schrater, 1998), Bayesian inference and decision theory (Kersten, 1990; Yuille & Bültoff, 1996), and pattern theory (Mumford, 1996; Yuille et al., 1998). "Pattern theory" was developed by Ulf Grenander to describe the mathematical study of complex natural patterns (Grenander, 1993, 1996; Mumford, 1996; Yuille et al., 1998). Central features of pattern theory are the importance of modeling pattern generation, and that natural pattern variation is characterized by four fundamental classes of deformations.[3] Further, the generative model is seen as an essential part of inference (e.g. via flexible templates to fit incoming data in a feedback stage) to deal with certain types of deformation, such as occlusion (Mumford, 1994). Our particular emphasis is based on the synthesis and application of pattern theory and Bayesian decision theory to human vision (Yuille et al., 1998). As an elaboration of signal detection theory, we choose the words *pattern* and *inference* to stress the importance of modeling complex natural signals, and of considering tasks in addition to detection, respectively. We argue that pattern inference theory provides the best language for formulating quantitative theories of visual perception and action at the level of the naturally behaving (human) visual system.

Our goal is to derive probabilistic models of the observer's world and sensory input, restricted by task. Such models have two components: the objects of the theory, and the operations of the theory. The objects of the theory are the set of possible image measurements I, the set of possible scene descriptions S, and the joint probability distribution of S and I: $p(S, I)$. The operations are given by the probability calculus, with decisions modeled as minimizing expected cost (or risk) given the probabilities. The richness of the theory lies in exploiting the structure induced in $p(S, I)$ by the regularities of the world (laws of physics) and by the habits of observers. A fundamental assumption of pattern inference theory is that Bayesian decision theory provides the best language both to describe complex patterns, and to model inferences about them. For us, the essence of a Bayesian view is not the emphasis on subjective prior probabilities, but rather that all variables are random variables. This assumption has ramifications for the central role, in perception, of generative (or synthetic) models of image patterns, as well as prior probability models of scene information. An emphasis on generative models, we believe, is essential because of the inherent complexity of the causal structure of high-dimensional image patterns. One must model how the multitude of variables (both the needed and unneeded variables for a task) interact to produce image data in order to understand how to decode those patterns. But perhaps equally importantly, the Bayesian view underscores the importance of *confidence-driven* visual processes. This latter idea leads us to the view that perception consists of sequences of computations on probabilities, rather than a series of estimations or decisions. We illustrate this with recent work on Bayes nets.

In the next section, we will show that pattern inference theory is a logical elaboration of ideal observer analysis in classical signal detection theory. However, it goes beyond standard applications of ideal observer analysis by emphasizing the need to take into account the full range of natural image patterns, and the intimate tie between perception and successful behavior.

PATTERN INFERENCE THEORY: A GENERALIZATION OF IDEAL OBSERVERS

Signal detection theory (SDT) was developed in the 1950s to model and analyze human sensory decisions given internal and external background noise (Peterson et al., 1954; Green & Swets 1974). The theory combined earlier work in statistical decision theory (Neyman & Pearson 1933; Wald, 1939, 1950; Grenander 1950) with communication systems theory (Shannon & Weaver, 1949; Rice, 1944). Signal detection theory made two fundamental contributions to our understanding of human perception. First, statistical decision theory showed how to analyze the internal processing of sensory decisions. The application of statistical decision theory to psychophysics showed that sensory decisions were determined by two experimentally separable factors: sensitivity (related to an inferred internal signal-to-noise ratio) and the decision criterion. Second, communication theory showed that there were inherent physical limits to the reliability of information transmission, and thus detection, independent of the specific implementation of the detector, i.e. whether it be physical or biological. These limits can be modeled by a mathematically defined ideal observer, which provides a *quantitative* computational theory for the information in a task. For the ideal observer, the signal-to-noise ratio can be obtained from direct measurements of the variations in the transmitted signal. The ideal observer presaged Marr's ideas of a computational theory for an information processing task, as distinct from the algorithm and implementation to carry it out (Marr, 1982). The top panel of Figure 7.1 illustrates the basic causal structure for the "signal plus noise" problem in classical signal detection theory.

Experimental studies of human perceptual behavior are often left with a crucial, but unanswered question: To what extent is the measured performance limited by the information in the task rather than by the perceptual system itself? Answers to this question are critical for understanding the relationship between perceptual behavior and its underlying biological mechanisms. Signal detection theory

Perception and the Physical World

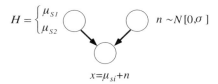

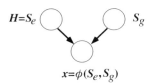

Figure 7.1 The top panel shows an example of generative graph structure for an ideal observer problem in classical signal detection theory (SDT). The data are determined by the signal hypotheses plus (usually additive gaussian) noise. Knowledge is represented by the joint probability $p(x, u, n)$. The lower panel shows a simplified example of the generative structure for perceptual inference from a pattern inference theory perspective. The image measurements (x) are determined by a typically non-linear function (ϕ) of primary signal variables (S_e) and confounding secondary variables (S_g). Knowledge is represented by the joint probability $p(x, S_e, S_g)$. Both scene and image variables can be high dimensional vectors. In general, the causal structure of natural image patterns is more complex and consequently requires elaboration of its graphical representation (see "Graphical models of statistical structure" below). For SDT and pattern inference theory, the task is to make a decision about the signal hypotheses or primary signal variables, while discounting the noise or secondary variables. Thus optimal perceptual decisions are determined by $p(x, S_e)$, which is derived by summing over the secondary variables (i.e. marginalizing with respect to the secondary variables): $\int_{S_g} p(x, S_e, S_g)\, dS_g$.

provided an answer through ideal observer analysis. One of the first applications of the ideal observer in vision was the determination of the quantum efficiency of human light discrimination (Barlow, 1962). By considering both the external and internal sources of variability, Barlow showed that an ideal photon detector could get by with about one-tenth the number of photons as a human for the same combination of hit and correct rejection rates. This success of classical signal detection theory demonstrated the need for probability in theories of visual performance, because light transmission is fundamentally stochastic (emission and absorption are Poisson processes) and any real light measurement device introduces further noise.

The example of ideal observer analysis of light detection further illustrates a fundamental strategy for studying perception, consisting of three modeling domains. First, how does the signal (i.e. light switch set to "bright" or "dim") get encoded into intensity changes in the image? The answer must deal with light variations due to quantal fluctuations. Second, how should the received image data be decoded to do the best job at inferring which signal was transmitted? Answers to this question rely on theories of ideal observers, or more generally of optimal inference. Third, how does one compare human and ideal performance? This requires common performance measures on the same task.

LIMITATIONS OF SIGNAL DETECTION THEORY FOR THE GRAND CHALLENGE

Despite its successes, signal detection theory as typically applied in vision falls short when faced with our grand challenge. Define perceptual signals to be some underlying causes of image data that are required for a visual behavior. These signals include the shapes, positions, and material of objects. The first problem is that natural perceptual signals are complex, high-dimensional functions of image intensities. In typical applications of SDT and classical ideal observer analysis to visual psychophysics, the input data, the noise, and the signal, are treated as the same "stuff". For example, in contrast detection, the input data is signal plus noise (Kersten, 1984). The signal is based on a physical quantity (luminance) as a function of time and/or space), the noise is either physical contrast fluctuations, or internal variability treated as equivalent to the physical noise (Pelli, 1990). Perceptual decisions are typically limited to information which is explicit in the decoded signal. So to answer the question, Does the signal image have more light intensity than another?, the decoder simply measures whether the image intensity is bigger.

We need a theoretical framework for which the signals can be any properties of the world useful for the visual behavior; for example, estimates of object shape and surface motion are crucial for actions such as recognition and navigation, but they are not simple functions of light intensity. Natural images are high-dimensional functions of useful signals, and arriving at decoding functions relating image measurements to these signals is a major theoretical challenge. Both of these problems are expressible in terms of pattern inference theory.

In signal detection theory, the non-signal causes of the input pattern are called noise. A second problem, related to the first, is that "noise" in the perception of natural images is not simple. Useful information is confounded by more than added external or internal image intensity noise. Uncertainty is due to both variations in unneeded scene variables as well as by the fact that multiple scene descriptions can produce the same image data. In contrast to the above example of contrast detection, consider the problem of 3-D shape discrimination in everyday vision. The signal is shape, but the counterpart to the noise is very different stuff, and includes variation in viewpoint, illumination, other occluding objects, and material (Liu et al. 1995). Further, although the discrimination decision may be able to rely on a primary image measurement that is explicit in the image (e.g. a contour description), this is rare. Because of projection and the confounding variables, the true 3-D shape is not explicit in any simple image measurement.

Pattern inference theory deals directly with the problem of multiple and diverse causes of image variation by modeling the generative process of image formation. Below, we distinguish between the needed *primary* and unneeded *secondary* variables.[4] The primary variables are those which the system's function is designed to estimate. By contrast, the secondary variables are not estimated but nor are they ignored, and there are principled methods for getting rid of unwanted variables. It should be emphasized that the distinction between primary and secondary depends on the specific task the system is designed to solve. Variables which are secondary for one task may be primary for another. For example, estimating the illumination is unimportant for many visual tasks and so illumination variables are treated as secondary. The theory of generic views treats viewpoint as a secondary variable, enabling resolution of ambiguities in shape perception (Nakayama & Shimojo 1992; Freeman, 1994). Light direction as a secondary variable can be used to obtain a unique estimate of depth from cast shadows (Kersten, 1999). There is a close connection between the task (discussed in "optical decoding" below) and the statistical structure of the estimation problem (Schrater & Kersten 2000).

A third limitation is that natural images are not linear combinations of their signals, and that the probabilities describing the signal and image variables are not Gaussian. Much of the success of signal detection theory has rested on an assumption of linearity: the input is the sum of the signal and the noise. Except in rare instances (e.g. contrast detection limited by photon fluctuations at high light levels), natural perceptual tasks involve inputs which are non-linear functions of the signals and the noise (or secondary variables). For example, light intensity is a non-linear function of object shape, reflectance, and illumination.

There is a close relationship between linearity and the assumption that the random variables of interest are Gaussian.[5] Although classical signal detection explored the implications of non-Gaussian processes (Egan, 1975), most applications of signal detection theory to vision have typically approximated noise variations as Gaussian processes. A Gaussian approximation works very well in certain domains (as an approximation to Poisson light emission), but is extremely limited as a model of scene variability. Both the linear and Gaussian assumptions have had a striking success in the general problem of modeling human perceptual and cognitive decisions, where the variability is inside the observer (Green & Swets 1974; Swets 1988). But the Gaussian assumption generally fails when modeling external variability. For example, whenever a probability density involves more than second-order correlations, a multivariate Gaussian model is no longer adequate. Image samples from Gaussian models of natural images fail to capture the rich structure of natural textures (Knill et al., 1990). Simple image measurements, such as those made by simple cells of the visual cortex are highly non-Gaussian (Field, 1987). A goal of pattern inference theory is to let the vision problem determine the distributions.

Fourthly, perception involves more tasks than classification. Not surprisingly, for signal detection theory, the primary focus is on signal detection—was the signal sent or not? Perception involves a larger class of tasks: classification at several levels of abstraction, estimation, learning, and control. Past applications of signal detection theory have successfully handled certain kinds of abstraction (e.g. "is any one of 100 signals there or not?" or "which of 100 known signals was sent?") as well as estimation (Van Trees, 1968); but we also require a framework that can handle diverse tasks from continuous estimations (e.g. of distance, shape, and their associations) to more complex categorical decisions: e.g. is the input pattern due to a cat, a dog, or "my cat"? Tools for the former build on classical estimation theory, but include recent work on hidden Markov models. The latter requires additional tools, such as flexible template theories to model shape abstraction. A mathematical framework for perception requires tools for the generalization of ideal observers for the functional complex tasks of natural perception. Defining primary and secondary variables is part of task specification, and pattern inference theory handles this by incorporating decision theory to define a risk function.

Finally, we note that most of the interesting perceptual knowledge on priors and utility is implicit. Signal detection theory grew out of earlier work on decision theory. Two important components of decision theory are the specification of prior probabilities of scene properties or signals and the costs and benefits of actions, through a risk or cost function. In most applications of SDT, it has been the experimenter that manipulates the priors and the cost functions. The human observer is often aware of the changes, and can adopt a conscious strategy to take these into account. We argue that the most important perceptual priors are largely determined by the structure of the environment and can, in principle, be modeled independently of perceptual inference (i.e. in the synthesis phase of study).[6] Modeling priors (e.g. through density estimation) is a hard theoretical problem in and of itself, especially because of the large number of potential interactions. In classical SDT, probabilities are typically specified over small dimensional spaces. The costs and benefits are inherent to the type of perceptual task, and determine the primary and secondary variables. Thus, to elaborate on Helmholtz's definition of perception: *perception is (largely) unconscious inference involving unconscious priors, and unconscious cost functions.*

Thanks to the successes of signal detection theory, we know that perception is limited by two factors: (1) the available information for reliable learning, inference, and action; (2) brain mechanisms to process that information. But one of the principal differences between classical SDT and pattern inference theory is the greater emphasis on modeling the external limits to inference, including both synthesis and optimal decoding. Both problems are clearly challenging, and computer vision has shown that the second problem is surprisingly hard. We agree with Marr when he wrote in 1982: ". . . the nature of the computations that underlie perception depends more upon the computational problems that have to be solved than upon the particular hardware in which their solutions are implemented." Theories of human perceptual inference require an understanding of the limits of perceptual inference through optimal decoding theories (Barlow, 1981; Geisler, 1989). These theories, in turn, require an understanding of the transformations and variations introduced in pattern formation. We will argue here that the structure of the visual information for function is best modeled in terms of its probabilistic structure, and that as a consequence any successful system must reflect the constraints in that structure, and further that its computations should be in terms of probability operations.

So, in the next section, we focus on the first problem: How can we model the information required for a task? This modeling problem can be broken down into: (a) synthesis, modeling the structure of pattern information in natural images; and (b) analysis, modeling the task and extracting useful pattern structures.

ENCODING OF SCENES IN IMAGES: MODELING IMAGE PATTERN SYNTHESIS

Computer vision has emphasized the difficulty of image understanding, which involves decoding images to find the scene variables causing the image measurements. Although, a great deal of progress has been made in computer vision, the best systems are typically quite constrained in their domain of applicability (e.g. letter recognition, tracking, structure from rigid body motions, etc.). The focus has understandably been on decoding—e.g. solving the inverse optics problem. However, the success of image decoding depends crucially on understanding the encoding. Although the computational challenge of image understanding is widely appreciated, the difficulty and issues of image pattern synthesis are less so.

How do we model the information images contain about scene properties? Following Shannon and Weaver (1949), the answer is through probability distributions. Treating perception as a communication problem, we identify certain scene variables S as the messages, and the image formation and measurement mapping as the channel $p(I \mid S)$, by which we receive the encoded messages I. Given this identification, we can use information theoretic ideas to quantify the information that I gives about S as the transinformation

$$I(S; I) = H(I) - H(I \mid S) = E_{p(I)}[-\log p(I)] - E_{p(S.I)}[-\log p(I \mid S)].$$

These entropies are determined by $p(I) = \int_S p(S)p(I \mid S)\mathrm{d}S$, the likelihood $p(I \mid S)$, and the prior $p(S)$.[7] Thus, the physics of materials, optics, light, and image measurement, which determine the likelihood, just scratch the surface of what is required to model image encoding. In addition, we need to understand the types of patterns and transformations that result from the fact that images are caused by a structured world of events and potentialities for an agent, which is captured in $p(S)$. While probability and information theory provide the tools for understanding image encoding, constructing theories with these tools requires work. Let's look at the framework, tools, and principles for theory construction.

ESSENCE OF BAYES: EVERYTHING IS A RANDOM VARIABLE

A key starting assumption is that all variables are random variables, and that the knowledge required for visual function is specified by the joint probability $p(S_e, S_g, I)$. The basic ingredients are variable classes: image measurement data (I), variables specifying relevant scene attributes (S_e), and the confounding variables (S_g). All these variables are random variables, and thus subject to the laws of the probability calculus, including Bayes' theorem. So for pattern inference theory, a Bayesian view is more than acknowledging the role of priors, but also emphasizes the redundancy structure of images, and the importance of the generative process of visual pattern formation, expressible as a graphical model. Thus the essence of a Bayesian theory of perception is more than applying Bayes' rule to infer scene properties from images, or that likelihoods are tweaked by prior and labile subjective "biases". This interpretation

(*Myth 1: Bayesian models of perception are distinct only by virtue of emphasis on modeling priors*[8]) would miss the point of our view of pattern inference theory approach to perception. By starting with a model space completely determined by the joint probability, $p(S_e, S_g, I)$, we have the foundation to understand:
(1) input image redundancy, through:

$$p(I) = \int p(S_e, S_g, I) \, dS_e \, dS_g$$

(2) scene structure, through:

$$p(S_e, S_g) = \int p(S_e, S_g, I) \, dI$$

and (3) inference, through:

$$p(S_e, I) = \int p(S_e, S_g, I) \, dS_g.$$

Of course, modeling $p(S_e, S_g, I)$ in general may pose an insurmountable challenge. But there is reason for optimism, and recent work in density estimation and image statistics suggest that tractable high-dimensional models may be possible (Zhu et al., 1997; Zhu & Mumford, 1998; Zhu, 1999; Simoncelli, 1997; Simoncelli & Portilla, 1998).

The key point is that necessary knowledge to characterize the perceptual problem is specified by a joint probability over the given data (usually image measurements, but could include contextual conclusions drawn earlier or elsewhere), what the visual system needs (primary), and the variables that confound (secondary variables).

BASIC OPERATIONS ON PROBABILITIES: CONDITIONING AND MARGINALIZING

We really have only two basic computations on probabilities, which follow from the two basic rules of probability—the sum and product rules. Each of the rules has specific roles in an inference computation, related to the kind of variable in the inference. When inferring the values of a set of variables S_e, the remaining variables come in two types: those which we don't know and don't care to know, and those which are known either by sensory measurement or *a priori*. How is the joint probability affected by this knowledge? The answer is to sum over the unneeded variables (marginalization), and divide the joint by the probability of the known ones (conditioning).

Marginalization

Presuming the utility of only a subset of the scene variables (which we treat below, on page 208ff.), the values of some variables S_g are not known, and we don't care to know them. Marginalization is the proper way to remove the effect of these secondary, unknown, unwanted variables:

$$P(S_e, I) = \int_{S_g} P(S_e, S_g, I) dS_g$$

The reason we marginalize is that being unneeded doesn't mean these variables should be ignored! Most of the time, the unwanted variables (e.g. viewpoint) crucially contribute to the generation of the possible images, and hence cannot be ignored. The marginalization approach contrasts with traditional modular studies of vision, in which most of the unneeded variables for a given module are left out of the discussion entirely (e.g. independent estimation of reflectance, shape, and illumination). Often, the modularity is adopted based on general practical and theoretical arguments. Our position is not that we forgo modularity, but rather that modularity be grounded in the statistical structure of the problem, rather than by what the theorist finds convenient (Schrater & Kersten 2000). It is important to emphasize that this approach does not necessitate that marginalizations are executed on-line by the brain. The effects of marginalization could be built directly into the inference algorithm avoiding the need for perception to have an explicit representation of the unneeded variables.

Conditioning

Some of our variables are known, through data measurements, or *a priori* assumptions. In either case, once we know something about the variables, we base our inferences on this knowledge by conditioning the joint distribution on the known information:

$$P(S \mid I) = P(S, I)/P(I)$$

The way Bayes' rule comes into the picture is that it is often easier to separately model image formation and the prior model for the causal factors. Bayes' rule is a straightforward application of the product rule to $P(S, I) = P(I \mid S)P(S)$:

$$P(S \mid I) = P(I \mid S)P(S)/P(I)$$

The likelihood $P(I \mid S)$ is determined by the generative image formation model which produces image measurements from a scene description. The generative model produces the image patterns, and consists of the scene prior, and the image formation model. The likelihood is easier to model because we are conditioning on the scene, and the image is a well-defined function of the scene—forward optics plus measurement noise. Although the likelihood and prior terms are logically separable, the division has little bearing on the algorithmic implementation. When it comes to inference, Bayes is neutral with respect to whether *a priori* knowledge is used in a bottom-up or top-down fashion. (*Myth 2: Priors are top-down.*) The regularizers in computer vision can be expressed as priors, and these are typically instantiated as bottom-up constraints (e.g. weights in feedforward networks—Poggio et al., 1985; Poggio & Girosi, 1990).

Why should scene variables be treated probabilistically? In contrast to subjective Bayesian applications (*Myth 3: Priors only refer to subjective, and perhaps conscious biases*), prior probabilities on scene variables are objectively quantifiable. They result from physical processes (e.g. material properties such as albedo and plasticity covary due to common dependence on the substance, such as metal), and from the relative frequencies of the scene variables in the observer's environment. Thus, vision modelers have a big advantage over stock market analysts: they have a better idea of what the functionally important scene causes are, and can hypothesize and test probability density models of scene variables, independent of visual inference. They can also test the extent to which vision respects the constraints in the prior model (see "Testing models of human perception", on page 214). Why is probability essential for modeling pattern synthesis? Because an infinite set of scenes can produce a given image. Thus, in the decoding problem it is essential to have a model of the generative structure of images, given by $p(S \mid I)$ and $p(S)$. Below we discuss how several kinds of generative processes produce characteristic image patterns.

GENERATIVE MODELS IN VISION

Functional vision depends on the kind of abstraction required for the task at hand. But psychological abstractions such as scene categories, object concepts, and affordances rest on the existence of objective world structure. Without such structure, there would be no support for reliable inferences—in fact, there would be no basis for consistent action in a world in which each image is independent of any previous ones. From this perspective, it is not unreasonable for an otherwise functional visual system to hallucinate in response to visual noise, because the best world interpretations will be structured. Thus, understanding the objective generative structure is necessary although not sufficient for an account of human visual perception.[9] However, a central theme of this chapter is the importance of understanding the objective generative processes of the images received. It is an intriguing scientific question as to the degree with which perceptual inference mechanisms mirror or recapitulate the generative image structure. Theories of back-projections in visual cortex rest on internal generative processes to deal with "explaining away" (Dayan et al., 1995; Hinton & Ghahramani, 1997) (see page 211), the related idea of model validation through residual calculation (Mumford, 1992, 1994), and predictive coding (Rao & Ballard, 1999). As we discuss later, the task itself refines our model of the relevant statistical structure through Bayesian modularity.

Visual perception deals with two broad classes of generative processes that produce *photometric* and *geometric* image variation. Further, it is useful to distinguish scene variations (knowledge in $p(S)$) from those of image formation (knowledge in $p(I \mid S)$). We postpone the discussion of the experimental implications of these variations until later (see page 214).

Object and scene variations

A logical prerequisite for a full understanding of image variation is a study of the nature of illumination, surface reflectivities, object geometry, and scene structure quite independently of the properties of the sense organs. Consider geometrical object variations that occur for a single object. An individual object, such as a pair of scissors, or a particular human body consists of parts with a range of possible articulations.

The modeling problem is of significant interest in computer graphic synthesis because it provides the means to model the transformations, and ultimately characterize the probabilities of particular articulations and actions.

Objects (and scenes) can be categorized at more abstract levels, such as "dogs" or "books" (Bobick & Richards, 1986; Rosch et al., 1976). Examples of sources of *within-class* scatter include geometric variations that occur between different members of the same species, vehicles, or computer keyboards. Certain types of within-class geometric variation (e.g. "cats") can be modeled in terms of prototypes together with a description of geometric deformations (Grenander et al., 1991; Yuille, 1991; Mumford, 1996) which admit a probability measure $p(S)$. For this sort of within-class variation, it may be possible to find $p(S)$ through probability density estimation on scene descriptions. Estimating prior densities (e.g. via Principal Components Analysis or PCA) for the distribution of facial surfaces (variations across human face shapes) is now possible due to advances in technology for measuring depth maps (Atick et al., 1996; Vetter & Troje, 1997). Material or albedo variation also occurs across an object set–e.g. the set of books, with different covers. And of course there are mixtures of geometrical and photometrical effects, such as within-species variation among dogs. There is a considerable body of work on biological morphometrics whose goal is to understand the transformations connecting objects within groups (Bookstein, 1978, 1997; Kendall, 1989). Origin of concepts at certain levels may lie in the generative structure of objects, and debate has occurred as to whether an entry-level object concept is based on a prototype with (possibly) a metric model of variation, or a description of the structural relationships between parts. We touch on this point later in the context of object recognition models.

"Schemas" are an example of an even higher level of organization involving *spatial layout*, which recognizes the spatial relationships between objects, and their contextual contingencies. The fact that perceptual judgments are strongly influenced by scene context, (e.g. forest, office, or grocery store scene), suggests that $p(S)$ is not at all uniform across spatial layout, but rather is highly 'spiked' which allows scene type recognition and its exploitation for scene analysis. See Figure 7.2 for examples of scene variable variations.

Effects in the Image

At the most proximal stage, the images projected into the eyes are transformed by the optics, sampled by the retina, and have noise added to them. These operations produce the well-studied photometric variations of *luminance noise* and *blurring* in the images.

Due to the additivity of light and the approximate linearity of reflection, photometric variations due to *illumination* change are approximately linear so that under fixed view, an arbitrary lighting condition can be approximated by the weighted sum of relatively few basis images (Epstein et al., 1995). Further, it has been shown that the images of an object fall on or near a cone in image space (Belhumeur & Kriegman, 1996). Cast shadows are another form of illumination variation resulting from the occlusion of a light source from a surface.

Figure 7.2 Illustrations of variations in scene variables. *Top left:* A collection of bicycles shows variations in geometry (size, shape), albedo (paint patterns). *Top right:* Two images of the same bicycle from the same view but differing in articulation. *Bottom left:* A flat-tailed Gecko hides on a tree, showing how variation in skin pigment (albedo) can match the background pattern of the tree bark (copyright Martin Kramer). *Bottom right:* A river illustrates the complexities of spatial layout. The presence and directionality of the water is encoded in the complex array of specularities and light scatter, determined by the interaction between light source, water surface fluctuation, and viewpoint.

Specularity in an image is an interaction between material, shape, and viewpoint. *Surface transparency* is another source of photometric variation. Its effect in the image can be either additive or multiplicative (Kersten, 1991). One form of additive transparency results from the combination of reflections in a store-front window.

Variations in observer viewpoint (i.e. viewing distance and direction) produce *geometric deformations* in the image. The utility of multiple-scale analysis in human and machine vision is in part a consequence of the distribution of translations in depth of the eye (or camera) viewpoint. Over small changes in viewing variables, the image variations are fairly smooth, although rotations around the viewing sphere can cause large changes in the images due to significant self-occlusions. If we were only concerned with geometry, viewpoint variations and variation in object position and orientation would produce the same set of images. However, illumination interacts with viewpoint so that view rotation is only equivalent to object rotation if the lighting is rigidly attached to the viewer's frame of reference. Rotations in depth cause particularly challenging image variations for object recognition that we briefly discuss later.

The distribution of multiple objects in a scene affects the images of objects through *occlusion* and clutter. Because of the nature of imaging, the local correlations in surface features typically carry over to local image features. However, occlusion of one object by another breaks up the image into disconnected patches. Further, patches widely separated in the image can be statistically related, and the challenge is to link the appropriate image measurements likely to belong to the same objects. Like occlusion, *background* is a significant confounding source of image variation that thwarts segmentation. The intensity edges at the bounding contours of an object can vary substantially as the background is changed, even if the view and lighting remain the same. See Figure 7.3 for examples of illumination and viewing effects on images.

Occlusion is the result of the distribution of the kinds and spatial arrangements of objects within a scene relative to the viewpoint. But the *spatial layouts* of schemas also generate statisical dependence in images. Temporal variation in images is induced by object motion and observer actions (Bobick, 1997). Thus the spatio-temporal image distribution is affected by the distribution of observer *actions*, and object *dynamics* (e.g. freeway driving).

GRAPHICAL MODELS OF STATISTICAL STRUCTURE

In general, natural image pattern formation is specified by a high-dimensional joint probability, requiring an elaboration of the causal structure that is more complex than the simplified model in the bottom panel of Figure 7.1. The idea is to represent the probabilistic structure of the joint distribution $P(S, I)$ by a Bayes' net (Pearl, 1988; Ripley, 1996), which is simply a graphical model that expresses how variables influence each other. There are just three basic building blocks: converging, diverging, and intermediate nodes. For example, multiple (e.g. scene) variables causing a given image measurement, a single variable producing multiple image measurements, or a cause indirectly influencing an image measurement through an intermediate variable (see Figure 7.4). These types of influence provide a first step towards modeling the joint distribution and, as we describe below, the means to efficiently compute probabilities of the unknown variables given known values.

Influences between variables are represented by conditioning, and a graphical model expresses the conditional independencies between variables. Two random

Figure 7.3 Variations in illumination and viewing. *Top left:* A young man's face shows shading variation due to the extrinsic shadows cast by leaves. *Top right:* Reflection of a face on the glass door of a bookcase creates a transparent image. *Bottom left:* Two images of the same bicycle differing in viewpoint. *Bottom right:* A deer hides behind foliage, illustrating occlusion/background clutter. (copyright Mark Brady).

variables may only become independent, however, once the value of some third variable is known. This is called *conditional independence.*[10]

Using labels to represent variables and arrows to represent conditioning (with $a \rightarrow b$ indicating b is conditioned on a[11]), independence can be represented by

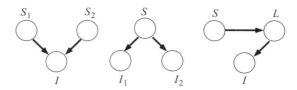

Figure 7.4 Components of the generative structure for image patterns involve converging, diverging, and intermediate nodes. For example, these could correspond to: multiple (scene) causes $\{S_1, S_2\}$ giving rise to the same image measurement, I; one cause, S influencing more than one image measurement, $\{I_1, I_2\}$; a scene (or other) cause S, influencing an image measurement through an intermediate variable L.

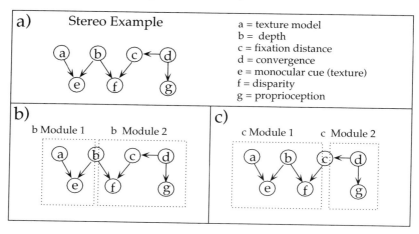

Figure 7.5 Example of a Bayes' net. **(a)** A Bayes' net representing the factored distribution $p(a, b, c, d, e, f, g) = p(a)p(b)p(c \mid d)p(d)p(e \mid a, b)p(f \mid b, c)p(g \mid d)$. The graphical model can express the probabilistic structure of depth from stereo and texture inference. **(b)** When estimating the depth variable b, the net can be decomposed into two separate depth modules (depth from texture and depth from stereo). The dashed boxes show the modules. **(c)** When estimating the fixation distance c, the net can be decomposed into two separate distance modules (distance from texture and stereo, and distance from proprioception). Note that the left-hand side of the graph does not decompose as before. This illustrates *Bayesian modularity*.

the absence of connections between variables. For example, if the joint probability $p(a, b, c, d, e, f, g)$ factors by independence into

$$p(a, b, c, d, e, f, g) = p(a)p(b)p(c \mid d)p(d)p(e \mid a, b)p(f \mid b, c)p(g \mid d),$$

then the variables can be represented by the graph in Figure 7.5. Had the variables factored into two independent groups the graph would have shown two separate nets. The example graph can represent a Bayes' network for computing structure from stereo and texture if we allow some of the nodes to represent multiple variables. To illustrate, let the node a represent the geometric and material causes of a particular image texture, and e represent the collection of texture measurements made by the observer. The node b represents absolute depth from the observer and is the variable of interest for the task. The horizontal and vertical disparity measurements are bundled into f, which depends on both the depth variable b and the direction and distance of the observer's fixation point, c, in space. The fixation point distance is determined by the convergence angle, d, between the eyes. The convergence angle can be inferred from non-visual proprioceptive feedback from the eyes represented by the data variable g.

Note that the graphical structure captures the structure of the data formation. The top layer of the graph represents the scene and viewing variables, whose causal effect on the sensory data in the bottom layer is represented by the directed arrows.

OPTIMAL DECODING: MODELING THE TASKS

The basic tenet is that perception enables successful behavior, and thus any decoding scheme is designed to extract useful information about the true state of the world. But the essence of decision theory analysis is the trade-off between truth and utility. A complete characterization of optimal behavior cannot dispense with either dimension. Even the simple problem of deciding whether a flash of light is bright or dim is only a useful visual function, if the task is to decide whether one or the other determines a true state of the world. Was the light switch set to high or low? Was the object closer or nearer? The fundamental computational problem of vision is: given visual data, how can the system determine the environmental causes of that data, when it is confounded by other variables. If one accepts this, then we can make the case that visual perception is fundamentally image decoding. But whether to draw an inference, or the precision with which it must be drawn is determined by the visual function. As with any decoding system, perception operates with target goals that depend on the task. A complete theory of vision needs to account for three classes of behavioral tasks:

1. The visual system draws discrete (categorical) conclusions about objective world. These decisions invariably involve taking into account potentially large variations in confounding secondary variables. For example, to reliably detect a face, a system must allow for variations in view, lighting, background, as well as the geometrical variations in individual facial shape, expression, and hair. Finer-grain identifications require more estimates of primary variables, and less marginalization with respect to secondary variables (Kersten, 1997). Because the causes are objective, decisions have a right or wrong answer. Further, the cost due to incorrect decisions can be large or small. A mistake in animal identification can have serious consequences. Failing to anticipate the change in color of a sweater going from indoor to outdoor lighting may cause only mild social embarrassment, requiring little investment in perceptual (vs. learned cognitive) resources.
2. The visual system provides continuously valued estimations for actions. For example, visual information for depth and size determine the kinematics of reach and grasp. Like discrete decisions, estimations can have degrees of utility.
3. The visual system adapts to environmental contingencies in the images received. This adaptation is at longer time scales than inference required for perceptual problem solving, occurring over both phylogenetic and ontogenetic scales. One form of adaptation requires implicit probability density estimation.

Can we describe these processes from the point of view of pattern inference theory— i.e. as image decoding by means of probability computations? To do so requires a probabilistic model of tasks. We consider a task as specifying four things, the required or primary set of scene variables S_e, the nuisance or secondary scene variables S_g, the scene variables which are presumed known S_f, and the decision to be made. Each of the four components of a task plays a role in determining the structure of the optimal inference computation. First, we review how to model the decision as a risk functional on the posterior distribution, then we show that S_e and S_f can be used to simplify the joint distribution through independence relations, while S_g and the decision rule can make one choice of S_e simpler than another.

Bayesian decision theory provides a precise language to model the costs of errors determined by the choice of visual task (Yuille & Buelthoff, 1996; Brainard & Freeman, 1997). The cost or *risk* $R(\Sigma; I)$ of guessing Σ when the image measurement is I is defined as the expected *loss*:

$$R(\Sigma; I) = \int_S L(\Sigma, S) P(S \mid I) dS,$$

with respect to the posterior probability, $P(S \mid I)$. The best interpretation of the image can then be made by finding the Σ which minimizes the risk function. The loss function $L(\Sigma, S)$ specifies the cost of guessing Σ when the scene variable is S. One possible loss function is $-\delta(\Sigma - S)$. In this case the risk becomes $R(\Sigma; I) = -P(\Sigma \mid I)$, and then the best strategy is to pick the most likely interpretation. This is standard *maximum a posteriori* (MAP) *estimation*. A second kind of loss function assumes that costs are constant over all guesses of a variable. This is equivalent to marginalization of the posterior with respect to that variable.

The introduction of a cost function makes Bayesian decision theory an extremely general theoretical tool. However, this flexibility has drawbacks from a scientific perspective. We could potentially introduce a loss function for each scene variable, which makes it impractical to independently test cost function hypotheses empirically—and we are stuck with an additional set of free parameters. However, we can achieve modeling economy by assuming the delta function or constant loss functions depending on whether the variable is needed (primary) or not. Thus, we advocate initially constructing simpler Bayesian theories in which we estimate the most probable relevant scene value (MAP estimation), while marginalizing with respect to the irrelevant generic variables. Bloj and colleagues have an example of this strategy applied to the interaction of color and shape (Bloj et al., 1999).

We now describe how the statistical structure and task interact in determining the inference computations. While the statistical structure of the joint distribution determines which variables interact, the choice of decision rule and marginalization variables determine the details of how they interact. In the next section, we show how the task, in choosing the relevant variables, partitions the scene variables through statistical independence.

PARTITIONING THE SCENE CAUSES: TASK DEPENDENCY AND CONDITIONAL INDEPENDENCE

Considering a single task allows us to focus our attention on a particular set of variables S_e. In some cases, we may be justified in ignoring a number of scene properties irrelevant to the task. This idea can be expressed in terms of the distributions through statistical independence. We may factor $p(S, I)$ into two parts, one of which contains all the variables which are statistically independent of S_e and the other which contains all of the dependent variables,

$$p(S, I) = p(I_{ind} \mid S_{ind})p(I_{dep} \mid S_{dep})p(S_{ind})p(S_{dep})^{12}.$$

In terms of a graphical model, this partitioning corresponds to unconnected subgraphs. Specifying a task restricts our base of inference to $p(I_{dep}, S_{dep})$.

In addition, the nature of a task or context fixes some of the scene variables S_f. For instance, if an observer is doing quality checking on an assembly line, then the lighting variables and viewpoint can be considered fixed. Note that constraints used to regularize vision problems can often be expressed as fixing a set of scene variables. For instance, in a world of polynomial surfaces, the constraint that the task only involves flat surfaces can be rephrased as all non-linear polynomial coefficients are fixed at zero.

Since the variables in S_f are presumed known, we can subdivide the dependent variables still further, $S_{dep} \rightarrow S'_{dep}, S_f$ and condition $p(I_{dep}, S_{dep})$ on S_f, $p(I_{dep}, S'_{dep} \mid S_f)$, which increases the statistical independence of the variables. This is true because variables which are not statistically independent, because they are dependent on a common variable, become independent when conditioned on the common variable. Thus we expect the conditional distribution to further decompose into relevant and irrelevant scene variable components.

Thus given the task, we can first factor

$$p(S, I \mid S_f) = \prod_{i=1}^{N} p(S_i, I \mid S_f).$$

To do inference we need only consider the factors in which the S_i contain the variables in S_e. Let S_j denote the minimal set of statistically dependent variables containing S_e. The variables in S_j excluding S_e are just the secondary variables S_g. Then, $p(S_e, S_g, I \mid S_f)$ contains all the information we need to perform the inference task, and has automatically specified the task relevant and irrelevant variables, i.e. the primary and secondary variables. Thus the independence structure determines which variables should be involved in an inference computation. This is an important issue for modeling cue integration.

In terms of graphical models, the set of variables S_e and S_g for the task have the property that they are connected by the image data. In other words, S_e and S_g are both involved in generating the image data. The basic generative structure of the perceptual inference problem is illustrated in the lower panel in Figure 7.1 from the point of view of pattern inference theory. Comparing this diagram to the generative diagram for the standard signal detection theory above it, we can better see how pattern inference theory is a generalization of the typical way of using signal detection theory. In most applications of SDT to vision, the image data are generated by signals plus noise, which allow us to identify S_e as the signal set, and S_g as the noise. Thus, one of the key ideas of pattern inference theory is that unwanted variables act like noise in the context of a particular inference task. However, the noise is multivariate, highly

Table 7.1 Table illustrating how the visual task partitions the scene variables into primary (E) and secondary (G) variables. The pattern of image intensities is determined by all of the scene variables, object shape, material, object articulation (e.g. body limb movements or facial expression), viewpoint, relative position between objects, and illumination. Basic-level recognition involves more abstract categorization (e.g. dog vs. cat) than subordinate-level recognition (Doberman vs. Dachshund), and is typically thought to be shape-based, with material properties such as fur color discounted. Finer-grain subordinate-level recognition requires estimates of shape and material.

| | Object perception | | Spatial layout | | |
| | Object-centered (object recognition) | | World-centered | Observer-centered (hand action) | |
	Basic-level	Subordinate-level	Planning	Reach	Grasp
Shape	E	E	G	G	E
Material	G	E	G	G	G
Articulation	G	E	G	G	E
Viewpoint	G	G	G	E	G
Relative position	G	G	E	G	G
Illumination	G	G	G	G	G

structured and in general cannot be modeled by a unimodal distribution. While the set of generic variables, S_g, play the role of noise for one task, they form the "signal" for another task, because the distinction between primary and secondary depends on the visual function. What is a primary variable for one task may be secondary for another. Table 7.1 illustrates how various visual tasks determine the primary vs. secondary variables.

One of the consequences of deciding a task, is that ambiguity can be reduced through marginalization (Freeman, 1994; Knill et al., 1996b). The basic principle is: *perception's model of the image measurement (i.e. the generative consequence of the primary variable's prediction of the image measurement) should be robust with respect to variations in the secondary variables.* In fact, the general viewpoint principle is a consequence of viewpoint being a secondary variable (Freeman, 1994).

PARTITIONING IMAGE MEASUREMENTS: SUFFICIENT STATISTICS

Once we have determined which scene variables are relevant to the task, the independence structure of $p(S_e, S_g, I \mid S_f)$ specifies the image measurements to make. Assuming we have a set of measurements $\{m_1(I), m_2(I), m_3(I), \ldots\}$ which form a good code for $p(I)$, then we can determine which image measurements to use by partitioning the joint distribution. The joint distribution,

$$p(S_e, \{m_1(I), m_2(I), m_3(I), \ldots\} \mid S_f)$$

will further factor into relevant and irrelevant image measurements, yielding a set M of measurements required for the task. If we inspect the posterior distribution needed for inference $p(S_e \mid M, S_f)$, we can interpret the set M as the set of sufficient statistics for S_e, since $p(S_e \mid I, M, S_f) = p(S_e \mid M, S_f)$ fits the standard definition of a *sufficient statistic* (Duda & Hart, 1973). While many different sets of measurements can form sufficient statistics, *minimal sufficient statistics* are the smallest set of sufficient statistics and have the property that any other set of sufficient statistics are a function of them. This new perspective leads to the principle: a good image code for a visual system is one that forms a set of minimal sufficient statistics for the tasks the observer performs.

PUTTING THE PIECES TOGETHER: NEEDED SCENE ESTIMATES, SUFFICIENT IMAGE MEASUREMENTS, AND PROBABILITY COMPUTATION

We have shown for optimal inference, how the choice of required variables determines which scene variables we need to consider through statistical independence, and the set of image measurements through the notion of sufficient statistics. We now illustrate how the variables interact in optimal inference, which is determined by the details of the generative model and the choice of loss functions. The generative model, in specifying how the secondary variables interact with the primary variables to produce an image, determines to a large extent how the primary and secondary variables interact in an inference computation. However, the choice of cost function, by specifying different costs for errors, modulates the relevance of errors induced by the ignorance of particular secondary variables.

To be more specific, we return to the generative model for texture, disparity and proprioceptive data. (Figure 7.5), but now from the point of view of decoding— estimating depth from measurements of disparity and texture. In Bayesian inference, the change in certainty of the scene variables causing the image after receiving image data respects the generative model. Both prior knowledge and image measurements fix values in the network, and the problem is to update the probabilities of the remaining variables. Updating the probabilities is straightforward for simple networks, but requires more sophisticated techniques such as probability or belief propagation, or the junction-tree algorithm for more complex networks (Frey, 1998; Weiss, 1997; Jordan, 1998). The primary effect of receiving image data is to change the certainty of all the variables which could possibly generate the image data. One effect of having more than one image measurement is known as "explaining away" in Bayes nets. For example, suppose we observe that the texture measurements e are compressed in the y direction relative to an isotropic texture. The compression might be the result of our texture being non-isotropic (i.e. attributing the observation to the texture model a), it might be due to the surface having a depth gradient (i.e. attributing the measurement to the surface depth b), or it might be due to a little of both. Given only the texture measurement, the data supplies evidence for both a and b. However, if we have additional disparity data f which is consistent with a depth gradient, then our best inference is that both the texture compression and the disparity gradient are caused by a depth gradient. This second piece of information drives the additional inference that our texture model should be isotropic—a common depth gradient "explains away" the coincidence between the disparity gradient and the texture compression. Bayesian inference does this naturally by updating probabilities of each needed but unknown variable. The process of updating probabilities in a network is more powerful than estimating a single state. For example, if the random variables in the network are Gaussian, then updating probabilities requires new estimates of the mean *and* variance.

The task also affects the algorithmic structure. To illustrate, consider trying to do inference based on the total probability distribution. We would need to maintain a probability distribution on more than seven dimensions (one for each node in the network plus the nodes with multiple variables). Thus, computing using the entire distribution would be computationally prohibitive. However, the statistical independencies show a kind of modularity we call *Bayesian modularity*. In Bayesian modularity, the independence structure allows us to produce separate likelihood functions for the variable of interest, which can be combined by multiplication. For instance, if we are doing inference on b in the above example,

$$p(e \mid b) = \int_a p(e \mid a, b) \mathrm{d}a$$

produces one likelihood function and

$$p(f, g \mid b) = \int_c \left[\int_d p(g \mid d) p(c \mid d) p(d) \mathrm{d}d \right] p(f \mid b, c) \mathrm{d}c$$

produces the other. This division creates two "modules" illustrated in Figure 7.5(b). The division also creates enormous computational savings, as we only need to maintain three likelihoods over two variables: $\{a, b\}$, $\{b, c\}$ & $\{c, d\}$. Modularity is modulated by the task. Figure 7.5(c) shows how Bayesian modularity changes as a function of which variables are estimated.

The quantitative influence of the data on the inference depends critically on both the likelihood and the knowledge we have about the secondary variables. The value of priors on secondary variables is clear, however the effect of likelihood is more subtle, as it depends on the number of possible scene causes for an image and the change in the image given a change in the scene variables. For example, Knill has shown that texture information is less reliable for frontal parallel surfaces than for strongly slanted surfaces because large changes in slant for fronto-parallel surfaces cause small changes in image texture compared to slant changes for strongly slanted surfaces (Knill, 1998b).

Now depending on our cost function, the two likelihood functions $p(e \mid b)$ and $p(f, g \mid b)$ for the depth b will have different influences on the decision. For example, consider a depth task in which the cost of depth errors is only high when the depth gradient is small (i.e. the surfaces are nearly fronto-parallel). In this case the depth from texture module will be nearly irrelevant to the decisions, because texture information is only reliable for large depth gradients (Knill, 1998b), whereas disparity information can be reliable for small depth gradients.

LEARNING GENERATIVE STRUCTURE

In pattern inference theory, learning is estimating the density $p(S, I)$, and discovering the appropriate cost function for the task. For example, learning to classify images of faces as male or female requires knowledge of intragender facial variability (i.e. $p(S)$), knowledge about how faces produce images (i.e. $p(I \mid S)$), and the decision boundary set by the cost of incorrectly identifying the faces. The two components, density estimation and cost function specification, have a rough correspondence to what we might call task-general and task-specific constraints respectively. Task-general constraints are those which hold irregardless of the specific nature of the task, which correspond to the fundamental constraints on inference set by the structure of the joint density. On the other hand, the choice of cost function is always task-specific, since it involves specifying the costs for a particular task. For generality, we focus on density estimation below.

It is one thing to talk about what one could do given the joint probability for a visual problem, and it is quite another matter to actually obtain it. High-dimensional probability density estimation is notoriously difficult. This observation has lead to radically different alternatives to learning, which place focus on the decision boundaries, largely ignoring the within-class structure (e.g. support vector machines (Vapnik, 1995)). We discuss here several reasons to be optimistic.

An essential requirement for density estimation is to have a rich vocabulary of possible densities, which are typically parametric, from which a best fit to the image data can be achieved. The second requirement is having a sensible error metric to assess the best fitting density model. Zhu et al. (1997) have developed a general method for density estimation based on the *Minimax Entropy Principle* which allows the consideration of both the best fitting model and what image measurements should be used. They assume that the density can be approximated well by a Gibbs distribution. Given a set of image measurements, they fit the best Gibbs distribution using the maximum entropy principle (Jaynes, 1957),[13] which in essence chooses the least structured distribution consistent with the image measurements. They then use the Kullback–Leibler divergence to select between different models and sets of image measurements. Maximum entropy fits prevent model overfitting and choose the Gibbs distributions for which the set of image measurements are sufficient statistics.

Another approach to density estimation works by evaluating the *evidence* (MacKay, 1992). Let G represent an index across the set of generative models we are considering. Then we select the best fitting model by maximizing the evidence

$$p(G \mid I) = p(I \mid G)p(G),$$

where

$$p(I \mid G) = \int_{S_G} p(I \mid S_G, G)p(S_G)dS_G.$$

Assuming we have a lot of image data, the prior across models does not matter much and the decision is based on $p(I \mid G)$. Choosing models by maximizing the evidence naturally instantiates Occam's Razor, i.e. models with lots of parameters are penalized (MacKay, 1992). Schwarz (1978) has found an asymptotic approximation to $\log p(I \mid G)$ for well-behaved priors which makes the penalty for the number of parameters of G explicit:

$$\log p(I \mid G) \simeq \log p(I \mid G, \hat{S}_G) - \frac{\log N}{2} \, \mathrm{Dim}(G),$$

where N is the number of training samples, $\hat{S}_G$ is the maximum likelihood estimate of the scene parameters and $\mathrm{Dim}(G)$ is the number of parameters for the model G. A similar formula arises from the *Minimum Description Length* (MDL) principle, which through Shannon's optimal coding theorem, is formally equivalent to MAP. While embodying Occam's Razor, evaluating the evidence works by choosing the model which is the best predictor of the data.

There have also been a few studies that try to directly learn a mapping from image measurements to scene descriptions (Freeman & Pasztor, 1999; Kersten et al., 1987). However, these approaches are limited in requiring the availability of sample pairs of scene and image data. While general methods could be used by the visual system for learning, the visual system may employ quite impoverished models of the joint density. The key point is that learning algorithms for both objective physical modeling or biological learning can be expressed in the Bayesian language of pattern inference theory.

TESTING MODELS OF HUMAN PERCEPTION

In order for the pattern inference theory approach to be useful, we need to be able to construct predictive theories of visual function which are amenable to experimental testing. While we have discussed the elements of constructing Bayesian theories throughout the paper, it is important to distinguish the role of the mathematical language from the elements of a theory of vision.

PATTERN INFERENCE THEORIES OF VISION

How do Bayesian or pattern inference theories of vision differ from other theories (e.g. Gestalt)? The answer so far is that they express observer principles in terms of probabilities and cost functions. Thus, these theories will involve explicit statements about the scene variables and image measurements used, the prior probabilities on scene variables, the image formation and measurement model assumed by the observer, and the relative costs assigned to potential outcomes in a task. We also hope however, that pattern inference theory will lead to a set of fundamental and deep principles akin to the laws of thermodynamics, also expressible in the same framework. The importance of such principles for scientific economy should not be underestimated. From the right first principles, an infinite set of experimentally testable consequences can be derived, not all of which are testable. Instead, it is enough to focus on testing the surprising consequences, which, when enough are verified, make it possible to reliably predict perceptual performance in unstudied domains. Past and recent work has built on the Bayesian perspective to advance a number of what we might call "deep principles" applicable to human perception.

1. The visual system seeks codes which minimize redundancy in the input (Barlow, 1959; Olshausen & Field, 1996; Atick & Redlich, 1992; Bell & Sejnowski, 1997). This principle exists in various forms, such as MDL encoding, minimax entropy (Zhu et al., 1997), principal components analysis (Bossomaier & Snyder, 1986) and independent components analysis (Bell & Sejnowski, 1997).

2. Given equally likely causes of an image, the visual system chooses the model with the least number of assumptions. In this sense, quantitative versions of the Gestalt principle of simplicity (e.g. via MDL realization of Occam's Razor) apply as a principle to resolve ambiguity (Restle, 1982; Leeuwenberg, 1969). The pattern inference theory distinctive is that it has the (yet to be obtained) goal of deriving the rules of simplicity from density models based on ensembles of natural image (e.g. Zhu, 1999).

3. The visual system actively acquires new information by maximizing the expected utility or minimizing entropy of the information for the task (Amit & Geman, 1997). This principle has been applied to an ideal observer model of human reading (Legge et al., 1997).

4. Perceptual decisions are confidence-driven. This requires that computations take into account both estimates and the degree of uncertainty in those estimates. Evidence that human perception does this comes from studies on cue integration (Landy et al., 1995), orientation from texture discussed above (Knill, 1998a), motion perception, discussed below (Weiss & Adelson, 1998), and visual motor control (Wolpert et al., 1995).

5. Perception's model of the image measurement should be robust with respect to variations in the secondary variables. We noted above that the general viewpoint principle is a consequence of viewpoint being a secondary variable (Freeman, 1994), and that ambiguity in depth from shadows can be resolved by treating illumination direction as secondary.

6. The visual system predictively models its behavioral outcomes. Until recently, the Bayesian approach to perception has been largely static; however, Bayesian techniques can be used to model both learning (Jordan, 1998) and time-variant processes (Dean & Kanazawa, 1988; Barker et al., 1995). (*Myth 4: Bayes lacks dynamics.*) For example, the Kalman filter provides a good account of kinematics of visual control of human reach (Wolpert et al., 1995). Consistent with the probability computation theme of this chapter, the Kalman filter goes beyond estimates of central tendency, and estimates both the mean and variance of control parameters.

7. The visual system performs ideal inference given its limitations in representing image data, but only for a limited number of tasks (Schrater & Kersten, 2000). In the next section, we discuss using this principle to develop models of ideal performance as a default hypotheses. It is essentially a statement that the visual system should be optimally adapted to perform certain visual tasks relevant to the observer's needs.

For Bayesian theory construction to be useful, we must show that the theories admit experimental testing. In the next section we discuss practical aspects of testing pattern theoretic hypotheses at several levels of specificity. In particular, we return to Principle 7.

IDEAL OBSERVERS AND HUMAN SCENE INFERENCE

How do we formulate and test theories of human behavioral function within a pattern inference theory framework? In psychophysical experiments, one can: (a) test at the constraint level—what information does human vision avail itself of?, or (b) test at the mechanism level—what neural subsystem can account for performance? Pattern inference theory is of primary relevance to hypotheses testable at the former level. Tests of human perception can be based on hypotheses regarding constraints contained in: the two components of the generative model, (1) the prior $p(S)$ and (2) the likelihood $p(I \mid S)$; (3) the image model $p(I)$; or (4) the posterior $p(S \mid I)$. A distinction based on the source of a constraint serves to clarify the otherwise confusing idea of "cue" which muddles scene and image constraints (Knill et al., 1996b). For example, the "occlusion cue" is sometimes defined in terms of "overlapping surfaces", and sometimes as a "T-junction" in the image contours. But surface occlusion is the *causal source* of a "T-junction". (*Myth 5: Identifying "Bayesian constraints" provides no advantage over identifying traditional "cues".*)

1. *The prior.* The well-known "light from above" assumption in shape-from-shading is an example of an hypothesis expressed solely in terms of a prior distribution on a scene variable, light source direction. Given that primary lighting for most of human history has been the sun, a prior bias on lighting from above is an example of a prediction which could be generated by a study of the natural distribution of scene variables, which can be quantitatively documented using density estimation. A fruitful first pass could be a more widespread use of principal components analysis as a way of seeking economical density models. Indeed, empirical measurements of the distribution of spectral reflectance functions of natural surfaces have shown that the set of naturally occurring spectral reflectance functions can be well-modeled as linear combinations of three basis functions (Maloney & Wandell, 1986). When restricted to natural illumination conditions, this result supplies an especially simple interpretation of trichromacy: three spectral measurements are usually enough to determine spectral reflectance. Earlier we noted research on prior models for facial surfaces (Atick et al., 1996; Vetter & Troje 1997). In a different example, an observer's assessment of the 3-D position of a moving ball is affected by moving cast shadow information. The observer's data can be qualitatively described in terms of a prior "stationary light source" constraint (Knill et al., 1996a). The subjective biases in the perception of shape from line contours have been studied by Mamassian and Landy & (1998). An interesting problem for the future will be to relate these subjective priors to ones discovered objectively through density estimation (Zhu, 1999).

2. *The likelihood term.* The independent variables in a psychophysical experiment can be specified in terms of the scene or image variables, or in the language of

perceptual psychology, in terms of the distal or the proximal stimulus. Even if one doesn't have an ideal observer model, it is still possible to manipulate the scene variables in the generative model to test hypotheses at these levels, if one has some way to account for changes in performance due to changes in image information. For example, object recognition must deal with variations in both viewpoint and illumination. View-based theories of object recognition rest on experiments showing that human vision doesn't compensate for all view variations with equal facility (Tarr & Bülthoff, 1995). Scale changes are handled with less sensitivity to view familiarity than either rotations in the image or rotations in depth. However, the degree to which the human visual system is view-dependent will require developing ideal observer models for object recognition, because part of performance variation due to viewpoint can be due to the informativeness of the viewpoint for the recognition task. In fact, Liu et al. (1995) showed that human observers are more efficient than simple view-based algorithms at recognizing simple wire objects (Liu et al., 1995).

Object recognition must also compensate for illumination variations. The fact, mentioned above, that under fairly general conditions, the space of images generated by an object under fixed view is a cone in image space makes predictions regarding how object recognition should generalize under illumination change, as well as the discriminability of two objects with distinct illumination cones (Belhumeur & Kriegman, 1996; Tarr et al., 1998).

3. *The image density.* Given a model, $p(I; \Lambda)$, of an image ensemble in a domain Λ (i.e. natural image prior, or more specific texture priors, such as "fur"), one can test how well the human visual system is "tuned" to the statistical structure specified by the parameters Λ. An example of this approach is the ideal observer analysis of human discrimination of Gaussian textures with $1/f^\alpha$ spatial frequency spectra (Knill et al., 1990). Current theoretical work on non-Gaussian texture modeling (e.g. Minimax entropy discussed above) is providing richer models of natural images that provide testable psychophysical hypotheses (Buccigrossi & Simoncelli, 1997; Zhu et al., 1997; Ruderman & Bialek, 1994). More domain-specific density models, e.g. using PCA, have been used to model face variation in the image domain (Sirovich & Kirby, 1987; Turk & Pentland, 1991), and have motivated psychological theories (Valentin et al., 1997).

4. *The posterior.* A full quantitative model (the grand challenge) requires tests at the level of the posterior. A statistical theory of visual inference plays two roles, it *normalizes* performance and *models* perception. An ideal observer model, which bases its performance on $P(S \mid I)$, provides the benchmark to normalize human performance relative to the information available for the task (Barlow, 1962). The importance of this normative measure cannot be overstated. Without carefully assessing how the information changes across experimental conditions, the mechanisms underlying changes in performance become nearly impossible to determine. In fact, normalizing human performance with respect to the available information can lead to the opposite conclusions from those based on the unnormalized performance (Eagle & Blake, 1995).

But in what sense does an ideal observer serve a modeling function? The fact that perception enables successful behavior has a non-trivial impact on the principles required to understand perception. In this regard, pattern inference theory is sympathetic with one aspect of the ecological approach to perception, namely that theories of visual perception cannot be built in isolation from functional visual tasks. If this is indeed the case, our grand challenge is unavoidably grand. This raises a dilemma for scientific methodology. If we have to worry about the large set of variables involved in normal perception, how can we manage controlled experimental tests of the theory? We believe the answer is to use the ideal observer as the default experimental hypothesis—in other words, first test whether human vision utilizes the information available for the task optimally. Of course, in general it won't. However, because the ideal starts off (at least in principle) with no free parameters, a sub-optimal theory can still achieve economy through modification of the ideal theory through the frugal introduction of free parameters. Further, any parameters introduced should be related to some biologically (or ecologically) relevant limitation on processing. This idea is very much in the spirit of sequential ideal observer analysis of photon and biological limits to resolution (Geisler, 1989). In the domain of surface perception, Knill has shown that human discrimination of surface slant improves with slant–a behavior that can be predicted from an ideal observer analysis of the information (Knill, 1998a).

As mentioned earlier, the true test of a quantitative framework such as pattern inference theory is its ability to generate economical and predictive theories. A rather striking recent success story is Weiss and Adelson's Bayesian theory of motion perception in which they tackled the problem of combining local motion measurements. Previously, distinct models (often with distinct hypothesized physiological realizations) have been proposed for various classes of motion effects. Weiss and Adelson were able to account for a wide and diverse range of human perceptual results with only one free parameter, the uncertainty in the local motion measurement (Weiss & Adelson, 1998). By assuming that the visual system takes into account the uncertainties in local motion measurements, rather than just the motion estimates (i.e. confidence-driven processing), and assuming simple priors for slower speeds and smooth velocity fields, the MAP estimate from the resulting posterior modeled: the barber-pole effect, the biases in the direction and speed of moving plaids due to differences in component orientation and contrast, the wagon-wheel effect, non-rigid contour perception, as well as others.

A crucial aspect to the success of such a program is to choose an information processing task for which the human visual system is well-suited. Our assumption is that if this is done, the ideal performance will be a good first-approximation to a model for human performance. This argument is similar to those made with regard to adaptability in cognitive tasks (Cosmides, 1989; Murray 1987; Gigerenzer, 1998). Pattern inference theory provides the language to express experimentally testable theories in a way analogous to calculus being useful for expressing quantitative theories in science generally. As such it is a mathematical theory, not a falsifiable experimental theory. However, pattern inference theory provides the means to generate testable scientific theories of perception with few free parameters; such theories should be more easily falsifiable than, for example connectionist theories with lots of free parameters. (*Myth 6: Bayesian theories are not falsifiable.*)

DOES THE BRAIN COMPUTE PROBABILITIES?

COMPUTING PROBABILITIES IS NOT PROBABILISTIC COMPUTING

Shortly before his death in 1957, John von Neumann wrote "The language of the brain is not the language of mathematics" (von Neumann, 1958). He went on to predict that brain theory would eventually come to resemble the physics of statistical mechanics and thermodynamics. His argument was based on the apparent imprecision in neural pulse-train coding, rather than an underlying computational function for stochastic processing elements. Nevertheless, von Neumann would no doubt have been intrigued by the algorithms, developed since, that do in fact rely on stochastic processing. But it is one thing to say that brain processing is limited by neural noise, or that it uses noise to compute, and quite another to state that the brain computes probabilities. An information processing system can compute probabilities quite deterministically (see example below).

The main purpose of this chapter is to argue that the perceptual system must necessarily do statistical inference, and thus compute probabilities. The degree of sophistication of such processes and the brain mechanisms are open questions. For example, a standard assumption in vision has been that probability computations are limited to computing central tendencies of distributions, which produce estimates of quantities of interest for decisions. But this leads to a premature commitment by discarding the information about the uncertainty in the estimate. In addition to the empirical worked discussed earlier, it has also been shown from work in Bayes nets that significant improvements in computational convergence time are obtained when probabilities are propagated (e.g. Weiss, 1997), thus preserving information about the degree of uncertainty.

HOW COULD PROBABILITY DENSITIES
BE REPRESENTED IN THE BRAIN?

Although Bayesian theories require the computation of probabilities, they do not necessarily require probabilities to be explicitly computed. For example, the knowledge regarding probability densities could be *implicitly* encoded in neural non-linearities and neural weights. For example, the form of the photoreceptor transducer can be interpreted as the result of mapping a non-uniform distribution of contrasts to a uniformly distributed response variable—i.e. histogram equalization (Laughlin, 1981). Knowledge of the image probability density function is implicit in the photoreceptor in the sense that the density is the derivative of its transducer function.[14]

At a higher level, for a classification task the visual system need only deterministically map the image data onto an appropriate decision variable space and then choose the category boundaries, neither of which require probabilities to be explicitly computed.

On the other hand, the visual system may *explicitly* compute probabilities in terms of population codes across a variable of interest. The basic idea is straightforward: the firing rate of a labeled line code for an image or scene variable is proportional to the posterior probability for the variable. Population codes occur in the coding of motor planning for eye movements in superior colliculus (Lee et al., 1988) and for reaching (Georgopoulos et al., 1989) in motor cortex, and they have been proposed for the representation of sensory information such as a population code for image velocities (Simoncelli, 1993; Schrater, 1998). Population codes hold the promise of being able to represent probabilities for computation. For instance, the uncertainty can be represented as the entropy over the ensemble or spread of activity across the population, and multiple values can be represented as multi-modal distributions of activity. Probability information can be transmitted from one functional group of neurons to the next by transforming the distributions between parameter spaces using the density mapping theorem. In contrast, a system that performs "estimation propagation" would summarize the population first (e.g. mean or mode) into an estimate of state, and then only propagate the estimate. Of course, making discrete decisions is one of the main types of task discussed above, and at some point the probability distribution could be collapsed to one decision variable.

The connection between population codes and probability distributions goes back to early work in communication engineering, where it was shown that an array of linear filters could produce a *sampled* log likelihood function (Van Trees, 1971). As an example, assume the input visual signal $r(\vec{x})$, is a sum of components of interest, $s(\vec{x}, \theta_i)$, plus Gaussian noise N: $r(\vec{x}) = \sum_i s(\vec{x}, \theta_i) + N$. The components could be oriented edge segments, in which case $s(\vec{x}, \theta_i)$ are prototypical edge images, parameterized by the orientation θ_i. Given the input signal $r(\vec{x})$, it is straightforward to show that the likelihood function for the signal given an orientation is given by $\log p(r(\vec{x}) \mid \theta_i) = \int_{\vec{x}} r(\vec{x}) s(\vec{x}, \theta_i) \, d\vec{x}$. This likelihood can be converted into an unnormalized posterior probability by adding a constant equal to the log prior probability θ_i, and running the outputs through an accelerating exponential non-linearity (see Figure 7.6). The limitation to sampled likelihood functions can be overcome by using "steerable filters" (Freeman, 1992), which allow the likelihood values between the samples to be computed as weighted sums of the samples. Given the linear receptive fields in visual area V1, this simple example may have an analog in the brain. The key idea is that a simple filtering operation yields a neuron whose firing rate can represent a likelihood. For local image velocity estimation, Simoncelli (Simoncelli et al., 1991; Simoncelli, 1993) showed how the posterior distribution for local image velocity could be computed in terms of simple combinations of the outputs of spatial and temporal derivatives of Gaussian filters. More recently, Schrater (1998) has shown how the likelihood for image velocity could be computed by the weighted sum of a set of units similar to V1 complex cells.

Several authors have proposed more general ways in which probability distributions could be represented by a population of neurons (Anderson, 1994; Sanger, 1996; Zemel, 1997, 1998). The basic idea is that a population of neurons which are tuned to some parameter can act like a kernel density estimate, in which a probability density is approximated as a combination of simpler densities. To illustrate, assume we have a posterior distribution $p(x \mid D)$ of some scene variable x (like position), given a set of image measurements D, and a set of receptive fields $f_i(x)$. Then the firing rates

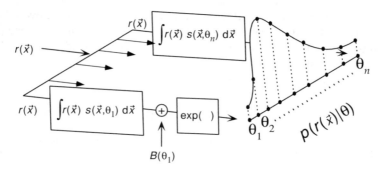

Figure 7.6 Computing probabilities in visual cortex. Probabilities can be computed across "labeled line" maps of neurons. The diagram shows an example of how a set of linear receptive fields can compute a posterior distribution. Assume the visual signal $r(\vec{x})$ can be decomposed into a sum of basis signals which vary according to some parameter θ plus some gaussian image noise: $r(\vec{x}) = \sum_i s(\vec{x}, \theta_i) + N$. For instance, the image could be decomposed into a sum oriented Gabor patches. The sampled (unnormalized) posterior probability of the parameter θ can be computed using an array of linear filters, each corresponding to a particular value of θ. The inner product of the signal with the receptive field produces the log likelihood for the presence of the component $s(\vec{x}, \theta_i)$ The log prior probability and needed bias are lumped as the additive constant $B(\theta)$, and the result is mapped from log likelihoods to probabilities by passing the results through a point-wise accelerating exp() non-linearity.

of the neurons will be given by the projection $r_i = \int_x p(x \mid D) f_i(x) dx$. Unlike the previous examples, the firing rate computed this way is not explicitly proportional to a probability or likelihood. Instead, the posterior is coded implicitly by the firing rates. To explicitly compute the posterior from the r_i, a fixed set of interpolation kernels $\phi_i(x)$ is used to invert the projection. Zemel et al. (1998) discuss two similar schemes to do the encoding and decoding of posterior distributions from firing rates. The number of ways of encoding posterior distributions by similar methods is limitless, and whether or not the brain uses a particular scheme of this sort is an intriguing problem for the future.

SUMMARY

We have argued that probability computation by the visual system is a necessary consequence of nature's visual signal patterns being inherently statistical. The origins of this perspective on perception began with the development of signal detection theory, and in particular, with ideal observer analysis. The basic operations of probability theory provide the means to model information for a task, and decision theory provides tools to model task requirements. The application of these tools to natural pattern understanding falls in the domain of what we have referred to as pattern inference theory—the combination of Bayesian decision theory and pattern theory. Pattern inference theory is clearly more powerful than any specific experimentally testable theory of human perception. However, it provides a sufficiently rich language

222   *Perception and the Physical World*

to develop theories of natural perceptual function. In addition to reviewing a number of principles that fall out of the Bayesian formalism, we highlighted two relatively new principles: (1) a Bayesian principle of least commitment, in which one propagates probabilities, rather than estimates, thereby weighting evidence according to reliability; (2) a Bayesian principle of modularity, in which Bayes nets show how statistical structure and task determine modularity.

ACKNOWLEDGMENTS

We thank Larry Maloney for providing exceptionally thoughtful and constructive criticisms on the first draft of this paper. This research was supported by NSF SBR-9631682 and NIH RO1 EY11507–001.

NOTES

1. Our level of analysis falls between the computational/function and representation/algorithmic levels in the Marr hierarchy.
2. Because it is rare to find a visual cue that is sufficiently reliable to unambiguously determine a perceived scene property, perception should be viewed as satisfying multiple constraints simultaneously. Examples are the constraint that light sources tend to be from above, or that a sharp image edge is more likely a reflectance or depth change than a shadow.
3. These four classes are intended to apply generally to natural patterns of all sorts, and not just to visual patterns. For spatial vision, these classes would correspond to: blur and noise, geometric deformations, superposition (e.g. of basis images), and occlusions (Mumford, 1994).
4. Primary and secondary variables have also been referred to as explicit and generic (or nuisance) variables, respectively.
5. Because the log of a multi-variate Gaussian is quadratic, extrema can be found using linear estimators.
6. We emphasize an empirical Bayesian approach in which, as is discussed below, one can test an hypothesis relating a subjective prior to an objective prior.
7. For simplicity, we've restricted our expressions to probability densities on continuous random, rather than discrete, random variables. There are well-known subtleties in translating results between discrete probabilities and continuous densities. Examples: (1) A change of representation (e.g. changing distance to vergence angle) will in general change the form of the density—e.g. change a uniform density into a non-uniform one. (2) Entropy for continuous variables is inherently relative, and thus transinformation is more useful (Cover & Joy, 1991). (3) If the range of a random variable is unknown, then the principle of insufficient reason leads to "improper" priors (Berger, 1985).
8. At several points in this chapter, we address what we see as misconceptions of the Bayesian framework for vision. We identify these as "myths".
9. This is one way of distinguishing the Bayesian perspective from a strict Gibsonian view which could be interpreted as assuming that objective structure is also sufficient to explain functional vision.
10. Two random variables are independent if and only if their joint probability is equal to the product of their individual probabilities. Thus, if $p(A, B) = p(A)p(B)$, then A and B are independent. If $p(A, B \mid C) = p(A \mid C)p(B \mid C)$, then A and B are conditionally independent. When corn prices drop in the summer, hay fever incidence goes up. However, if the joint on corn price and hay fever is conditioned on "ideal weather for corn and ragweed", the correlation between corn prices and hay fever drops. Corn price and hay fever symptoms are conditionally independent.

11. In graph theory, a is called the *parent* of b.
12. For notational convenience, here we use S to indicate the set of scene variables to be partitioned, $\{S\}$.
13. The Maximum Entropy Principle is a generalization of the symmetry principle in probability, and is also known as the principle of insufficient reason. For example, it says that one should assume a random variable is uniformly distributed over a known range unless there is sufficient reason to assume otherwise.
14. This is a consequence of the density mapping theorem: $p_y(y) = \int \delta(y - f(x)) f^{-1}(x) p_x(x) \, dx$ over each monotonic part of f.

REFERENCES

Amit, Y. & Geman, D. (1997). Shape quantization and recognition with random trees. *Neural Computation*, **9**(7), 1545–1588.

Anderson, C.H. (1994). Basic elements of biological computational systems. *International Journal of Modern Physics C*, **5**(2), 135–137.

Atick, J.J., Griffin, P.A. & Redlich, A.N. (1996). Statistical approach to shape from shading: Reconstruction of three-dimensional face surfaces from single two-dimensional images. *Neural Computation*, **8**(6), 1321–1340.

Atick, J.J. & Redlich, A.N. (1992). What does the retina know about natural scenes? *Neural Computation*, **4**(2), 196–210.

Barker, A., Brown, D. & Martin, W. (1995). Bayesian estimation and the Kalman filter. *Computers and Mathematical Applications*, **30**(10), 55–77.

Barlow, H. (1959). Sensory mechanisms, the reduction of redundancy, and intelligence. *Proceedings of the Symposium on the Mechanization of Thought Processes*. National Physical Laboratory: HMSO, London.

Barlow, H. (1962). A method of determining the overall quantum efficiency of visual discriminations. *Journal of Physiology (London)*, **160**, 155–168.

Barlow, H. (1981). Critical limiting factors in the design of the eye and visual cortex. *Proceedings of the Royal Society, London B*, **212**, 1–34.

Belhumeur, P. & Kriegman, D. (1996). What is the set of images of an object under all possible lighting conditions? *IEEE Conference on Computer Vision and Pattern Recognition* (pp. 270–277). San Francisco, CA.

Bell, A.J. & Sejnowski, T.J. (1997). The "independent components" of natural scenes are edge filters. *Vision Research*, **37**(23), 3327–3338.

Berger, J. (1985). *Statistical decision theory and Bayesian analysis*. Springer.

Bloj, M.G., Kersten, D. & Hurlbert, A.C. (1999). Perception of three-dimensional shape influences colour perception through mutual illumination. *Nature*, **402**(6764), 877–879.

Bobick, A. (1997). Movement, activity and action: The role of knowledge in the perception of motion. *Philosophical Transactions of the Royal Society B*, **352**, (1358), 1257–1265.

Bobick, A. & Richards, W. (1986). *Classifying objects from visual information*. Technical Report A.I. Memo No. 879, Artificial Intelligence Laboratory Massachusetts Institute of Technology.

Bookstein, F.L. (1978). *The measurement of biological shape and shape change*. Springer-Verlag, New York.

Bookstein, F.L. (1997). *Morphometric tools for landmark data: Geometry and biology*. Cambridge University Press.

Bossomaier, T. & Snyder, A. (1986). Why spatial frequency processing in the visual cortex? *Vision Research*, **26**(8), 1307–1309.

Brainard, D.H. & Freeman, W.T. (1997). Bayesian color constancy. *Journal of the Optical Society of America A*, **14**(7), 1393–1411.

Buccigrossi, R. & Simoncelli, E. (1997). Progressive wavelet image coding based on a conditional probability model. In *ICASSP*, Munich, Germany.

Cosmides, L. (1989). The logic of social exchange: Has natural selection shaped how humans reason? Studies with the Wason selection task. *Cognition*, **31**, 187–276.

Cover, T.M. & Joy, A.T. (1991). *Elements of information theory*. Wiley Series in Telecommunications. New York: John Wiley & Sons, Inc.

Craik, K.J.W. (1943). *The nature of explanation*. Cambridge: Cambridge University Press.

Dayan, P., Hinton, G.E., Neal, R.M. & Zemel, R.S. (1995). The Helmholtz machine. *Neural Computation*, **7**(5), 889–904.

Dean, T. & Kanazawa, K. (1988). Probabilistic temporal reasoning. In *AAAI-88* (pp. 524–528).

Duda, R. & Hart, P. (1973). *Pattern classification and scene analysis*. New York: John Wiley & Sons.

Eagle, R.A. & Blake, A. (1995). Two-dimensional constraints on three-dimensional structure from motion tasks. *Vision Research*, **35**(20), 2927–2941.

Egan, J.P. (1975). *Signal detection theory and ROC-analysis*. Academic Press series in Cognition and Perception. New York: Academic Press.

Epstein, R., Hallinan, P. & Yuille, A. (1995). 5 ± Eigenimages suffice: An empirical investigation of low-dimensional lighting models. In *IEEE Workshop on Physics-Based Modeling in Computer Vision* (pp. 108–116), Boston, MA.

Field, D.J. (1987). Relations between the statistics of natural images and the response properties of cortical cells. *Journal of the Optical Society of America A*, **4**(12), 2379–2394.

Freeman, W.T. (1992). *Steerable filter and local analysis of image structure*. Technical Report 190, Massachusetts Institute of Technology.

Freeman, W.T. (1994). The generic viewpoint assumption in a framework for visual perception. *Nature*, **368**(7 April), 542–545.

Freeman, W.T. & Pasztor, E.C. (1999). Learning to estimate scenes from images. In M.S. Kearns,S.A.S & Cohn, D.A. (Eds.) *Advances in Neural Information Processing Systems 11*. Cambridge, MA: MIT Press.

Frey, B.J. (1998). *Graphical models for machine learning and digital communication*. Adaptive Computation and Machine Learning series. A Bradford Book. Cambridge, MA: MIT Press.

Geisler, W. (1989). Sequential ideal-observer analysis of visual discriminations. *Psychological Review*, **96**(2), 267–314.

Georgopoulos, A., Lurito, J., Petrides, M., Schwartz, A. & Massey, J. (1989). Mental rotation of the neuronal population vector. *Science*, **243**, 234–236.

Gibson, J.J. (1966). *The senses considered as perceptual systems*. Boston, MA: Houghton Mifflin.

Gigerenzer, G. (1998). Ecological intelligence: An adaptation for frequencies. In D.D. Cummins, & C., Allen (Eds.), *The evolution of mind*. Oxford: Oxford University Press.

Green, D.M. & Swets, J.A. (1974). *Signal detection theory and psychophysics*. Huntington, NY: Robert E. Krieger Publishing Company.

Gregory, R. (1980). Perceptions as hypotheses. *Philosophical Transactions of the Royal Society B*, **290**, 181–197.

Grenander, U. (1950). Stochastic processes and statistical inference. *Arkiv. Mathematik*, **1**(17), 195.

Grenander, U. (1993).*General pattern theory* Oxford: Oxford University Press.

Grenander, U. (1996). *Elements of pattern theory*. Baltimore, MD: Johns Hopkins University Press.

Grenander, U., Chow, Y. & Keenan, D.M. (1991). *Hands. A pattern theoretic study of biological shapes*. New York: Springer.

Helmholtz, H. v. & Southall, J.P.C. (1924). *Helmholtz's treatise on physiological optics*. Rochester, NY: The Optical Society of America.

Hinton, G. & Ghahramani, Z. (1997). Generative models for discovering sparse distributed representations. *The Philosophical Transactions of the Royal Society*, **352**(1358), 1177–1190.

Jaynes, E.T. (1957). Information theory and statistical mechanics. *Physical Review*, **106**, 620–630.

Jordan, M. (1998). *Learning in graphical models*. Cambridge, MA: MIT Press.

Kendall, D. (1989). A survey of the statistical theory of shape. *Statistical Science*, **4**(2), 87–120.

Kersten, D. (1984). Spatial summation in visual noise. *Vision Research*, **24**, 1977–1990.

Kersten, D. (1990). Statistical limits to image understanding. In C. Blakemore (Ed.) *Vision: Coding and efficiency* (pp. 32–44). Cambridge, UK: Cambridge University Press.

Kersten, D. (1997). Perceptual categories for spatial layout. *Philosophical Transactions of the Royal Society B*, **352**(1358), 1155–1163.

Kersten, D. (1999). High-level vision as statistical inference. In M.S. Gazzaniga (Ed.) *The new cognitive neurosciences* (2nd edn., pp. 353–363). Cambridge, MA: MIT Press.

Kersten, D., O' Toole, A., Sereno, M., Knill, D.C. & Anderson, J. (1987). Associative learning of scene parameters from images. *Applied Optics*, **26**, 4999–5006.

Kersten, D.J. (1991). Transparency and the cooperative computation of scene attributes. In M. Landy & A. Movshon (Eds.) *Computational models of visual processing* (pp. 209–228). Cambridge, MA: MIT Press.

Knill, D., Field, D. & Kersten, D. (1990). Human discrimination of fractal images. *Journal of the Optical Society of America, A*, **7**, 1113–1123.

Knill, D. & Richards, W. (1996). *Perception as Bayesian inference*. Cambridge, UK: Cambridge University Press.

Knill, D.C. (1998a). Discrimination of planar surface slant from texture: Human and ideal observers compared. *Vision Research*, **38**(11), 1683–1711.

Knill, D.C. (1998b). Surface orientation from texture: Ideal observers, generic observers and the information content of texture cues. *Vision Research*, **38**(11), 1655–1682.

Knill, D.C., Kersten, D. & Mamassian, P. (1996a). The Bayesian Framework for visual information processing: Implications for psychophysics. In D. Knill & W. Richards (Eds.) *Perception as Bayesian inference* (pp. 239–286, Ch. 5). Cambridge: Cambridge University Press.

Knill, D.C., Kersten, D. & Yuille, A. (1996b). A Bayesian formulation of visual perception. In D. Knill & W. Richards (Eds.) *Perception as Bayesian inference* (Ch. 0). Cambridge: Cambridge University Press.

Landy, M.S., Maloney, L.T., Johnston, E.B. & Young, M.J. (1995). Measurement and modeling of depth cue combination: In defense of weak fusion. *Vision Research*, **35**, 389–412.

Laughlin, S. (1981). A simple coding procedure enhances a neuron's information capacity. *Z. Naturforsch.*, **36**, 910–912.

Lee, C., Rohrer, W.H. & Sparks, D.L. (1988). Population coding of saccadic eye movements by neurons in the superior colliculus. *Nature*, **332**(6162), 357–360.

Leeuwenberg, E. (1969). Quantitative specification of information in sequential patterns. *Psychological Review*, **76**, 216–220.

Legge, G.E., Klitz, T.S. & Tjan, B.S. (1997). Mr. Chips: An ideal-observer model of reading. *Psychological Review*, **104**(3), 524–553.

Liu, Z., Knill, D.C. & Kersten, D. (1995). Object Classification for Human and Ideal Observers. *Vision Research*, **35**(4), 549–568.

MacKay, D.J.C. (1992). Bayesian interpolation. *Neural Computation*, **4**(3), 415–447.

Maloney, L. & Wandell, B. (1986). Color constancy: A method for recovering surface spectral reflectance. *Journal of the Optical Society America*, **3**, 29–33.

Mamassian, P. & Landy, M.S. (1998). Observer biases in the 3D interpretation of line drawings. *Vision Research*, **38**(18), 2817–2832.

Marr, D. (1982). *Vision: A computational investigation into the human representation and processing of visual information*, San Francisco, CA: W.H. Freeman & Company.

Mumford, D. (1992). On the computational architecture of the neocortex. II. The role of cortico-cortical loops. *Biological Cybernetics*, **66**, 241–251.

Mumford, D. (1994). Neuronal architectures for pattern-theoretic problems. In C. Koch & J.L. Davis (Eds.), *Large-scale neuronal theories of the brain* (pp. 125–152). Cambridge, MA: MIT Press.

Mumford, D. (1996). Pattern theory: A unifying perspective. In D. Knill & W. Richards (Eds.) *Perception as Bayesian inference* (ch. 2). Cambridge: Cambridge University Press.

Murray, G. (1987). *Cognition as intuitive statistics:* New Jersey: Erlbaum.

Nakayama, K. & Shimojo, S. (1992). Experiencing and perceiving visual surfaces. *Science*, **257**, 1357–1363.

Neyman, J. & Pearson, E. (1933). On the problem of the most efficient tests of statistical hypotheses. *Philosophical Transactions of the Royal Society London, Series A*, 289.

Olshausen, B. & Field, D. Emergence of simple-cell receptive field properties by learning a sparse code for natural images. *Nature*, **381**, 607–609.

Pearl, J. (1988). *Probabilistic reasoning in intelligent systems.* San Mateo, CA: Morgan Kaufmann Publishers Inc.

Pelli, D.G. (1990). The quantum efficiency of vision. In C. Blakemore. (Ed.) *Vision: Coding and efficiency*. Cambridge: Cambridge University Press.

Peterson, W., Birdsall, T. & Fox, W. (1954). The theory of signal detectability. *Transactions of the IRE Professional Group on Information Theory*, PGIT-4, 171–212.

Poggio, T. & Girosi, F. (1990). Regularization algorithms for learning that are equivalent to multilayer networks. *Science*, **247**, 978–982.

Poggio, T., Torre, V. & Koch, C. (1985). Computational vision and regularization theory. *Nature*, **317**, 314–319.

Rao, R.P. & Ballard, D.H. (1999). Predictive coding in the visual cortex: A functional interpretation of some extra-classical receptive-field effects [see comments]. *Nature Neuroscience*, **2**(1), 79–87.

Restle, F. (1982). Coding theory as an integration of Gestalt psychology and information processing theory. In J. Beck (Ed.) *Organization and representation in perception* (pp. 31–56). Hillsdae, NJ: Erlbaum.

Rice, S.O. (1944). Mathematical analysis of random noise. *Bell System Technical Journal*, **23**, 282–332.

Ripley, B. (1996) Pattern recognition and neural networks. Cambridge, UK: Cambridge University Press.

Rock, I. (1983). *The logic of perception*. A Bradford Book. Cambridge, MA: MIT Press.

Rosch, E., Mervis, C., Gray, W., Johnson, D. & Boyes-Braem, P. (1976). Basic objects in natural categories. *Cognitive Psychology*, **8**, 382–439.

Ruderman, D. & Bialek, W. (1994). Statistics of natural images: Scaling in the woods. *Physical Review Letters*, **73**, (No. 6; 8 August), 814–817.

Sanger, T.D. (1996). Probability density estimation for the interpretation of neural population codes. *Journal of Neurophysiology*, **76**(4), 2790–2793.

Schrater, P. (1998). *Local motion detection: Comparison of human and model observers*. Ph.D. Thesis, University of Pennsylvania.

Schrater, P.R. & Kersten, D. (2000). The role of task specification in optimal cue integration. *International Journal of Computer Vision*, **40**(1), 71–89.

Schwarz, G. (1978). Estimating the dimension of a model. *Annals of Statistics*, **6**, 461–463.

Shannon, C.E. & Weaver, W. (1949). *The mathematical theory of communication*, Champaign, IL: University of Illinois Press.

Simoncelli, E.P. (1993). *Distributed analysis and representation of visual motion*. Ph.D. Thesis, Massachusetts Institute of Technology, Department of Electrical Engineering and Computer Science.

Simoncelli, E.P. (1997). Statistical models for images: Compression, restoration and synthesis. *Proc. 31st Asilomar Conference on Signals, Systems and Computers.* Pacific Grove, CA. © IEEE Signal Processing Society.

Simoncelli, E.P., Adelson, E.H. & Heeger, D.J. (1991). Probability distributions of optical flow. *IEEE Conf on Computer Vision and Pattern Recognition*, Mauii, Hawaii.

Simoncelli, E.P. & Portilla, J. (1998). Texture characterization via joint statistics of wavelet coefficient magnitudes. *5th IEEE International Conference on Image Processing*, Chicago, IL.

Sirovich, L. & Kirby, M. (1987). Low-dimensional procedure for the characterization of human faces. *Journal of the Optical Society of America*, **4**(3), 519–524.

Swets, J.A. (1988). Measuring the accuracy of diagnostic systems. *Science*, **240**(4857), 1285–93.

Tarr, M. & Bülthoff, H. (1995). Is human object recognition better described by geon-structural-descriptions or by multiple-views? *Journal of Experimental Psychology: Human Perception and Performance*, **21**(6), 1494–1505.

Tarr, M.J., Kersten, D. & Bülthoff, H.H. (1998). Why the visual recognition system might encode the effects of illumination. *Vision Research*, **38**(15–16), 2259–2275.

Turk, M. & Pentland, A. (1991). Eigenfaces for recognition. *Journal of Cognitive Neuroscience*, **3**(1), 77–86.

Valentin, D., Abdi, H., Edelman, B. & O'Toole, A.J. (1997). Principal component and neural network analyses of face images: What can be generalized in gender classification? *Journal of Mathematical Psychology*, **41**(4), 398–413.

Van Trees, H.L. (1968). *Detection, estimation and modulation theory. Part I* (vol. 1). New York: John Wiley & Sons.

Van Trees, H.L. (1971). *Detection, estimation and modulation theory. Part III* (vol. 3). New York: John Wiley & Sons.

Vapnik, V. (1995). *The nature of statistical learning.* New York: Springer-Verlag.

Vetter, T. & Troje, N. (1997). Separation of texture and shape in images of faces for image coding and synthesis. *Journal of the Optical Society of America A*, **14**(9), 2152–2161.

von Neumann, J. (1958). *The computer and the brain*, New Haven: Yale University Press.

Wald, A. (1939). Contributions to the statistical estimation and testing of hypotheses. *Annals of Mathematical Statistics*, **10**, 299–326.

Wald, A. (1950). *Statistical decision functions.* New York: JohnWiley & Sons.

Weiss, Y. (1997). Interpreting images by propagating Bayesian beliefs. In M.C. Mozer et al. (Eds.) *Advances in neural information processing systems 9* (pp. 908–915). Cambridge, MA: MIT Press.

Weiss, Y. & Adelson, E.H. (1998). *Slow and smooth: A Bayesian theory for the combination of local motion signals in human vision.* Techhnical Report A.I. Memo No. 1624, M.I.T.

Wolpert, D.M., Ghahramani, Z. & Jordan, M.I. (1995). An internal model for sensorimotor integration. *Science*, **269**(29 September), 1880–1882.

Yuille, A. (1991). Deformable Templates for Face Recognition. *Journal of Cognitive Neuroscience*, **3**(1), 59–70.

Yuille, A.L., & Bülthoff, H.H. (1996). Bayesian decision theory and psychophysics. In D.Knill & W. Richards (Eds.), *Perception as Bayesian inference.* Cambridge, UK: Cambridge University Press.

Yuille, A.L., Coughlan, J.M. & Kersten, D. (1998). Computational vision: Principles of perceptual inference, *http://publications.kersten.org*

Zemel, R.S. (1997). Combining probabilistic population codes. *International Joint Conference on Artificial Intelligence*, Denver, CO. Morgan Kaufmann.

Zemel, R.S. (1998). Probabilistic interpretation of population codes. *Neural Computation*, **10**(2), 403–430.

Zhu, S. (1999) Embedding Gestalt laws in Markov random fields. *IEEE Trans. Pattern Analysis and Machine Intelligence*, **21**(11), 1170–1187.

Zhu, S. & Mumford, D. (1998). GRADE: A framework for pattern synthesis, denoising, image enhancement, and clutter removal. *Proceedings of International Conference on Computer Vision*, Bombay, India. Morgan Kaufmann.

Zhu, S.C., Wu, Y. & Mumford, D. (1997). Minimax entropy principle and its applications to texture modeling. *Neural Computation*, **9**(8), 1627–1660.

8

Perception and Evolution

BRUCE M. BENNETT,
Department of Mathematics, University of California, USA

DONALD D. HOFFMAN,
Department of Cognitive Science, University of California, USA

CHETAN PRAKASH
Department of Mathematics, California State University, USA

INTRODUCTION

The freshwater eel is notable not only for great sushi, but also for chromophore substitution (Beatty, 1984; Lythgoe, 1991). As young adults these eels spend most of their time in fresh water and, like many other freshwater creatures, have a long-wavelength visual pigment known as porphyropsin, with a maximal sensitivity at 522 nanometers. As the time draws near for the first leg of their breeding migration, which takes them into coastal waters, the porphyropsin changes to a rhodopsin with maximal sensitivity at 500 nanometers. And as the time draws near for the last leg of their breeding migration, which takes the eels into the deep sea, the rhodopsin changes its maximal sensitivity to 487 nanometers, a value typical for many deep-sea creatures. This is but one of many engaging examples of the adaptation, both phylogenetic and ontogenetic, of perceptual systems to environments.

The variety of adaptations in vision alone is remarkable. The optical systems used include: pigmented pits without lenses or mirrors, found in some platyhelminthes, protochordates, coelenterates, annelids, and molluscs (Salvini-Plawen & Maxx, 1977); multiple pigmented tubes, found in some tube-worms; spherical lens eyes, found in fishes, some molluscs, alciopid annelids, and copepod crustaceans (Pumphrey, 1961); corneal refraction, found in many terrestrial vertebrates and arachnids (Land, 1985); apposition compound eyes, found in many diurnal insects and crustacea; refracting superposition compound eyes, found in nocturnal insects and some crustacea (Exner, 1891; Kunze, 1979; Nilsson, 1989); simple mirror eyes,

Perception and the Physical World: Psychological and Philosophical Issues in Perception.
Edited by Dieter Heyer and Rainer Mausfeld. © 2002 John Wiley & Sons, Ltd.

found in the *Pecten* bivalve mollusc and the *Gigantocypris* crustacean; and reflecting superposition compound eyes, found in shrimps, prawns, crayfish, and lobsters (for an excellent review, see Land, 1991). Each solution works in its niche. Even something as simple as a pinhole eye has served the cephalopod *Nautilus* well for 400 million years (Lythgoe, 1991, p. 4).

Then there is the variety of visual pigments and colored oil drops used in vision. Humans are trichromats, as are some species in almost every animal class (Jacobs, 1981, p. 153). Squirrels, rabbits, tree shrews, some fishes and male New World monkeys are dichromats. Goldfish and turtles are tetrachromats (Crawford et al., 1990; Neumeyer, 1985, 1986). Pigeons may be pentachromats (Delius & Emmerton, 1979; Emmerton & Delius, 1980; Wright, 1979). The mantis shrimp has at least ten spectral types of photoreceptors (Cronin et al., 1994; Cronin & Marshall, 1989). Some visual pigments respond to ultraviolet (Neumeyer, 1985) and some to near infrared (Lythgoe, 1988).

The variety explodes when it comes to the neural processing and interpretation of visual images. On one extreme there is almost no processing, as in creatures with simple eye spots. On the other extreme there is human vision, with tens of billions of neurons devoted to image interpretation.

So if we are interested in perceptual evolution, and in particular how the perceptual interpretations of organisms are adapted to their environments, we must admit at once that the topic encompasses an incredible diversity of phenomena. Indeed the diversity is such that one might be tempted to conclude that there is little useful to be said in general about perceptual adaptation, but much to be said about individual cases.

That may yet turn out to be true. But recent developments in the formal study of perception, and developments with a longer history in the formal study of evolution, offer hope for a formal theory of perceptual adaptation that captures the unity behind the many cases while respecting the remarkable diversity. In this chapter we take initial steps directed toward making this hope a reality.

Currently the most rigorous and comprehensive formal theories of perception are Bayesian (see, e.g., Knill & Richards, 1996), and the most successful theories of evolution are neo-Darwinian. We will begin by developing the Bayesian approach to perception, and then place this approach in a neo-Darwinian context. This leads to concrete mathematical problems, regarding the convergence of certain probabilistic processes, whose resolution will provide key insights into the scope and limits of perceptual evolution.

BAYESIAN PERCEPTION

In the case of vision, the simplest motivation for the Bayesian approach is as follows. We are given an image or sequence of images, I, and we wish to reach conclusions about the visual scenes, S, responsible for I.

In general, countless different scenes could, in principle, be responsible for I. This ambiguity arises because the relationship between scenes and images is typically one of *projection,* e.g., from the three dimensions of the visual world to the two dimensions of retinal images. Since the mapping from scenes to images is many to one, the mapping from images to scenes is one to many.

So, given an image I, there are many scenes to be considered as possible interpretations since there are many scenes that could in principle be responsible for I. An observer would like to pick the "right" one, but might not have sufficient information to know with certainty which one to pick. If a guaranteed "right" choice is not possible, a probabilistic assessment over all possible choices is next best. Ideally, in this case, an observer would like to find a conditional probability,

$$\Pr(S \mid I) \tag{8.1}$$

which specifies the probabilities of various scenes given the image I.

As a simple example, suppose our image I_{line} has just one straight line segment in it. Consider the following two sets of scene interpretations. In the first, S_{line}, the interpretation is as some (any) straight line in 3-D which projects to the given line in the image. There are many such lines, at different orientations in space, all of which project to the same line in the image. Together these lines constitute the set S_{line}. In the second, S_{curve}, the interpretation is as some (any) curve in 3-D which projects to the given line in the image. There are many such curves, including semicircles, various sinusoidal curves, and so on, all of which project to the same line in the image. Together these curves constitute the set S_{curve}. What we would like to compute are the conditional probabilities

$$\Pr(S_{\text{curve}} \mid I_{\text{line}}) \text{ and } \Pr(S_{\text{line}} \mid I_{\text{line}}) \tag{8.2}$$

Each set of interpretations, S_{line} and S_{curve} is uncountably large. So set size alone won't help us much in computing these conditional probabilities. What we need is the apparatus of Bayes' rule:

$$\Pr(S \mid I) = \frac{\Pr(I \mid S)\Pr(S)}{\Pr(I)} \tag{8.3}$$

It is conventional to call $\Pr(S \mid I)$ the posterior probability, $\Pr(I \mid S)$ the likelihood function, and $\Pr(S)$ and $\Pr(I)$ the prior probabilities. What we want to compute are the posterior probabilities $\Pr(S \mid I)$. They will give us the relative confidence we should place in the various possible interpretations. We can compute them, by Bayes' rule, if we know the likelihood function $\Pr(I \mid S)$ and the prior probabilities $\Pr(S)$ and $\Pr(I)$.

Do we know the likelihood function $\Pr(I \mid S)$? We do, if we know how scenes get rendered as images. In fact $\Pr(I \mid S)$ is sometimes called the rendering function for this reason. If we know, for instance, that the projection is orthographic and noise free, then we know that for each possible scene S, the likelihood function is a dirac delta function on that image I which is the orthographic projection of S. If instead we know that the projection is orthographic and noisy, and that the noise is distributed as a gaussian $N(0, \sigma)$, then we know that for each possible scene S, the likelihood function is a gaussian of variance σ^2 centered on that image I which is the orthographic projection of S. So if we know how images are rendered as scenes, and we often do have a reasonable idea about this, then we know the likelihood function $\Pr(I \mid S)$.

Do we know the prior probability $\Pr(I)$? Not really. But this might not be a problem in practice. As long as $\Pr(I)$ is not zero, it really doesn't much matter what it is when computing the posterior by Bayes' rule. We can simply view it as a normalizing factor, to make all the conditional probabilities sum to one. Or we can ignore it and just look at the ratios of various posterior probabilities to find the relative likelihoods of various scene interpretations. Of course if $\Pr(I)$ is zero, as may be the case if the space of possible images is nondiscrete, then there is a serious technical issue to deal with. One must reformulate Bayes' rule in a more sophisticated setting, using Radon–Nikodym derivatives and kernels, to get a rigorous result (Bennett et al., 1996). This has been done, but is outside the purview of this chapter.

Do we know the prior probability $\Pr(S)$? To know this would be to know, under a frequentist interpretation of probability, in fact how frequently different scenes in the world actually occur. This is surely a lot to know. It is hard to imagine how, in practice, one could empirically obtain such information. One cannot, in practice, measure all scenes. There simply is not enough time, phylogenetically or ontogenetically, to do so. And one cannot, in principle, arrange for an appropriate statistical sample of scenes from which one can infer the proper population statistics. It's not clear even how one would try to do this. When pollsters sample voters prior to an election, they try to obtain a stratified random sample. They stratify their sampling based on their prior knowledge about properties of the population of voters. Such knowledge about the population of scenes is not at hand.

So a frequentist interpretation of $\Pr(S)$ seems to lead us into trouble. But if we adopt a subjectivist interpretation, then $\Pr(S)$ is the prior probability that the observer assumes to hold for purposes of computing interpretations. $\Pr(S)$ codifies the assumptions of the observer. These assumptions heavily influence, via Bayes' rule, the posterior probabilities assigned by the observer to various scenes, and thus heavily influence what the observer sees. In the example at hand, however, it is hard to imagine a principled assumption to make about the prior probabilities of lines versus curves. Intuitively one might expect that there are more curves than lines, but beyond this it's hard to assign specific probabilities. Let's assume, for now, that both are just given some positive probability.

Assumptions can also affect the likelihood function. For instance, one assumption that the observer might hold in the example at hand is the assumption of a generic view. That is, the observer might assume that all possible viewing directions are equally likely. If one thinks of the set of viewing directions as being isomorphic to the unit sphere, where each point on the sphere represents a different view directed toward the center of the sphere, then the probability of a given set of views is proportional to the area of that set on the unit sphere. Under this assumption it is easy to prove that the set of viewing directions for which curves in space project to the given line in the image is a set which has no area. Indeed this set is a great circle on the unit sphere.

Since this set has no area, it has probability zero. Thus the probability

$$\Pr(I_{\text{line}} \mid S_{\text{curve}}) = 0 \tag{8.4}$$

On the other hand, the set of viewing directions for which straight lines in space project to the image I_{line} is the entire unit sphere. Thus the probability

$$\Pr(I_{\text{line}} \mid S_{\text{line}}) = 1 \tag{8.5}$$

If we assume that $\Pr(S_{\text{curve}}) > 0$, $\Pr(S_{\text{line}}) > 0$, and $\Pr(I_{\text{line}}) > 0$, then by putting (4) and (5) respectively into Bayes' rule (3), we find that

$$\Pr(S_{\text{curve}} \mid I_{\text{line}}) = 0 \tag{8.6}$$

and that

$$\Pr(S_{\text{line}} \mid I_{\text{line}}) = 1 \tag{8.7}$$

Thus an observer who makes the plausible assumption of a generic viewpoint, and who also assumes that curves and lines occur with nonzero probability, is led inexorably to the conclusion that a straight line in an image must be interpreted as a straight line in space.

This example is simple, in that the critical probabilities involved in the computation, namely the likelihoods, are either zero or one so that the resulting posteriors are also zero or one. This simplicity is intentional, to illustrate how Bayesian approaches to vision work, but without getting bogged down in detailed mathematical computations. However the Bayesian approach is, of course, not restricted to these simple cases. The priors and likelihood functions, and therefore the posteriors, can be as nasty as you like. In this manner many interesting problems of vision have been successfully addressed within a Bayesian framework, including visual motion (Bennett et al., 1996; Jepson et al., 1996; Knill et al., 1996), texture (Blake et al., 1996; Witkin, 1981), stereovision (Belhumeur, 1996), shading and lighting (Adelson & Pentland, 1996; Freeman, 1996), and color constancy (Brainard & Freeman, 1994). In many of the cases just cited, the Bayesian analysis leads to an effective computational procedure, thus allowing one to build a process model that can be implemented by computer. So in addition to providing interesting theoretical insights, the Bayesian approach also aids in the construction of working computer vision systems.

TWO APPROACHES TO ONTOGENETIC ADAPTATION

Perceptual adaptation is a refining of an observer's perceptual conclusions in consequence of its interactions with its environment.

In the simple example of the previous section, we saw that (usually unconscious) assumptions by the observer play a key role in the perceptual conclusions it reaches.

These assumptions are modeled in a Bayesian framework by priors and likelihood functions. Changes in the observer's assumptions must, on the Bayesian formulation, be modeled by changes in the observer's priors and likelihoods. These changes will, in general, also lead to changes in the resulting posteriors, i.e., in the observer's perceptual conclusions.

Therefore one way to model perceptual adaptation within a Bayesian framework is to model changes in the likelihoods and priors an observer uses as it interacts with its environment. These changes will systematically affect the perceptual conclusions of the observer, resulting in systematic perceptual adaptation. This approach seems to us most natural, and is the one we will pursue in some detail here. We call it the *structural adaptation* approach.

But there is another approach that one might take. If one never alters the priors or likelihoods, one can still get changes in the posteriors, and therefore perceptual adaptation, by simply conditioning on more and more data. As the observer has more and more commerce with its environment, the observer obtains a larger pool of data on which to do its Bayesian computations and arrive at a posterior. This accumulated data need not affect the *structure* of the likelihood function or priors at all. It can simply change the *argument* given to the likelihood function, and thus lead to a different posterior. This approach seems to us less natural as a model either of ontogenetic or phylogenetic adaptation. It seems unlikely that adaptation is simply a matter of conditioning on more data, without concomitant structural changes in the priors and likelihoods effectively used by the organism. But it is a logical possibility, one that we call the *nonstructural adaptation* approach. In a later section we formally compare the structural and nonstructural approaches to adaptation. This provides clearer insight into both.

BAYES MEETS DARWIN: BASIC IDEAS

Whether one chooses a structural or nonstructural approach to ontogenetic adaptation, there remains the problem of placing this ontogenetic adaptation in a phylogenetic context in such a way that satisfies, at least in broad outline, neo-Darwinian accounts of evolution by natural selection. What will not work, of course, are Lamarckian-style theories of either the structural or nonstructural types, in which a parent passes on to its offspring the results of its ontogenetic adaptation. The parent cannot, on a structural approach, pass on to its offspring the structural changes in its likelihoods and priors that took place in the course of its perceptual interactions with its environment. Moreover the parent cannot, on a nonstructural approach, pass on to its offspring the body of data it has accumulated in the course of its perceptual interactions with its environment.

What it can pass on, and all it can pass on, is its genome. On the Bayesian hypothesis this genome encodes, inter alia, the various Bayesian structures and processes (including priors and likelihoods) involved in perception and ontogenetic perceptual adaptation. This genome is subject to random mutations, so that the offspring can, in principle, have slightly different Bayesian structures and processes than the parents.

The key idea (and an old one) is this. If an organism's genetic endowment allows its perceptual system to adapt so well and so quickly to its environment that it can, with greater probability than its competitors, reproduce and pass on its genes, then in succeeding generations the offspring will inherit this advantaged perceptual ability, with minor random mutations. Some of these mutations will be beneficial to perceptual adaptation, more will be harmful. But natural selection will, in this manner, tend to grant higher frequency of offspring to those whose mutations are beneficial.

So there are two evolutionary processes intertwined. There is the ontogenetic evolution of the perceptual system within the life of an individual. And there is the phylogenetic evolution of the perceptual system across generations. Those genomes which grant more effective ontogenetic evolution tend to persist in the phylogenetic evolution.

This story sounds promising in broad outline. To see if it really works it is necessary, of course, to formalize structural and nonstructural Bayesian approaches to perceptual adaptation and to prove that they have the ability to properly converge to or track with those aspects of a changing environment that are crucial to an organism's survival to reproductive age. We now turn to these formal issues.

STRUCTURAL AND CLASSICAL BAYES UPDATING

To recapitulate: The *classical* model operates by sequentially updating the posterior as data arrive, while holding the prior and likelihood function fixed. The sequencing here is based upon successively richer conditioning on present and past data; the strategy of instantaneous inference remains unaffected by such information. In our notation, given a data sequence $(I_1, \ldots, I_k)$, the posterior is updated to

$$\Pr(S \mid (I_1, \ldots, I_k)) = \frac{N((I_1, \ldots, I_k) \mid S)\, \Pr(S)}{\Pr((I_1, \ldots, I_k))} \qquad (8.8)$$

where N is a markovian kernel known as the "likelihood function". Classical updating is also known as Bayesian statistical inference and has a long history in the statistical literature (see, e.g., Diaconis & Freedman, 1986 and references cited therein). A different scheme has been proposed by Bennett and Cohen (1999) as part of their "directed convergence" scheme for acquiring stable percepts. In this scheme, their *structural* procedure involves updating not only of posteriors but also of priors consequent to an observation. When the image I_1 arrives, Bayes' rule produces a posterior $\Pr_1(S) = \Pr(S \mid I_1)$. This posterior is then taken as the new candidate prior to be used for a Bayesian inference at the next arrival of a premise. In contrast to the *iterative* character of classical updating, the structural variety is *recursive*: the result at any given stage changes the very strategy of computation at the next stage.

In order to clarify the differences between these two kinds of procedure, we will develop our notation somewhat. The space of punctual premises will be denoted Y. We wish to include the possibility, in a performance model, of probabilistic premises: those that arrive as a *probability measure*. We will denote such premises (e.g., the data I) by $\lambda(\mathrm{d}y)$. Thus a punctual premise y_0 reappears as the "Dirac measure", or "point mass" $\delta_{y_0}(\mathrm{d}y)$ at y_0: the measure that assigns to any set $B \subset Y$ the value 1 if $y_0 \in B$ and 0 otherwise. The space of punctual percepts, on the other hand, will be denoted X. A probabilistic premise will, in general, lead to a probabilistic percept: we are therefore interested in percepts which are themselves measures on X. Conversely, in the presence of noise, even a punctual state of affairs in the world—say $x \in X$—will lead to the appearance of a probabilistic premise. In this sense, the "noise kernel" or likelihood function N plays the role of an image-rendering function which assigns, to each punctual percept x, the corresponding *probabilistic* premise $N(x, \mathrm{d}y)$. That is, for x in X, $N(x, \mathrm{d}y)$ is the probability distribution on Y which expresses the likelihood that premises will be acquired assuming that the system is subject to an ambient state of affairs represented by x. As a final motivation for probabilistic premises and percepts, note that Bayes' rule gives a procedure whereby premises (probabilistic *or* punctual) are transformed to (probabilistic) conclusions: we will call this updating procedure the *updating law* and denote it by P. Thus, given a premise λ, the updating law produces a posterior probability $\mu(\mathrm{d}x)$ on X by integrating over the premise distribution:

$$\mu(\mathrm{d}x) \underset{\mathrm{def}}{=} \lambda P \underset{\mathrm{def}}{=} \int \lambda(\mathrm{d}y) P(y, \mathrm{d}x) \tag{8.9}$$

Of course, this updating law[1] P has further structure that depends on the image rendering function N and the current prior μ_0. Bayes' rule in the discrete case expresses this dependence as

$$P_{(\mu_0, N)}(y, A) = \frac{\sum_{x \in A} \mu_0(x) N(x, y)}{\sum_{x \in X} \mu_0(x) N(x, y)} \tag{8.10}$$

where we have explicitly displayed the dependence on the current prior and on the likelihood function as subscripts. In the continuous case we have

$$P_{(\mu_0, N)}(y, A) = \frac{\mathrm{d}\left(\int_{x \in A} \mu_0(\mathrm{d}x) N(x, \mathrm{d}y)\right)}{\mathrm{d}\left(\int_{x \in X} \mu_0(\mathrm{d}x) N(x, \mathrm{d}y)\right)}(y) \tag{8.11}$$

Here the right-hand side is given as a Radon–Nikodym derivative (see Bennett et al., 1996, equations (5.21) and (5.28)). The likelihood, or image rendering function N takes percepts and yields premises, according to physical laws of projection, refraction, noise, etc. P, in turn, accepts prior probabilities and, employing the offices of N, gives a procedure for transforming those priors into posteriors upon the arrival of a premise.[2]

In classical updating, P remains the same regardless of the sequence of percepts. In structural updating, by contrast, at stage n, where the prior is μ_n, the law is $P_{(\mu_n, N)}$. Then, in the $(n + 1)$th stage, a premise λ_{n+1} is acquired; this results in the new conclusion μ_{n+1} by

$$\mu_{n+1} = \lambda_{n+1} P_n \tag{8.12}$$

This μ_{n+1} then becomes the prior at the next stage. It is a fact, though we shall not prove it here, that the two procedures are identical for the sequences of punctual premises, i.e., Dirac measures, that the classical case considers. However, the structural procedure is vastly more general, in that it allows the use of nonpoint masses and therefore of much more general kinds of premise. Moreover, the structural procedure allows us to improve on the efficiency of convergence: Even with a sequence $(y_1, \ldots, y_k)$ of punctual premises, the structural method allows us to use, at stage n, the premise

$$\lambda_n(dy) = \frac{1}{n} \sum_{k=1}^{n} \delta_{y_k}(dy) \tag{8.13}$$

We expect the structural posteriors using this sequence of premises to converge more rapidly than the classical posteriors (which, perforce, use punctual premises) to the true state of affairs.

Let us use a simple example to illustrate updating. Suppose we are to infer the relative probabilities of heads and tails for a biased coin. The probability of a head, to be inferred, is some number $x \in X = [0, 1]$. Successive premises y_k consist of tossing the coin and observing the outcome. So $y_k = 1$ or 0, depending on whether we observe a head or a tail. Now if the probability of a head were actually x, the distribution of premises y would be governed by $N(x, dy) = x^{|y|}$, where $|y| = \sum_{k=1}^{n} y_k$ is the number of heads in the n observations. Then the random vector $\{y_k\}_{k=1}^{n} = (y_1, \ldots, y_n)$ is distributed binomially, i.e., the probability of any n-long sequence of heads and tails equals a product of x's (one for each $y_k = 1$) and of $(1 - x)$'s (one for each $y_k = 0$). This is just $x^{|y|}(1 - x)^{n-|y|}$. Finally, the random variable x is itself taken to be distributed according to the prior μ_0, so in terms of the posterior probability on $[0, 1]$, the previous expression is proportional to a *density* with respect to μ_0. Hence classical Bayesian statistical inference says that, after n observations have been obtained, and given a prior probability μ_0 (on the x's), the posterior probability is

$$\mu_n\left(dx \mid \{y_k\}_{k=1}^{n}\right) = \frac{x^{|y|}(1 - x)^{n-|y|}\mu_0(dx)}{\int x'^{|y|}(1 - x')^{n-|y|}\mu_0(dx')} \tag{8.14}$$

The denominator in (8.14) is the normalization which makes the left-hand side a probability.

We would like these posteriors in Equation (8.14) to converge to the point mass (or Dirac delta) at the true value $\bar{x}$, given that the data $\{y_k\}$ are independent and identically distributed with a probability of $\bar{x}$ for heads. Such a convergence of the posteriors to the true coin probability is called *consistency* in the literature. It is well known that whenever the prior μ_0 assigns positive measure to every open interval around $\bar{x}$, we have consistency: The measures μ_n converge *weakly* to Dirac measure at $\bar{x}$. That is, if A is any (measurable) subset of the interval $[0, 1]$,

$$\mathrm{Lim}_{n \to \infty} \mu_n\left(A \mid \{y_k\}_{k=1}^{n}\right) = \begin{cases} 1 & \text{if } \bar{x} \in A \\ 0 & \text{otherwise} \end{cases} \tag{8.15}$$

for almost all[3] input sequences $\{y_k\}_{k=1}^{\infty}$. In other words, the limit is the point mass at $\bar{x}$.

This is satisfying; there are, however, more complicated situations where consistency does not obtain, in a generic sense (Diaconis & Freedman, 1986).

In general, consistency for Bayes updating is defined as follows: Given that the data arrive under the law $N(\bar{x}, dy)$ for a (punctually) true state of affairs $\bar{x}$, then we say that the pair $(\mu_0, \bar{x})$ consisting of the initial prior and the actual situation $\bar{x}$ is *consistent* if , the posteriors μ_n defined in (8.9) and (8.10) (or (8.11)) above *converge weakly* to Dirac measure at $\bar{x}$. This means that for every bounded, continuous, real-valued function f on X, if we define

$$\mu_n(f) \underset{\text{def}}{=} \int_X \mu_n(dx) f(x) \qquad (8.16)$$

then

$$\mu_n(f) \longrightarrow \delta_{\bar{x}}(f) = f(\bar{x}) \qquad (8.17)$$

as $n \to \infty$. Weak convergence is a natural notion, in that the collection of bounded continuous functions on X can be thought of as *observables* for the states of the world: in state x, the observable f has the value $f(x)$. Thus consistency is the requirement that in the Bayes updating scheme, the limiting values of all observables are their true values – surely an operationally sound notion. Moreover, weak convergence has the technical advantage that it is the easiest of the various kinds of convergence criteria to satisfy: if a given sequence of measures is weakly convergent, then it is so in other ways too.

We will refer to the above definition of consistency as *classical adaptability*: the pair (μ_0, N) is (classically) adaptable to the state of affairs $\bar{x}$ if $(\mu_0, \bar{x})$ is consistent as in (8.16) above. That is, for almost all input sequences $y_1, y_2, y_3, \ldots$, the sequence of distributions $\mu_1, \mu_2, \mu_3, \ldots$ on X obtained as $n \to \infty$, by successively conditioning on the first n terms of $y_1, y_2, y_3, \ldots$, converges weakly to Dirac measure at $\bar{x}$. Classical adaptability corresponds, in evolutionary situations, to the capability of an organism to attain a *stable* perceptual representation of the persistent environmental feature represented by $\bar{x}$, beginning with the initial perceptual representation μ_0. Note, however, that this definition of adaptibility is of practical value only if punctual inputs are received according to the law $N(\bar{x}, \cdot)$ for some *fixed* $\bar{x}$ in X.

We now state the natural generalization of classical adaptability to the structural situation:

> The pair (μ_0, N) is *adaptable* to the probability measure μ on X if the structural process with initial prior μ_0 and repeated premise $\lambda = \mu N$ converges weakly to a probability measure μ_∞. We call this weak limit μ_∞ the *adaptation* of (μ_0, N) to μ.

Structural adaptability corresponds, in evolutionary situations, to the capability of an organism to attain a stable perceptual representation of the stable environmental feature represented by μ, beginning with the initial perceptual representation μ_0. Clearly the faster the rate of adaptation, the more likely is it that this particular adaptability will persist through generations.

BAYES AND DARWIN MEET: DIRECTED CONVERGENCE

Consider an inferencing system (X, Y, N, μ_0), where X is the space of conclusions for the inference, Y is the space of premises, and N is the 'image rendering kernel'. μ_0 is the 'prior' measure on X which encodes the system's initial subjective probabilities for conclusions in X.

The classical process can reasonably be used to acquire stable inferences only in situations where (i) the points of Y represent premises which are acquired with perfect discrimination by the system, and where (ii) the points in X irredundantly parameterize, via N, *all* possible distributions of images which might occur in practice. In fact, with regard to (ii), given N and the prior μ_0, the question of whether or not classical adaptibility holds is meaningful only when the law governing the punctual inputs at each stage is $N(\bar{x}, \cdot)$ for some fixed $\bar{x}$ in X. If for some $\bar{x}$ in X, (μ_0, N) is not adaptable to $N(\bar{x}, dy)$, then a state of affairs corresponding to $\bar{x}$ (i.e., a state of affairs which generates premises according to the law $N(\bar{x}, dy)$) will never be stably inferred. On the other hand, if there is more than one $\bar{x}$ in X with the same $N(\bar{x}, \cdot)$ then classical adaptability becomes almost meaningless. This suggests that we should weaken the definition to be something like: (μ_0, N) is adaptable to $\bar{x}$ if the posteriors in the classical process converge to a measure supported on the set $V_{\bar{x}} = \{x' \in X : N(x', \cdot) = N(\bar{x}, \cdot)\}$. Putatively this measure will be the restriction of μ_0 to $V_{\bar{x}}$, normalized to a probability measure. Without additional information there is no way to make a stronger inference than this, so this weaker type of adaptability at least provides a "platform" for a more specialized inference that might permit discrimination within $V_{\bar{x}}$. Note that if $V_{\bar{x}}$ has more than one element in it, such a measure on $V_{\bar{x}}$ represents a *multistable* percept.

We will assume that we have a standard way to measure the rate of weak convergence. Then if (μ_0, N) is adaptable to $\bar{x}$, we will denote by $f(\mu_0, N; \bar{x})$ the *reciprocal* of the rate of convergence to Dirac measure at $\bar{x}$ of the classical process starting with (μ_0, N). We might then interpret $f(\mu_0, N; x)$ as the 'length of time required for convergence'. For example, if (μ_0, N) is not adaptable to x then $f(\mu_0, N; x)$ will be infinite.

For our purposes we can define an *environment* to mean the collection of possible ambient states of affairs, together with their probabilities of occurrence. Suppose an organism's perceptual inferencing system utilizes (X, Y, N, μ_0). In the case of systems which employ the classical process to acquire stable percepts, we will assume that these "possible ambient states of affairs" are represented by points of X. Thus, a *(classical) environment E is specified by a probability measure ρ_E on X*. This measure, called the *underlying environmental measure*, is meant to give a much more global and long-term description of the environment than does μ_0, or do the measures on X which embody perceptual inferences. In fact ρ_E is intended to provide comprehensive information about the relative frequency of occurrence, *over an extended period of time*, of the various states of affairs represented by points of X. By contrast, an inference is intended to describe the state of affairs encountered by the organism more instantaneously, i.e., an inference intends to describe a much more specific and transient state than does the underlying environmental measure ρ_E.

In addition to frequency of occurrence of environmental states of affairs, we will also assume that the underlying environmental measure ρ_E contains information about the degree to which the states of affairs are adaptively critical, i.e., information about the *survival value* of the inference. Consider, for example, a creature which must drink water every few days for survival, and which is also the prey of an extremely deadly predator which comes into the vicinity, say, once every few months. For purposes of survival the abilities to correctly infer the presence of the predator, or to correctly infer the presence of water, are of equal importance. So, in spite of the fact that the corresponding states of affairs occur with very unequal frequency, they may be given equal weight by ρ_E. We conclude that if $\rho_E(S)$ is large for some $S \subset X$, then the environmental states of affairs represented by S are collectively significant for survival, perhaps because they are only moderately critical but occur frequently, or perhaps because they are enormously critical but occur only rarely.

We can now define the *classical adaptivity of the organism to an environment E* for the case where stable inferences are acquired via the classical process. We assume X and Y are fixed, so that in effect we are defining the adaptivity $A_{cl}(\mu_0, N; E)$ of (μ_0, N) to E as

$$A_{cl}(\mu_0, N; E) = \frac{1}{\int_X \rho_E(dx) f(\mu_0, N; x)} \qquad (8.18)$$

The adaptivity is an indicator of the time required for the organism to arrive at stable percepts which stably represent environmental states of affairs as they are encountered. This indicator takes into account, via ρ_E, the relative likelihood of encountering the various states of affairs, as well as the survival value of a correct inference in the context of the encounter. The smaller the average value of f, i.e., the less the average time required for adaptation, the larger will be the value of the adaptivity. Hence the larger the value of the adaptivity, the more rapidly does the organism's perceptual system make correct inferences about environmental states of affairs. To say that the adaptivity is infinite means that the function $f(\mu_0, N; x)$ on X has value 0 except possibly on some subset of X which has ρ_E-measure 0. This means that stable percepts are instantaneously inferred in almost all environmental conditions, i.e., in all conditions except those represented by the ρ_E-measure zero subset of X. On the other hand, to say that the adaptivity is 0 means that there is a class of environmental states of affairs which are significant for survival (i.e., they are represented by a set S in X for which $\rho_E(S) > 0$), but the perceptual adaptation to these environmental states is very slow (i.e., f takes large values on S). In particular, if (μ_0, N) is *not adaptable* to x in X, then we must take $f(\mu_0, N; x)$ to be ∞, so if nonadaptability holds on any set S in X with $\rho_E(S) > 0$, then the adaptivity will be 0.

We now consider the case of an organism which acquires stable percepts using the structural process; we will indicate the appropriate definitions of adaptability and adaptivity. In this case, as in the classical case, we assume that the basic data for the organism's perceptual inferencing system is (X, Y, N, μ_0), where these symbols have the same meanings as above. But in this case the priors, beginning with μ_0, are updated recursively, based on premises which are probabilistic, i.e., the premises are probability measures λ on the scene space Y. To review the updating procedure, suppose that at time n the updated prior is μ_n. We then have the Bayesian posterior kernel $P_{(\mu_n, N)}$ for this prior μ_n and the likelihood kernel N.

(Recall that $P_{(\mu_n, N)}$ is the kernel from Y to X which has the following interpretation: Assume that the distribution of states of affairs is given by the probability measure μ_n on X, and assume that $N(x, \cdot)$ describes the probabilities of scenes in Y being acquired as premises given that the actual state of affairs is x. Then, for $y \in Y$, $P_{(\mu_n, N)}(y, S)$ is the probability that an environmental state of affairs which is represented by some point of S was transduced, given that the scene y was acquired as a premise.)

Suppose that at the next $(n + 1)$th instant the premise λ_{n+1} is acquired. Recall that the system then infers the measure $\lambda_{n+1} P_{(\mu_n, N)}$ on X, which becomes the next prior μ_{n+1}, i.e., the priors are updated recursively according to the law $\mu_{n+1} = \lambda_{n+1} P_{(\mu_n, N)}$, where μ_n denotes the prior at time n, $P_{(\mu_n, N)}$ is the Bayes' posterior kernel for this prior and for the likelihood kernel N, and λ_{n+1} is the premise at time $n + 1$. Thus, for $A \subset X$,

$$\mu_{n+1}(A) = \int_Y \lambda_{n+1}(dy) P_{(\mu_n, N)}(y, A) \qquad (8.19)$$

In this situation, a stable percept is a weakly convergent sequence of measures μ_n on X which arises from this updating procedure for some sequence of premises λ_n.

Now suppose that an environmental state of affairs is described as a probability measure μ on X. Here, the meaning of the likelihood kernel N is that the premise scene transduced from μ is described by the probability measure μN on Y, defined by $\mu N(B) = \int_X \mu(dx) N(x, B)$. We will say that (μ_0, N) *is structurally adaptable to* μ if the sequence of measures μ_n on X, defined recursively by (8.19) (beginning with μ_0), converges weakly *for the constant sequence of premise measures* $\lambda_n = \mu N$ on Y. In other words, (μ_0, N) is adaptable to μ if, beginning with μ_0, the system acquires a stable percept in the presence of that persistent environmental state of affairs which corresponds to μ. Let μ_∞ denote the weak limit of the sequence μ_n; this μ_∞ exists by definition in case of adaptability as above. For the definition here of structural adaptability of (μ_0, N) to μ it is too much to require that $\mu_\infty = \mu$, just as for classical adaptability of (μ_0, N) to x in X it is too much to require that the classical process converges to x. All that we can ask is that a stable percept be acquired in the presence of the given persisting environmental state of affairs. In the classical case, if an environmental state corresponds to the punctual x in X, then for the system to be in the "presence of a persistent environmental state" means that the system obtains sequences of punctual premises y_n in Y which are independent and identically distributed with the law $N(x, \cdot)$. In the structural case, if an environmental state corresponds to the probability measure μ on X, then for the system to be in the "presence of a persistent environmental state" means that the system obtains a sequence of probabilistic premises λ_n which are identically equal to μN.

We now consider the meaning of adaptivity in the structural case. As in the classical case, we assume we have a measure of the rate of weak convergence, and we denote its reciprocal by f. If (μ_0, N) is adaptable to μ, then $f(\mu_0, N; \mu)$ may be interpreted as the length of time required for the convergence of the structural process $\{\mu_n\}$, beginning with μ_0 generated by the constant premise sequence $\lambda_n = \mu N$. If (μ_0, N) is not adaptable to μ, then we may set $f(\mu_0, N; \mu) = \infty$. We must also specify a precise definition of "environment" as we did for the classical case; the idea again is that an environment E is represented by an underlying environmental measure ρ_E, which is a measure on the space of environmental states of affairs. In the structural case, while X is a "configuration space" for these states, the actual states are identified with probability measures μ on X. Thus, denoting the set of probability measures on X by $\mathcal{P}(X)$, we will define a *(structural) environment* to be a probability measure ρ_E on $\mathcal{P}(X)$.[4] We can now define the *structural adaptivity of an organism* (μ_0, N) *to an environment* E as

$$A_{st}(\mu_0, N; E) = \frac{1}{\int_{\mathcal{P}(X)} \rho_E(d\mu) f(\mu_0, N; \mu)} \qquad (8.20)$$

Note that μ is now the variable of integration on $\mathcal{P}(X)$. As in the classical case, the number $A_{st}(\mu_0, N; E)$ may be interpreted as the expected rate of perceptual adaptation to the environment, a rate which is adjusted for survival value of the various environmental conditions.

CONCLUSIONS

One significant distinction between structural and classical Bayesian updating of perceptual inferences is that a *directed convergence* strategy is available in the structural case (Bennett & Cohen, 1999). Directed convergence is a strategy for acquiring stable percepts, i.e., convergent sequences of instantaneous percepts, even in a noisy environment with ubiquitous distractors. The idea is to decide whether or not to incorporate a premise λ into the updating procedure based on (i) how close λ appears to be to the current percept, and (ii) how strong is the belief that the current percept is close to a "correct percept". To make this precise, suppose at time n an organism (μ_0, N) which uses structural updating has percept μ_n, so that its updating law is the Bayesian posterior kernel $P_{(\mu_n, N)}$. Suppose that there is a strong belief that μ_n is close to a correct percept "μ". In fact the degree of that belief may be expressed as the distance within which it is believed that μ_n lies from μ. Then $\mu_n N$ should be correspondingly close to μN, since N is continuous as a function from $\mathcal{P}(x)$ to $\mathcal{P}(Y)$ ($\mathcal{P}(X)$ denotes the probability measures on X, etc.). Now when we say that μ is a "correct percept" we mean that it represents a stable environmental feature *of interest* to the organism. Because it represents a stable environmental feature, we expect that it will be transduced, i.e., there is a nontrivial probability that any given premise transduces that feature. And if a premise λ does transduce the feature represented by μ, then λ will be close to μN and consequently close to $\mu_n N$. Thus, to the extent to which the degree of belief in μ_n is justified, within a reasonable time interval the organism will receive a premise λ that *confirms the degree of belief in* μ_n, in the sense that it lies sufficiently close to $\mu_n N$. Thus, suppose that at the next $(n + 1)$th instant a premise λ is received. If λ confirms the degree of belief in μ_n, since the organism is *interested* in the feature μ, λ will be accepted as λ_{n+1}, and hence incorporated in the updating procedure. Indeed we will then have $\mu_{n+1} = \lambda P_{(\mu_n, N)}$. On the other hand, if a λ which confirms the degree of belief in μ_n is not received within a reasonable time, then there will be reason to modify the degree of belief to suppose that μ_n lies at a greater distance from a correct percept than was originally thought, and hence justifying acceptance of premises λ which lie further from $\mu_n N$ than was acceptable previously.

The use of such a strategy introduces a "flexibility of direction" into the updating procedure, that maximizes the possibility of convergence to a conclusion which represents one of a possible multitude of environmental phenomena, each of which may be responsible for a share of the raw premises obtained by the organism. By using the directed convergence strategy, the conclusions are updated only in response to the premises in a recursively selected subsequence (of the sequence of *all* premises); the actual selection occurs as the result of an ongoing balancing dance of belief and confirmation.

It seems clear that the organism (μ_0, N) must use something similar to a directed convergence strategy to selectively incorporate premises into the updating procedure. Otherwise, given the complexity of the environment, with numerous features being transduced on the sensorium in the presence of noise and other perturbations, it is hard to imagine that the raw sequence of incoming premises would correspond to just one of those features, and would do so in a manner which would produce, via updating, a convergent percept sequence. But in any case it is unreasonable to expect that, in practice, the premise sequences that yield the stable percepts (i.e., that yield convergent percept sequences), are *constant*. In other words, suppose the organism obtains a sequence of premises λ_n which give rise to the convergent percept sequence μ_n, whose limit μ represents a stable environmental feature. In fact, suppose for simplicity that this premise sequence arose from transduction of that very feature. In practice, this does *not* mean that $\lambda_n = \mu N$ for all n. For, because of various perturbations whose effect is not completely subsumed in the "noise" kernel N, the transduction will result in premises which are close to μN but not equal to it. Therefore the most we can reasonably expect in this situation is that the premises λ_n converge to $\lambda = \mu N$ (as the percepts μ_n converge to μ). Indeed if we imagine that a raw sequence of premises which are random perturbations of μN is obtained, then the directed convergence procedure will lead to the recursive selection of a subsequence which optimizes the possibility of convergence of the μ_n to μ.

But recall that the *adaptivity* of (μ_0, N) to μ and the associated function $f(\mu_0, N; \mu)$ were previously defined in terms of the sequence of percepts μ_n which is generated in response to the *constant* premise sequence $\lambda_n = \lambda = \mu_n N$ for all n. How is this definition relevant to the "real world" situation where the adaptivity of the organism to μ depends on its response to a non-constant premise sequence λ_n which converges to λ? The idea is that the adaptivity defined in terms of the constant sequence λ is an idealized version of the response of the organism to a random premise sequence which converges to λ. And in this spirit, if μ and μ' are measures on X, the relative values of $f(\mu_0, N; \mu)$ and $f(\mu_0, N; \mu')$ represent the relative expected rates of convergence of the percepts, in response to random premise sequences which converge on the one hand to μN and on the other hand to $\mu' N$.

We expect that ongoing mathematical investigations will clarify these intuitions, and lead ultimately to computable models.

Acknowledgement. Supported in part by a grant from the US National Science Foundation to Don Hoffman.

NOTES

1. Note that we often write the argument *before* a function, rather than after it: this leads to a certain notational convenience, as we shall see.
2. So far, these notational changes are purely formal and seek to express the essential functional relationships in Bayes' rule. We will see, however, that there is much more than formality to the content of this notation.
3. By "almost all" input sequences we mean "with respect to the usual measure extended from that defined on cylinder sets of the set of sequences, i.e., infinite product set $Y \times Y \times \cdots$, given by $N(\bar{x}, dy)$ in each factor.
4. For this purpose we should assume that X *is a complete separable metric space*, whose σ-algebra of measurable sets is generated by the open sets of its metric topology. Then, by theorems of Prohorov [Billingsley, 1968], $\mathcal{P}(X)$ is also a complete separable metric space, with its corresponding σ-algebra of measurable sets; ρ_E is a measure for this σ-algebra.

REFERENCES

Adelson, E.H. & Pentland, A.P. (1996). The perception of shading and reflectance. In D.C. Knill & W.A. Richards (Eds.), *Perception as Bayesian inference* (pp. 409–423). Cambridge: Cambridge University Press.

Beatty, D.D. (1984). Visual pigments and the labile scotopic visual system of fish. *Vision Research*, **24**, 1563–1573.

Belhumeur, P.N. (1996). A computational theory for binocular stereopsis. In D.C. Knill & W.A. Richards (Eds.), *Perception as Bayesian inference* (pp. 323–364). Cambridge: Cambridge University Press.

Bennett, B.M. & Cohen, R.B. (1999). L-infinity metric criteria for convergence in Bayesian recursive inference systems. *Advances in Applied Mathematics*, **23**, 255–273.

Bennett, B.M., Hoffman, D.D., Prakash, C. & Richman, S.N. (1996). Observer theory, Bayes' theory, and psychophysics. In D.C. Knill & W.A. Richards (Eds.), *Perception as Bayesian inference* (pp. 163–212). Cambridge: Cambridge University Press.

Billingsley, P. (1968). *Convergence of probability measures*. Wiley, New York.

Blake, A., Bülthoff, H.H. & Sheinberg, D. (1996). Shape from texture: Ideal observers and human psychophysics. In D.C. Knill & W.A. Richards (Eds.), *Perception as Bayesian inference* (pp. 287–321). Cambridge: Cambridge University Press.

Brainard, D.H. & Freeman, W.T. (1994). Bayesian method for recovering surface and illuminant properties from photosensor responses. *Proceedings of SPIE, 2179*. San Jose, California, February 1994.

Crawford, M.L.J., Anderson, R.A., Blake, R., Jacobs, G.H. & Neumeyer, C. (1990). Inter-species comparisons in the understanding of human visual perception. In L. Spillman &

J.S. Werner (Eds.) *Visual perception: The neurophysiological foundations.* San Diego: Academic Press.

Cronin, T.W. & Marshall, N.J. (1989). A retina with at least ten spectral types of photoreceptors in a stomatopod crustacean. *Nature*, **339**, 137–140.

Cronin, T.W., Marshall, N.J. & Land, M.F. (1994). The unique visual sysem of the mantis shrimp. *American Scientist*, **82** (4), 356–365.

Delius, J.D. & Emmerton, J. (1979). Visual performance in pigeons. In A.M. Granda & J.H. Maxwell (Eds.) *Neural mechanisms of behavior in the pigeon.* New York: Plenum Press.

Diaconis, P. & Freedman, D. (1986). On the consistency of Bayes estimates. *The Annals of Statistics*, **14** (1), 1–26.

Emmerton, J. & Delius, J.D. (1980). Wavelength discrimination in the "visible" and ultraviolet spectrum by pigeons. *Journal of Comparative Physiology A*, **141**, 47–52.

Exner, S. (1891). *The physiology of the compound eyes of insects and crustaceans.* Translated by R.C. Hardie (1989). Berlin: Springer.

Freeman, W.T. (1996). The generic viewpoint assumption in a Bayesian framework. In D.C. Knill & W.A. Richards (Eds.), *Perception as Bayesian inference* (pp. 365–389). Cambridge: Cambridge University Press.

Jacobs, G.H. (1981). *Comparative color vision.* New York: Academic Press.

Jepson, A., Richards, W. & Knill, D. (1996). Modal structure and reliable inference. In D.C. Knill & W.A. Richards (Eds.), Perception as Bayesian inference (pp. 63–92). Cambridge: Cambridge University Press.

Knill, D.C. & Richards, W.A. (Eds.) (1996). *Perception as Bayesian inference.* Cambridge: Cambridge University Press.

Knill, D.C., Kersten, D. & Mamassian, P. (1996). Implications of a Bayesian formulation for processing for psychophysics. In D.C. Knill & W.A. Richards (Eds.), Perception as Bayesian inference (pp. 239–286), Cambridge: Cambridge University Press.

Kunze, P. (1979). Apposition and superposition eyes. In H.-J. Autrum (Ed.) *Handbook of sensory physiology* (vol. VII/6A, pp. 441–502). Berlin: Springer.

Land, M.F. (1985). The morphology and optics of spider eyes. In F.G. Barth (Ed.) *Neurobiology of arachnids* (pp. 53–78). Berlin: Springer.

Land, M.F. (1991). Optics of the eyes of the animal kingdom. In J.R. Cronly-Dillon & R.L. Gregory (Eds.) *Evolution of the eye and visual system* (pp. 118–135). Boca Raton, FL: CRC Press.

Lythgoe, J.N. (1988). Light and vision in the aquatic environment. In J. Atema, R.R. Fary, A.N. Popper & W.N. Tavolga (Eds.) *Sensory biology of aquatic animals* (pp. 57–82). New York: Springer.

Lythgoe, J.N. (1991). Evolution of visual behavior. In J.R. Cronly-Dillon & R.L. Gregory (Eds.) *Evolution of the eye and visual system* (pp. 3–14). Boca Raton, FL: CRC Press.

Neumeyer, C. (1985). An ultraviolet receptor as a fourth receptor type in goldfish color vision. *Naturwissenschaften*, **72**, 162–163.

Neumeyer, C. (1986). Wavelength discrimination in the goldfish. *Journal of Comparative Physiology*, **158**, 203–213.

Nilsson, D.-E. (1989). Optics and evolution of the compound eye. In D.G. Stavenga & R.C. Hardie (Eds.) *Facets of vision* (pp. 30–73). Berlin: Springer.

Pumphrey, R.J. (1961). Concerning vision. In J.A. Ramsay & V.B. Wigglesworth (Eds.) *The cell and the organism* (pp. 193–208). Cambridge: Cambridge University Press.

Salvini-Plawen, L.V. & Maxx, R. (1977). On the evolution of photoreceptors and eyes. *Evolutionary Biology*, **10**, 207–263.

Witkin, A. (1981). Recovering surface shape and orientation from texture. *Artificial Intelligence*, **17**, 17–45.

Wright, A. (1979). Color-vision psychophysics: a comparison of pigeon and human. In A.M. Granda & J.H. Maxwell (Eds.) *Neural mechanisms of behavior in the pigeon.* New York: Plenum Press.

9

The Very Idea of Perception as a Process of Unconscious Probabilistic Inference

MARK KAPLAN

Department of Philosophy, University of Wiscousin-Milwaukee, USA

I

The very idea that perception is a process of unconscious inference (probabilistic or otherwise) appears to make nonsense out of the distinction between what requires inferential support and what does not.[1]

The idea that perceptual knowledge involves inference is one that, at least until recently, enjoyed wide currency in philosophy. The thought was that perceptual judgments about the location and visible characteristics of tables, chairs and other medium-size dry goods are sufficiently immodest that they require some sort of inferential support if they are to count as justified or (better yet) knowledge. There was considerable controversy about exactly what characteristic perceptual judgments have that makes them immodest in this way. (Is it, for example, their being uncertain, open to revision, dependent for their truth on facts about the world "external" to the perceiver?) But about this much all were in agreement: (i) perceptual judgments are immodest in a way certain other judgments, which invariably accompany perceptual judgments, are not (typically, these more modest judgments were taken to concern themselves solely with the perceiver's introspectible psychological states); and (ii) it is only by an argument that appeals to these more modest judgments that a perceptual judgment can be justified.

Now, while it was thought that a perceptual judgment requires justification via an argument whose premises include one or more of these relatively modest judgments, it was also recognized that one cannot expect a person to be able to produce on

Perception and the Physical World: Psychologicaal and Philosophical Issues in Perception.
Edited by Dieter Heyer and Rainer Mausfeld. © 2002 John Wiley & Sons, Ltd.

demand the requisite argument. Even the most eminent of philosophers had difficulty determining exactly what form of argument was called for. (Roderick Chisholm, to take the most eminent among them, revised his account of how the argument should go for over four decades.) And, given what they *had* determined, anyone was guaranteed to find the task of producing such an argument—replete, as it came to be thought it must be, with an extremely demanding coherence constraint—difficult, if not impossible.[2]

So, rather than have to claim that we have few, if any, justified perceptual beliefs and, thus, little if any perceptual knowledge (a claim that they found unpalatable), the philosophers about whom I am writing opted for the view that it is not necessary for a perceptual belief to count as justified or as knowledge that the perceiver be able to produce the justification required. We can, they maintained, rest easy in the assumption that the appropriate argument is "tacitly or implicitly involved in the actual cognitive state"[3] of the perceiver. We can safely assume, as we pursue the research project of trying to discern the shape an argument must take if it is to confer justification on a particular one of our perceptual judgments, that "the truth we are seeking is 'already implicit in the mind that seeks it, and needs only to be elicited and brought to clear reflection'."[4]

You don't have to be a philosopher to find the foregoing pretty familiar. The idea that perception is a process of unconscious inference is very much alive in current work in the psychology of perception. That idea is motivated by much the same line of thought: that perceptual judgments (gaudy with commitments to a three-dimensional world) are sufficiently immodest as to require the inferential support of other, more modest, judgments (about two-dimensional representations) that invariably accompany them; and that the putative inference from modest premises to immodest conclusions, far too complicated to be elicited, must be classified as unconscious. And the idea leads to the same unhappy result: we are to regard perceptual knowledge of medium-sized dry goods as involving a judgment that requires inferential support—but not any inferential support that the perceiver must be able to produce.

Why is the result unhappy? Not because it is wrong to shrink from requiring, as a condition of our being justified in harboring perceptual beliefs, that we be able to produce on demand the sort of arguments philosophers or perceptual psychologists think are required to justify the beliefs. The consequence of such a requirement would be intolerable. Patently unable to do what is required to render our perceptual beliefs justified, we would be forced (insofar as we embraced the foregoing view of perceptual knowledge) to draw the methodologically mad conclusion that we have no business harboring these beliefs—no more business than we would have believing what is printed on the front page of a tabloid newspaper.

The trouble is that it is hard to see what comfort we are supposed to derive from jettisoning the offending requirement. What, after all, are we to make of the view that, while my current perceptual judgments require justification by appeal to judgments more modest in character, I don't need be able to provide now (or for that matter ever) the requisite argument in order to be justified in making those judgments?

There are two possibilities. The first is that we are to take this view to be an instance of a more general principle. This principle states that, even if the judgment that *P* is one you recognize requires substantive justification, you may happily persist in the belief that *P* without the slightest worry about whether you could now or ever produce the requisite justification for that belief. If so, we're back in the territory of methodological madness. For this principle licenses a methodology on which one is free to persist in believing anything at all, about any matter at all, with no regard for whether one can produce even the most meager argument in the belief's favor. Obviously this is a methodology very much at odds with our own.[5]

The second possibility is that we are not to take the view as an instance of a more general principle—we are to understand it as applying only to perceptual judgments. But then it becomes difficult to make sense of the fundamental thought behind this entire endeavor: the thought that perceptual judgments are sufficiently immodest that they require some sort of inferential support if they are to count as justified. The reason it *seemed* to make sense when it was initially broached is that we were able to assimilate perceptual judgments to predictions, historical theses, scientific hypotheses—all claims we recognize as sufficiently immodest as to require inferential support if they are justifiably to be believed. But now it turns out that this assimilation is mistaken: these other claims require inferential support in order to be justifiably believed in the sense that we cannot with good methodological conscience believe them unless we can produce the appropriate inferential support. Perceptual judgments, on the view under discussion, do not in this sense require inferential support in order to be justifiably believed. On the contrary, we are perfectly free to persist without any methodological qualm in our perceptual judgments without paying even the slightest heed to whether we can produce any inferential support for them. But, if so, it is difficult to see the sense in which justified perceptual judgments can properly be said to *require* inferential support at all.

That is to say, the doctrine that perception is process of unconscious inference appears to be no more tenable than the doctrine that perception is a process of conscious inference. It makes one wonder whether one really wants to—whether one really has to—think of perception as a process of inference at all.

II

It is hard to see how the probabilities involved in the putative inferences can be interpreted in a way that (i) makes them into things that can properly thought to obey the axioms of the probability calculus, and (ii) enables them to do the work they must do to capture the phenomenon of perception.

In "Unity of Perception", Bennett, Hoffman and Prakash offer an elegant summary and development of the inference model of perception they elaborated in their book, *Observer Mechanics*.[6]

On their view, perception consists of a set of inferences, each of which goes from a set of premises to which probabilities are assigned to a set of conclusions to which probabilities are assigned. How are these probabilities to be interpreted? They write of the probability measure over the set of conclusions (here they constitute three-dimensional rigid fixed-axis interpretations of two-dimensional motion of dots on a video monitor).

One can think of this probability measure as stating the degree of confirmation or belief assigned to each interpretation. Or one can think of it as describing the ease or frequency with which each interpretation is perceived (op. cit., p. 307).

It seems to me, however, that one's options are actually more limited than this, and in a somewhat unfortunate way.

Consider the frequency interpretation. The frequency interpretation has an obvious attraction: one thing a theory of perception might be expected to do is to predict, and account for, the (say) frequency with which people perceive depth as a result of being exposed to a given trajectory of dots on videotape. But estimating the frequency with which such perception occurs is something that scientists do by way of pursuing their science (or amateurs do by way of indulging their fascination with perceptual phenomena); contrary to the frequency interpretation, it is nothing a *perceiver* does when she sees (or fails to see, or oscillates between seeing and failing to see) depth. She just sees depth, or fails to see depth, or oscillates between seeing depth and failing to see depth—*period*. It is, indeed, perceivers' perceivings of depth and so on that provide the data upon which our conscious estimates of the frequency of depth perception are based.

The ease interpretation has the same attraction and suffers the same difficulty. It is easy to see how, as cognitive scientists and amateurs, we would want, in the course of our investigations, to draw conclusions about how easy it is to perceive depth in certain circumstances. But it is hard to see how we could possibly be drawing such conclusions as perceivers; as perceivers, we just find it easy or we don't.

That leaves the degree-of-belief interpretation. The difficulties attending the frequency and ease interpretations are entirely absent. If unconscious inference is anything, it is a transition from prior conviction to posterior conviction—something that degrees of belief are ideally equipped to represent. But what is also absent is the attraction of the other two interpretations. Unconscious inference construed as a transition from prior conviction to posterior conviction seems insufficient for perception. It would seem entirely compatible with a person's coming via the required inference to the conviction that there is before her a moving three-dimensional object, that she does not actually *see* it as (i.e., that she merely *infer* it to be) three dimensional. And if so, a theory of perception understood as a probabilistic inference under the degree-of-belief interpretation, seems ill-equipped to get at least one thing we really want: i.e., a theory that can predict, and account for, the circumstances in which people *see* objects as three dimensional.

Now, I recognize that this criticism of the degree-of-belief interpretation admits of response. The criticism, it might be replied, presupposes that there is some qualitative feel in perception that is essential to it. This, it may be pointed out, is a not an uncontroversial presupposition—nor is it a helpful one. It makes it difficult to talk of machine perception as being of a kind with its human counterpart; it does not allow us (in the words of Bennett et al., p. 310) "to uncover observers [by which they mean 'perceptual capacities'] in biological perceptual systems and implement them in silicon".

But let me say in my defense that I make no claim about qualitative feels. Nor do I deny that generality and abstraction have their uses. I claim only (i) that there is a distinction between seeing something as three dimensional and (merely) inferring that it is three dimensional and (ii) that any view that cannot distinguish the two is unable to capture what is peculiar to perception.

III

It is also hard to see how the ultimate premises of the putative inferences (the prior probability distributions) could be justified—and, indeed, how any such ultimate premise could fail to be completely unjustified.

Claims to inferential knowledge live and die by the cogency of the inferences they invoke: impeach the cogency of the inference and you've impeached the claim to knowledge. So it is with perceptual knowledge if perception is just a process of inference: our claims to perceptual knowledge are only as secure as the inference involved in perception is cogent. One way of impeaching the cogency of an inference is to challenge the capacity of its premises to support its conclusion. Another way is to deny the integrity of the premises themselves.

A probabilistic inference from modest information (call it I) to immodest perceptual judgment (call it P) is going to require a prior probability assignment to P. After all, by Bayes' Theorem,

$$\text{prob}(P \mid I) = \text{prob}(I \mid P)\text{prob}(P)/\text{prob}(I)$$

Thus the probability you assign to immodest P given modest information I is going to depend, in part, on how probable you antecedently regard P. But if P is the sort of claim that requires support—if the judgment that P is true is too immodest to stand on its own, if the justification of our judging that P depends on our having information of a modest sort—how, antecedent to our acquisition of the required information, can this prior probability assignment to P be warranted?

The issue of how to justify prior probability distributions in the case of ignorance— of how the ultimate premises of probabilistic inferences in such cases are to be defended—has been much debated. Some have thought there are a priori principles— such as the principle of indifference—available to secure the integrity of prior probabilities. But none of these principles—and certainly not the principle of indifference— has proved very compelling and, in any event, if perception is a process of inference, then research indicates that the priors it employs are biased in a way not plausibly sanctioned by a priori considerations.

Others have thought prior probabilities to be unimpeachable on other grounds: because they are ultimately inconsequential given how the influence of priors on posteriors tends to be swamped by the acquisition of evidence. But it turns out that the swamping referred to only occurs in certain rather special circumstances.[7]

Another idea is to defend priors by appeal to a posteriori considerations—by appeal, in particular, to the efficacy and utility of the process of perception in which they figure. But while this seems an attractive way to justify a design feature of a process for accomplishing a certain task, it is no way to defend the cogency of an inference. If the cogency of an inference could be defended simply by appealing to its utility—say, its efficacy in producing and sustaining true belief—then, so long as it was commonly found to be convincing, any inference with a true conclusion could be defended as cogent, no matter how fallacious it might be.

A final, very Bayesian, approach to the matter is to insist that priors require no defense: they are unimpeachable because they are unavoidable. The thought is that every state of opinion—even rank ignorance or uncertainty—is expressible by a probability distribution. We cannot avoid being *some* state of opinion or other. But if we thus cannot avoid being in some such state, and no such state has any special claim to be the right one or a wrong one, then any state of opinion we end up adopting must be regarded as permissible. We are safe no matter which we pick.

The trouble with this line of thought is that not every state of opinion—and, in particular, not every state of ignorance—is representable by a probability distribution. After all, when one is at a loss for any reason to pick one distribution rather than another, there is an alternative to just picking one: one can simply refuse to adopt any distribution at all. Indeed, in the absence of any good reason to choose one prior rather than another, refusing to choose any at all would seem just what one *should* do. If one does refuse to attach any prior to P, then one will have adopted an attitude toward P that, far from being characterizable by a definite probability distribution, is characterizable by the absence of a definite probability distribution: a state of ignorance about the truth of P that is characterized by an infinite set S of probability distributions such that, for each rational number r in the closed interval between 0 and 1, there is a probability distribution in S that assigns r to P.[8] But if one thus assigns no prior probability to P, one cannot get a posterior for P. That is, if one does what one should, given the absence of any reason to choose any particular prior, one cannot, on the receipt of information I, make any inference at all.

Now, I cannot claim to have canvassed every possible strategy for defending the priors postulated to be involved in perception. But this much is, I think, clear enough: if perception is a process of probabilistic inference that delivers perceptual knowledge, the prior probabilities involved require defense. And if perceptual judgments are immodest in the way they are supposed to be on the inference model of perception, it is by no means easy to see how such a defense can be mounted.

IV

Fortunately, however, the interest of a research project that attempts to employ probabilistic machinery to capture input/output relations in the process of perception does not depend on the project's being construed as an attempt to reconstruct a process of unconscious inference; and it is only when so construed that the research project is beset by the foregoing difficulties.

All the foregoing problems arise from a single theoretical commitment of the probabilistic-inference model of perception: the commitment to regarding perception as a process of inference. But it is remarkable how little the true appeal of the model—its ability to bring to bear the formal machinery of probability theory on the phenomena of perception—depends on that theoretical commitment. Recast the model as one that seeks to understand in probabilistic terms the conditions under which we perceive depth and so on—*sans* any mention of inference—and the problems evaporate. We need no longer make any claims about what requires inferential support: we are now investigating the dispositions of perceptual systems. We are free to interpret probabilities however we like: no longer do they have to figure in the premises of the perceiver's inferences. We need no longer worry about the cogency of inference: inference is no longer an object of our study. And we can enjoy all the advantages of—all the scientific progress engendered by—construing perception as probabilistic inference without the pain of having to answer for tendentious claims about inference. Not least among the pains we can thus avoid is that unhappy trip into the quagmire of disputes over our access to the external world that the inference model of perception (with its insistence that perceptual judgments must be justified by appeal to ultimate premises of a very different, more modest, sort), has led so many philosophers. In my view the calculus is clear. The probabilistic-inference model of perception has liabilities the probabilistic-disposition model does not have and no advantages the latter model lacks. The probabilistic-inference model should be abandoned.

POSTSCRIPT

I recognize that this may seem a draconian prescription to some researchers on perception. The idea that perception is a process of unconscious probabilistic inference, they will say, has served as a useful metaphor, as a provocative heuristic, in their research. Were they to take to heart the terminological fastidiousness that I am urging upon them, they will say, they would lose the use of this productive metaphor and heuristic. The trade is simply not worth it.

But I have issued no injunction against useful metaphors and heuristics. I am happy to see researchers on perception use whatever metaphors or heuristics (or, for that matter, diets or exercise regimens) that lead to good ideas. All I have urged is that, once the metaphors and heuristics have done their work, they be *recognized* as the metaphors and heuristics they are—that they be set aside for the purpose of describing the scientific results for whose attainment they have served as instruments.

Let me put the point another way. When I was first taught to swim the sidestroke, I was told to imagine that I was picking apples—that I was reaching above my head for an apple with my left hand, transferring the apple at about chest height to my right hand and placing it in a basket slung about my right hip. I went into the water, imagined what I was told to imagine and the heuristic/metaphor worked. But, for all that, I have never been tempted to describe—and I do not see how the mere fact that the heuristic/metaphor was useful could have entitled me to describe—what I went on to do in the water that day as apple-picking. I cannot see why the mere fact (which I am perfectly prepared to grant) that it is of heuristic value to think of perception as a process of unconscious inference should offer any of us any more entitlement to describe what actually happens in perception as unconscious inference.

254 *Perception and the Physical World*

Might it entitle us to say something more modest: that in perceiving we behave *as if* we were making a conscious inference?[9] I think not, and for two reasons. First, to say that in perception we behave as if we were making conscious inferences is to presuppose that we have some robust account of the psychology of conscious inference—of the sort of thing that perception (on this view) mimics. We have nothing of the sort.[10] Second, as far as we can tell, the credence we invest in the conclusion of an inference tends to be somewhat sensitive to—indeed, even, eradicable as a consequence of—criticism of the cogency of the inference. But, while what we *believe we see* is sensitive to criticism in this way, what we *see something as* is not. So (i) we don't know enough about conscious inference to say what it would be like for something to be behaving as if it were a process of conscious inference and (ii) what little we *do* know suggests that in perceiving we do not behave quite as we do when we make conscious inferences.

NOTES

1. This chapter was prepared for presentation to the conference, "Perception and the Role of Evolutionary Internalized regularities of the Physical World", sponsored by the *Zentrum für interdisziplinäre Forschung*, the University of Bielefeld, 28 November–1 December 1995. The last section (Postscript) was written in response to the discussion that ensued after the paper was read.
2. Laurence Bonjour concedes that this is true of the argument from the coherence of a person's belief system he favors, allowing that no person has a sufficient explicit grasp of her system of beliefs to furnish such an argument [*The Structure of Empirical Knowledge* (Cambridge, MA: Harvard University Press, 1985), pp. 151–152]. Given that there is no foundationalist alternative that does not itself involve some strong coherence constraint [see, for example, the coherence constraint that Roderick Chisholm imposes in chapter 6 of his *Theory of Knowledge*, 3rd edn. (Englewood Cliffs, NJ: Prentice-Hall, 1989)], it would seem that a comparable concession is warranted from the foundationalist quarter as well.
3. Bonjour op. cit., p. 152.
4. Roderick M. Chisholm, *Theory of Knowledge*, 2nd edn. (Engelwood Cliffs, NJ: Prentice-Hall, 1977), p. 17. Chisholm is here quoting from C. I. Lewis, *Mind and the World Order* (New York: Dover, 1929), p. 19.
5. The principle is not, however, so mad that it has failed to find philosophical voice. See, for example, Isaac Levi, *The Enterprise of Knowledge* (Cambridge MA: MIT Press, 1983), pp. 1–2; Gilbert Harman, *Change in View* (Cambridge, MA: MIT Press, 1986), ch. 4. But see David Christensen, "Conservatism in Epistemology", *Nous*, 28 (1994): 69–89.
6. Bruce Bennett, Donald D. Hoffman & Chetan Prakash, *Observer Mechanics* (San Diego: Academic Press, 1989).
7. On this, see John Earman, *Bayes or Bust* (Cambridge, MA: MIT Press, 1992), pp. 137–149.
8. I offer a more detailed argument for the propriety of this representation of ignorance in Chapter 1 of my *Decision Theory as Philosophy* (New York: Cambridge University Press, 1996); see especially section v.
9. This was suggested in discussion by Ansgar Beckermann.
10. I owe this point to Robert Schwartz.

Part III

Aspects of Picture Perception

10

Two Paradigms
of Picture Perception

ROBERT SCHWARTZ

Department of Philosophy, University of Wiscousin-Milwaukee, USA

The psychological study of picture perception has been dominated by a particular understanding of the nature and function of pictures. This paradigm has largely set the problems in the field, as well as oriented empirical and theoretical approaches to their solutions.[1] But this paradigm is not the only one available, and in many contexts it may not be the most profitable to adopt. For it frames issues in ways that underestimate both the full diversity of pictorial representations and the full range of problems an adequate theory of picture perception must face.

After presenting a broad outline of this dominant paradigm—one I call the "surrogate paradigm"—I will sketch an alternative perspective for exploring picture perception. This other paradigm, the symbolic paradigm, plays down some of the central problems of the standard position, raises a number of new questions, and suggests a different approach to investigating the perception of pictures. In turn, the incongruities between the two paradigms may help to explain some of the tensions and fragmentation of research in this area.[2]

THE SURROGATE PARADIGM

According to this paradigm, pictures represent by virtue of being *surrogates* for items and scenes in the world. The main difference between perceiving pictures and perceiving the actual environment is that in viewing pictures we are looking at stand-*in* objects, not the real things. Pictorial representation succeeds only when the surrogate "mimics" the original, thus making it possible to find out about the latter by looking at the former.

Perception and the Physical World: Psychological and Philosophical Issues in Perception.
Edited by Dieter Heyer and Rainer Mausfeld. © 2002 John Wiley & Sons, Ltd.

It is, of course, acknowledged that this account is something of an idealization. Pictures are two dimensional, while the things rendered in pictures are usually three dimensional. So a picture can never replicate completely the world it depicts. Still, the basic idea holds sway. A picture serves to convey information about the world by being an appropriate substitute. Representation is achieved to extent the two-dimensional picture is alike, resembles, copies, or otherwise mimics what it represents. Once this paradigm is in place, much else usually is thought to follow:

1. Since pictures are replicas of real things in the real world, they can be employed as substitutes for them in vision experiments. There is no need for subjects to deal with messy actual environments; pictures can serve in their stead. Hence, a wide variety of perceptual phenomena may be and are studied using pictures as the stimuli (Ittelson, 1996).
2. In this context, the domain of pictures employed is highly restricted. It does not include many, if not most, of the things we ordinarily call "pictures". No one, in experiments on vision, thinks of using caricatures, cartoons, ancient Egyptian, Haitian folk-primitive, German Expressionist, or Cubist pictures as probes or substitutes for actual spatial layouts. "Realistic" pictures are the coin of the realm.
3. Significantly for our concerns, the study of picture perception, itself, tends to focus on issues associated with this narrower domain of pictures. For only realistic pictures—roughly, photographs and depictions constructed according to the rules of linear perspective—are thought to resemble, copy, or otherwise function as true substitutes or surrogates. Accounts of the understanding and cognitive role of other sorts of pictures, if these depictions are even called "pictures", are considered somewhat tangential to visual theory.
4. As a first approximation, there is nothing special about the study of picture perception, since *real*istic pictures, as opposed to written words or Cubist and Egyptian "pictures", represent by replicating what they are about. So we perceive these real pictures the same way we see the objects or scenes for which they serve as substitutes. The problems of picture perception, again to a first approximation, are just the problems of perception.
5. Understandably, the particular problems surrogate theorists encounter and take as important in the study of picture perception depend on the approaches they take to ordinary perception. Theorists, say, who stress the role of "pictorial" cues in perceiving the everyday environment, conceive matters differently than theorists who assign such cues little weight and emphasize the role of information gained by movement and other non-pictorial cues.

PROBLEMS WITH THE SURROGATE PARADIGM

A number of problems facing the surrogate paradigm's account of pictorial representation are well documented in the art and philosophical literature (Gombrich, 1961; Goodman, 1968), and they are often noted in psychological writings as well (Arnheim, 1969; Kennedy, 1974; Hochberg, 1978). I intend, here, only to highlight some of the issues that are most germane to this chapter.

Issue 1

In order to explain the function of pictures to guide behavior and inform cognition, it is necessary to understand the *referential* aspects of pictorial representation, what object or objects a picture is about. Replication or resemblance, however, are not *sufficient* for establishing pictorial reference. Multiple copies of an engraved print of the Cologne Cathedral each represent the Cathedral, they do not represent each other. Although the prints may be able to serve as substitutes for one another, what they individually depict is a particular structure in Cologne. Being an "exact" copy or replica does not entail representation. Nor can a picture be assumed to represent that which it is "most alike".

Nor is accurate replication *necessary* for representation. If it were, there could be no mistakes or errors in pictorial representation. Yet it is a commonplace that pictures can misguide action and misinform mind. A picture that represents the Cologne Cathedral as being of reddish tint or as not having flying buttresses will mislead the tourist, because it misrepresents that singular Cologne attraction. Similarly, a real estate company's promotional picture depicting a beautiful lake where there is none is a fraud. It deceives, because it represents the landscape in ways that do not reflect how that parcel of land actually is. And in the case of fictive representations, such as the depiction of centaurs or Santa Claus, any account that makes it necessary to copy or replicate the "real" thing is in trouble.

Issue 2

Every object has an unlimited number of properties, and no representation—linguistic, iconic, or other—can capture them all. A picture can only depict some aspects of what it represents. But then which shall it be? An ordinary picture of Tabby the tiger does not show the animal's heart, kidneys, brain, the DNA that makes him the animal he is, the skin beneath his hairs, or the fine structure of the hairs depicted. It merely tells us about some of Tabby's properties, quite likely his outward appearance. The picture is a surrogate for Tabby, then, not in embodying or conveying information about most of Tabby's "essential" properties but in resembling the way he looks.

Even this more modest account of surrogatehood status, though, is rife with problems. The idea of there being "*the* way an object looks" makes little sense. Tabby the tiger looks different in full view or partly occluded, from the front, back, side, or above, in good light, green light or the dark, and from one inch, one foot or one mile away. A picture cannot depict all of Tabby's "appearances" any more than it can depict all of his other properties. At most, it will depict Tabby *as seen* under certain viewing conditions, from a certain vantage point. Pictures, therefore, do not serve as surrogates by mimetically rendering or copying most of the properties of the object represented. Instead, they *convey* highly selected information about the represented scene.

Issue 3

Conveying information about the world or the way the world looks is not limited to "realistic" pictorial representations. Linguistic descriptions do so, as do diagrams, graphs, and gestures, as do forms of depiction that do not fall within the scope of the surrogate paradigm. For example, a "picture" done in reverse perspective can offer as much and much the same information as one in standard linear perspective (Goodman, 1971; Arnheim, 1986). And a Cubist representation, not being limited to a single viewpoint, may actually provide more information about the layout than a realistic depiction.

Nevertheless, it is quite common to assume that a distinction between pictorial representation and other kinds of representation, descriptive as well as iconic, is obvious and can be readily drawn in terms of resemblance. True or real(istic) surrogates just look phenomenally like what they represent. Unfortunately, the idea of "phenomenal likeness" needed to underpin this account of pictorial representation is notoriously vague. We seldom misperceive pictures for the objects they represent. So in one good sense, depictions and the depicted do not look the same. We are not ordinarily deceived by the substitute. Attempts to characterize a less stringent notion of "phenomenal likeness" and make it do substantial explanatory work, however, have not proven very fruitful.

People do, of course, judge some pictures to resemble their referent or to look more like it than other pictures. This is not to be denied. Crucially missing is a satisfactory, non-circular account of the basis of such judgements and a plausible theory of how such perceived resemblance explains the facts about representation. As Black (1972, p. 122) has remarked: "The objection to saying some paintings resemble their subjects is not that they don't, but rather so little is said when only this has been said."[3]

Issue 4

Another prominent attempt to distinguish pictorial representation from other forms of symbolization rests on the idea that *realistic* pictures, at least, afford the same stimuli, the same bundle of light rays, as those projected from the scenes they represent.[4] With other forms of representation there is no like match or agreement with their subject matter. This proposal, too, runs into obstacles. For what matches are to be considered? Trivially, it is possible to get stimulus agreement between as disparate items as the actual Cologne Cathedral and a picture of Tabby. Viewed from different but suitably far distances, they will each cast a single matching point on the retina. But the fact the stimuli match under *these* conditions says nothing about the representational content of the picture.

The match that surrogate theorists have in mind is between the object, as seen from a single vantage point and under particular viewing conditions, and the picture, as seen from its station point (the center of its perspective projection), also under restricted conditions of observation. These observation points and viewing conditions typically will not be the same for the object and picture, and in order to match light rays, both object and picture must be viewed monocularly.[5]

But then the significance of picture/object stimulus agreement thus achieved is not readily apparent. For we hardly ever view a picture monocularly *and* from its station point. We usually view pictures binocularly, from various angles and distances, and in changing illumination. In all these other circumstances there is no match in the arrays of light afforded by the depiction and the depicted.[6]

Issue 5

Discrepancies between the stimulus arrays afforded by pictures and their real-life counterparts pose *the* central theoretical and empirical problem for surrogate theories of picture perception. And the discrepancies are many, as soon as the viewer is allowed to use both eyes and move off the station point. First, the stimulus arrays pictures make available for seeing the spatial layout are comparatively impoverished. Powerful depth cues such as binocular disparity and motion parallax are lacking. In addition, strong cues do become available indicating that the picture surface is itself flat. So surrogate theorists feel obliged to explain how it is possible to *see* pictorial depth given the presence of these "conflicting" cues.

Second, and more problematic, the differences between the stimulus array provided by a picture and its object do not greatly affect what the picture is taken to represent. A picture of the Cologne Cathedral is typically perceived as representing the same view and shape of the building whether the picture is looked at straight on or from a side. The stimuli the picture affords, however, change with such movement. Moreover, these changes do not mimic those the real layout would provide after comparable movement. Thus, it is often said in such circumstances that the stimuli the picture affords "distort" or provide distorted information of the actual layout. But then how is it that we see the rendered objects and space correctly? (Pirenne, 1970; Kubovy, 1986; Rogers, 1995).[7]

THE SYMBOLIC PARADIGM

Put briefly, the major difference between the surrogate and the symbolic paradigms is this. The surrogate paradigm assumes as basic a notion of a "depictive surrogate" and tries to explain pictorial representation in its terms. The symbolic paradigm, in contrast, starts with a quite generic conception of "representation" and attempts to locate the pictorial within this wider framework.

According to the symbolic paradigm, all that is required for representation, in its broadest sense, is that an item purports to refer, be about, stand for, denote, in other words, serve as a *symbol* for something. Thus conceived, the range of representational systems in everyday use is large and diverse. In addition to languages (artificial, as well as natural), and pictures (Egyptian, Haitian, Cubist, as well as realistic), there are: music notation, diagrams, graphs, maps, gestures, mime, models, traffic signals, fabric samples, gauges, and a lot more. Each of these systems can convey accurate or inaccurate information about real and imaginary worlds, and each can and does play a role in guiding behavior and informing the mind.

On the symbolic account, these varied systems of representation are to be distinguished by their structural properties, not by features of the modality or modalities used to access them. Words, for example, can be seen, felt, or heard, but their reference and meaning are independent of the modes of presentation. At the same time, our visual system is clearly involved in processing not only pictures and words, but a host of other representational systems, including music notation, diagrams, graphs, gestures, maps, and also a lot more. What is distinctive of pictorial representation are the syntactic and semantic principles governing its use, not some unique alliance with vision that fixes and determines depictive meaning.[8] Once this alternative paradigm is in place, issues of pictorial representation and picture perception take on a different complexion.

Issue 1

The symbolic paradigm does not presuppose that referential aspects of representation, including that of pictures, are to be explained solely, if at all, in terms of resemblance or other mimetic notions. No one, or example, believes that the link between the words, ' Cologne Cathedral" and the cathedral in Cologne is based on replication or likeness. Although it is necessary to perceive the marks on paper, "Cologne Cathedral", as having the appropriate shape (i.e. spelling), the referential function of the words is determined by causal and communicative features of their use. Similarly, we need not assume that shared properties, or natural resemblance is what determines that a picture refers to or represents the Cologne Cathedral. A photograph of the Cathedral may be distorted, from an unusual angle, or from far enough away that no one would recognize its object. In such circumstances, it is not likeness or other surrogate equivalence that fix the reference of the photograph, but typically the causal story linking the Cathedral to the exposed film (Black, 1972).

Issue 2

Separating, in this way, the referential underpinnings of pictures from claims about replication and substitution allows for a more natural account of *mis*representation and fictive representation. That a picture depicts a cathedral as red and without flying buttresses is compatible with the picture being of or referring to the real Cologne Cathedral. Similarly, there is nothing impossible or very troubling with a picture representing a fictive cathedral, a cathedral like none that actually exists.

Issue 3

The symbolic approach also offers a different perspective on the issue of cue "distortion". Surrogate theorists, we noted, are troubled to explain how a picture can be seen to (re)present Tabby or the Cologne Cathedral accurately, if the picture is not looked at from its center of projection. In various guises, this station point puzzle has become one of the most studied issues in picture perception (Rogers, 1995). The puzzle as customarily understood, however, only has bite for perspective renderings having a center of projection, i.e. "realistic" pictures. It is not clear what the issue even amounts to outside of this circumscribed domain of pictures. And even within the domain of realistic renderings, the bite loses much of its sting, if the symbolic paradigm is adopted.

To see why, consider first the situation with the sentence, "Tabby is in his cage", appearing on a sign. The sentence is about Tabby and offers information about his location. There is nothing perplexing, though, how this sign can be taken to represent these spatial relations when the sign is viewed from the side instead of straight-on. The stimuli and visual experiences of the written sentence may change somewhat as we move about, but, within limits, we perceive the shapes of the letters correctly. Veridical perception of the written sentence, the representation, is what is required to properly assess its content or meaning.

The symbolic paradigm suggests a similar approach to picture perception. A picture of Tabby may depict him lying asleep on the floor of his cage. It makes no difference to the representational content of the picture whether it is viewed straight-on, from a side, forward, or back from its station point. True, the stimuli the picture affords change as we move about, and the perceptual experience of the picture may differ to an extent. Yet, within limits, it is possible to perceive the shapes and relationships within the picture pretty much as they are, or as they need to be seen, in order to comprehend correctly the picture's representational content.

The whole idea of analyzing the "distortion" problem along these lines is obscured when surrogate theorists fall into talking of the represented pictorial space as though it is "part of" or "continuous with" the space occupied by the observer and the picture (Goldstein, 1979, 1987). Then the perceiver is supposed to "see through" the picture locating and orienting objects in the picture's "virtual space", behind or in front of its surface. Accordingly, representation is thought at its best or most correct, if the observer is not even aware he or she is looking at a picture, that is, if the real space and pictorial space meld. Given this understanding of the issue, the enormous attention devoted to *trompe l'oeil* paintings and experiments aimed at fooling the viewer is not surprising, nor is the considerable attention accorded phenomena, such as the perceived orientation shift of Uncle Sam's beckoning "I want you" finger as the viewer moves from side to side.

In contrast, the symbolist has no temptation to collapse depicted space and environmental space. The symbolist, as well, finds the surrogatist's idea of an "ideal" picture misleading. By and large pictures are not viewed under the highly constricted conditions needed to fool an observer, and *trompe l'oeil* paintings are the exception not the rule. Concern, too, about the perceived direction of depicted objects with respect to the observer's real space is minimal, for such matters normally are not germane to determining a picture's representational content. The symbolist, however, does not reject the findings concerning pictorial deceptions and distortions, but rather questions their place in an account of pictorial representation.[9]

Issue 4

Evolutionary worries, alluded to earlier, are given a new twist on the symbolic model. The problem arises most acutely for those troubled by the discrepancies between the stimuli afforded by the depiction and the depicted. The more the difference they find, the harder it has seemed to offer an evolutionary account of how our ability to perceive pictures evolved.

Adopting the symbolic paradigm shifts the locus of this dilemma, along with possible approaches to its resolution. It suggests treating the problem not in isolation but in the context of other forms of representation. There is, for example, much controversy about the correct evolutionary account of the human language capacity. Yet no one supposes that our ability to understand the representational content of written sentences is a deep problem for an evolutionary account of *vision*. Language comprehension depends on mastering the interpretive principles of the system, and the failure of written words to replicate what they represent does not stand in the way. Our ability to understand pictures, especially when this is understood to include the full range of pictorial representations, not just "realistic" renderings, might be construed along similar lines. Appreciation of the representational content of pictures requires having the requisite skills of interpretation. Failure of pictures to duplicate the light bundle or otherwise replicate what they represent need not be an insurmountable obstacle to attaining this competence.

Humans do have an amazing, perhaps species-defining, capacity to comprehend and use many kinds of representational systems. Among the systems humans master are languages, graphs, and music notations, systems whose representational schemes are relatively unconstrained and conventional. Other systems of representation, including diagrams, mime, Egyptian, and "realistic" pictures are more constrained and in this way less arbitrary. Mastering the interpretative principles of these systems would appear the easier task, and hence their development should pose less, not more, of an evolutionary puzzle.[10]

Issue 5

In contrast to the surrogate approach, the symbolic paradigm is not under any pressure to isolate, marginalize, or exclude from study the many styles of depiction ordinarily classified as pictorial. Caricature, cartoons, Egyptian, Haitian, German Expressionist and Cubist pictures fall squarely within the domain. Proponents of the symbolic paradigm *do* recognize that there are differences among these depictive systems. And most emphatically, symbolists do *not* claim that all systems of representation, depictive and non-depictive, operate on the same principles. Diagrams, music notations, graphs, and mime differ from each other, as well as from natural languages and realistic pictures.

How best to delineate the syntactic and semantic principles that serve to distinguish systems of representation does remain a delicate and controversial issue (Goodman, 1968, 1988). In fact, the most appropriate place to draw the boundaries is somewhat obscure. For example, intuitions vary as to the proper placement of maps, Chinese ideographs, and assorted kinds of scale models. Should they be aligned with languages or with pictures, or do they all together, or each individually, constitute distinct categories of representation? Also, proponents of the symbolic paradigm differ in their analyses of the distinction between realistic and non-realistic styles of depiction. Some think the distinction is itself neither fixed nor firm, but more a matter of shifting habits and familiarity, others believe the distinction to be less conventionally drawn (Schwartz, 1974) .

Lack of unanimity in drawing the boundaries among systems does not erase the significant differences in form, acquisition, and use that do exist. The symbolist claim that pictures, like maps, graphs, models, music notation, and language must be "interpreted" does *not* mean that processes of production and comprehension are alike. The considerable variability in syntactic and semantic principles governing these systems gives excellent reason to believe the underlying capacities, mechanisms, and experience needed to master them will not be identical. With maps and music notation, for example, the ability to comprehend one set of representations may transfer to novel cases. This is not so with an arbitrary list of English nouns (Schwartz, 1974; Elgin, 1988).

Failure to appreciate the symbolic paradigm's acceptance of such differences has led some, whose views might otherwise be more congenial, to reject the paradigm prematurely. These critics (e.g. Hochberg, 1972; Kennedy, 1974; Hagen, 1986) are convinced that "reading" pictures is not exactly the same as reading text.[11] They assume the symbolist must deny this, and thus they find the paradigm untenable. This, though, is a misconception that turns the symbolic paradigm upside-down. Symbolists admit, indeed insist, that depictive and linguistic systems differ in structure and principle, and that reading pictures is not identical with reading words. But symbolists find here no basis for rejecting the paradigm. Reading pictures is also "not exactly the same as" perceiving the real three-dimensional environment. This, after all, is one of their primary reasons for rejecting the surrogate thesis.

THE PROPER SUBJECT MATTER

Proponents of the surrogate paradigm tend to sidestep many of these issues, presupposing that the concept of a "realistic" picture is clear enough to do its work. They often assume, as well, that *the* significant break among kinds of representational systems is at the juncture between realistic pictures and all the other forms of description and depiction. In turn, the class of perspective renderings is thought to constitute a distinct set of items to study, a "natural kind" for research in visual theory. This class is also presumed to be the repository of substitute probes for use in other vision experiments. But is there a satisfactory rationale or justification for so orienting the field?

Merely to be told that the class of "realistic" pictures forms a coherent domain, whose members have a lot in common, is not a satisfactory answer. Cubist pictures, German Expressionist pictures, and caricatures each constitute significant, coherent kinds too. Yet accounts of these representations are not taken to fall strictly within the purview of visual science. What, then, underlies the surrogate paradigm's insistence on drawing the boundaries where it does?

I think a main and formative intuition is that understanding realistic pictures is something our *visual* system does, without *cognitive* intrusion. The use and comprehension of other kinds of depictions and descriptions involve more than the visual faculty. Extracting the representational content of cartoons or Egyptian pictures, like comprehending sentences in English, involves cognition or mind. By contrast, it is not necessary to interpret or read realistic pictures. They are simply *seen* to represent what they do.

The pervasiveness of this core intuition should not be mistaken for clarity of formulation. For there is no agreement among vision theorists as to what it means for a process to be mental and no consensus at all where vision leaves off and cognition begins (Schwartz, 1994, 1996). Nor is it obvious how to give empirical significance to the claim that the representational content of other symbol systems cannot be *simply* seen.

At times in these discussions, "cognition" is equated with conscious thought or deliberation, and the perception of realistic pictures is said to be free of such mental intrusion. This conception of cognition, however, cannot serve to underwrite the surrogate theorist's intuition. Comprehending sentences is in this sense as "thoughtless" a process as understanding photographs. Everyday language comprehension is rapid and automatic, not conscious or deliberative. Once having mastered the relevant syntax and semantics, we cannot help but understand a presented sentence.

Another account of cognitive intrusion, prominent in the picture perception literature, appeals to *learning*. Cognitive processes are those depending on prior experience. In order to comprehend a sentence, we must learn the syntactic and semantic features of the language. This is what makes understanding a sentence a cognitive act. The same is said to hold for music notation, maps, diagrams, Egyptian and Cubist pictures. Skill at extracting the representational content of realistic pictures is different. It does not require experience or practice.[12]

This attempt to buttress the core intuition runs into its own difficulties. First, there is much dispute over the proper interpretation of the anthropological and experimental data on untutored picture perception. Second, evidence for untutored comprehension of real pictures must be understood in light of evidence that comprehension of cartoons, caricatures, and other non-paradigm kinds of depiction may not be very different on this score (see Kennedy, 1974; Jones & Hagen, 1980). Third, the identification of learned processes with cognitive processes is, in this context, not well motivated. In contemporary theories of vision, the learned/innate distinction does not pair up with the cognitive/non-cognitive dichotomy that supposedly underlies the core intuition. Many current models of perception claim to involve mental or thought-like processing, yet allow that the processes are not learned but the result of innate structures. Alternatively, Gibsonians, who disparage the claim that ordinary vision involves mental participation, allow that various perceptual skills are learned.

The misgivings I have just expressed with various accounts of the central surrogate intuition, does not mean there is nothing to it (Schwartz, 2001). In this section, I have only pointed out some of the difficulties involved when uncritical appeals to a visual/cognitive dichotomy are used to support the surrogate paradigm.

THE STATE OF RESEARCH

The above account of the competing paradigms, I believe, sheds light on the uneasy state of research in picture perception. A survey of the field would show considerable disagreement over what are the important problems, why they are important, and how they should be studied. Usually in work on vision the symbolic framework is ignored, for the problems it raises are thought to lie outside the scope of a theory of vision.

If understanding a picture is like understanding a sentence, it is not a job for the *visual* scientist to investigate. At the same time, if by severely restricting the viewing conditions, the stimuli from picture and object are made identical, there is nothing really left to explain about *picture* perception per se. Subjects will not know they are viewing a picture, and will see whatever the stimuli would cause him or her to see in an environment unmediated by pictures.

Once outside these observational confines, however, the stimuli afforded by pictures and objects diverge considerably, the more so as motion is allowed. Then there does seem to be separate or distinctively pictorial phenomena for the visual scientist to investigate. Yet, the greater the discrepancy between the stimuli afforded by depiction and depicted, the less sense can be made of the claim that the picture is a true surrogate, in the way the paradigm seems to demand. What's more, with each step beyond the limited domain of realistic pictures, the surrogate idea loses plausibility and application. Hence, the paradigm has difficulty accommodating the vast, full range of representations ordinarily classified as pictures.

A related tension lies in attempts to restrict the domain of pictures to which the paradigm is claimed to apply. The basis for claiming that certain pictures constitute a "natural kind" for visual science gets its life, in part, from the assumption that there is a significant demarcation between the products of vision and the products of mind. The comprehension of written language and non-realistic depictions is regarded as a two-stage process. Vision stops after generating an un-interpreted sentence or depictive display. Higher level cognitive structures and mechanisms take over from there and extract the representational content. In the case of realistic pictures, the story is supposedly different. The representational content is extracted by the visual system. There is no need for a second stage to interpret or read the visual data.

Although this one-stage/two-stage distinction is easy to avow, as previously indicated, it is not so easy to explain or give empirical content. In earlier times, matters may have seemed more straightforward and the intuition more transparent. The sensory domain was identified pretty closely with features thought to correspond to the retinal image, and not much processing was assumed to take place until central, cognitive centers of the brain were reached. Now we know there is selection, supplementation, deletion, and elaboration beginning at the periphery and continuing to the end. The "innocent eye" appears to lose its innocence at the retina. So where is the surrogate theorist to draw an empirically and theoretically well-motivated line?

On the one hand, the more *in*clusively the scope of the visual is conceived, the harder it becomes to exclude the perception of cartoons, Egyptian or Cubist pictures, and perhaps sentences and music notation from its scope. On the other hand, a minimalist understanding of the visual raises opposite problems. A natural minimalist position might be to draw the boundary of the strictly visual at the extraction of "basic" spatial information about the layout. This, however, threatens to collapse the enterprise. To treat a flat surface as a *picture* requires more than seeing it as a two dimensional colored object of a particular size, at a certain distance and direction. It must be perceived not just as an object in the environment like all others, but as a representation, that is a *symbol*. Stripped of this something more, of "interpretation," of "reading," of the accretions of experience and all else that constitutes or contributes to referential and representational significance, a picture cannot readily function to guide behavior, inform cognition, or enhance aesthetic experience.

POSTSCRIPT

Some months into the ZiF project a subgroup formed to discuss picture perception. It seemed, however, we lacked a common base of assumptions about what might be taken for granted, what needed explaining, and how the disputed matters could fruitfully be explored. There was not even a consensus on what made a form of representation a picture, and accordingly, on what items and issues fell within the proper domain of picture perception. This latter point was highlighted by a feature of the everyday work of the ZiF project. In the majority of the experiments presented, pictures, not real objects or environments were employed as stimuli. Yet no one considered this work as being about picture perception. I found this phenomenon not only intriguing but suggestive of an explanation of some of the difficulties facing the picture subgroup. It seemed to me that there were two competing paradigms underpinning conceptions of pictorial representation and picture perception. These paradigms, the surrogate and the symbolic, structure both the problems examined and the solutions entertained.

In this chapter, I have attempted to articulate these two paradigms and spell out implications they each have for the study of picture perception. Although I believe there is something worth while to be obtained from both, most of my efforts are directed at urging vision scientists to explore more sympathetically the symbolic paradigm. I am aware that I have left a lot undefended and unsaid. In subsequent work (Schwartz, 1997 and 2001), I have begun to make amends. In particular, I have tried to dispel the misguided conviction that in treating pictures as symbols the symbolic paradigm ignores the distinctive "visuality" of pictures.

ACKNOWLEDGMENTS

I wish to thank Carl Zuckerman and members of the ZiF picture perception group, especially Heiko Hecht and Dejan Todorovic, for input and comments. My indebtedness to the work of Nelson Goodman should be apparent.

NOTES

1. See Hochberg (1978) and Rogers (1995) for reviews of the literature, as well as reservations about some of the prevalent assumptions guiding the research.
2. As I am using the label "surrogate paradigm", what links its proponents is their rejection of the symbolic paradigm and not their sharing a single model of picture perception. Tellingly, differences among surrogate theorists' models of picture perception are largely a reflection of the differences in their approaches to non-pictorial vision.

3. For an appreciation of just how much work really remains to be done, along with an effort to do some of it, see Hopkins (1995).
4. Note again the limited domain of pictures to which the analysis can apply.
5. Less noticed, surrogate theorists are also reluctant to abide by some of the decisions their own model would seem to sanction. For example, they are uncomfortable admitting that a single pictorial dot can be a true surrogate for the Cologne Cathedral or for Tabby, although when viewed from its station point the light projected from the dot picture may duplicate that coming from the distantly located Cathedral or Tabby.
6. Kubovy (1986) seems to mistake Goodman's related concerns about the implications of observation point variability with an unmade claim that the geometry of the projection of light is arbitrary or conventional.
7. To some in the ZiF group, and others with whom I have subsequently discussed the issue, these differences are thought to make it most difficult to offer an evolutionary account of our capacity to comprehend pictures. Since picture perception could not have had independent survival value, how, they ask, could the ability have evolved, if seeing pictures was not largely the same as seeing anything else.
8. Conflating these matters has caused much mischief in debates over imagery (Schwartz, 1982).
9. I recognize that the sketchiness of my remarks leave much to dispute. I develop these issues in more detail in Schwartz (1997 and 2001).
10. In particular, the mapping scheme of linear perspective may be a relatively simple one to master and perhaps is biologically favored by built-in properties of our visual system.
11. Gibson's rejection of the symbolic paradigm stems, in part, from similar worries (Goodman, 1971). Gibsonians do have other related concerns that I address below.
12. The voluminous research attempting to discover if adults from far removed cultures or infants from our own can comprehend "real," or realistic pictures, attests to the sway of these ideas.

REFERENCES

Arnheim, R. (1969). *Visual thinking*. Berkeley: University of California Press.
Arnheim, R. (1986). Inverted perspective and the axiom of realism. In *New essays on the psychology of art* (pp. 159–85). Berkeley: University of California Press.
Black, M. (1972). How do pictures represent? In *Art, perception, and reality* (pp. 95–129). Baltimore: Johns Hopkins University Press.
Elgin, C. (1988). Confronting novelty. In N. Goodman & C. Elgin (Eds.) *Reconceptions in philosophy and other arts and sciences* (pp.101–120). Indianapolis: Hackett Publishing.
Gibson, J.J. (1971). The information available in pictures. *Leonardo*, **4**, 27–35.
Goldstein, E.B. (1979). Rotation of objects in pictures viewed at an angle: Evidence for different properties of two types of pictorial space. *Journal of Experimental Psychology: Human Perception and Performance*, **5**, 78–87.
Goldstein, E.B. (1987). Spatial layout, orientation relative to the observer, and perceived projection in pictures viewed at an angle. *Journal of Experimental Psychology: Human Perception and Performance*, **13**, 256–266.
Gombrich, E.H. (1961). *Art and illusion*. Princeton: Princeton University Press.
Goodman, N. (1968). *Languages of art*. Indianapolis: Bobbs-Merrill.
Goodman, N. (1971). Professor Gibson's new perspective. *Leonardo*, **4**, 359–360.
Goodman, N. (1988). Representation re-presented. In N. Goodman & C. Elgin (Eds.) *Reconceptions in philosophy, and other arts and sciences* (pp. 121–131). Indianapolis: Hackett Publishing.

Hagen, M. (1986). *Varieties of realism*. Cambridge: Cambridge University Press.

Hochberg, J. (1972). The representation of things and people. In *art, perception, and reality* (pp. 47–94). Baltimore: Johns Hopkins University Press.

Hochberg, J. (1978). Art and perception. In E.C. Carterette & M.P. Friedman (Eds.) *Handbook of perception: Vol. X. Perceptual Ecology* (pp. 225–258). New York: Academic Press.

Hopkins, R. (1995). Explaining depiction. *Philosophical Review*, **104**, 425–455.

Ittelson W. (1996). Visual perception of markings. *Psychonomic Bulletin & Review*, **3**, 171–187.

Jones, R. & Hagen, M. (1980). A perspective on cross-cultural picture perception. In M. Hagen (Ed.) *The perception of pictures* (vol. II, pp. 193–226). New York: Academic Press.

Kennedy, J. (1974). *A psychology of picture perception*. San Francisco: Jossey-Bass.

Kubovy, M. (1986). *The psychology of perspective and Renaissance art*. Cambridge: Cambridge University Press.

Pirenne, M.H. (1970). *Optics painting and photography*. Cambridge: Cambridge University Press.

Rogers, S. (1995). Perceiving pictorial space. In W. Epstein & S. Rogers (Eds.) *Perception of space and motion* (pp. 119–163). New York: Academic Press.

Schwartz, R. (1974). Representation and resemblance. *Philosophical Forum*, **4**, 499–511.

Schwartz, R. (1982). Imagery: There's more to it than meets the eye. In N. Block (Ed.) *Imagery*, (pp. 109–130). Cambridge: MIT Press.

Schwartz, R. (1994). *Vision: Variations on some Berkeleian themes*. Oxford: Blackwell Publishers.

Schwartz, R. (1996). Direct*ed* Perception. *Philosophical Psychology*, **9**, 81–91.

Schwartz, R. (1997). Pictures, puzzles, and paradigms. *Philosophia Scientiae*, **2**, 231–242.

Schwartz, R. (2001). Vision and cognition in picture perception. *Philosophy and Phenomenological Research*, **3**, 707–719.

11

Ecological Optics and the Creative Eye

JAN J. KOENDERINK, ANDREA J. VAN DOORN

Department of Physics,Utrecht University, The Netherlands

LARRY AREND

AMES Research Center, NASA, USA

HEIKO HECHT

Man-Vehicle Laboratory, Massachusetts Institute of Technology, USA

In this chapter we will not so much regard normal everyday visual perception as *pictorial* perception. We will concentrate on the perception of three-dimensional relations (such as the curvature of surfaces) in photographs of natural scenes. In the sense that photographs are *pictures* of scenes, not *actual* scenes, we deal with pictorial perception. However, the "cues" available to the observer on which to base visual judgments pertaining to the scene seen "in the picture" are only a subset (dynamical cues, precise structure of the light field, contextual information and multimodal perceptions are lacking) of the cues available when the observer would be confronted with the actual scene. Apart from this there exists another set of cues that pertains to the perception of the picture as a simultaneous order of luminous dots on a CRT screen (as in the computer representation in many of our experiments) or albedo variations on a piece of paper (as when you look at photographic prints). The observer is at all times aware of the double nature of the picture as a thing and as a carrier of information about some scene. Even when the observer is attending to the pictorial scene it can be shown through psychophysical methods that the subsidiary awareness of the pictorial surface plays a role (Pirenne, 1970). In most cases the perceived three-dimensional structure of the scene is a compromise with the pictorial surface. This can be shown when the relative saliences of the two are varied as when the picture is viewed monocularly or binocularly (Koenderink et al., 1994; Todd et al., 1996).

Perception and the Physical World: Psychological and Philosophical Issues in Perception.
Edited by Dieter Heyer and Rainer Mausfeld. © 2002 John Wiley & Sons, Ltd.

The cues on which the observer may base the perception of the scene can be tightly controlled in pictorial perception. For instance, when the picture is stored as an image file it is exactly described in terms of a matrix (of less than 1000×1000 pixels) of eight bits per pixel, in total about 10^6–10^7 bits of information. In practice this may be compressed (taking redundancies into account) by a factor of 10 or 100 without loss. This is reasonable in the case of vision where the observer sees uniform patches as such, not as a large collection of identical pixels. Thus a full description involves a finite information volume of the order of perhaps 100 kilobytes to a megabyte. This makes the pictorial presentation highly suitable for psychophysical investigation of the perception of scenes.

Of course modern man is continuously confronted with pictorial information, thus the study of pictorial perception is also intrinsically important. However, here we concentrate primarily on the natural cues. This is why we use photographs of real scenes in preference to conventional artefacts such as drawings or computer renderings.

ECOLOGICAL OPTICS

"Ecological Optics" is a term coined by James Gibson (1950) in the early 1950s rather than an actual field of scientific endeavor. In our opinion Gibson was dead right in holding that ecological physics is a prerequisite to the study of vision, that is to say, the study of vision in the sense of the perceptual exploration of the world by optical means, rather than the study of the physiology of the visual system. It is a sad fact that vision research has failed to provide this prolegomena to any study of vision. There isn't even much interest among researchers in the field! Fortunately, a quite different field, namely that of "machine vision" has discovered the hard way that it is not really feasible to design vision systems without a thorough understanding of ecological optics. Since the serious launching of this engineering discipline in the 1980s ecological optics has been developed far beyond what vision scientists achieved since Gibson. We use this type of background extensively in our studies in pictorial perception. For the purposes of the present work we need to deal mainly with two subtopics: natural perspective and the structure of light fields. We present a short, nontechnical introduction in the following sections.

Ecological optics pertains to the possibilities of optical interaction with the environment by perceiving agents. Its limits are determined by the sets of agents (we assume biological organisms of mammal size) and the possible environments (we assume the terrestrial environment). Thus the discipline is not overly (although somewhat) anthropocentrically oriented. *A priori* one envisages two major sources of ecological knowledge. One pertains to *generic* regularities, say the laws of physics. An example would be that things grow in the visual field when the agent approaches them. The other would be a corpus of generic to specific *accidental* facts. Examples would be that elongated large things tend to stand vertically upward or lie (horizontally) on the floor, that things are typically irradiated from above (both generic), another that a spectral shift toward longer wavelengths means shame in a face (specific). Such regularities may be either deterministic or statistical, it doesn't really matter.

NATURAL PERSPECTIVE

"Natural Perspective" is the study of the structure of "visual rays" in the sense of Euclid. The first serious treatise on natural perspective is indeed Euclid's *Optics* (Euclid, 1945). Due to an unfortunate historical accident (the European renaissance's preoccupation with artificial or painter's perspective) Euclid's text has been misinterpreted as a (faulty) treatise on linear perspective. It isn't. Instead, the *Optics* has theorems that relate to the angular configuration of visual rays that connect the eye to objects in the scene. The theorems are more easily interpreted in terms of "optic flow" and indeed, Euclid is perhaps best read as a precursor of Gibson.

In natural perspective one regards the propagation of radiation as taking place by way of "rays", whereas the actual direction of travel is immaterial. It makes no difference to the theory when you let the rays issue forth from the eye as Euclid did or from the source as one thinks reasonable today. Formally then, the theory boils down to the geometry of congruences of straight lines. The eye itself is modeled as a point, the common intersection (or caustic) of certain pencils of straight lines. The straight lines are labeled by fiducial points in the scene, thus you have really to think of thin pencils of rays that give rise to a small mark in the visual field. The actual imaging in the eye is irrelevant to the theory, thus the—even today not infrequent—discussions on the relevance of planar focal planes (of cameras) or the spherical orb of the eye are quite inconsequential.

Perhaps the most important fact of life from the perspective of vision is that the overwhelming majority of objects in our ken are opaque, diffusely scattering solids (we're thinking of rocks, tables, human bodies and so forth). That most objects have indeed diffuse scattering properties is most fortunate, for it means that you can see them from any vantage point as long as the visual rays are not intercepted and there is sufficient radiation around. That most objects are opaque means roughly that you can see only half of their surfaces (the "front") and that objects may occlude each other. In real life objects will often be partly or wholly occluded by other objects and because they also occlude themselves you have to walk around them or rotate them in your hand in order to come to know their whole surface.

That you can only see things by their surfaces has many important consequences (for optical exploration that is). One aspect that is important in the setting of this chapter is that things tend to appear as bounded visual objects in the visual field. The boundaries of visual objects are not boundaries of the objects themselves, in fact you are not able to trace any marks on the surfaces that correspond to the boundaries in the visual field (Koenderink & van Doorn, 1976, 1982; Koenderink, 1984, 1987; Richards et al., 1987). The boundaries—which we will designate "contours"—correspond to the virtual curves on the surfaces that divide these surfaces into areas that are at least potentially visible from the given vantage point and areas that are even potentially invisible from that vantage point. "Potentially" here means only "proving no occluders intervene"; when you change your vantage point potentially invisible areas may become (potentially) visible. These virtual curves on the surfaces of objects we will designate "rims". The contours are the images of the rims, that is to say, the contours correspond to conical surfaces that have the eye as apex and that are tangent to the objects. The generators of these conical surfaces are "limiting visual rays". These conical surfaces serve to unify the concepts of "contour" and "rim" in a single geometrical configuration (Koenderink & van Doorn, 1976, 1982; Koenderink, 1984, 1987; Richards et al., 1987).

Even when the contours are actually visible in the context of natural perspective, an observer may fail to discern them in the visual field. For instance, one may fail to find a marble egg on a marble floor in very diffuse radiation because the "contrast" at the contour fails to reach the visual threshold. Thus, the theory of natural perspective has to be augmented with a theory of light fields, and we will return to that key issue in the next section.

When you consider the cones of limiting visual rays there are a few features that deserve careful attention. First you may concentrate on the cone itself and disregard the rim (which is a curve on the cone mantle). The cone corresponds to a region in the visual field that is the contour. The contour is an *oriented* or one-sided curve in the sense that the object is on one well-determined side, where the "background" is on the other side of the curve. The background may actually be part of the same object (as when an arm is seen in front of the chest) of course. If one considers only those parts of the contour that delimits the object one usually speaks of the "silhouette". The contour of a smooth object (such as a human body) is generically smooth, with the exception of certain singular points, namely transversal crossings of contours and cusps of the contour. At a transversal crossing the silhouette has a discontinuity of direction. This singularity is usually designated "T-junction", because half of one of the contours is occluded and the visual parts form a "T" configuration. The cusp always occurs in the interior of the silhouette. Due to occlusion only one branch of the cusp is visible and one often speaks of an "ending contour". Both T-junctions and ending contours are ubiquitous in the appearance of typical objects (Koenderink & van Doorn, 1982; Koenderink, 1984, 1987). (See Figures 11.1 and 11.2.)

The generic, smooth stretches of contour are typically curved. The curvature can be conveniently measured as the curvature of the trace of the cone of limiting visual rays on a unit sphere centered at its apex, the so called "conical curvature". It is a signed quantity because the contour is a one-sided curve. We use the convention that the contour of a convex body like (the outside of) an egg is positive or *convex*. *Concave* stretches of contour also occur frequently. They do not correspond to concave surface patches (like the inside of an egg shell) as is often—erroneously—assumed, but to saddle-shaped or "hyperbolic" surface patches (both the inside and the outside of an egg shell are known as "elliptic"). The curvature of an ending contour at its limit is necessarily concave because the surface has to be saddle-shaped for the singularity to occur (Koenderink & van Doorn, 1982).

The rim is a curve on the conical surface of limiting visual rays. It cannot be *seen* in pictures, the image reveals only the contour. The rim itself is a twisted space curve and varies in distance to the eye from point to point. Since the rim is not optically specified, there exist *infinities* of objects that might have generated a given (that is to say: *observed*) contour. For instance, a circular contour can be due to any (arbitrary!)

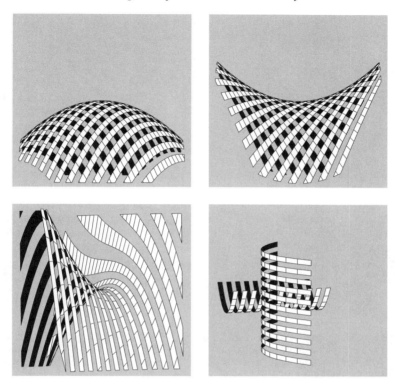

Figure 11.1 *Upper left:* The contour of an elliptic region is convex. *Upper right:* The contour of a hyperbolic region is concave. *Lower left:* An ending contour. The region is hyperbolic and the contour is necessarily concave at the point where it ends. *Lower right:* A "T-junction".

triaxial ellipsoid, but also to many other objects. The only cues available are due to the structure of the contour. Thus you can distinguish convex elliptic from hyperbolic surface patches in the immediate environment of the rim and you can establish a radial order at the T-junctions and ending contours. Therefore the contours fail to *specify* the geometry of the scene, they merely constrain it. In the case of pictorial perception (single vantage point) the ambiguity is mind boggling. Even when a variety of vantage points is admitted much ambiguity remains.

At points of the visual field *inside* of the contour natural perspective maps a local surface patch isomorphically on a patch of the visual field since both manifolds are two dimensional. The local surface patch is geometrically determined by its spatial location and attitude. Two degrees of freedom of the location are immediately specified in the visual field (the direction), the third is not immediately specified (the distance). The attitude is determined by two degrees of freedom (say the conventional slant and tilt), neither of which is immediately specified. Distance can only be inferred conditional on an assumed absolute length (say average human size, in

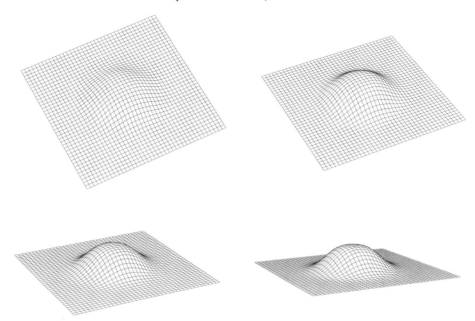

Figure 11.2 Contours for various views of a local elevation on a plane. In the first picture (upper left) there is no contour at all. Notice that the contour—though convex on the summit— is concave near its ending points. For this particular elevation a closed contour never occurs. The shading for this elevation is illustrated in Figure 11.3.

which case you will arrive at non-veridical results for giants or dwarfs). Slant and tilt are generally believed (Gibson, 1966) to be specified by "texture gradient", but this is highly debatable. Examples in text books use planar textures that are isotropic and have a well-defined scale. Real textures in the visual field are due to structures that are not planar (tree bark, foliage, . . .) and have more of a fractal structure (many relevant scales). In a photograph of a natural scene the smallest elements (not pixels, but scene elements) depend on the resolution of the camera, rather than distance or slant. The foreground image granularity may be due to gravel, the background granularity to rocks, but there is hardly a classical "texture gradient". Due to the three-dimensional structures responsible for texture the texture gradients in images of scenes are typically determined by the slant with respect to the source, rather than the slant with respect to the eye. Near a body shadow boundary the texture is strong (high contrast), it peters off as you move toward the regions of more frontal irradiation. (This can be easily observed in pictures of the moon in various phases.)

THE LIGHT FIELD

The "Light Field" is a term introduced by Gershun (1939) in the context of photometry, it has little to do with the "fields" of modern physics (like the electromagnetic fields that underlie optical phenomena). It is a very useful concept in ecological optics because natural scenes are quite different from the typical set ups considered in optics texts. The light field has properties that are germane to professionals like interior decorators, photographers or cinematographers and visual artists. We discuss it summarily, giving only sufficient detail to follow later arguments pertaining to pictorial perception.

Radiometry is the science of "counting light rays". The major entity in radiometry is the *radiance*. The concept applies to *beams*, that are ray congruences with five degrees of (geometrical) freedom: At each location (three degrees of freedom) you have rays in a continuum of directions (the remaining two degrees of freedom). Beams are quite distinct from the *pencils* (often called "beams") that figure in the optics text books. At each location in a pencil one has only rays in a *finite* number (typically just one) of directions. One typical beam is the sun beam. It is *almost* a pencil, for the spread in direction is only half a degree. Yet the spread is important as is evident from the sharpness of shadow edges in natural scenes (half a degree is about a centimeter at one meter). For insects with very low resolving power the sun appears as a star in the sky and the sun beam is practically a pencil. Another typical beam is that of the overcast sky. Here the spread in directions is much larger, about 180°. In such a beam cast shadows are almost absent. Both beams are very "large" in the sense that they are essentially the same if you move by a mile. The beam of a candle flame or a typical light bulb is much smaller in this respect.

The radiance is an important invariant in the sense that it doesn't vary along any ray of the beam. This is something that you know from experience: When you walk toward something (say a white wall) it doesn't change brightness (in the physical sense of course). For beams one doesn't have anything like the "inverse square law of photometry", that law applies strictly to pencils. The best way to understand radiance intuitively is as a huge filing cabinet containing photographs of the scene from all locations taken in all directions. Of most importance is the radiance at your eye. There the location is fixed and the radiance simply describes the brightness (again, in the physical sense) in your visual field in all directions. Thus the radiance describes all possible optical input you might conceivable gather about the scene. It "sews the flesh on the bones" of natural perspective as it were.

Any surface facing a beam is irradiated by it. The number of intercepted rays per unit area is known as the irradiance of the surface. It depends on the radiance of the beam and the attitude of the surface. When a ray hits the surface it interacts with the material of the surface and it may be scattered into another direction, thus changing the radiance. In a natural scene one has an equilibrium distribution of radiation. Although rays ultimately derive from the sun beam, the rays arriving at your eye may have suffered many scattering events in the scene (in the clouds, the air, that tree over there, . . .). The total radiance accounts for all that.

When you look at a surface you perceive a distribution of radiance within its silhouette and a contrast with the radiance distribution of the background at the parts of the contour that make up the silhouette. The distribution of radiance depends on the light field in the absence of the object as well as on the optical properties of the surface of the object (Koenderink & van Doorn, 1980, 1993).

The object interferes with the light field in that it occludes the beams impinging on other objects and in that it adds scattered rays to the light field. When an object is darkened through the interception of a beam by another object one says that the other object "throws a cast shadow" on the former object. The side of the object facing the major source also darkens the other side of the object itself, known as the "attached shadow". Both the cast and the attached shadow may show very diverse properties (sharpness, local texture contrast, . . .) depending on the nature of the light field, the textural properties of the surface and (in the case of the cast shadow) the distance between the objects and the attitude of the receiving surface (Koenderink & van Doorn, 1996; Hattersley, 1979).

When the beam is very diffuse the shadows become *very* indistinct. The point is that the source may be *partly* occluded instead of all or none. When this partial occlusion dominates one speaks of "vignetting", rather than "shadow casting". The irradiance of a surface patch then depends primarily on the extent of source (*the overcast sky (say)*) that irradiates it (Koenderink & van Doorn, 1983, 1996, 1998). In such cases crevasses and depressions in surfaces (space between fingers or toes, arm against the trunk, between legs pressed together, eye sockets and so forth) tend to appear as dark. The degree of darkening is immediately related to that of the vignetting ("how much of the source can be seen" from the surface).

The object—when irradiated—acts as a "secondary source", that is to say, as a cause of irradiance of other surfaces. This effect can be very important radiometrically and it is even more important visually for it causes relations between objects to become visible.

In the literature (Erens et al., 1993a, b, c) one has—almost singularly—focused on the irradiance of "Lambertian" surfaces by "point sources" or "ambient illumination". Lambertian surfaces are diffuse scatterers such that the radiance of the scattered beam is independent of the viewing direction. The generic examples are white washed walls and pieces of white blotting paper: They look equally bright from wherever you are. Most surfaces are not Lambertian, nor are most sources point sources. The deviations are typically *extremely* important quantitatively, even qualitatively. "Ambient illumination" is the supposed summary effect of secundary sources. Ambient illumination is popular in computer graphics to patch up faulty results. For instance, if you use simplified (wrong would be a better term actually) methods, radiances often turn out *negative* in parts of the image (Koenderink & van Doorn, 1996). This is clearly objectionable, since no one understands what "negative light" might mean. One then invokes the beneficial effect of "ambient illumination" to justify the addition of a constant term: Any faulty result can be cured by the addition of something positive that is sufficiently huge. Unfortunately, such hacks even dominate the preparation of stimuli for vision research nowadays with the result that many studies are rendered irrelevant from their very start. Here we avoid such pitfalls by using photographs of real scenes throughout instead of relying on (in all probability physically unrealistic) computer graphics.

The "Lambertian assumption" is dear to the hearts of machine vision people because it ensures that the loci of equal radiance (isophotes in the visual field) are the projections (by natural perspective) of the loci of equal irradiance (on the surfaces).

Figure 11.3 The shading for the local elevation on a plane whose contour was illustrated in Figure 11.2. All views are frontoparallel, that is to say, there is no contour. Notice the ridge of the darkest shaded area. It is a full circle when the source direction is fully frontal, part of a circle (or almost) when the illumination is at some finite elevation. It seems likely that the shading ridges rather than the contours often determine the marks made by draughtsmen.

Thus the isophotes are true *landmarks*. (See Figure 11.3.) For real surfaces this is generally not the case. Then the preimages of the isophotes on the surface *don't* match the loci of equal irradiances. Then "shading" becomes much less of a shape cue than it is for the "Lambertian" surface class. An extreme example would be a purely *specular* surface (like a polished bronze sculpture): There is no shading in the proper sense, the radiance that gets at your eye is a (distorted) image of the environment.

When a surface element receives the full impact of a beam the actual irradiance depends on the attitude of the surface element. When the surface is roughly Lambertian, the radiance scattered to the eye will be proportional to the cosine of the slant of the surface with respect to the "effective source direction" (the "light vector" in Gershun's terminology). This is generally known as "shading". When vignetting, non-Lambertian properties and unaccounted for secundary radiators can be neglected (which will seldom be the case in real life) one may estimate the attitude variation

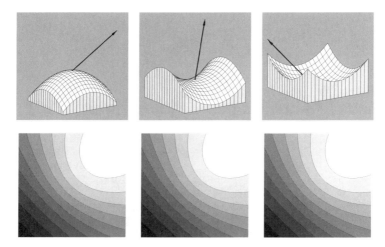

Figure 11.4   Three surfaces which are illuminated from different directions: The shading patterns (seen frontoparallelly) are printed beneath. Notice that—in absence of prior knowledge concerning the source direction—the surfaces cannot be discriminated on the basis of their shading. In this figure the source direction azimuth differs by 180° for the two elliptic surface patches and 90° for the hyperbolic patch as compared to an elliptic patch.

from the radiance distribution. Even in this ideal case there exist infinitely many scenes that could have given rise to the observed radiances. However, these possible scenes form a relatively well-defined family. This is known as "shape from shading".

Even when the Lambertian assumption holds true, the shading is not very informative when the direction of the source is unknown (see Figure 11.4). Figuring out the source direction is much less easy than it is sometimes made out to be (you're not "done" when you know where the sun is) because it is the *rule* rather than the exception that parts of the scene are illuminated by different sources. (For instance, in a portrait in sunlight the shadow side of the face is clearly not illuminated by the sun but by the environment.)

PICTORIAL CUES ASSOCIATED WITH NATURAL PERSPECTIVE AND THE LIGHT FIELD

The pictorial cues typically associated with natural perspective are:

- the contour, its curvature
- T-junctions
- ending contours

and those typically associated with the light field are:

- shading
- shadows
- specularities.

The cues from natural perspective either reveal partial information concerning the nature of local surface patches (on the rim; the generic and the ending contour), or mere depth order (the T-junction). The cues from the light field yield similar information, except for the shading cue, which is special in that it (partly) specifies pictorial relief all over the illuminated areas. This is why the shading cue is generally thought highly of. Reality is different though. Full use of the shading cue assumes knowledge of the (local) source direction and constant albedo of a truly Lambertian surface. Both assumptions are generally unjustified and indeed likely to be false.

AMBIGUITY AND VERIDICALITY

Both the observation of the geometry (the natural perspective) and the light field (the radiance distribution as seen from the vantage point, on visible surfaces: shading and shadow) do not *specify* the scene in front of the observer (or a camera, it makes no difference to the argument). An infinity of *different scenes* could have given rise to the *same image*. Suppose you make a photograph of an actual scene in front of you. Then that scene is the "fiducial solution" to the photograph if one poses the photograph as a riddle. Here the "scene" not only includes the geometry but also the material properties of the objects, the radiant properties of the sources, and so forth. Since you actually pressed the shutter release you are dead sure you know "the" solution. But what about the next guy? Suppose you mail the photograph (as many people do to friends), then can you be sure of the perception the photograph will evoke?

Well, there's no way to be *sure*. Indeed, when you don't know the fiducial scene by revelation (say) there is no way to figure it out. The closest you can get is to delimit the set of all *possible solutions* and be happy in the knowledge that the fiducial scene has to be a member of that set. But this set will include such obvious solutions as a plane with a certain distribution of surface albedo (what else *is* a photographic print anyway?) and such monsters as a starry sky with stars at various distances but close together in direction and of the correct intensity ("pixels" in outer space that are actually objects light years apart). All members of the set have equal claims to being "veridical solutions". However, both the fiducial scene and the plane covered with pigments are eminently *probable* solutions whereas the starry sky is—to say the least—somewhat improbable. "Probable" solutions are scenes that you might feel at home in, that is to say, they fit your ideas of "ecologically valid" scenes. It seems likely to us—although we have no proof—that the set of probable solutions has measure zero in the set of veridical solutions and that it roughly is the "fiducial scene with slop", where the "slop" means various "reasonable" perturbations that would leave the picture invariant (within the observational accuracy). Reasonable means something like displacement in depth with matching magnification, continuous fields of deformations in the depth dimension with matching changes in beam direction, small albedo variations with matching beam inhomogeneities, and so forth.

Suppose we do a psychophysical experiment and suppose we figure out exactly what the perception is like (not something feasible today). Suppose the perception differs from the fiducial solution. Do we have to conclude that such a perception is wrong? The answer is that *we can't say*. The perception might well be a veridical solution (in which case it is certainly a "true" perception) but we are in no position to figure out since there is really no way to delimit the set of veridical solutions. Even to verify that any specific solution is in the veridical set is very hard because it would necessitate an exact computer graphics rendering to compare with the picture. Technology will probably catch up with that, so in the next decade or so we may at least be able to check veridicality in this weak sense. Of course even a true enough perception may differ widely from the fiducial solution! In that sense "true perception" doesn't do one much good.

There are a few things one might address with confidence. For instance when perceptions pertain to physically impossible scenes they must be *wrong*. Likewise, when perceptions are clearly outside the veridical set they must be *wrong*. In some cases it is actually easy to check whether solutions are outside the veridical set, for instance, you cannot photograph a cube (in reasonable ways) such as to look like a sphere.

THE CREATIVE EYE

Since any photograph (no matter how "realistic") does in no way specify any unique *fiducial scene*, but at best an infinity of equally *veridical*, though by no means equally *ecologically probable* scenes, it is of considerable interest to try to specify the structure of the visual *perceptions* of observers of the photograph in as much quantitative detail as possible. As we all know, most observers immediately arrive at clear cut perceptions when confronted with photographs of an "obvious" type. Indeed, such photographs are often used to "document" a scene with a cheerful ignorance of the veridicality problem. From a scientific perspective this is highly remarkable. Reasons have to be sought in the application of expertise in ecological optics of both the generic and the accidental kind. Presently we understand neither the ecological optics, nor the physiological or psychological processes involved.

Unfortunately, there are currently no psychophysical techniques that enable one to measure perceptions of scenes in any great quantitative detail. There are several reasons for this. One is that "perceptions" are very volatile entities indeed. They may be more or less articulated depending upon various conditions, one being the *psychophysical procedure* itself. Depending on the method of operationalization one has to expect a variety of results. Such results may even seem incompatible if one approaches them in a naive manner. For instance, suppose we have two methods A and B (say) to "measure property Ξ (say) of perception" and suppose the results Ξ_A and Ξ_B turn out to be different: Does one have a problem? In our opinion not, because there is no reason to expect $\Xi_A = \Xi_B$ given the difference in operationalization

($A \neq B$). There is indeed no reason to expect equality of a distance measured via radar or pacing unless when one is in possession of a theory that connects both. In psychophysics one generally lacks such connecting theories. Does this mean we are in a hopeless predicament? By no means, it means that one should not rely on any one method, but should apply all tools at one's disposal and compare them with an open mind. Many unfortunate debates in the literature are indeed due to such apparent contradictions as $\Xi \neq \Xi$ by failing to see that $\Xi_A \neq \Xi_B$ because $A \neq B$, usually because both *nominally* measure "the same" entity. In this chapter we will apply two simple psychophysical methods that will be described summarily in the next sections. They have been compared with various alternative methods in the past.

The general problem area we address is that of contour or shading cues to surface shape and their interaction. In pictorial perception these (when taken in a sufficiently broad sense) are the major cues for photographs of single objects against simple backgrounds (say a person against a wall). Contour and shading are intricately interwoven. For instance, normally a contour only becomes visible through tonal contrast, that is to say, through shading. Contours have to be distinguished from (either attached or cast) shadow boundaries (again due to shading). In order to interpret shading one needs a notion of the direction of the light vector. When the source is not visible in the photograph one has to infer this direction from the shading. Such a chicken and egg circle can be broken when one has an independent cue to surface orientation at some locations in the picture: Here the contour comes in since it specifies the local surface attitude at the rim.

We start the investigation with the (summary) discussion of a few well-known facts of visual perception pertaining to contour and shading.

A contour becomes visible through radiance contrast with the background. In real life this contrast may have either polarity, it may even vanish (with a "dipolar" contrast it vanishes at at least two places). In many cases a large part of the contour may be invisible, either through occlusion or vanishing contrast. Typically, observers are not a whit abashed in such situations, perhaps even more remarkable, they may not even notice. One sometimes says that the contour is "amodally completed". But such an assumption clearly stands in need of empirical verification. For instance, do observers actually know where the amodally completed contour is? Does it depend on the mode of operationalization? These are quite important questions in view of the fact that "lost contours" are *the rule*, rather than the exception and that painters and draughtsmen apply the lost contour frequently to increase the "realism" of their renderings.

An object that appears as a silhouette against a contrasting (mostly uniform) background tends to appear quite *flat*. Examples are distant mountains or clouds, persons against the light (in a door opening seen from the inside), objects emerging from the fog, and so forth. More generally, a strong, unipolar contrast with the background tends to flatten an object perceptually, the visual object assumes a silhouette-like appearance. Photographers use a "wrap around illumination" (dipolar contrast) or a partially lost contour to make objects look more "solid". When the rendering approaches the silhouette, objects approach a "flat cardboard cut out" look.

"Shape from shading" is very ambiguous in the absence of contours. One is easily misled in interpreting surface articulations in terms of smudges and vice versa. This can often be seen in whitewashed walls or not quite flat paper. When "shape from shading" was approached psychophysically one tried to get as "clean" a stimulus as possible: All other cues—including "shape from contour"—had to be removed. The result turned out to be that shape from shading wasn't operational any more (Erens et al., 1993a, b, c). However, the conclusion that "shading is only a weak cue" is overly hasty. In a full cue situation a variation of the shading cue does lead to a change of percept (Koenderink et al., 1996a, b; Koenderink, 1997, 1998). Apparently shading needs contour and contour needs shading. Isolating such cues leads to sterile results.

In many cases it is quite unclear whether a certain mark inside the silhouette is a contour or a *ridge of darkness* due to shading. Try to locate the exact ending of an "ending contour": You can't. In many cases the lines draughtmen make to indicate surface relief within the silhouette may stand equally well for shadow-like ridges as for (inner) contours. This is indeed to be expected because it is quite probable that a contour is also a light or dark ridge in the image.

STIMULI

We prepared a number of stimuli in such a way that

- all pictures are geometrically identical in the sense that they are photographs of the same object from the same vantage point; thus all contour and geometrical landmarks such as local pits or edges coincide perfectly;
- some pictures are also photometrically identical, except for the tone of the background;
- in some pictures the left side of the contour of the object is lost, in others the right side, in yet others both sides, either through vanishing contrast with the background, or due to occlusion by a second object;
- in some pictures the *silhouette* is the major aspect.

Because we wanted generic, smooth objects of a non-trivial kind we used (fiberglass) torsos of the kind sold for shop windows to display clothes. The main torso we used had the classical posture (*déhanchement*) with a weight bearing and a "playing" leg that effectively removed much of the natural bilateral symmetry. The surface was quite smooth, thus avoiding local landmarks and texture gradients. We selected a female torso in order to avoid the deep V-grooves between muscle groups that provided obvious landmarks in the male exemplars that were also on sale.

The objects were photographed in a studio with black painted walls (an absolute requirement if the light field is to be controlled). Backgrounds could be large papers of various gray levels. We implemented an independent illumination of background and objects, thus the radiance of the background could also be controlled optically.

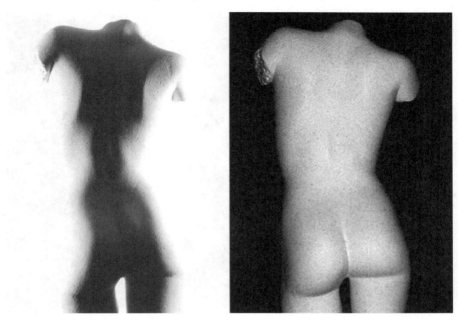

Figure 11.5 The first stimulus pair. *Left:* Contours at both sides lost in the light background. *Right:* Contours at both sides lost in the dark background (one believes to see contours here, but they really run in the dark area).

Variable light sources at either side enabled the production of horizontal irradiance gradients in the background. For the illumination of the main object we used a variety of sources, from very diffuse to collimated. During the photo session the luminances of various points in the scene were carefully controlled and monitored via a one degree spot meter device.

Photographs were made with a Leica equipped with 90 mm optics. The 35 mm monochrome film was processed under carefully controlled conditions. Negatives were scanned into computer images and cropped to exactly the same view with pixel accuracy. The stimuli were presented on a calibrated monitor and viewed in a semidark room.

The stimuli were paired for the purposes of our experiments (see Figures 11.5–11.10). The observers were confronted with these pairs in such a sequence that gradually more and more of the true nature of the surface was revealed. Thus in the first presentation the contours were lacking on both sides, in the final presentation the contour was visible throughout and the observers had seen pictures with a revealing shading pattern. Such a technique is indeed required because observers tend to use *all* the available data, not simply the pictorial cues in the actual image, but also any prior information at their disposal. Since our observers were fully naive, the sequence of the stimuli is a relevant datum: It is necessary to know how much was already

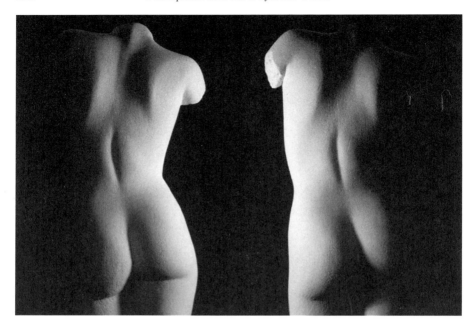

Figure 11.6   The second stimulus pair. *Left:* Left-side contour lost in the dark background. *Right:* Right-side contour lost in the dark background.

"disclosed" to the observers in judging their performance on a given stimulus. The importance should become obvious from a study of Figure 11.5. If this is all one has it is obviously quite hard to arrive at a clear concept of the shape.

PSYCHOPHYSICAL METHODS

We used two quite distinct psychophysical methods. One method allowed us to *compare two distinct pictures* with respect to the apparent location of visible features of the scene, the other allowed us to probe the local apparent surface attitude at various locations in the scene.

Simultaneous Comparison of Corresponding Locations

This is a method we have used before (Koenderink et al., 1997). The idea is very simple (Figure 11.11): Suppose the observer looks at a pair of photographs that are obviously of the "same scene" (say St. Peter's square in Rome) but may otherwise be quite different (taken from different positions, showing changes in the scene, taken in different lighting situations, and so forth). A dot is placed on one photograph: The observer localizes the dot *in the scene*. The observer is then asked to place a dot on the other photograph at such a place that it appears at the corresponding position *in the scene*. This is actually very natural and observers have no problems with it: When

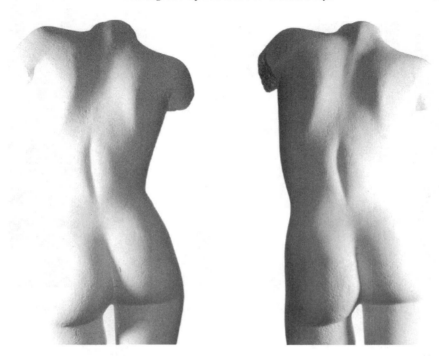

Figure 11.7   The third stimulus pair. *Left:* Left-side contour lost in the light background. *Right:* Right-side contour lost in the light background.

you look at a pile of photographs of the same scene with a friend it is quite natural to point out "the same" feature or object in quite different shots.

Yet it remains a mystery (scientifically that is, intuitively it couldn't be more obvious) *how* people are able to do this. Most certainly, it cannot be done on the basis of local image structure for this can be quite different. In order to do the task one needs an interpretation of the scene, that is to say, the correspondence is found in the scene, not in the picture (in the sense of a simultaneous distribution of pigments in the plane). This makes this apparently very simple method a very powerful one indeed: One immediately addresses "pictorial space" in such a way as to obtain an easily interpretable quantitative datum (the coordinates in the picture plane which can easily be measured).

We have found that observers can accurately perform the task (this has been checked in cases the fiducial scene was known to the experimenter) even when the object has been rotated between photographs (Koenderink et al., 1997). In our present case the difference is only of a photometric nature though. In the latter case observers might conceivably relate to the picture frame and solve the task trivially. However, it turns out they don't. Apparently it seems more natural to relate to pictorial space than to the picture frame.

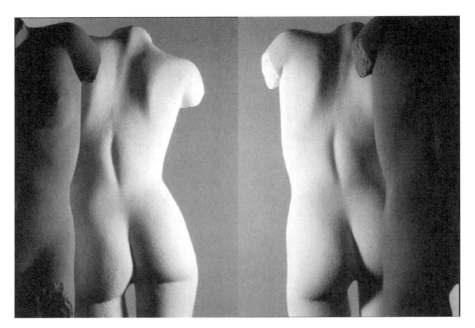

Figure 11.8 The fourth stimulus pair. *Left:* Left-side contour occluded. *Right:* Right-side contour occluded.

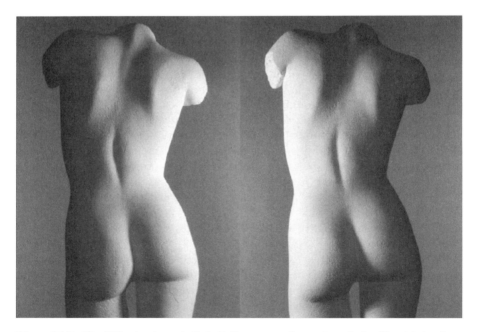

Figure 11.9 The fifth stimulus pair. *Left:* Full contours of opposite polarity, illumination from the right. *Right:* Full contours of opposite polarity, illumination from the left.

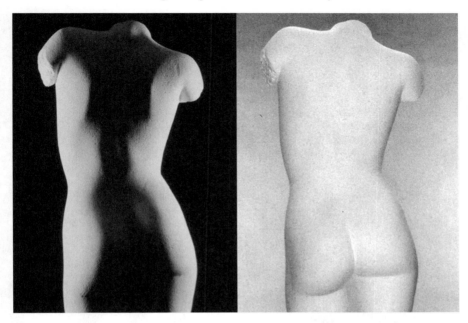

Figure 11.10   The sixth stimulus pair. *Left:* Full contours of same polarity, background dark. *Right:* Full contours of same polarity, background light.

Probing of Local Surface Attitude

There is a very simple, general procedure to obtain a measure of things: Compare them to a standard. The idea is that even though you may not be able to describe any particular thing in quantitative detail, it tends to be easy to judge whether two things are the same or whether they "match up" in some dimension. The classical example is *length*. You apply a yardstick to the object and judge whether specific marks on the yardstick match up with certain features (the extremities say) of the object. Even people that appear to have no trustworthy sense of length can come up with dependable lengths measurements this way. The only expertise needed is the ability to judge a "fit" (notice the coincidence of a needle with a mark on a dial say), it is by no means required that you know what you're doing. This method is easily transferred to measurement in pictorial space. In order to measure some property you design a suitable "gauge figure" (the "yardstick" or "template") and you apply the image of the gauge figure to the image of the scene (this can be done using a transparent overlay for instance). Then you have your observer judge the *fit in pictorial space*. There is no practical problem here even if no one knows how to locate "pictorial space" (it has to be "in the mind" somewhere), for all operations—except for the judgment—are performed in the picture which is simply a physical thing.

Local *surface attitude* is a two parameter entity, in the conventional parameterization one specifies two angles, the "slant" and the "tilt". The slant is the angle

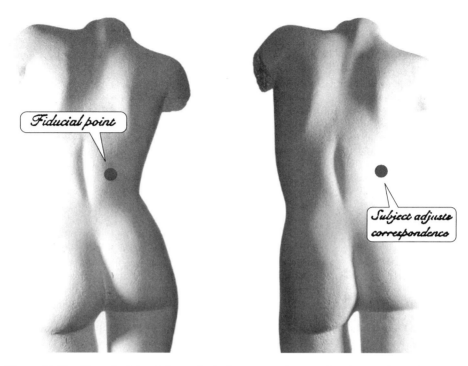

Figure 11.11 The principle of the method of correspondences: The observer is confronted with a pair of pictures. On one picture a mark singles out some point. The task of the observer is to place a mark on the other picture such as to match the location of the formal mark in pictorial space.

subtended by the surface normal and the visual direction. It takes values in the range from zero (frontoparallel attitude) to 90° (surface seen "edge on", that is to say: at the contour). The tilt is the direction of the depth gradient in the visual field. It needs to be measured from a fiducial direction (e.g., from the vertical, clockwise) and is periodic with a period of 360°.

Any flat object can be used as a gauge figure, we use a circular disk (Figure 11.12) with a pin sticking out in the normal direction (the pin resolves the "depth reversal" ambiguity). The gauge figure is rendered in red wire frame and superimposed upon the gray tone photograph. The observer is given active control over the attitude of the gauge figure and is supposed to orient it such that the circular disk looks like it lies flat upon the surface of the pictorial object.

By repeating attitude probing for many points we easily collect sufficient information to attempt the construction of a smooth (as smooth as possible), curved surface in three-dimensional space that has the measured attitudes at the sample points. Such a surface is the (operationally defined) quantitative measure of "pictorial relief" (Koenderink et al., 1992, 1994, 1995, 1996a, b, c; Koenderink & van Doorn, 1995; Todd et al., 1996; Koenderink, 1997, 1998). (See Figures 11.13 and 11.14.)

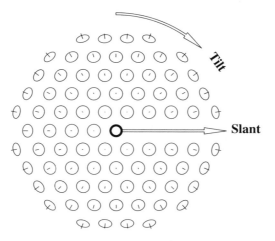

Figure 11.12 The gauge figure used to probe surface attitude (slant and tilt). In this figure we have drawn a large number of gauge figures of various slants and tilts. In an experiment only one gauge figure is visible at any time. The observer has control over the slant and tilt of the gauge figure and adjusts it such as to "fit" the attitude of the local pictorial relief.

LOCATION OF THE PERCEIVED CONTOUR

In a first experiment we studied the location of amodal contours in photographs of real scenes. Contours could be "lost" due to occlusion or due to vanishing contrast with the background. In the latter case the lost contour can be located either in the lights or in the darks. We studied cases in which the contour either at one side, or at both sides was lost. We use the method of correspondences, which involves *pairs* of pictures. In case the contour on the left side in the first and the right side of the second picture are lost the two pictures do not hold any contour in common. In such cases the correspondences must be due to either "completion" of the lost contour or to the shading (which is typically different for the two pictures). We always found correspondences for many fiducial points, thus we obtain a *field* of displacements which might be expected to yield some insights in the possible influence of the "amodally completed" lost contours.

In the leftmost two subfigures of Figure 11.15 we show the triangulation on the left and the results for observer GM on the first stimulus pair (Figure 11.5) as second from the left. The triangulation was the same in all our experiments. Indeed, it need not be changed because all pictures are geometrically identical as far as the contours are involved. The triangulation is never revealed to the observers, but it is used in our experiments to select the locations of the fiducial marks in the correspondence task and the gauge figure in the attitude task. In the correspondence task the fiducial mark always coincides with one of the vertices of the triangulation. During the course of an experiment we visit all vertices several times, in randomized order. The observers are not even aware of the regular triangulation that underlies the fiducial marker positions because the edge length of the triangulation is quite small: This is indeed

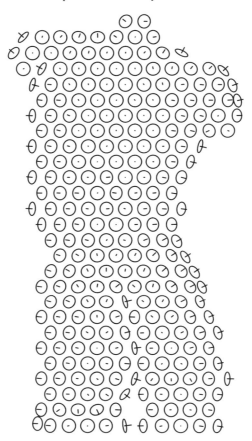

Figure 11.13   Average gauge figure settings for a specific experiment. Notice that only a single gauge figure is visible at any time in the course of the experiment! This figure is a compilation of results obtained in the course of a session (about an hour.) The ellipses can be interpreted as the so called "Tissot indicatrices" of differential geometry that indicate the attitudes of the tangent planes.

obvious from the results, often the deviations exceed an edge length. The underlying triangulation is very useful in the analysis of the results, we obtain a discretized sample of a continuous field of deformations in which the discretization is conveniently fine.

In the result of observer GM on the first stimulus pair (Figure 11.15, second from the left) we notice that the deformation field has both random and systematic components. Because we visit each vertex of the triangulation several times in the course of the experiment we have a good estimate of the statistical scatter and we know that the apparent irregularities are indeed "noise". In this case there is still a rather obvious systematic pattern left: The resulting triangulation is quite severely "shrunk" in the horizontal direction. It is clear that the observer didn't know how to pinpoint the contours, there is certainly no sign of "amodal completion" here. We found this result

Figure 11.14 A profile of a smooth approximation to the tangent plane samples shown in Figure 11.13. The horizontal direction coincides with the "depth dimension" for the observer: We have turned the picture plane into a threedimensional "pictorial surface".

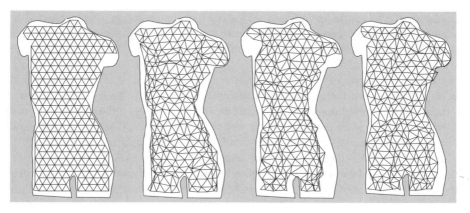

Figure 11.15 *Left:* The triangulation used to define the fiducial points; *Second from the left:* Observer GM, first stimulus pair (Figure 11.5); *Third from the left:* Observer HH, second stimulus pair (Figure 11.6); *Right:* Observer AD, second stimulus pair (Figure 11.6).

for all four observers. Given the structure of the stimuli this result is not surprising. In the photograph on the left in Figure 11.5 one sees a dark core whereas both the left- and right-hand contours are lost against the light background. The dark core derives from an illumination from both sides by sources that are located slightly behind the object. Such a "core lighting" is not infrequently used by professional (portrait and model) photographers. Although the picture looks weird one clearly gains a reasonable impression of the shape of the object. The right-side photograph has been taken with a frontal illumination by a small source against a dark background. The contours at both sides are lost against the dark. Such an illumination is frequently used to de-emphasize the horizontal extension of corpulent people. In neither picture does one have a clear impression of the silhouette, although the overall impression of the shape seems OK. But apparently observers have little idea of the actual location of the contours.

The two subfigures on the right-hand side of Figure 11.15 are the results for the second stimulus pair for the observers HH (third from the left) and AD (far right). In this stimulus pair (Figure 11.6) both photographs look solid and yield an excellent impression of the shape, but in the left-side picture the contour on the left and in the right-side picture the contour on the right is lost against the dark background. Notice that both photographs look very natural (this type of lighting is quite common in photography) and neither one looks "incomplete": Observers don't "miss" the lost contour. In this case there is no contour available that can be seen on *both* pictures and thus the correspondence cannot be obtained by using such a common contour as a convenient anchor. The observers have to use the interior features of the shading to arrive at the correspondences. A comparison of the results of these observers reveals the fact that perceptions are rather idiosyncratic in such cases and that large systematic deviations occur. Observer AD locates the right-side contour in the background for the upper side of the figure (above the waist) and in the interior at the lower side (below the waist), whereas observer HH locates the right-hand contour inside the interior throughout. The results of observer AD show that the "solution" is constructed in a piecewise manner, and not for the figure as a whole. This means that observers might well differ in their judgment of the *pose* of the figure. This is an effect that we have noticed before, often observers show idiosyncratic rotations of the major body parts (rotations of the thorax, arms or legs) (Koenderink et al., 1996c; Todd et al., 1996). Again, there is no indication whatsoever of any "amodal completion". The observers simply don't know how to locate the contours although they are not particularly worried by that in the sense that no one complains that the pictures show "incomplete" objects, or that the correspondence task is an unreasonable one.

In the case of the third stimulus pair (Figure 11.7) we find results very much like those in the case of the second pair (Figure 11.6). Indeed, the only difference between these stimuli is that in the case of the third pair the contours are lost against a light background, whereas in the case of the second pair the same contours are lost against a dark background. The internal details due to shading are similar.

In Figure 11.16 we show the field of displacements generated by observer GM for the fourth (Figure 11.8) and fifth (Figure 11.9) stimulus pairs. We use this illustration to demonstrate the fact that in the results for the fourth pair there exist large deviations,

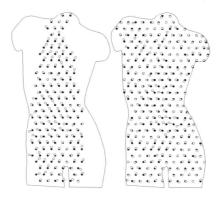

Figure 11.16   *Left:* Observer GM, fourth stimulus pair (Figure 11.8); *Right:* Observer GM, fifth stimulus pair (Figure 11.9).

both in the horizontal and in the vertical directions, whereas for the fifth pair the deformations are relatively minor. In the case of the fourth stimulus pair the left-side picture has its left contour occluded, whereas the right picture has its right contour occluded. The internal detail is due to shading from opposite sides, thus the observers can use neither a common contour, nor common shading features as "landmarks". That they do use some kind of landmarks is clear from the fact that they commit large errors in the vertical. In fact, they would do better on an empty picture since the correspondence is necessarily at the same height in the picture frame. Apparently the observers find it hard to indicate corresponding locations in this case. This need not surprise us since (when one is not permitted to solve the task in a trivial manner, say by using the picture frame as a reference) one has to use features of pictorial relief as landmarks. In the case of the fifth stimulus pair the shading is opposite, but all contours are visible. This is the type of lighting known as "wrap around" by photographers: The figure is illuminated from the side by a diffuse source (no areas hidden in the attached shadow) and the background has a medium gray tone leading to opposite contrast edges at the two sides (light figure dark ground or dark figure light ground). This type of lighting is generally agreed upon to lead to the best impression of solid shape. Thus the good performance of the observers in this case may be due to the availability of common contours as well as on the improved perception of pictorial relief. The results of the correspondence task for the fifth stimulus pair is indeed the best one ever encounters in this paradigm. Near the contours the observers are near to perfect, in the interior of the silhouette the performance depends on the nature of the pictorial relief. Ambiguities are indeed due to the nature of the relief, for instance, the correspondences on a spherical surface would be totally ambiguous, on a cylindrical surface they would be ambiguous in the direction of the cylinder axis, and so forth. In cases like this the magnitude of the error is distributed over the picture in a similar way for all observers.

The sixth stimulus pair (Figure 11.10) is similar to the first one (Figure 11.5), except for the tone of the background. However, this difference is a crucial one in

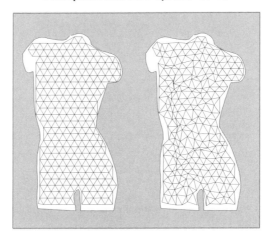

Figure 11.17   Observer HH, sixth stimulus pair (Figure 11.10).

that both contours are strongly accentuated (most certainly "found"), rather than hidden. These are the lighting conditions that photographers use when they want to emphasize the outline of a shape and de-emphasize its interior. These methods are preferred over true silhouettes (which are rarely used by professional photographers) because they do show interior detail and thus appear much more lively than true silhouettes which tend to look rather dull. In the case of core lighting the edges are light against a dark background, in the case of the frontal illumination they are dark against a light background (this is called the "limb effect"). Clearly the interior details yield no landmarks that might be used in the correspondence task, here we can be almost sure that the observers will solve the task by anchoring on the (common) contours. This is indeed very clear from an analysis of the deformation field (shown for observer HH in Figure 11.17): Whereas the deviations are minor near the edges we see a "wrinkle" in the interior. Apparently the observer propagated inwards from both sides and failed to meet up in a synchronized way! This is what we find for all four observers. There always exists an elongated, vertical strip of either elongated horizontal triangulation edges (gap left in the middle) or of collapsed horizontal triangulation edges (collision in the middle). In fact, an analysis of the shrinkage or expansion in the horizontal direction yields a very direct insight in the relation of the deviations to the (predominantly vertical) contours. We present this analysis for all observers and stimuli (Figures 11.18–11.23).

In the case of the first and second stimulus pairs we see two types of major effect. One effect is a vertical banding of shrinkage or expansion (which type seems essentially arbitrary). This is very clear for observers GM, HH and LA in the case of the first stimulus pair and observers HH and LA in the case of the second stimulus pair. The other effect is that of a clear piecewise "solution". This is seen in the case of observer AD for the first stimulus pair and observers AD and GM in the case of

Stimulus #1

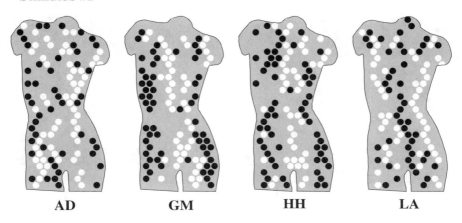

| AD | GM | HH | LA |

Figure 11.18   First stimulus pair (Figure 11.5).

the second stimulus pair. In these cases the vertical banding can still be discerned, but phase shifts occur between parts (for instance thorax and pelvic region) of the figure.

Quite similar effects are seen in the case of the third and fourth stimulus pairs, and even in the case of the fifth where almost full information (both from the contours and the shading) is available to the observers.

In the case of the sixth stimulus pair we obtain almost purely vertical banding. This is understandable since effectively only contour information is available to the observers. There is still some indication of regional effects though.

Stimulus #2

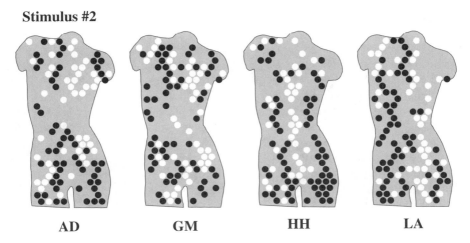

| AD | GM | HH | LA |

Figure 11.19   Second stimulus pair (Figure 11.6).

Stimulus #3

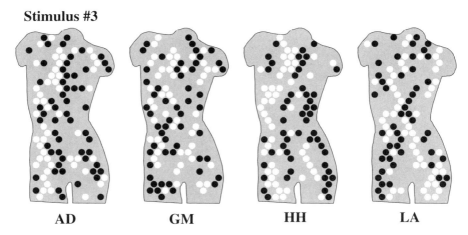

AD   GM   HH   LA

Figure 11.20   Third stimulus pair (Figure 11.7).

The results of the correspondence task have revealed a number of important observations:

* There is no indication whatsoever that contours are "amodally completed". Observers obviously have difficulty to locate lost contours.
* Observers use shading to do the correspondence task, even when the gray tones proper cannot be used as landmarks. Observers clearly apply some variety of "shape from shading".
* When shading is not available or obviously very ambiguous, the correspondence task is "solved" by propagating inwards from the contours. Large errors may

Stimulus #4

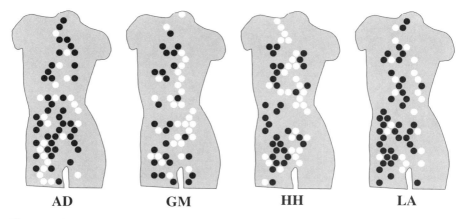

AD   GM   HH   LA

Figure 11.21   Fourth stimulus pair (Figure 11.8).

Stimulus #5

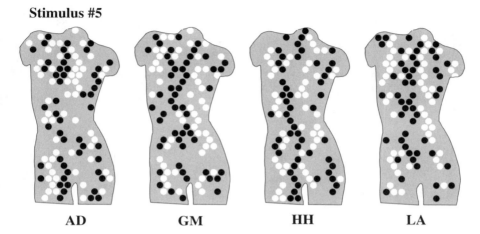

| AD | GM | HH | LA |

Figure 11.22 Fifth stimulus pair (Figure 11.9).

accumulate in the interior. In such cases observers effectively treat the picture as a silhouette.

PERCEIVED SHAPE

We studied "perceived shape", or "pictorial relief", through the gauge figure task, sampling surface attitudes at many points. It seems *a priori* likely that the pictorial relief will be influenced by both the contours (lost or found) and the shading. Since the fiducial solution is the same for all pictures, we can do an immediate comparison. In this study we used one new and two of the original observers (namely observers AD and GM).

Stimulus #6

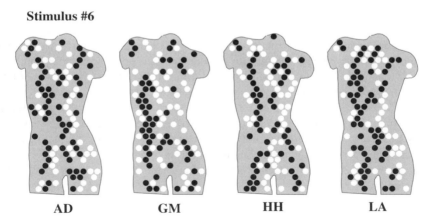

| AD | GM | HH | LA |

Figure 11.23 Sixth stimulus pair (Figure 11.10).

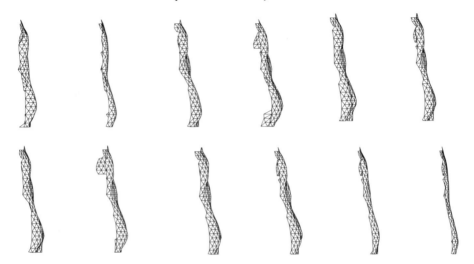

Figure 11.24   Profiles of the pictorial relief (as determined by way of the gauge figure task) for observer AD. The stimuli are ordered from top left to bottom right and are first pair left and right, and so forth till sixth pair left and right. Notice that the horizontal direction is the depth dimension for the observer. The profiles are shown via a rendering of the triangulation (shown earlier) in three dimensions.

In Figure 11.24 we present profile views of the pictorial reliefs for all pictures for the observer AD. Notice that the pictorial relief may differ appreciably from picture to picture, even though all pictures are geometrically identical and represent one and the same fiducial geometrical configuration. The conclusion has to be that these pictorial reliefs are not fiducial solutions. There is no way to find out whether they represent "true" or "false" perceptions. The differences in pictorial relief are apparently due to the differences in contour (lost or found) and/or shading information.

In Figure 11.25 we present scatterplots of the pictorial depths for all stimulus pairs. The data are of observer AD. In each subfigure the pictorial depths for all vertices of the triangulation obtained for one picture are plotted against those for the other pictures. Since the pictorial depths are only determined up to an arbitrary additive constant, the actual values are unimportant. All scales are the same in these plots, thus perfect correlation would show up as a line with unit slope.

It is immediately apparent that enormous differences exist. For the pairs where both pictures are rich in cues (contours and shading) the correlations are very high (R squares over 95%, often over 99%), but when one or both of the pictures only contains tenuous cues the correlations may drop precipitously (R squares down to values as low as 60%). Moreover, one sees that the scatterplots that are only somewhat correlated fail to have a random character. In most cases one sees a fibrous structure. This is illustrated in somewhat better detail in Figure 11.26.

Indeed, when you isolate such fibers (Figure 11.26) you find nice linear correlations, but even more interesting, when you trace the points that make up such a fiber, they

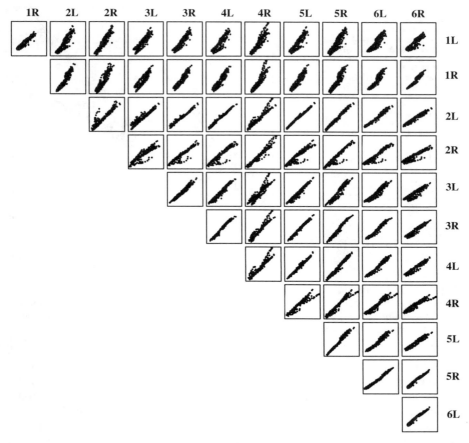

Figure 11.25 Scatter plots for the pictorial depths for observer AD. The results of each picture are plotted against all others. All scales are identical.

turn out to fill out contiguous areas. Such areas typically coincide with body parts that tend to move as roughly piecewise rigid with respect to other parts (examples are the thorax, the pelvic girdle, buttocks, shoulders, legs).

THE INFLUENCE OF SHADING AND LOST OR FOUND CONTOUR ON PICTORIAL RELIEF

So what are our final conclusions? Clearly this type of research is unlikely to lead to fast, easy answers. Many aspects must remain undecided. For instance, we are in no position to figure out whether the perceptions of the observers were veridical or simply false. What is clear is that they rarely coincide with the fiducial solution as was indeed to be expected.

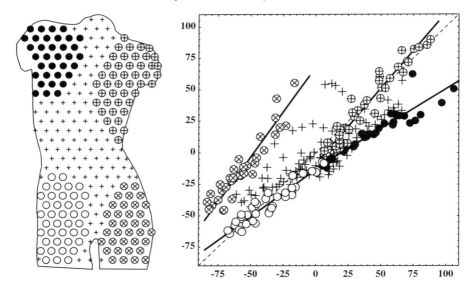

Figure 11.26   *Left:* The vertices have been marked with the same symbols as used in the scatterplot on the right. *Right:* Scatterplot of pictorial depths for subjects AD and GM for the case of stimulus three-right. The drawn lines indicate the linear regressions for the subgroups of vertices indicated in the left-hand map. The dashed line indicates the identity.

We have found no compelling reasons to believe that our observers "amodally complete" lost contours. We have found much reason to believe that contours play a very important role in the perception of pictorial relief, even in case where strong shading cues are available. In the case of the correspondence task we find evidence of propagating from the contours, even in cases where excellent shading information is available. In the latter cases the contour influence is much diminished as compared to cases where the shading cues are really poor, in such cases the relief seems predominantly due to the contours.

When there is a good shading pattern there are various reasons why the contours might still be important. A simple reason might be that the two cues contribute complementary information that is simply pooled. But it might also be the case that the shading can only be really effective when the contour information is present. Indeed, we have found indications that the shading cue is somehow dependent on the contour information before (Erens et al., 1993a, b, c; Koenderink et al., 1996a, b).

The pictorial cues leave the observers much freedom because infinitely many different perceptions can be true enough in the sense that physically possible scenes exist that would have led to the picture. The pictorial reliefs measured in these experiments show that only a tiny fraction of possible interpretations actually occurs in perception. The reasons are clear enough: Observers don't go for veridical interpretations, but for ecologically probable ones. This puts a strong constraint on the acceptable interpretations, and it seems that perceptions are constrained in this way. Such constraints must be due to experience, either ontogenetically or phylogenetically.

Although one would expect the ecological validity constraints to act towards the pruning of idiosyncrasies, we do see clear signs of such interindividual differences in pictorial relief, sometimes quite significantly so. This means that the "creative eye" plays an important role in pictorial perception. It is by no means the case that observers, when looking at the same photographic documentation of even a simple scene see quantitatively, or even qualitatively similar structures. We have clearcut evidence for significant differences in the perceptions of various observers in even the geometrical relations of parts of a pictorial scene with respect to each other.

It would appear that the perceptions are organized quilt-like in the sense that observers come up with internally coherent interpretations in parts of the scene, but that different parts of the scene are only loosely coupled. This makes sense from an ecological perspective, since it is indeed quite common for different parts of a scene to be illuminated by different sources even. In sufficiently limited compartments it may be assumed that there is a dominant source direction (we take the photometric structure as an example here) whereas such an assumption is most likely to be violated for any extensive scene. The boundaries of the compartments are likely to be "natural boundaries" such as shadow and sunlit areas or thorax and pelvic region as in our paradigms (Koenderink, 1987; Richards et al., 1987; Hoffman & Richards, 1984).

ACKNOWLEDGMENTS

We thank Hans Kolijn for technical assistance and Gitendro Mukherjee for running part of the experiments.

REFERENCES

Erens, R.G.F., Kappers, A.M.L. & Koenderink, J.J. (1993a). Estimating the gradient direction of a luminance ramp. *Vision Research*, **33**, 1639–1643.

Erens, R.G.F., Kappers, A.M.L. & Koenderink, J.J. (1993b). Perception of local shape from shading. *Perception and Psychophysics*, **54**, 145–156.

Erens, R.G.F., Kappers, A.M.L. & Koenderink, J.J. (1993c). Estimating local shape from shading in the presence of global shading. *Perception and Psychophysics*, **54**, 334–342.

Euclid (1945). *The optics of Euclid* (H. E. Burton, Trans.). *Journal of the Optical Society of America*, **45**, 357–372.

Gershun, A. (1939). The light field. *Journal of Mathematical Physics*, **18**, 51–151.

Gibson, J.J. (1950). *The perception of the visual world*. Boston: Houghton Mifflin.

Gibson, J.J. (1966). *The senses considered as perceptual systems*. Boston: Houghton Mifflin.

Hattersley, R. (1979). *Photographic lighting: Learning to see*. Englewood Cliffs, NJ: Prentice-Hall Inc.

Hoffman, D. & Richards, W. (1984). Parts of recognition. *Cognition*, **18**, 65–96.

Koenderink, J.J. (1984). What does the occluding contour tell us about solid shape? *Perception*, **13**, 321–330.

Koenderink, J.J. (1987). An internal representation for solid shape based on the topological properties of the apparent contour. In W. Richards & S. Ullman (Eds.) *Image understanding 1985–86*. Norwood, NJ: Ablex Publishing Corporation.

Koenderink, J.J. (1997). Pictorial relief. In C. Arcelli, L.P. Cordella & G. Sanniti di Baja (Eds.) *Advances in visual form analysis*. Singapore: World Scientific.

Koenderink, J.J. (1998). Pictorial relief. *Philosophical Transactions of the Royal Society London*, **A356**, 1071–1086.

Koenderink, J.J. & van Doorn, A.J. (1976). The singularities of the visual mapping. *Biological Cybernetics*, **24**, 51–59.

Koenderink, J.J. & van Doorn, A.J. (1980). Photometric invariants related to solid shape. *Optica Acta*, **27**, 981–996.

Koenderink, J.J. & van Doorn, A.J. (1982). The shape of smooth objects and the way contours end. *Perception*, **11**, 129–137.

Koenderink, J.J. & van Doorn, A.J. (1983). Geometrical modes as a general method to treat diffuse interreflections in radiometry. *Journal of the Optical Society of America*, **73**, 843–850.

Koenderink, J.J. & van Doorn, A.J. (1993). Illuminance critical points on generic smooth surfaces. *Journal of the Optical Society of America*, **A10**, 844–854.

Koenderink, J.J. & van Doorn, A.J. (1995). Relief: Pictorial and otherwise. *Image and Vision Computing*, **13**, 321–334.

Koenderink, J.J. & van Doorn, A.J. (1996). Illuminance texture due to surface mesostructure. *Journal of the Optical Society of America*, **A13**, 452–463.

Koenderink, J.J. & van Doorn, A.J. (1998). Phenomenological description of bidirectional surface reflection. *Journal of the Optical Society of America, A15*, 2903–2912.

Koenderink, J.J., van Doorn, A.J. & Kappers, A.M.L. (1992). Surface perception in pictures. *Perception and Psychophysics*, **52**, 487–496.

Koenderink, J.J., van Doorn, A.J. & Kappers, A.M.L. (1994). On so-called paradoxical monocular stereoscopy. *Perception*, **23**, 583–594.

Koenderink, J.J., van Doorn, A.J. & Kappers, A.M.L. (1995). Depth relief. *Perception*, **24**, 115–126.

Koenderink, J.J., van Doorn, A.J, Christou, C. & Lappin, J.S. (1996a). Shape constancy in pictorial relief. *Perception*, **25**, 155–164.

Koenderink, J.J., van Doorn, A.J, Christou, C. & Lappin, J.S. (1996b). Perturbation study of shading in pictures. *Perception*, **25**, 1009–1026.

Koenderink, J.J., van Doorn, A.J. & Kappers, A.M.L. (1996c). Pictorial surface attitude and local depth comparisons. *Perception and Psychophysics*, **58**, 163–173.

Koenderink, J.J., Kappers, A.M.L., Pollick, F. E. & Kawato, M. (1997). Correspondence in pictorial space. *Perception and Psychophysics*, **59**, 813–827.

Pirenne, M.H. (1970). *Optics, painting and photography*. Cambridge: Cambridge University Press.

Richards, W.A., Koenderink, J.J. & Hoffman, D.D. (1987). Inferring three-dimensional shapes from two-dimensional silhouettes. *Journal of the Optical Society of America*, **A4**, 1168–1175.

Todd, J.T., Koenderink, J.J., van Doorn, A.J. & Kappers, A.M.L. (1996). Effects of changing viewing conditions on the perceived structure of smoothly curved surfaces. *Journal of Experimental Psychology: Human Perception and Performance*, **22**, 695–706.

Part IV

Epilogue

12

Hidden Agenda: A Sceptical View of the Privacy of Perception

HORACE BARLOW

Physiological Laboratory, University of Cambridge, UK

INTRODUCTION

As a biologist who puzzles over perceptions I am asking different questions from a psychologist or a philosopher, for I am continually thinking about biological survival: How do perceptions help us? How would we be worse off if we didn't have them? Are all possible representations of sensory experience equally good for the purposes we use our perceptions for? And so on. As a result of thinking along these lines I have a rather different viewpoint from others who were present at the ZiF meetings. It seems to me that the representation of the world that we experience subjectively— i.e. perceive—is specialised in two ways: first it is specialised to be suitable for the formation of new associations; and second it is specialised to be in a form that can be described and hence relayed to other people.

It is often not appreciated that the same body of information can be represented in totally different forms, and the form has a very large effect on what you can readily do with that information. For instance, when a library is catalogued, author, publication date, subject matter, and size of the volume may or may not be used as cataloguing features and hence may or may not be deducible from the catalogue reference. Even if the catalogues were all complete with unique references for each volume, they would vary greatly in their usefulness; for instance, if you wanted to know how often books above a certain size were withdrawn from the library it would be useful for the size to be used in the catalogue reference, and likewise for questions about author, date of publication, or subject matter. These are just the sort of questions

Perception and the Physical World: Psychological and Philosophical Issues in Perception.
Edited by Dieter Heyer and Rainer Mausfeld. © 2002 John Wiley & Sons, Ltd.

we need to know about the world around us: How often have I seen this before? Was there a happy outcome to my last encounter with it? What else did I see at the same time? The key point is that each item used in the representation, or in the catalogue reference, should correspond to a meaningful and significant subset of all sensations, or all the books. We must catalogue our sensory experiences according to very definite principles if important questions about them are to be readily and accurately answerable, and I think the form of our perceptions is to a large extent dictated by these requirements. But I have written about this before (Barlow, 1994, 1995), and here I shall develop the second idea, that perceptions are specialised to be communicable to other people.

Vision can occur without this communicable component, as in blindsight (see Weiskrantz 1997, for an up-to-date review), or in the system for controlling hand movements described by Milner (1997). These, and no doubt the visual systems of many animals, perform interesting and effective information processing, and it is arguable that they deserve to be called perception because they share so many features with the mechanisms we use in ordinary conscious vision. But what is the biological role of the component lacking in blindsight and the system for movement control? What does the conscious component of perception do for us? Weiskrantz suggested that his blindsight patients lacked a "commentary system" that enabled them to communicate about the visual image, and it is this idea that leads to the different viewpoint I shall present here.

MODELS OF CONSCIOUS PERCEPTION

Let us consider alternative views of our conscious perceptual experience. An ancient idea says that conscious experience results from the direct interaction of our perceptual apparatus with the outside world, and this is shown in the top box of Figure 12.1. The double-headed arrow indicates the feeling we have that our eyes and fingers actively explore the world, with conscious experience resulting from this intimate interaction. Although we know it is wrong, this is still the way we treat perception at a common-sense level and in everyday discourse.

What is wrong is its failure to incorporate the knowledge acquired about the senses over the last three centuries and more, so the internal loop shown in the second box must be added. We are endowed with eyes, ears, senses of touch, taste and smell, and these are acted upon by physical stimuli from the world around us. Through the sensory messages thereby aroused we can, to some extent, reconstruct the physical events going on in the external physical world, and this reconstruction gives rise to our conscious perceptions. This is a crude sketch of the view presented by Marr (1982), and I accept most of it, but there are two problems. First the relation between subjective experience and the world that gives rise to it is now much less intimate, so the double-headed arrow has to be abandoned; perception loses its interactive, explorative, character and the C is moved to a later stage in the internal loop. Second, it suggests that perception is a purely private affair, completely uninfluenced by other people, past or present. This is the point that worries me here, for we can, and frequently do,

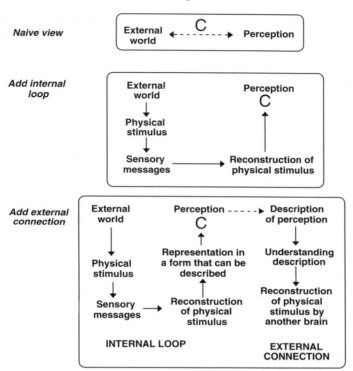

Figure 12.1 One must make two additions to the naive view that our perceptual apparatus directly interacts with the external world. First one must recognise that there is an internal loop through sense organs and reconstructing mechanisms. Then one must recognise that the representation so formed is communicated to other people through an external link, and this requires the addition of mechanisms that make the reconstructed scene communicable. It is argued in this article that conscious experience occurs when the communicable representation is activated, and that the communications that may result provide the main survival value of our conscious perception.

tell other people about our perceptions, while there is nothing in the second box of Figure 12.1 that would make this possible.

One cannot assume that neural activity can be described to other people just because it occurs in the brain and influences our actions. On the one hand, think of the complexity of the neural mechanisms required to make neural activity communicable: acquiring a schema of communicable terms, classifying the activity according to this schema, connecting the outcome of the classification to the language and then the speech centres, and so on. On the other hand, think of the fact that we have no need to communicate much of the work our brains do for us, just as a busy commercial company has no need to communicate the work dealing with specific transactions to other businesses or the world at large. It makes good sense to me to believe that the communicable aspects of brain work are pretty much the same as the conscious aspects; consciousness is, if you like, the public relations department of the brain company. I know that many people feel that their conscious wills are in total control of their behaviour, so that consciousness is more like the executive office or board room of the company, but it seems to me that this is an illusion. Those same people often conduct their lives very effectively and influentially, but are neither able nor willing to communicate the reasons for their actions—in other words they are driven by unconscious brain work, not conscious thoughts. Furthermore, there is nothing wrong with that: there is no reason why the work the brain does unconsciously should be any less efficient or effective than what it does consciously, and the only difference I can see is that the unconscious part cannot be communicated to others. But it is not important for the present argument how much we consciously control our behaviour; what matters is that there are *some* influences we are not aware of, so let us return to perception.

The bare internal loop consisted of: physical stimulus–sensory message–reconstruction of physical event–perception. What must be added is a stage producing a describable representation that can be communicated verbally or by some other means to other people, and this is added in the third box. You will say, "Yes but I know this external connection is not necessary, for I still perceive the world even when I do not tell other people about it." That is true, and we must suppose that conscious perception occurs simply when a communicable representation is activated, not only when it is communicated, but the fact that it is not always communicated does not diminish the importance of communicability. This is where the biological viewpoint is important, as the following analogy makes clear.

Flowers look, and indeed are, the same whether or not bees are currently extracting their nectar, yet no one doubts that the bees' activities are genuinely responsible for the appearance of flowers. Flowers attract bees searching for nectar and thus get pollinated: flowers are the way they are because this leads to them getting pollinated. In the same way, some aspects of perception surely owe their origin to the requirement of communicability. If the survival value of conscious perception lies in the communication mediated by the externally directed link, then any biologist will expect its mechanisms to be evolutionarily adapted in ways that will improve the survival value of these communications.

That perception should be open to such influences may seem false to introspection, but it is not a new idea. The internal loop is obviously useful (as in Milner's patients), but the conscious experience would have no survival value without its external connection; this is precisely what Friedrich Nietzsche (1887) implied when he said: "Consciousness is really only a net of communication between human beings; it is only as such that it had to develop; a solitary human being who lived as a beast of prey would not have needed it." On this view, the mechanisms of conscious perception will have evolved to suit the external connection, not for the purely private experience, just as the form and colour of flowers have evolved for their effects on the bee's visual system. It would be a serious error for psychologists and philosophers to neglect the requirement of communicability if this is how perception promotes survival.

The external loop added to the third box of Figure 12.1 is passive and has no effect on the internal loop, so a defendant of the exclusively private, personal, view of perception might say, "OK there *is* an external connection, but there is no means by which this can influence the inner loop: the arrow points externally, and there are no causal arrows pointing the other way." But even in the fully developed adult nervous system there is some feedback, for we usually cease to communicate items that lead to unpleasant consequences or are persistently misunderstood. And if I am right that the survival value of the conscious component of perception lies in this being the communicable part, then evolutionary forces will have moulded the properties of this part just as it has every other detail of our brains. If the external connection gives perception its survival value, natural selection is smart enough to ensure that the whole system will be effective in enabling us to relay knowledge gained through our senses to other people. The constraints on the inner loop implied by the need for effective communication will therefore be incorporated; for instance, the requirement that perceptions be describable in the language of the external recipient must surely constrain their nature.

Moving from the first to the second box raised doubts about the intimate connection between perception and the external world indicated by the double-headed arrow, so we had to move the C to the representation of the reconstructed world. For the third box we move it again, and my view is that conscious perception results from activation of the communicable representation rather than any earlier stage, but I have reservations in stating that there is a definite, localised site in the brain where conscious experience arises. Introspectively we *feel* perceptions arise in the external world, and this is surely a useful notion to stick to when putting our perceptions to their most important use: communicating them to others. We *have* to feel this, for why should those we communicate with trust us if we don't feel they arise in the real world? The physiological facts show that our introspections are a bit misleading for it is only an indirect connection, but in this case one need not be too particular in aligning common sense with science.

As Marcel (1983) has pointed out, those towards whom the external arrow points can have powerful and deep influences. Like the PR department of a company, we tailor our communications to the background knowledge and expectations of those with whom we are communicating. Furthermore, as I shall explain below, our perceptions have certainly been tailored before we are aware of them, and there are powerful forces determining our beliefs and motivations that we are also unaware of.

I think these unconscious forces have written a hidden agenda for perception, but rather than continuing the argument along the lines I have started, I shall now approach the problem in a different way and tell you how and why I have come to believe this. I cannot give a scholarly account of the ideas that have influenced me and their sources, but shall describe brief personal incidents that I look back upon as being important in forming my opinions, though of course there may be others that I do not recall. For example, Wittgenstein was a much-talked-about figure when I was an undergraduate at Cambridge, and it is quite possible that my emphasis on the *use* to which perceptions are put may be derived, second or third hand, from his famous dictum about language "Don't ask for the meaning, ask for the use" (see Fann, 1971).

FREUD AT FOURTEEN ˙

I am the youngest of a large family, and when I was about 14 an older brother who had just started medical school brought back two volumes of Freud over the summer holidays—*Psychopathology of Everyday Life,* and *Totem and Taboo,* as far as I can remember. I read quite a lot of the two books, and Freud was a frequent topic of family conversation. The general attitude was sceptical rather than hostile, and I remember my own response was to be unconvinced by the detailed arguments and unsatisfied by the examples, but enormously interested in one general message: people do not, and perhaps cannot, give accurate reasons for their actions and beliefs, even when they are convinced that they can. Observation of other people's behaviour and of the explanations they gave for it was sufficient to verify for me the truth that people have unconscious, as well as conscious, minds, and this is very generally accepted today, though it was not 60 years ago. I realised that what was true for other minds was likely to be true for my own, and from that summer to the present day I have been a little wary of taking my direct conscious experiences of the world and my introspections about them at their face value, for there could be hidden forces at work.

But if there is a hidden agenda, who writes it? A schoolboy has no difficulty introspecting about father figures and their surrogates, so *their* agenda did not seem to be hidden, but I recall an episode that, subsequently at least, seems revealing. At that time I was at a boarding school, and the day started at 7 am with a cold bath, followed by a cup of cocoa; then we had to walk 7 minutes to a religious service in the college chapel. A straw hat was a compulsory part of the uniform, and one day I forgot it and had walked most of the way to chapel when I suddenly became aware that it was missing. I can still to the present day feel the sense of shame and horror at something that felt 1000 times more disgraceful than complete nudity! I rushed back to get the hat, but arrived late for chapel, and can remember that moment of late arrival too. I probably received a mild reprimand, but if so I cannot remember that; what I recall so vividly is the self-administered reprimand for having transgressed the tribal code.

How can such a trivial episode make such a deep impression? A few years later I found what I think is the answer in another book I came across at home, Wilfred Trotter's *Instincts of the Herd in Peace and War.* This is not very well known, and I think my parents had the book through personal acquaintance with the author, a brilliant surgeon with broad interests in neurology, psychology and sociology. Although a surgeon, he had some knowledge of the Freudian doctrines that were just beginning to create a stir in 1909, when the book was sketched out. It was published in 1916, no doubt because he realised it was relevant to problems of shell-shocked soldiers and the civilian mass-hysteria of the First World War. Its message is that humans are deeply social animals and the herd instinct is a force as powerful in humans as the other primary instincts of self-preservation, nutrition, and sex, though it is largely unrecognised by our conscious minds. He was more charitable towards Freud's interpretations than is fashionable today and does not directly challenge them, but he implies that it is the herd instinct that gives internal power to the repressive forces that conflict with the infant's egotistical drives during early development; this seems a very sensible modification of Freud's stark and over-stated assertions. He gives a convincing account of the way that instinctively driven, non-rational, beliefs appear to their owners, and of the way such beliefs are expounded by their owners. Many of the things we feel and say about our perceptions fit this description all too well.

I have just looked at the book again, and although it is in some ways less satisfactory than I remember it to have been, its message has, deservedly I think, become part of my world view, and a part that continues to help me to make sense of the behaviour of others, as well as myself. I think the external connection of Figure 12.1 shows one means by which we pay our dues to the herd, and in view of the power of the herd instinct it is not unreasonable to suspect a reciprocal influence of herd opinion on our perception.

NOISE AND SENSORY THRESHOLDS

The next autobiographical episode I shall recount occurred much later, when I had started work in vision. In 1949 the view of rigorous psychophysicists, among whom I wished to be counted, was that the doorway to perception had a threshold: if a stimulus was not strong enough to cross this threshold, then it had no effect on the sensorium. Through my membership of a group called the Ratio Club[1] that met in London from time to time, and also through reading R.A. Fisher (1925), I realised that responses to weak stimuli could not be considered properly without taking noise into account, and once this was done the idea of a threshold required modifying. It was natural to replace the senseless idea of a step at the doorway to perception by the notion that, because of the noise, there was a minimum intensity below which stimuli could not be detected reliably. This view implied that there was an element of convention in deciding whether to say "seen" or "not seen" to a weak visual stimulus, namely the standard of reliability that was deemed acceptable to the recipients of the message. There would be a distribution of values of the internal representations that resulted from noise alone, and convention would decree the point on this scale, the criterion, that had to be exceeded in order to claim that a stimulus was present. If a high criterion was selected, there would be virtually no false positive responses to non-existent stimuli, but a stronger added stimulus would be needed to exceed that value so there would be the penalty of insensitivity; choice of a low criterion would improve sensitivity but bring the penalty of an increased rate of false positive responses. This notion, therefore, legitimised false positive responses, and also implied that the criterion might be adjustable according to the standard of reliability that was expected.

At about that time I started a series of experiments with two other psychophysicists, both now world-famous in their own fields. Even though false positive responses were known to occur quite regularly, one of my colleagues regarded them as discreditable errors that could be avoided. Just before starting a run as an observer he made the remark that, even if the record of the results showed that he had made a false positive response, he would not believe that he had seen something that was not there but would attribute it to a recording error or some other mistake. I was running that particular experiment, recording the responses, changing filters, and occasionally inserting a thick piece of black card to give a blank stimulus. Quite soon he gave a "seen" response when I knew the black card was in place, so although it meant abandoning the run I said, "Hey, did you really see that?" He confirmed that he had, so I said, "Come and look which filter is in place." He looked at the black card and acknowledged glumly that he had experienced a visual sensation from a blank stimulus, but he was very seriously upset; we could never persuade him to come anywhere near that equipment ever again and the collaboration had to be abandoned. I think he felt he had done something discreditable according to his tribal code and was torn whether to abandon the code or accept the discredit.

About a year later I went to Steve Kuffler's lab in Baltimore to work on the retinal ganglion cells of the cat. He had found that they give a rapid, highly irregular, discharge even in the absence of any stimulation by light, and if human ganglion cells behaved anything like that it seemed at first surprising that we can ever do anything other than give false responses! I was one of those who was arguing for the existence of noise in the visual pathway, but I was expecting that it would be hard work to prove its existence in the optic nerve, just as it had been hard work to prove psychophysically that there could be a background of noise to our perceptions. I was not expecting anything as loud and obvious as Kuffler had found, and we did many experiments testing whether it was an artefact due to electrode pressure, anaesthetic, or some other factor. We decided it was not (Kuffler et al., 1957), and on reflection the result became perfectly reconcilable with my quantitative predictions (Barlow, 1957), provided that the retina's sensitivity to light was high enough. It is the ratio of signal to noise that matters, not the absolute amount of noise, and we went on to show that the sensitivity was indeed high enough (Barlow et al., 1957).

This is an example of how my own hidden agenda, derived from the cryptic nature of noise in perception, had warped my perception of new facts, but there is something genuinely seditious in the way that noise is suppressed in perception. We do not usually notice the background noise at all, although it is true that those who know about noise often do become aware of it, and those who know nothing about noise can be persuaded to reveal its presence by being asked to "guess" instead of reporting "seen" or "not-seen". But noise is undoubtedly much less prominent in perception than it is in the sensory messages upon which perception is based, so reducing the prominence of noise must be an example of one item in the hidden agenda. Its reduced prominence clearly supports the influence of communicability on perception, for external communication would be quite useless if there were no generally accepted standards of reliability.

PERCEPTION IS NOT PRIVATE

These autobiographical anecdotes should by now have made clear what I am driving at: it is the external connection in Figure 12.1 that gives conscious perception its survival value, and the need for the effectiveness of this link has ensured that our perceptual apparatus can deliver appropriate messages to be transmitted down that

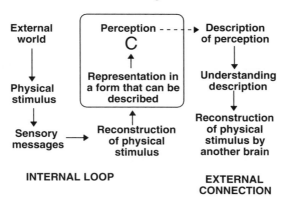

Figure 12.2 The box shows the stages in the mechanisms of perception that might be influenced evolutionarily by the survival value of the external connection.

link. But this process does not stop with the innately determined formation of our perceptual apparatus. During life, our herd instinct gives the tribal voice extraordinary power and insistence, though we do not consciously recognise this. Through our social antennae we know very well what the tribe expects of us, and since we have evolved to interact beneficially with the tribe, our perceptions are also likely to be modified to promote the interactions. Figure 12.2 shows the parts of the inner loop and external connection that might be influenced in this way.

I think the main influences are those connected with the use of language, for it is of course advantageous for the external link to be used for correct messages that are correctly understood by the recipient, and many facts already fit this view well. For instance, constancy phenomena can be regarded as steps to make our perceptual knowledge transferable, because other people are not interested in angular subtenses or ratios of cone excitation, but in absolute sizes and reflectances. We already recognise that sensory messages have been acted on in complex ways to yield our perceptions, and the three additions I have pointed to—reducing the prominence of noise, demanding that perceptions be verbally describable, and paying attention to the requirements of our conspecific tribal companions—are comparatively minor additions. I don't want to exaggerate the role of the hidden agenda, but it is often strenuously denied that there could possibly be any social influence on our apparently private perceptual experience, and I think this is a mistake: perception is not the purely private matter it seems to be, and the public aspects are genuinely important because they give conscious perception its survival value.

ACKNOWLEDGMENTS

I would like to thank those with whom I've discussed these ideas for their criticisms and for explaining what they have found unconvincing—especially Paul Whittle and Gary Hatfield for their comments on this particular article.

NOTE

1. The club had been started by John Bates, an electro-encephalographer from Queen's Square Hospital for Neurological Diseases, to discuss Shannon's newly published Information Theory, which Bates realised had relevance to the brain. The club included Donald MacKay, Albert Uttley, Phillip Woodward, Tommy Gold, Pat Merton, William Rushton, and occasional visitors such as Alan Turing and Warren McCulloch.

REFERENCES

Barlow, H.B. (1957) Increment thresholds at low intensities considered as signal/noise discriminations. *Journal of Physiology, London*, **136**, 469–488.
Barlow, H.B. (1994). What is the computational goal of the Neocortex? In C. Koch & J. Davis (Eds.) *Large scale neuronal theories of the brain*. Cambridge, Mass.: MIT Press.
Barlow, H.B. (1995). The neuron doctrine in perception. In M. Gazzaniga (Ed.) *The cognitive neurosciences* (pp. 415–435). Cambridge, Mass: MIT Press.
Barlow, H.B., FitzHugh, R. & Kuffler, S.W. (1957). Dark adaptation, absolute threshold and Purkinje shift in single units of the cat's retina. *Journal of Physiology*. **137**, 327–337.
Fann, K.T. (1971). *Wittgenstein's conception of philosophy*. Berkeley: University of California Press.
Fisher, R.A. (1925). *Statistical methods for research workers*. Edinburgh: Oliver & Boyd.
Kuffler, S.W., FitzHugh, R. & Barlow, H.B. (1957). Maintained activity in the cat's retina in light and darkness. *Journal of Genetics and Physiology*, **40**, 683–702.
Marcel, A.J. (1983) Conscious and unconscious perception: an approach to the relations between phenomenal experience and perceptua;l processes. *Cognitive Psychology*, **15**, 238–300.
Marr, D. (1982). *Vision*. San Francisco: W.H. Freeman.
Milner, A.D. (1997) Vision without knowledge. *Philosophical Transactions of the Royal Society, series* **B352**, 1249–1256.
Nietzsche, F. (1887). *Die Fröhliche Wissenschaft* . Leipzig: Verlag von E.W. Fritzsch. (Translated as *The Gay Science* by W. Kaufmann. New York: Vintage Books, Random House, 1974).
Trotter, W. (1916). *Instincts of the herd in peace and war*. London: T. Fisher Unwin.
Weiskrantz, L. (1997). *Consciousness lost and found*. Oxford: Oxford University Press.

Author Index

Index compiled by Rainer Mausfeld

Subject Index

Index compiled by Rainer Mausfeld